Understanding Communication Research Methods

Using an engaging how-to approach that draws from scholarship, real life, and popular culture, this textbook, now in its third edition, offers students practical reasons why they should care about research methods and offers a practical guide to actually conducting research themselves.

Examining quantitative, qualitative, and critical research methods, this new edition helps undergraduate students better grasp the theoretical and practical uses of method by clearly illustrating practical applications. The book features all the main research traditions within communication including online methods and provides level-appropriate applications of the methods through theoretical and practical examples and exercises, including sample student papers that demonstrate research methods in action. This third edition also includes additional chapters on experimental design and methods of performance, as well as brand new case studies throughout.

This textbook is perfect for students and scholars using critical, cultural, interpretive, qualitative, quantitative, and positivist research methods, as well as students of communication studies more generally.

It also offers dedicated student resources on the Routledge.com book page and instructor resources at https://routledgetextbooks.com/textbooks/instructor_downloads/. These include links, videos, outlines and activities, recommended readings, test questions, and more.

Stephen M. Croucher is a Professor and the Head of the School of Communication, Journalism, and Marketing at Massey University, New Zealand. He is also Lead Research Fellow at the National Research University, Higher School of Economics, Russia. He serves on the editorial boards of more than 10 journals and served as the editor of the *Review of Communication* (2022-2025), *Frontiers in Communication* (2019-2022), *Journal of Intercultural Communication Research* (2010-2019), and *Speaker & Gavel* (2010-2015). He has held and holds various leadership positions in the National Communication Association, the International Communication Association, and the World Communication Association. He serves as President of the World Communication Association from 2019-2023.

Daniel Cronn-Mills is a Professor and Distinguished Faculty Scholar at Minnesota State University, Mankato, USA. He has authored and co-authored three books, five book chapters, and a stack of journal articles. He served for more than a decade as the editor of *Speaker & Gavel* (1997-2010) and has served on the editorial board of 11 scholarly journals. Dan has served in numerous leadership roles from local to national levels including the National Communication Association, the American Forensic Association, and the Communication and Theatre Association of Minnesota.

UNDERSTANDING COMMUNICATION RESEARCH METHODS

A Theoretical and Practical Approach

Third edition

Stephen M. Croucher and Daniel Cronn-Mills

Routledge
Taylor & Francis Group

NEW YORK AND LONDON

Third edition published 2022
by Routledge
605 Third Avenue, New York, NY 10158

and by Routledge
2 Park Square, Milton Park, Abingdon, Oxon, OX14 4RN

Routledge is an imprint of the Taylor & Francis Group, an informa business

First edition published by Routledge 2015

Library of Congress Cataloging-in-Publication Data
Names: Croucher, Stephen Michael, 1978– author. | Cronn-Mills, Daniel, author.
Title: Understanding communication research methods : a theoretical and
    practical approach / Stephen M. Croucher and Daniel Cronn-Mills.
Description: Third edition. | New York, NY : Routledge, 2022. | Includes
    bibliographical references and index.
Identifiers: LCCN 2021020261 (print) | LCCN 2021020262 (ebook) | ISBN
    9780367623685 (hardback) | ISBN 9780367623661 (paperback) | ISBN
    9781003109129 (ebook)
Subjects: LCSH: Communication–Research–Methodology.
Classification: LCC P91.3 .C73 2022 (print) | LCC P91.3 (ebook) | DDC 302.2/0721–dc23
LC record available at https://lccn.loc.gov/2021020261
LC ebook record available at https://lccn.loc.gov/2021020262

ISBN: 978-0-367-62368-5 (hbk)
ISBN: 978-0-367-62366-1 (pbk)
ISBN: 978-1-003-10912-9 (ebk)

DOI: 10.4324/9781003109129

Typeset in Interstate
by Apex CoVantage, LLC

Access the Support Material: www.routledge.com/9780367623661

Contents

Section One
Research Paradigms

1 Introduction and Ethics

Chapter Outline

- Why Take Research Methods?
- A Few Key Terms
- Ethics
- Ethics and the Scientific Community
- Ethics and Human Subjects
- Ethical Practice in School and Scholarship
- Outline of the Book
- Summary
- Key Steps and Questions to Consider
- Discussion Questions
- Key Terms

Welcome to Communication Research Methods

Sir Edmund Hillary (1919-2008), a New Zealand-born explorer, mountain climber, and philanthropist is best known for being the first confirmed person to reach the summit of Mt. Everest in 1953. Sir Hillary sought out new areas of exploration and challenges and devoted a great deal of his efforts to building schools, hospitals, and other facilities for the Sherpa people of Nepal. He was known for believing all people are capable of great things. In fact, he is known for saying, "I have discovered that even the mediocre can have adventures and even the fearful can achieve."

Stephen and Daniel (authors of your textbook) agree with Sir Hillary when thinking about research methods. We've seen students who are resistant to conducting research. However, we have seen all kinds of students excel in communication research, including those who did not think they would ever "reach the summit." The key is to look at learning research methods, as corny as it sounds, as a journey. You will confront challenges, face frustrations, celebrate milestones, and sometimes wander off the path. Yet, in the end, we can all can achieve and experience the journey. Look around your classroom and you will see other students on the journey. Enjoy the trip—your textbook is your map, and your teacher is the guide. Let's start by establishing a few good reasons to study communication research methods, second, identify key terms to help you progress, third, discuss the importance of ethics in research, and, finally, provide an overview for the rest of the chapters in the textbook.

DOI: 10.4324/9781003109129-2

Why Take Research Methods?

Understanding research methods has both academic and practical benefits. Let's first talk about the academic benefits. First, research methods will improve your ability to locate, critique, and use academic materials. In many research classes, students must look up information on a subject. With the university library and the Internet at your disposal, you can find stacks of information. The key is to know what is "good" information. This kind of class will help.

Second, you will likely have to write one or more papers in the course. Stephen and Dan have their students conduct research papers of various lengths. The students are graded on content, ability to follow a research design, and their writing abilities. Effective writing is important. Even if we have the best ideas but cannot communicate them properly, our ideas lose merit.

Third, as you progress through the course, you will be introduced to a variety of concepts and theories. Critical analysis of new concepts is important. What we mean by critical analysis: 1) know what the concept means, 2) evaluate the concept, and 3) make a judgment about the concept. You will learn these skills in your research course, particularly when you discover concepts such as reliability, validity, and claims. Critical thinking is a great skill to have and crosses into every aspect of life.

Learning research methods has practical reasons and benefits. All teachers have stories of students who have taken their research skills into other avenues. Stephen recently spoke with a former student who is now the coordinator of human resources for a group of 15 hospitals. The student told Stephen:

> Research skills are integral to my responsibilities. I would be lost without them. Every day I need to make our hospitals better places to work. To do this I regularly propose new programs to the Board. When I do this, I have to be perfect in my proposal . . . the numbers have to add up, and it must be well-written. I constantly ask questions such as: is this plan valid, are the measures reliable? My team and I regularly do reviews of current literature to see the state of our industry, we always are analyzing data, and constantly writing reports. I am grateful I took this course. Whenever I interview applicants, this is one thing I look for . . . research skills.

A former student of Dan's had plans to become a pharmaceutical sales representative. She conducted a research project focused on the communication interactions between sales reps and physicians. She conducted interviews with reps and doctors and identified the strengths and weaknesses of what occurred when the groups met. She was able to take her findings and effectively use the results to advance her career.

A second student of Dan's worked at a popular local restaurant during college. The restaurant had a high rate of employee turnover. The restaurant was constantly hiring new staff. The student conducted a study, with permission of the restaurant management, comparing communication expectations between staff and management. The student identified several levels of mismatched expectations. The findings helped the restaurant improve communication and reduce employee turnover. The student listed the research report on his resume. During his first post-graduation interview, the potential employer was intrigued by the study, and they spent more than an hour discussing the research project.

With these students and many others, research methods enabled them to better communicate (e.g., prepare presentations, reports), understand the professional world, and compete in the world after graduation. As you can see, taking this course (and reading this textbook) has lots of practical benefits. With benefits in mind, let's move forward on this journey. Before we begin learning about research methods, we need to define a few key terms.

A Few Key Terms

So that we're all on the same page, let's review some terms we use in this book. The first term we want to define is communication. While communication has many definitions, we believe **communication** is a process of sharing meaning with others. A process explains how communication has a sender, a message, and a receiver. When the receiver provides feedback (a response of some kind), a transaction occurs. Think about a conversation: person A (the sender) says "Hi" (the message), person B (the receiver) receives the messages and responds with "Hi." This is the classic sender–receiver model. However, not all communication involves a direct response like the example we just provided. In some cases, person B may just nod (a nonverbal response), or person B may not respond at all. No response means you have one-way or unilateral communication.

Another key element of the definition is the idea of sharing meaning. When we "communicate," we are sharing something with others. You may have heard the saying, "you cannot not communicate." This means we are always communicating, even when we do not mean to communicate. The sending of messages to others, verbally or nonverbally, is always happening. The thoughts/feelings we share with others is done through the sender–receiver process we call communication.

A second key term to define is communications. **Communications** (notice the "s" on the word) is a technological system for the transmission of information. Examples of communications systems include telephone, cable, television, fiber optics, the Internet, etc. A key difference between *communication* and *communications* is the technology. *Communication* is a human process of sharing meaning with others; *communications* is a technological system for the transmission of information. Stephen and Dan have both known professors and industry professionals who are very particular about the difference, so make sure you know the difference.

The third term to define is theory. A **theory** is a formal statement of rules on which a subject is based or an explanation of the relationship between variables. Basically, a theory is a statement intended to explain facts in the social or scientific world. Chapters 2–4 each discuss different ways communication researchers define and approach the study and research of "theory."

The fourth term is research. **Research** is the detailed or in-depth study of a subject (often a theory) to reach a greater understanding or to obtain new information about the subject. This is what you will be doing when asked to do research; you will be reaching a greater understanding or obtaining new information about a subject (like a theory).

The fifth term is method. A **method** is a systematic technique or procedure to conduct research. In Chapters 8–20 we describe various methods you can use in communication research. Each method is different, systematic, and has its own "rules" or guiding principles. As you read through the textbook you will find one or more methods that "speak to you."

The final term is methodology. While method and methodology may sound similar, they are quite different. **Methodology** is the study of one or more methods. A method is how you conduct your research, for example, using interviews to collect data for your project. Methodology is the study of interviews as a method. In a methodology, you would explain what makes interviewing an appropriate choice for your research, what the history of interviewing as a method is, what your data analysis technique was, etc. Essentially, in a methodology, you discuss the theory behind the method. So, remember, the method is the "how to," and the methodology is the theory behind the method.

Ethics

Ethics has many different definitions. Aristotle considered ethics as living well and doing good things. Quintillian, a Roman orator, identified a clear relationship between communication and ethics when he defined an ethical man as one who speaks well. English philosopher Thomas Hobbes in his 1651 book *Leviathan* described ethics as the actions one takes in order to maintain a social contract in society. In *Leviathan*, Hobbes praised ideas such as autonomy, preservation of relationships, justice, and fairness. All of these ideas are essential for maintenance of the social contract, which is an ethical aspect of life. The *Cambridge Dictionary of Philosophy* defined ethics as the "principles of right and wrong that govern our choices and pursuits" (Audi, 1999, p. 286). Arnett et al. (2009) defined ethics as "practices that enact or support a good, a central value or set of values associated with human life and conduct" (p. xii). We define *ethics* as the actions, thoughts, values, principles and communicative practices one enacts in determining how to interact with and treat others.

If you were to write a paper on ethics, paying particular attention to how Western (European and North American, for example) scholars conceptualize ethics, you would find many of the same attributes as outlined in *Leviathan*. An ethical person, from a Western perspective, is one who typically upholds justice, fairness, the preservation of relationships, and autonomy (Pojman, 2005). Let's take a closer look and compare the two largest religious populations in the world today—Christianity and Islam. The emphasis among Christians for such qualities in an ethical person stems from the Bible and the teachings of Jesus Christ (Croucher, 2011). The 39 books of the *Old Testament* provide a litany of rules, or ways one should live their life to be a "good" or "ethical" Christian. While many Christians do not follow everything in the *Old Testament*, the rules and laws set forth paint a picture of what was meant at the time of the *Testament's* writing of what was needed to be "good" (Croucher, 2011). For many Fundamentalist Christians (strict followers), many aspects of the books hold true as roadmaps to ethical behavior and salvation. The 27 books of the *New Testament* describe, among many things, the importance of autonomy, preservation of relationships, justice, forgiveness, and fairness in order to be a "good" or "just" person. In the *New Testament*, readers are taught these values and actions lead to salvation. These actions and values have served as the bedrock of classical and modern Western thought on ethics (Croucher, 2011).

Traditional ethics in Islam, the second largest religious group in the world, differs a bit from traditional Christian ethics. Traditional Islamic ethics is based on the Koran and the teaching of the Prophet Muhammad. Three principles are of keen importance—forgiveness, shame, and patience. The Koran states that Allah (God) is forgiving and merciful. Thus, forgiving an individual who wrongs you is more valued and ethical than to demand justice and/or punishment (Croucher, 2011). The tenets are similar to the Christian philosophy, "To err is human, to forgive divine." Shame is a trait of an ethical person, particularly in conflict situations. Let's say you have been disrespected in some way; it is easy to remain upset instead of being a better person and trying to work out the problem. The ethical solution is to work through the conflict with the person, maybe using a third party to avoid shame for all parties involved. An escalation of conflict only brings more shame to all involved. Patience is an important part of the Islamic ethic. One should not rush to judgment. One should contemplate a situation, pray for God's guidance, and seek the help of a third party if needed in situations. A decision should be based on a logical, patiently thought-out plan. The different approaches to ethics between these two religious groups reveal various ways to think about "What is ethical?"

Ethics and the Scientific Community

The place of ethics in philosophy, science, and medicine used to be a much more contentious issue than today. Philosophers like John Locke and John Stuart Mill argued that ethical concerns had no real place in science because ethical issues belonged to a priori knowledge (or knowledge independent of experience and evidence). For philosophers like Locke and Mill, science should be amoral, detached, and separate from moral obligations to best ascertain truth. These scientists were responding to fears in the days of Copernicus and Galileo. Science was silenced by the Catholic Church because scientific discoveries and knowledge questioned/challenged Catholic doctrine. A fear of scientific knowledge hindered by religious dogma led philosophers like Locke and Mill to call for scientists who were amoral. Mary Shelley's 1818 novel, *Frankenstein; or the Modern Prometheus*, can be interpreted as a challenge to Locke, Mill, and Max Weber and their call for amoral science. For Shelley, amoral scientific experiments lead to the Frankenstein monster. Mill (1861–1957) disagreed with Shelley on the place of morals/ethics in science. His philosophy of utilitarianism proposed a different view of science/research. Mill argued that individuals should have full liberty except when harming others. The concept of **utilitarian ethics**, which stems from utilitarianism, means one should have full freedom to conduct research, as long as the benefits outweigh any potential harms of the research (Christians, 2000).

The utilitarian ethic was misconstrued in the 20th century. During World War I, medical researchers working for the United States, Germany, France, and the United Kingdom, and other European powers experimented on humans with chemical and biological agents. Researchers argued that the experiments were carried out to better advance science and to protect national security. In World War II, Nazi and Japanese doctors conducted experiments on prisoners. The experiments explored pain thresholds, responses to poisons and temperatures, injecting individuals with viruses, and many other experiments. Numerous doctors were tried for crimes against humanity at Nuremberg for unethical and inhumane treatment of humans during the war. The doctors argued they were following orders, or the work was for the benefit of mankind.

The history of the United States during the 20th century includes numerous instances when researchers and doctors violated ethical principles in the "name of science." From the 1930s to the 1970s, Black men in Tuskegee, Alabama with syphilis were told they did not have the disease and were denied treatment. Many of the men were airmen in the U.S. military. Other men and women were intentionally injected with the disease. Researchers were studying the progression of syphilis. The experiments lasted until the 1970s (Kampmeier, 1972). Countless people died, and generations of lives were damaged by the government-sponsored experiments. Another horrendous experiment was conducted in 1963 by Southam and Mandel at the Jewish Chronic Disease Hospital in New York. They injected 22 patients with live cancer cells without their consent (Mulford, 1967). The physicians were exploring the effects of cancer on the human body.

In the social sciences, researchers have been questioned about their ethics. The 1961 Milgram experiments at Yale University explored individuals' obedience to authority figures. While the experiment offered valuable insights into people's behaviors under pressure from authority, the techniques used by Milgram and his colleagues have been deemed less than ethical (Baynard & Flanagan, 2005). The psychological stress suffered by the participants is something you do not want when conducting research. The 1971 Stanford Prison Experiment is a classic example of psychology run amuck. The experiment conducted by Phillip Zimbardo concluded that, given the right circumstances, just about anyone's personality could shift from follower to leader and vice versa (Stolley, 2005). These results are of particular interest to the military and prisons. The study, which examined conflict between superiors and subordinates, was wrought with problems, such as physical abuse between participants and poor debriefing of participants (we will talk about debriefing later in the chapter).

In response to many of these incidents (Tuskegee in particular), the National Commission for the Protection of Human Subjects of Biomedical and Behavioral Research, a federally funded Commission, was created in 1974. The commission met and wrote the Belmont Report, which outlined ethical guidelines and principles for research with human subjects. Three key principles were identified in the report: 1) respect for individuals, 2) beneficence, and 3) justice. Due to the Belmont Report, the federal government requires all organizations receiving federal funds to have an Institutional Review Board (IRB). IRBs monitor, direct, and are responsible for enacting codes of conduct. Every American university/college has an IRB. IRBs consist of faculty members from diverse backgrounds (sex, ethnicity, race, discipline). An IRB is staffed by research faculty from a variety of specializations. An IRB has at least one outside member (not affiliated with the university/college) to ensure rules are followed.

Any research involving human subjects must receive IRB approval before data is collected. Research involving human subjects must meet at least three minimum requirements (the same three principles as outlined by the Belmont Report). First, the researchers must *respect* the rights of participants. Second, the benefits of the research should outweigh any potential harms to the participants (*beneficence*). Third, participants should be treated fairly (*justice*).

Based on these three principles and the procedures used in a research project, IRBs make determinations about levels of risk. An **exempt** research project has minimal risk–similar to the risk a person faces in a normal day. Examples include research conducted on existing data, research in educational environments, and surveys and interviews without high-probing questions. Exempt requests receive **expedited** review by the IRB. To qualify for exempt research, the human participants must personally consent to the research.

If a project involves higher levels of risk for participants, or if individual participants are not able to consent for themselves (children, individuals with mental disabilities, prisoners and other protected groups), a project is **nonexempt**. Nonexempt projects are sent to the full board for review. Such projects need close scrutiny to make sure they fulfill the three principles from the Belmont Report. We include at the end of this chapter an example IRB application. Now that you know a bit more about the relationship between ethics and the scientific community and how an IRB monitors ethics, the following section discusses ethical practices we should all follow when working with human subjects.

Ethics and Human Subjects

Along with the principles outlined in the Belmont Report, one should adhere to three additional procedural and ethical guidelines. The three elements are informed consent, level of participant privacy, and debriefing.

Informed Consent

When conducting research we must get informed consent from participants. **Informed consent** is where you tell your participants, in a written document, what they will be doing in the study, explain the risks and benefits of their participation, explain that individuals have a right to stop participation at any time, provide the researchers' contact information, and obtain participant permission to take part in the study. Important!–the consent document must be in a language the participants can understand. Avoid jargon, acronyms, and other phrasing that may confuse participants. Informed consent documents are signed by participants, showing they have given permission. In such cases, the researcher should keep names confidential (private). We will talk more about the difference between confidentiality and anonymity in a bit. Figure 1.1 is a sample informed-consent document for a study on conflict styles among Muslim immigrants and non-Muslims in France. Figure 1.2 details the eight elements for an informed consent form.

Figure 1.1 Sample Informed Consent Document

INFORMED CONSENT
TO PARTICIPATE IN A RESEARCH STUDY

You are being asked to volunteer for a research study. Please read this form and ask any questions that you may have before agreeing to take part in this study.

Project Title: "A comparative analysis between Muslim and non-Muslim conflict styles."
Principal Investigator: Stephen M. Croucher
Co-Investigators: _____
Contact Information: INSERT ADDRESS AND PHONE NUMBER HERE

Purpose of the Research Study
The purpose of this study is to measure the conflict styles of individuals who reside in France, the United Kingdom, Germany, Spain, Costa Rica and the United States.

Procedures
If you agree to be in this study, you will be asked to do the following things: you will be asked to complete an 11-page survey that examines how you rationalize and manage conflict. This survey should take you approximately 35–50 minutes.

Risks and Benefits of Being in the Study
There are no foreseeable risks to participating in this study.
The benefits to participation are: that you will be able to voice your opinion(s) anonymously on a controversial issue, which can help relieve stress. Also, this study is important because it examines how individuals from different cultures rationalize and manage conflict.

Anonymity
Because you have not signed a sign-up sheet or any other form that includes your name, your participation in this study is completely anonymous. Furthermore, because your survey will be combined with other surveys (approximately 3,000–4,000) your responses will be virtually impossible to separate from the other responses.

Voluntary Nature of the Study
Participation in this study is voluntary. Your decision whether or not to participate will not result in penalty or loss of benefits to which you are otherwise entitled. If you decide to participate, you are free not to answer any question or to withdraw at any time.

Contacts and Questions
The researcher conducting this study can be contacted at (INSERT E-MAIL HERE). You are encouraged to contact the researcher if you have any questions.

You may also contact the chair, Human Subjects Review Board, Bowling Green State University, (419) 372-7716 (hsrb@bgsu.edu), if any problems or concerns arise during the course of the study.

You will be given a copy of this information to keep for your records. If you are not given a copy of this consent form, please request one.

Figure 1.2 Required Elements of Informed Consent

1. Title of the project. A title is required for an IRB application.
2. Names of the investigators. List your name and the names of anyone else in your research group. A student researcher will need to list their teacher as a faculty-sponsor of the research.
3. Contact information. Contact information provides participants with means to reach the researchers in case they have questions. Provide your physical address, e-mail address, and phone number(s). Second, a student researcher should also provide the teacher's contact information. Finally, provide the contact information for the IRB chair.
4. Purpose of the study. Provide a brief description of the study. The description needs just enough to inform the participants of what you are studying.
5. Procedures. This is where you inform the participants of what they need to do in the study. Let participants know how much time you need to use and any other obligations.
6. Risks and benefits. First, tell the participants about any risks/harms from participating in the study. Second, let them know any benefits to them, society, or the academic discipline from their participation.
7. Anonymity. Let the participants know if you are keeping track of their names. If so, tell them what steps you will take to protect their identities.
8. Voluntary nature of the study. Make sure participants know their involvement is voluntary. Voluntary participation means they can end their involvement in the study at any time.

Focusing on key issues in an informed-consent form supports ethical research for participants. Participant privacy is the next issue you must consider when collecting research.

Participant Privacy

An important part of informed consent is the privacy of your participants. People may provide insight into their private lives, and only in rare circumstances should participants be identifiable. Researchers often use pseudonyms for participants. In quantitative studies with statistical results, participant names are never reported. It is important for participants to speak freely and answer questions without fear of being "outed" to the public. Thus, participant privacy is very important.

You can take two approaches with participant privacy. One approach is **confidentiality**. Confidentiality is when the researcher knows the names and personal information of the participants but does not share the information. The information can be very helpful if you need to contact the participants (e.g., follow-up interviews). **Anonymity** is when not even the researcher knows the participants' names or personal information. In Stephen's study on conflict styles among Muslims and non-Muslims in France, anonymity was used. Stephen did not know the participants' personal information because the participants were filling out anonymous surveys. As long as you are upfront with your participants as to what kind of privacy you are using, you are being ethical. Only in rare cases are participants' real names used.

Debriefing

In Milgram's studies at Yale University, he explored the power of control on individuals' actions. He showed that, with the right amount of influence exerted on an individual, most people will do just about anything to another person. Milgram had two people in separate rooms who could not see one another. One person read a series of numbers and the other person had to read the numbers back. If they got the series wrong, they were given an electric shock. The voltage increased each time they got an answer wrong. Over time, the person receiving the shocks would scream in pain, complain of their heart, and ask to end the experiment. The person giving the shocks would ask a helper if they could stop and were told they could not. The helper giving the order was a **confederate** (a person in on the project and assisting with data collection). The confederate would guide the participants to continue the electric shocks. Some participants stopped, but many continued to shock the other person until the screams ended. The person could have been dead from a heart attack. At the end of the experiment, the confederate reunited the two individuals. The one giving shocks realized they did not kill the other person. They were told the other person was in on it all along.

Our recounting of the Milgram experiment is necessary to provide an example of a debriefing exercise. **Debriefing** is when a researcher explains the research process after the research is completed. Debriefing provides participants a chance to ask questions and to remove any of their data from the study if they wish. The purposes of the study should be explained in the informed-consent form. However, deceiving participants may be necessary in some cases. If you are trying to study how people respond to persuasive messages in the media, you do not want to predispose them to your persuasive tactics. You might tell participants in the informed-consent form you are studying individuals' preferences for media messages. The IRB will weigh whether the benefits of your research outweigh deceiving your participants. Many IRBs will, in fact, ask you for a copy of your debriefing script, especially if your research includes any kind of deception.

Ethical Practices in School and Scholarship

As a college/university student, you have ethical responsibilities in your academic studies and in any research you conduct. If you are conducting research for a methods class, you must consider the ethical issues we have outlined. You may be asking, "I don't plan on presenting or publishing this paper. It's just a class project, so why do I need to go through the entire IRB process?" However, you have an ethical responsibility to get approval for your project. Formal approval ensures your project follows appropriate research guidelines. Your instructor will know if you are required to get official approval for a research project. Many instructors require their students to complete an IRB application even for in-class research projects.

Next, we must all work to avoid plagiarism. **Plagiarism** is using someone else's words or ideas without giving credit to the person or institution. Blatant examples of plagiarism include borrowing, buying, or stealing a paper and calling it your own. However, most examples of plagiarism are not this blatant. In the years Dan and Stephen have been teaching, the two have encountered borrowing, buying, or stealing someone else's paper less than five times (even five is too many). The most common form of plagiarism is when people use a quotation without using quotation marks or citing the source. We may find a great source that helps us make a great point in a paper but struggle with explaining the source in our own words. So, what happens is people "paraphrase" almost word for word. Changing a word or two in a sentence does not make it your own.

Remember, even an effective paraphrase must be cited. Author(s) deserve credit for their ideas. Most students do not intend to plagiarize when trying to paraphrase. This is why many faculty members will ask students about their intent in these situations. If you are aware of the need to avoid this situation and make things your own, you can avoid plagiarism.

Outline of the Book

Whenever we approach a textbook, we like to know the organization of the book and what we will be reading. This textbook is divided into three main sections: 1) Research Paradigms, 2) Research Design, and 3) Research Methods. At the end of each chapter, you will find a list of activities, discussion questions, and key terms to help clarify each chapter.

The first section is an introduction to research and research paradigms and has four chapters. The chapters define the various approaches to research (paradigms) and discuss ethical practices in research.

1. Chapter 1–Introduction and Ethics (you are reading it right now) discusses reasons for taking research methods, identifies key terms, reviews the importance of ethics and following ethical practices in research, and outlines the other chapters in the textbook.
2. Chapter 2–The Social Scientific Paradigm presents the first of the three research paradigms. The chapter defines the social scientific paradigm, discusses the development of the paradigm, and outlines key questions underlying this paradigm.
3. Chapter 3–The Interpretive Paradigm presents the second of the three research paradigms. The chapter defines the interpretive paradigm, discusses the development of the paradigm, describes the three main approaches to theory and method within this paradigm, and outlines key questions supporting this paradigm.
4. Chapter 4–The Critical Paradigm presents the final of the three research paradigms. The chapter defines the critical cultural paradigm, discusses the development of the paradigm, describes approaches to theory and method within this paradigm, and outlines key questions for the paradigm.

The second section focuses on Research Design and has three chapters. The chapters address issues related to what data is, how we evaluate research, and what constitutes hypotheses and research questions.

5. Chapter 5–Data explores research data. The chapter describes the various sources of data, defines data sampling, explains the various data collection settings, and discusses the different levels of measurement (types of variables) available.

6. Chapter 6—Evaluating Research discusses the various approaches to evaluating research. The chapter describes warrants for social scientific research, interpretive research, and critical/cultural research.

7. Chapter 7—Hypotheses and Research Questions describes hypotheses and research questions. The chapter describes the reasoning behind hypotheses and research questions, explains when to use which kind of hypothesis and/or research question, discusses how to test hypotheses and/or research questions, defines error, and provides a case study that applies the principles learned in the chapter.

The third section on Research Methods has 12 chapters. Each chapter introduces you to different methods you can use to explore, test, or analyze phenomena, theory, or research questions. The end of most chapters includes an example student paper of the method. These are real student papers written in a class like the one you are taking now. Maybe one of your papers will be included in a future edition of the textbook!

8. Chapter 8—Ethnography guides you in learning how to conduct ethnographic research. The chapter defines ethnography and the different approaches to ethnography; explains how to make claims with each approach, how to collect and analyze data, and what makes good ethnographic research; and provides a student paper example of ethnographic research.

9. Chapter 9—Interviewing describes how to conduct studies using interviews. The chapter defines interviewing and the different approaches to interviewing, describes data collection and grounded theory as a form of data analysis, and provides a student paper example of interviewing.

10. Chapter 10—Focus Groups develops skills to conduct focus groups. The chapter defines focus groups and explains why they are used, describes how to prepare and conduct a focus group, outlines the advantages and disadvantages of focus groups, and provides a student paper example of focus group research.

11. Chapter 11—Content Analysis explores the difference between quantitative and qualitative content analyses, different approaches to a content analysis, and the process for gathering and analyzing your data. The chapter concludes with a sample student paper.

12. Chapter 12—Discourse Analysis offers an approach for researching everyday communication. The chapter explores options for collecting and processing data to produce reliable research and identifies principles and practical advice for conducting a discourse analysis.

13. Chapter 13—Surveys helps you better understand the function of surveys. The chapter describes surveys, why they are used, survey creation, survey delivery, and data analysis. Next, the chapter explains the advantages and disadvantages of surveys and provides a student paper example of survey research.

14. Chapter 14—Descriptive Statistics breaks down the purpose of and the uses of statistics to organize and describe data. The chapter defines visual data, measures of central tendency, variability, and distribution and provides a student paper example that uses descriptive statistics.

15. Chapter 15—Inferential Statistics illustrates how statistics can be used to test for differences, relationships and prediction. The chapter explains the foundations of inferential statistics, tests of mean differences, tests of relationships and prediction, and provides a student paper example that uses inferential statistics.

16. Chapter 16—Experimental Design focuses on the purpose of experiments. The chapter defines experimental design and explains experiment preparation, variable selection, experimental design types, validity threats, and data analysis.

17. Chapter 17—Mixed Methods investigates the complex world of mixed-method research. The chapter sets the parameters for a mixed-method study, important issues to consider when planning a study, and the steps involved in conducting your research. The chapter concludes with a student paper using a mixed-methods approach.

18. Chapter 18—Rhetorical Criticism guides you in learning how to conduct rhetorical criticism. The chapter defines rhetoric, rhetorical criticism, and the various approaches to rhetorical criticism; explains how to conduct a rhetorical criticism; and provides a student paper example of a rhetorical criticism.

19. Chapter 19—The Process of Critique—guides you in learning how to conduct a critical/cultural study. The chapter explains the critical/cultural method, discusses various approaches, explains how to conduct a critical/cultural study, and provides a student paper example of a critical/cultural critique.

20. Chapter 20—Methods of Performance guides you through both the method and theory of using performance to illuminate communication. You will learn different ways to approach performance as a way of gathering and presenting qualitative data to understand communication and enact social change.

Summary

In this chapter, we explored the terrain of this course. Every class should be an adventure. Communication research methods are a process where you will exchange ideas on how to study a variety of different subjects. You will leave this class more prepared for your academic and nonacademic lives. In the next chapter we examine research ethics. As budding communication scholars, it is essential to start off on the right foot and understand the ethical principles of research.

Key Steps and Questions to Consider

1. Communication is a process of sharing meaning with others.
2. Communications is a technological system for the transmission of information.
3. Communication and communications are different. *Communication* is a human process of sharing meaning with others; *communications* is a technological system for the transmission of information.
4. A theory is a formal statement of rules on which a subject is based or an explanation of the relationship between variables.
5. Research is the detailed or in-depth study of a subject (often a theory) to reach a greater understanding or to obtain new information about the subject.
6. Method is the systematic technique or procedure used to conduct research.
7. Methodology is the study of a method or of multiple methods.
8. The method is the how to, and the methodology is the theory behind the method.
9. Ethics are the actions, thoughts, values, principles and communicative practices one enacts in determining how to interact with/treat others.
10. Utilitarian ethics comes from utilitarianism, which means one should have full freedom to conduct research as long as the benefits of the research outweigh the potential harms of that research.
11. Institutional Review Boards were developed after the Belmont Report was published.

12. Informed consent is where you tell participants, in a written document, what they will be doing in the study, explain the risks and benefits of their participation, explain that participants have a right to stop participation at any time, provide contact information for the researchers, get participant permission to participate in the study, and other things.
13. Two important elements of participant privacy are confidentiality and anonymity.
14. Debriefing is when a researcher explains all of the aspects and purpose(s) of the research process after the research is completed.

Discussion Questions

1. Why should we study communication?
2. Why are ethics important?

Key Terms

Anonymity	Ethics	Methodology
Communication	Exempt	Nonexempt
Communications	Expedited	Plagiarism
Confederate	Informed Consent	Research
Confidentiality	Institutional Review Board	Theory
Debriefing	Method	Utilitarian Ethics

References

Arnett, E. C., Harden Fritz, J. M., & Bell, L. M. (2009). *Communication ethics literacy*. Sage.

Audi, R. (Ed.). (1999). *Cambridge dictionary of philosophy* (2nd ed.). Cambridge University Press.

Baynard, P., & Flanagan, C. (2005). *Ethical issues and guidelines in psychology*. Routledge.

Croucher, S. M. (2011). Muslim and Christian conflict styles in Western Europe. *International Journal of Conflict Management, 22*, 60-74. Kampmeier, R. H. (1972). The Tuskegee study of untreated syphilis. *South Medical Journal, 65*, 1247-1251.

Mulford, R. D. (1967). Experimentation on human beings. *Stanford Law Review, 20*, 99-117.

Pojman, L. P. (2005). *How should we live? An introduction to ethics*. Wadsworth.

Shelley, M. W. (1992). *Frankenstein; or the modern Prometheus*. Everyman's Library.

Stolley, K. S. (2005). *The basics of sociology*. Greenwood Publishing Group.

2 The Social Scientific Paradigm

Chapter Outline

- Social Science Defined
- Development of Social Science
- Key Questions for Social Science
- Summary
- Key Steps and Questions to Consider
- Activities
- Discussion Questions
- Key Terms

What Will I Learn in This Chapter?

This is a photo of Professor Michael Pfau, the former chair of the Department of Communication at the University of Oklahoma. He passed away in 2009—but not before he taught and inspired generations of researchers, including Stephen. While he respected all paradigms, he was at his heart a social scientist. On Stephen's first day of the course, Introduction to Graduate Studies at the University of Oklahoma (many, many years ago), Michael said, "you should be any kind of researcher you want, as long as you are good at it." When he said he was a social scientist, a student asked what that was. He said his approach to research and theory closely resembled the natural sciences and that he looked for causal laws, looked to develop testable theories, gathered empirical data, and was value-free in his testing of theory. These four issues came up a lot in his discussions of social scientific theory and method. Michael made a prolific career out of being a social scientist; his work on inoculation has spawned countless studies (for reviews see Compton, 2013; Miller et al., 2013; Pfau & Burgoon, 1988; Pfau et al., 1990; Szabo & Pfau, 2002). Stephen became a social scientist largely due to Michael's influence and mentorship. When revising this textbook for the third edition, Stephen debated whether or not to discuss Michael in this chapter again or to bring in a new example. However, after consideration, he realized that Michael had such a profound effect on him and his understanding of social science that he deserved discussion again.

The social scientific paradigm is one of the three main paradigms or approaches to method discussed in this book; the other two are the interpretive (Chapter 3) and the critical/cultural

DOI: 10.4324/9781003109129-3

m (Chapter 4). Social scientists prefer to conduct research that looks for causal laws, es and predicts things, gathers empirical data, and tries to be as value-free as possible in research. This brings up a lot of questions. For example: 1) what is theory, 2) what are causal laws, 3) what is empirical data, and 4) what does it mean to be value-free in research? In Chapter 2, we answer these and other questions related to the social scientific paradigm.

Social Science Defined

Social scientific research borrows heavily from the scientific method. **Social science** is an organized method of research combining empirical observations of behavior with inductive and deductive logic to confirm and test theories that are then used to describe and/or predict human activity. For social scientists, describing and/or predicting human behavior, particularly through the testing of theory, is of the utmost importance. Theory testing is where the scientific method comes into play. However, before we jump into the scientific method, let's briefly differentiate between inductive and deductive logic.

In **inductive reasoning** our logical arguments move from specific observations to more broad generalizations, where one develops a pattern and then develops a theory. For example, Stephen recently induced the following about tūīs (a bird native to New Zealand) and their consumption of sugar water: one tūī liked sugar water (observation), tūīs like water with sugar (pattern), all tūīs like sugar water (theory). Stephen recently tested this theory using deductive reasoning. In **deductive reasoning**, our logical argument begins with a theory that we will test. Deductive reasoning is the result of inductive reasoning. Returning to the tūīs: his theory is that all tūīs like sugar water; his hypothesis is that adding a sugar water feeder in his backyard will increase tui visits to his backyard; he collects data and then analyzes the results. Stephen can report that it worked and there are a lot more tūīs when he has sugar water in a bird feeder in the yard.

The **scientific method** is a four-step systematic process in which a researcher conducts "research," which, as we discussed in the introductory chapter, can be done in various ways. The ancient Egyptians, Greeks, and Romans all created systems for conducting research that closely resembled today's scientific method. These systems were later modified by Sir Francis Bacon (1561–1626), René Descartes (1596–1650), David Hume (1711–1776), Charles Peirce (1839–1914), and many others. The scientific method has four basic steps that form the backbone of social scientific research: theory should be proposed or present, predictions should be made (hypotheses), observations should be made, and empirical generalizations should be generated.

The first step in the scientific method is proposing a theory. A **theory** is a conceptual representation or explanation of a phenomenon. Theories are attempts by researchers to represent processes. We all know Isaac Newton's (1642–1726) theory of gravity, simply put, "what goes up must come down." Countless scientists have made careers out of refining and expanding this theory into new horizons. Thanks to Newton's initial explanation of how gravity works, we have had breakthroughs in mathematics, architecture, and science. We identify eight critical things to know about theories in the following box (Craig & Tracy, 1995; Littlejohn, 1999).

Critical Things to Know About Theories

1. Theories organize and summarize knowledge and information. What we know about the world is organized into a collection of systematic theories created by researchers.

2. Theories focus attention on specific variables and the relationships between those variables. When you are thinking about a project and wondering what variables to look at, look to the body of theory for guidance on variable selection.

3. Theories clarify what is observed and how to study it in our research. Theories provide road maps for explaining and interpreting human behavior.

4. Theories allow for prediction of human behavior. As theories are systematic explanations of phenomena, we can make predictions based on certain kinds of data (we will talk more about predicting later in this chapter).

5. A "good" theory should generate research; this is the heuristic function of a theory.

6. No theory can reveal the whole truth about a phenomenon. Some descriptive and/or explanatory aspects will always be left out, which leave the theory partial and abstract.

7. People create theories. Theories represent how people see the world and not how some divine entity sees the world. It is important that we recognize that theories are not perfect. We need to continually test theories with new research. The issue of continued testing is at the heart of being a social scientist and represents what Popper (1968) argues is a key aspect of a theory; a theory must be **falsifiable** (or testable through empirical research).

8. Some theories have a generative function, which means the theory's purpose is to challenge existing cultural life and generate new ways of living.

The second step in the scientific method is developing predictions about the relationships between phenomena. Predictions usually come in the form of hypotheses. A **hypothesis** is a prediction about what a researcher expects to find in a study. Hypotheses are educated guesses (predictions) about relationships between variables. When conducting research, the purpose of hypotheses is to help researchers make predictions based on theories. We will talk much more about hypotheses in Chapters 5–7.

The third step in the scientific method is testing hypotheses—or the observation step. A researcher can test hypotheses in multiple ways. One purpose of this book is to provide new researchers (like you, maybe) with different ways to observe (test) your hypotheses. One important criterion for a social scientist when it comes to observation is that the method must be empirical, objective, and controlled. **Empiricism** is the notion that a researcher can only research what they can observe. Something you can't observe is generally outside of the realm of science. For example, most empirical researchers will not conduct research on the existence of God or gods. Why? The existence of God(s) is a matter of faith and something that cannot be empirically proven true or false. **Objectivity** refers to the need for a researcher to be sure his/her emotions and personal feelings do not interfere with his/her research. For a social scientist, objectivity is an important thing that they strive for in their research. For an interpretive or critical/cultural researcher, objectivity is not as much of a concern (more on this to come in the next two chapters). All researchers should recognize that the choice of method they make is a subjective choice. An interpretive or critical/cultural researcher relies more on subjectivity. For example, Dan is a qualitative and rhetorical researcher, while Stephen is a quantitative researcher. The fact that they use these methods represents a choice (subjectivity) on their part. In his work, Stephen discusses his role as an objective observer/researcher of human behavior. Dan, on the other hand, discusses his role as a more critical/subjective researcher.

Control is when the researcher makes sure personal biases and other influencing variables do not interfere with a project (or at least tries to prevent this). As much as social scientists attempt to make research value-free, we are human, and so our personalities and predetermined preferences will influence our research methods and findings to some extent (Condit, 1990). Researchers working in the natural sciences (like pharmaceuticals or medicine) take many steps to make research value-free. In medical experiments, researchers work to prove that the medicine (like a vaccine) is effectively combating the virus and not some other random variable interacting with the patient and the virus. This is why vaccines go through massive, long, and expensive clinical trials. We will talk more about such trials later in this book.

Once you have chosen a theory, generated a hypothesis/hypotheses, and tested them, you move to the fourth step of the scientific method, making empirical generalizations. **Empirical generalizations** are descriptions of phenomena based on what you know about them from previous research. Your generalizations should build on and/or refine theory in some way, and, if it is at all possible, provide some practical (real-world) implications from the research you conducted.

Michael Pfau's primary area of research was inoculation theory. The theory asserts that an individual can be inoculated against negative messages by giving them a small dose of the message before they encounter the full message. This is in essence a persuasive form of a flu shot. Michael and his research team developed numerous hypotheses over the years, and his students and colleagues continued to develop the theory after his death. They tested the hypotheses using surveys and experiments. Their research was empirical, they were objective, and they took numerous steps to control for interfering variables. His body of research has provided numerous refinements to inoculation theory and many practical implications for media, politics, economics, health, and many other walks of life. Michael argued that, if a message had the right level of persuasive elements in it, it could affect consumers enough so that they would not be impacted by future negative messages. Think about this in terms of the 2020 United States Presidential election and Trump's use of Twitter to build his base. Throughout 2020, Trump would post numerous tweets claiming that the Democrats, the FBI, the media, etc. would say or do this to hurt him and/or his political/economic agenda. While it may not have been his intent, such messages inoculated his base (to some extent) against any future messages that would criticise him. During the 2016 election, then-candidate Trump widely used Twitter to inoculate against negative campaign attacks (Baughman & Cali, 2017).

Now that we have gone over the basic definition of social science, the scientific method, and some critical things to know about theories, the next section of Chapter 2 provides a brief historical review of the development of social science.

Development of Social Science

The process of social science dates back to ancient Greece, Rome, and Egypt. During ancient times, ancient thinkers combined empirical observations of behavior (inductive logic) with deductive logic when confirming and discovering theories used to describe/predict human activity. Philosophers such as Hippocrates (460–370 BCE), whom you might know from the Hippocratic

Oath, would gather massive amounts of empirical data on issues and write about their observations. As the centuries progressed and data collection/scientific methods advanced, researchers continued to develop social science.

Great leaps forward were made in social science in Europe in the 1700s-1900s. Two British philosophers furthered a concept known as positivism, a highly social scientific paradigm. David Hume, in his *Treatise on Human Nature* (1739-1740), outlined how human nature affects scientific research and outlined his experimental method. John Stuart Mill (1806-1873), whom you might remember from his "Social Contract," discussed the relationships between logic and scientific research in his *A System of* Logic (1840). He specifically outlines five principles to inductive reasoning known as "Mill's method." Emile Durkheim (1858-1917), a French researcher, argued that science should be value-free in his *Rules of the Sociological Method* (1895). Durkheim argued that sociology must study social facts and that researchers must use the scientific method. Auguste Comte (1798-1858), in his *Cours de Philosophie Positivistic* (The Course of Positive Philosophy, 1830-1842), outlined the key principles of social science. He argued that the natural sciences were already being conducted properly, and that the social sciences should be conducted properly soon. Karl Popper (1902-1994), an Austrian, argued that a key aspect of social science was that theories and knowledge "can never be proven or fully justified, they can only be refuted" (Phillips, 1987, p. 3). This is the falsification aspect of theory mentioned earlier in this chapter. Collectively, these researchers paved the way for a wave of researchers who have continued to strive for value-free, logical, empirical, and predictive social scientific research.

With a basic understanding of the social scientific paradigm and some of its early researchers, the following section outlines nine key questions that guide social science.

Key Questions for Social Science

1. How do the social sciences differ from the natural sciences?

Social scientists are most concerned with describing and predicting human behavior. However, the "social" part of social science can be very unpredictable. While a biologist might be able to predict the exact composition of behavior of a single-cell organism, social scientists really cannot predict the exact behavior of human beings. For example, in 2020-2021, a social scientist would be very interested in an individual's intent to get vaccinated against COVID-19. Detoc et al. (2020) found that 75% of those they surveyed might get a vaccination. Issues such as fear of the virus and vaccine hesitancy all impacted people's willingness to say they would get the vaccine. While significant findings, the researchers could not definitively say (without question) who would or would not get a vaccine, as there are social variables that make it unpredictable. We will discuss more in-depth issues of significance and being able to definitively say something in later chapters. The key is that, even with a well conducted study, there is still the unknown.

2. What is the purpose of research?

As with every research paradigm, a key question to ask is: what is the ultimate purpose of the research? For a social scientist, the purpose of research is the discovery of theories that explain and predict human behavior and traits (Lindlof & Taylor, 2002; Littlejohn, 1999). To do this, social scientists collect data and test the data with systematically developed theories of human behavior and traits. The process of testing theories is endless, just as knowledge is endless (Neuman, 2011). It's important to note and remember that one of the reasons why the process is never-ending is because theories are not perfect. Theories are constantly refined as testing methods improve and as our understanding of phenomena changes.

3. What is reality?

For social scientists, reality can be observed by the researcher because reality is "out there" waiting to be observed, explained, and identified. Social scientists adopt a realist ontology (think back to the introductory chapter where we defined ontology). If we can see and/or touch something, then it really is not complex at its basic root. For example, we can see and therefore measure someone's biological sex, their age, and their income level. When variables relate to other variables, we work to explain why. For example, research on conflict styles in India has found that preference for conflict style differed based on participant sex (male/female) and education level (Croucher et al., 2011). Males tend to prefer the dominating style, while women prefer the avoiding, compromising, integrating, and obliging styles. Regarding educational level, the more educated a person was, the less likely they were to dominate in conflicts. Thus, when exploring conflict styles, it's important to consider the influence of variables like a person's sex and education level. Second, social scientists view reality as generally stable. Out traits and behaviors do not change *dramatically* over time; this is why we can conduct research today about human behaviors that can hopefully be viable in the future.

4. What is human nature?

Social scientists recognize that human beings are still animals (mammals). While we sometimes like to forget this fact, humans, unlike other mammals (as far as we know), are consciously self-interested, are rational, take steps to avoid pain, and seek out pleasure (Neuman, 2011). A social scientist typically tries to observe the stimuli occurring outside of the animal. These researchers understand the difficulties in isolating everything happening in the brain of an animal. As Durkheim (1938) argued, "social phenomena are things and ought to be studied as things" (p. 27).

5. Do humans have free will?

Social scientists are deterministic in their thinking. **Determinism** means social scientists believe humans and their actions are caused by identifiable external forces as well as internal attributes. This means a lot of our decisions in life are determined not only by our internal makeup (who we are) but also by our surroundings (culture, people around us, politics, economics, etc.). Social scientists, therefore, study how external behaviors affect humans. How these factors lead us to do certain things or act in certain ways is of critical interest. We are not saying humans are robots who bend to the will of external commands; however, some social scientists do think this way, unfortunately. With determinism backing social scientific thought, we are able to make our predictions about human behavior because we can estimate how specific stimuli may lead to a change in some behavior(s).

Michael Pfau's inoculation research showed that, if you give a person just the right amount of a persuasive message, you could inoculate them against a future negative persuasive message. This is powerful information if you consider how political candidates like Trump used messages to persuade people to vote for him. We are not making a political statement here, but as political campaigns try to reach their audiences and counter the messages of their opposition . . . they are regularly inoculating their base against their opposition. Thus, we have to ask, how are they influencing our free will?

6. What is theory?

Theory is one of the most important factors in research for a social scientist. Stephen fondly remembers Michael Pfau talking about how the goals of a social scientist are theory testing and theory building. In Stephen and Dan's early theoretical training, they were told social scientific theory involves the following. First, a theory can be descriptive, predictive, and/or causal in its explanation(s). If a theory is causal: X causes Y because Y and X are related in some way. If a theory is descriptive or predictive: X is related to Y because of A, B, C, D, etc. reasons. Second, a theory should clearly outline the situations under which it operates and/or applies. The situations are typically stated as boundary conditions (Dubin, 1978). One should not use a theory meant to study organizational dissent (Kassing, 1997) when studying how intimate partners express dissatisfaction about one another to their friends. Organizational dissent focuses on how organizational members express dissatisfaction or opinions about organizational issues. Third, for social scientists, a theory should typically have axioms, postulates, and theorems. These statements add to the testability of theories. Fourth, a theory should, if at all possible, be applicable in various cultural contexts.

7. How do you determine if an explanation is good or bad?

Social scientists use two criteria to determine whether an explanation or results are good or bad. First, you must ask yourself if the results are logical. Are contradictions evident in what you are presenting? If your results contradict previous research, can you offer a logical response as to why this might be the case? If your results are new, there needs to be a logical explanation as to why. In 2020, Stephen and his research team in New Zealand published a piece exploring prejudice toward Asians during the COVID-19 pandemic. Their analysis looked at prejudice levels members of the dominant groups in New Zealand, Spain, Italy, and the United States (whites) had toward Asians, who were largely blamed in each nation by media for the spread of COVID-19. Their results found that New Zealanders were the least prejudiced (Croucher et al., 2020). Research had not explored this before. Thus, it was essential for Croucher et al. to discuss how New Zealand's politically centric media and centralized government response that encouraged people to "be kind" more than likely led to lower levels of prejudice. Following this initial work, he has conducted additional analyses in New Zealand and other countries and found that government response and political position of the media does relate to prejudice levels. Thus, these initial thoughts have held true, thus far. Second, social scientists are fans of replication, more replication, and even more replication. A standard scientific practice is to repeat experiments to make sure they work the same way for every researcher every time. The same holds true for social scientific research. If you look at the method section of a journal article that uses statistics in a communication journal, you will find that most provide detailed information about how they conducted their research. The details are provided so that other researchers can replicate the work. While more details can always be provided to increase the chances of replication, replication is key to social science (Croucher & Kelly, 2020; Violanti et al., 2018).

8. How do you determine good and bad claims?

Claims are weighed based on our knowledge of empirical facts and theory. Popper argued that knowledge cannot be proven or entirely justified, it "can only be refuted" (Phillips, 1987, p. 3). In this sense, refuting claims to knowledge is the never-ending quest that social scientists consider the testing of theory.

9. What is the place of values in social science?

Social scientific researchers try to be value-free (objective). When conducting research from a social scientific paradigm, values and morals should not influence our research decisions and/or outcomes. Social scientists strongly believe that research should be free of interference from religious, political, and other personal influences that might alter the objectivity of a researcher's process and/or findings. A researcher should be a disinterested party, one who observes and reports on phenomena without allowing values/morals to interfere. Value-free research is the ideal for social science. However, this is not always the case, nor possible, as humans are by nature value-laden creatures. The job, then, of the social scientist is to recognize the place and impact of values on their research (Condit, 1990).

Michael Pfau told Stephen when he was a student that, to be a social scientist, he needed to do his best to be an observer and not to allow his personal feelings and/or other values to interfere with his research. Michael told his students that scientists like Copernicus and Kepler were persecuted because others around them allowed their religious views to interfere with how they interpreted research. For social scientists, research should be separate from values, but this is not 100% possible.

Summary

This chapter examined the first of the three paradigms, social science. As stated earlier, researchers who subscribe to this approach emphasize research that combines empirical observations of behavior with inductive and deductive logic to confirm and test theories that are used to describe and/or predict human activity. For social scientists, describing and/or predicting human behavior and activity, particularly through testing theory, is of the utmost importance. In the next chapter, we delve into a different research paradigm, the Interpretivist Paradigm.

Key Steps and Questions to Consider

1. Social science is a method of research combining empirical observations of behavior with inductive and deductive logic to confirm and test theories used to predict and/or predict human activity.
2. A theory is an explanation of a phenomenon. Theories are not perfect. Theories should be continually refined.
3. Social science is often based on hypotheses, which are educated guesses about relationships between variables.

4. Social scientists prefer objectivity over subjectivity.
5. While we try to describe, predict, and show causal relationships, human beings are not 100% predictable. Social science is, after all, the study of human beings.
6. Social scientists strive for value-free research. However, it is virtually impossible to have 100% value-free research.

Activities

1. Look back to the tūī example about deductive and inductive logic. Develop your own deductive and inductive logic reasoning theory.
2. Go to the most recent issue of one of the following communication journals: Communication Education, Communication Research Reports, or Journal of Intercultural Communication Research. Look through the articles and determine if the researchers are approaching their work from the social scientific approach. Look back to the criteria set in this chapter as guidelines for your arguments.

Discussion Questions

1. For a social scientist, what is the purpose of research?
2. What aspects of human behavior or life might be difficult to study for a social scientist? Why?
3. Why is the scientific method critical to research?

Key Terms

Control	Empiricism	Social Science
Deductive Reasoning	Hypothesis	Theory
Determinism	Inductive Reasoning	
Empirical Generalizations	Scientific Method	

References

Baughman, D., & Cali, D. D. (2017). Trump as troll: Personae and persuasive inoculation in the 2016 Presidential campaign. In R. Denton Jr (Ed.), *The 2016 US presidential campaign* (pp. 153–177). Palgrave Macmillan.

Compton, J. (2013). Inoculation theory. In J. P. Dillard & L. Shen (Eds.), *The SAGE handbook of persuasion: Developments in theory and practice* (pp. 220–236). Sage.

Condit, C. M. (1990). The birth of understanding: Chast science and the harlots of the arts. *Communication Monographs, 57*, 323–327.

Craig, T., & Tracy, K. (1995). Grounded practical theory: The case of intellectual discussion. *Communication Theory, 5*, 248–272.

Croucher, S. M., Holody, K. J., Hicks, M. V., Oommen, D., & DeMaris, A. (2011). An examination of conflict style preferences in India. *International Journal of Conflict Management, 22*, 10–34. https://doi.org/10.1108/10444061111103607

Croucher, S. M., & Kelly, S. (2020). Measurement in intercultural and cross-cultural communication. In E. E. Graham & J. P. Mazer (Eds.), *Communication research measures III: A sourcebook* (pp. 141–159). Routledge.

Croucher, S. M., Nguyen, T., & Rahmani, D. (2020). Prejudice toward Asian-Americans in the Covid-19 Pandemic: The effects of social media use in the United States. *Frontiers in Health Communication.* https://doi.org/10.3389/fcomm.2020.00039

Detoc, M., Bruel, S., Frappe, P., Tardy, B., Botelho-Nevers, E., & Gagneux-Brunon, A. (2020). Intention to participate in a COVID-19 vaccine clinical trial and to get vaccinated against COVID-19 in France during the pandemic. *Vaccine, 38,* 7002–7006. https://doi.org/10.1016/j.vaccine.2020.09.041

Dubin, R. (1978). *Theory building* (Rev. ed.). Free Press.

Durkheim, E. (1938). *Rules of the sociological method* (S. Solovav & J. Mueller, Trans. & G. Catilin, Ed.). University of Chicago Press.

Kassing, J. W. (1997). Articulating, antagonizing, and displacing: A model of employee dissent. *Communication Studies, 48,* 311–332. https://doi.org/10.1080/10510979709368510

Lindlof, T. R., & Taylor, B. C. (2002). *Qualitative communication research methods* (2nd ed.). Sage.

Littlejohn, S. W. (1999). *Theories of human communication* (6th ed.). Wadsworth.

Miller, C. H., Ivanov, B., Sims, J. D., Compton, J., Harrison, K. J., Parker, K. A., et al. (2013). Boosting the potency of resistance: Combining the motivational forces of inoculation and psychological reactance. *Human Communication Research, 39,* 127–155.

Neuman, W. L. (2011). *Social research methods: Qualitative and quantitative approaches* (7th ed.). Allyn & Bacon.

Pfau, M., & Burgoon, M. (1988). Inoculation in political campaign communication. *Human Communication Research, 15,* 91–111.

Pfau, M., Kenski, H. C., Nitz, M., & Sorenson, J. (1990). Efficacy of inoculation strategies in promotion resistance to political attack messages: Application to direct mail. *Communication Monographs, 57,* 25–43.

Phillips, D. C. (1987). *Philosophy, science and social inquiry: Contemporary methodological controversies in social science and related applied fields of research.* Pergamon.

Popper, K. R. (1968). *The logic of scientific inquiry.* Harper & Row.

Szabo, E. A., & Pfau, M. (2002). Nuances in inoculation: Theory and application. In J. P. Dillard & M. Pfau (Eds.), *The persuasion handbook: Developments in theory and practice* (pp. 233–258). Sage.

Violanti, M. T., Kelly, S. E., Garland, M. E., & Christen, S. (2018). Instructor clarity, humor, immediacy, and student learning: Replication and extension. *Communication Studies, 69,* 251–262. https://doi.org/10.1080/10510974.2018.1466718

3 The Interpretive Paradigm

Chapter Outline

- Interpretive Approach Defined
- Development of the Interpretive Paradigm
- Three Key Interpretive Approaches
- Key Questions for the Interpretive Paradigm
- Summary
- Key Steps Steps to Consider
- Activity
- Discussion Questions
- Key Terms

What Will I Learn About the Interpretive Paradigm?

The picture shows a cubistic face. We have always found abstract art fascinating because each image tells numerous stories. Anyone who looks at a picture will focus on different aspects, which is one of the purposes of abstract art and particularly cubist art. The artist's work compels us to think and feel. The use of color, shapes, shading, and myriad other techniques bring us into the picture and help the artist achieve their goals. What do you see in the face? What do you think the artist is trying to convey? The face will inspire multiple interpretations, since everyone's life is unique and we all have different lived experiences.

The concept of varied understandings is at the heart of the interpretive paradigm. The interpretive paradigm is the second of three paradigms we discuss. The other two paradigms are the social scientific and the critical/cultural. For interpretivists, the preference when doing research is to look for the varied interpretations or meanings. The multitude of interpretations and meanings in phenomena provide a wealth of information. Interpretivists are interested in theory, relationships, data, and value but have a different approach than social scientists. The four key questions for interpretivists are: 1) What is theory? 2) What is meaning? 3) What is data? 4) What is the place of value in the research process? In this chapter, we explore these four questions and other aspects of the interpretive paradigm to research.

DOI: 10.4324/9781003109129-4

Interpretive Approach Defined

The interpretive paradigm is one of the three main paradigms of research. The **interpretive paradigm** believes reality is constructed through subjective perceptions and interpretations. Interpretive researchers believe the study of human communication has different standards and methods than the natural sciences. Researchers using the interpretive paradigm study the social construction of meaning through the analysis of individualized purposes, goals, and intentions in communication.

You will find that interpretivists differ in their approach to the scientific method and scientific rigor. Interpretive research answers many of the same questions as social scientific and critical research, just in different ways than the other paradigms. As with the other research paradigms, interpretivists generate or test theories. However, an interpretivist has their own view of "theory." We will discuss this in depth in the "Key Questions for the Interpretive Paradigm" section of this chapter. Interpretivists rarely use hypotheses, instead using research questions to guide their work. Research questions are another form of educated guesses about the relationships between constructs (variables).

Interpretivists set aside the social scientific notion of empiricism (the notion that scholars can only research what they can observe). Instead, interpretivists generally embrace rationalism. **Rationalism** is the notion that we gain knowledge through the use of logic and reason. In this sense, we learn and describe the world around us through a variety of means. For example, most empiricists (e.g. social scientists) would not conduct research on the existence of God. However, a rationalist could conduct the research since individuals can describe in a variety of ways how they experience the existence of god(s).

Subjectivity is the condition for a researcher to be involved in or inseparable from the research context. A common practice for interpretive researchers is active participation in the research process, which means their personal connections (and identification of potential biases) to the research may be part of the research manuscript.

A researcher would have a hard time trying to explain from an empirical and objectivist (social scientific) point of view the varied interpretations of what the cubist face means to each one of us. We all come to the painting with different lived experiences and backgrounds. The subjective nature of art is interesting and brings to the table a broad diversity of perspectives.

We have now gone over the basics of the interpretive paradigm. The next section of the chapter offers a historical review of the paradigm. The review serves to help further define our understanding of the interpretive paradigm.

Development of the Interpretive Paradigm

Interpretivism developed as a response to the growth of social scientific inquiry in the 1800s and the 1900s. Social scientific calls to action from scholars such as Emile Durkheim (1858-1917) and Auguste Comte (1798-1857) began to grow, and many researchers, mostly German, questioned such calls to study human behavior from a more natural-science perspective. Scholars like George Wilhelm Hegel (1770-1831), Edmund Husserl (1859-1938), Ferdinand Töennies (1855-1936), Max Weber (1864-1920), and Georg Simmel (1858-1918) pioneered ideas such as *verstehen* (the interpretive approach to social science). The scholars claimed that the natural sciences were not effective for studying human behavior since the methods did not consider cultural norms, symbols, values, or individual social processes (Weber, 1991). Töennies, in fact, asserted that the major flaw of social science was failing to consider the influences of community (*gemeinschaft*) or society (*gesellschaft*) on human behavior (Cahnman et al., 1995). Through the work of these scholars, the interpretivist paradigm developed into various research fields still widely used today including hermeneutics, phenomenology, and symbolic interactionism.

Three Key Interpretive Approaches

Hermeneutics

Hermeneutics scholars were at first interested in studying and interpreting sacred texts, such as the Bible, the Talmud, and the Vedas. In the late 19th and early 20th centuries, this philosophy expanded into the examination of other kinds of texts. Wilhelm Dilthey (1833–1911) in his classic work (1977/1910) "The Understanding of Other Persons and their Expressions of Life" emphasized the importance of hermeneutics in understanding the individual spiritual experiences of others. Scholars such as Martin Heidegger (1889–1976), Hans-Georg Gadamer (1900–2002), and Jürgen Habermas (1929–) have all expanded hermeneutics to focus on how interpreting a text reveals something about the author(s) and the social context and provides a shared experience between the author(s) and the reader(s) (Gadamer, 2003).

Hermeneutic researchers in communication studies identify three key points. First, when exploring social activity, subjective understanding is paramount (not prediction, explanation, or control, which are key to the social scientific paradigm). For example, Waisanen (2013), in his analysis of a controversy with the Los Angeles County Seal, identified how different groups formed around the controversy. Each group had a different stake, different opinions, and a different way of experiencing the removal of a cross from the Los Angeles County Seal. Second, a variety of objects and concepts (things) are potential "texts" for analysis. Waisanen identified the texts as the seal, the cross, and a hearing between the Board of Supervisors and the public. Third, hermeneutic scholars argue that separating the observer from what they are observing is impossible and is the point where subjectivity comes into play. For Gadamer (2003), the observer is, in fact, an intrinsic part of the research process.

Phenomenology

Phenomenology is the systematic explanation and study of consciousness and subjective human experience (Husserl, 1970). The study of phenomena is how we experience things in life and the meanings things have for us. The key thinkers are Edmund Husserl (1859–1938), Martin Heidegger (1889–1976), Alfred Schultz (1899–1959), Jean Paul Sartre (1905–1980), and Maurice Merleau-Ponty (1908–1961). Husserl, in his concept of transcendental phenomenology, was keenly interested in the experiences we take for granted. All of our activities and experiences have a certain structure to them, and we often overlook these structures. Thus, the process is to step back—transcend the phenomenon—in order to better understand what is happening or has happened.

For example, every time you have class you may have a verbal exchange with your teacher. How does this exchange happen? What do you say and what does the teacher say? How do the two of you verbally and nonverbally interact? The interaction might have become second nature for both of you. However, if you investigate the interaction or experience, you are trying to transcend the taken-for-granted aspects. Why do we interact the way we do? The process of transcending is what Husserl called epoche—or trying to set aside taken-for-granted aspects of an experience to gain a deeper grasp of the experience. In Leonard's (2013) phenomenological analysis of a Polar-Eskimo language in northern Greenland, he explains his experiences of engaging with language and culture. In his analysis, Leonard dissects the experience of speaking and knowing a language, which are often things people take for granted.

Symbolic Interactionism

Symbolic interactionism is an area of research emphasizing the relationships between symbols, the social world, and social interaction. Primary credit with founding and furthering this approach to research goes to Charles Horton Cooley (1864-1929), George Herbert Mead (1863-1931), and Herbert George Blumer (1900-1987). Mead is credited with founding the approach even though he never used the term "symbolic interactionism". The interpretive symbolic interactionists are primarily associated with the "Chicago School of Thought" (since most were located in or near Chicago). In 1934, Mead outlined three connected ideas that have become essential for symbolic interaction studies. Human thought (the mind) and social interaction (self and others) help us make sense of the world in which we live (our society). When you consider these three essential ideas, we understand how researchers can conduct studies from this perspective.

MacLean (2008) explored framing organizational misconduct through deceptive sales practices. Using archival data, interviews, and a published report, MacLean found that organizational members acting on behaviors socially constructed by the organization and society shape the notion of misconduct. The three interpretive philosophies—approaches to research—can be conducted using a variety of research methods. You will find all three approaches may use ethnography, interviewing, focus groups, qualitative content analysis, and other methods.

With a basic understanding of the interpretive paradigm, its development, and three approaches to interpretive research, the following section outlines the same nine questions posed in Chapter 2 for the social scientific approach. The comparison will help you understand the interpretive approach and the differences between the paradigms.

Key Questions for the Interpretive Paradigm

1. How does the interpretive approach to science differ from the natural sciences?

In Chapter 2, we talked about how biologists and other natural scientists may predict the exact composition of an organism, but social scientists are not able to make similar predictions of human behavior. Interpretivists, on the other hand, are not interested in *predicting* human behavior but rather *understanding* human experiences. For example, while a social scientist might try to predict a relationship between *World of Warcraft* and violent behavior(s), an interpretivist might study how a player understands and/or experiences violence in the game. Klimmt et al. (2006) conducted interviews with players of violent video games. Their analysis explains why people play the games through the moral justification given for enjoying violent games. Such an analysis would be difficult to achieve through a social scientific approach.

2. What is the purpose of research?

The main goal of research for interpretivists is to understand how people construct meaning in life and understand experiences. If you look back at the definitions of hermeneutics, phenomenology, or symbolic interactionism, you will see all have one thing in common—they each study some aspect of meaningful social action or interaction. Geertz (1973) asserted that human actions are meaningless unless considered in their social and cultural contexts. This exploration of meaning is at the heart of the interpretive paradigm.

3. What is reality?

For interpretivists, reality is created through social interaction. Social interaction and reality are primarily what people perceive them to be (experiences and meaning). Our subjective experiences create our individual realities. While social scientists see the world in an objective, realist ontological point of view, interpretivists take a constructionist perspective (Neuman, 2011), meaning people construct reality out of their own experiences. For example, "snow." We all experience snow falling to the ground differently. For example, Stephen lived in Finland for a number of years (he now lives in New Zealand). In October and November, Finns look forward to snow because the months are normally rainy and dark with little sunlight. Finns typically feel a bit better when the snow reflects the stars. They know holiday lights are coming and soon things will get brighter. Stephen's parents live in the United States (Nebraska) and see snow as a sign of icy roads and shoveling, not happy things. The constructions of "snow" differ, which lead to different realities.

4. What is human nature?

While social scientists look for patterns leading to explanation, prediction, and control, interpretive researchers understand patterns differently. Interpretive researchers believe patterns exist in human nature, but the patterns are a result of ever-evolving meaning systems, norms, and conventions people learn through interactions. The study on video game moral concerns (Klimmt et al., 2006) is an excellent example of researchers' interest in how human nature evolves within a particular issue in a given context. A central idea is how the morality of the players is socially constructed (Klimmt et al., 2006).

5. Do humans have free will?

Many social scientists support the idea of determinism—the belief humans and their actions are mainly caused by identifiable external forces and internal attributes. Interpretive researchers generally advocate for **voluntarism**—the idea people are able to make conscious choices based on reason. Researchers must be considerate of subjects' feelings and decision-making processes. Such processes and feelings often reveal how participants understand phenomena (phenomenology) and interact with society (symbolic interactionism).

6. What is theory?

Social scientific research strives to be descriptive, predictive, or causal in its explanations. Interpretive theories try to describe or understand the lives of people in their social environment. Interpretive theorizing may make limited generalizations. However, interpretive theories focus on the social and lived experiences of individuals. For example, Collier and Thomas' (1988) cultural identity theory was designed as an interpretive theory (Collier, 1998). The theory explains how identities are negotiated in discourse.

7. How do you determine if an explanation is good/bad?

While social scientists are big fans of replication, interpretive researchers do not see replication as a major necessity. For interpretive researchers, two closely connected issues are key. First, the explanation must make sense to those the researcher is studying. As a researcher, you are studying a group of people and trying to convey their experiences. Your interpretation of their experiences should make sense if they read it. Second, the explanation should make enough sense so others can also understand the experiences of the group(s) you studied. When someone tells you a story and then you try to retell the story to someone else, you should try to be as true to the original story as possible. If you are not true to the original story, you may lose important information and the original intent of the storyteller.

8. How do you determine good/bad claims?

For social scientists, claims are weighed based on empirical facts and theory. For interpretive researchers, explanations/research should provide in-depth description of phenomena and offer coherent interpretation of experiences. A goal is to provide what Geertz (1973) called "thick description." Interpretive researchers detail the experiences of others by providing a "thick" or rich description to substantiate the analysis.

9. What is the place of values in social scientific research?

Interpretive researchers embrace and analyze their position in the research process. For these scholars, separating values and morals from research decisions/outcomes is impossible. An interpretive researcher is not a disinterested, objective scholar who reports on phenomena. Instead, an interpretive researcher is a subjective participant who is actively involved in the research process.

Let's return to the cubist face that starts the chapter. An interpretive researcher could conduct in-depth interviews with individuals on their understanding of the painting. The researcher will more than likely get numerous responses. How have the social interactions, upbringing, and culture shaped participants' perceptions of the face? How does the researcher's background influence how they see the face? The extent to which the researcher is involved in the process is an important factor to consider.

Summary

In this chapter, we examined the Interpretivist Paradigm. Unlike the Social Scientific Paradigm, the Interpretivists believe in the social construction of reality through subjective perceptions and interpretations. Such researchers, unlike the social scientists, believe the study of human beings should not and cannot be held to the same standards/methods as the natural sciences.

Key Steps to Consider

1. The interpretive paradigm believes reality is constructed through subjective perceptions and interpretations.

2. Rationalism is the notion that we gain knowledge through logic. In this sense, we learn and describe the world around us through a variety of means.
3. Subjectivity is the need and desire for a researcher to be involved in or inseparable from the research context.
4. Hermeneutics scholars were first interested in interpreting/studying sacred texts, such as the Bible, the Talmud, or the Vedas. This interest expanded into the examination of various kinds of texts.
5. Phenomenology is the study of phenomena, how we experience things in life, and the meanings things have for us.
6. Symbolic interactionism is an area of research that emphasizes the relationships between symbols, the social world, and social interaction.
7. Interpretivists are interested in understanding human experiences.
8. Interpretive researchers generally advocate for voluntarism—or the idea that people are able to make conscious choices based on reason.

Activity

1. Develop a "cheat sheet" for comparing the different research paradigms.
   a. Prepare a chart with four columns and 10 rows.
   b. Label the three columns (in the first row): 1) Key Questions; 2) Social Science; 3) Interpretive Paradigm; 4) Critical/Cultural.
   c. Fill in the rows of column 1 under your Key Questions heading with abbreviated versions of the Key Steps and Questions listed in each chapter (e.g., "interpretive approach vs. natural sciences").
   d. Fill in your Social Science and Interpretive Paradigm columns with significant components to help you remember how to distinguish between the different approaches. You can add to the Critical/Cultural column after reading Chapter 4.

Discussion Questions

1. How will following the interpretive paradigm alter approaches you might take for different communication research projects?
2. Researchers, while familiar with all the research approaches, tend to gravitate toward one of the paradigms. What aspects of the interpretative paradigm do you find compelling? What aspects do you find disquieting?

Key Terms

Hermeneutics	Rationalism	Voluntarism
Interpretive Paradigm	Subjectivity	
Phenomenology	Symbolic Interactionism	

References

Cahnman, W. J., Maier, J. B., Tarr, Z., & Marcus, J. T. (Eds.). (1995). *Weber and Töennies: Comparative sociology in historical perspective*. Transaction Publishers.

Collier, M. J. (1998). Researching cultural identity: Reconciling interpretive and post-colonial perspectives. In D. V. Tanno & A. Gonzales (Eds.), *International and intercultural annual: Volume 21, communication and identity across cultures* (pp. 121–147). Sage.

Collier, M. J., & Thomas, M. (1988). Cultural identity. In Y. Y. Kim & W. B. Gudykunst (Eds.), *Theories in intercultural communication* (pp. 99–120). Sage.

Dilthey, W. (1977/1910). The understanding of other persons and their expressions of life. In *Descriptive psychology and historical understanding*. Springer. https://doi.org/10.1007/978-94-009-9658-8

Gadamer, H.-G. (2003). *Truth and method* (2nd ed.). Continuum.

Geertz, C. (1973). *The interpretation of cultures*. Basic Books.

Husserl, E. (1970). *The crisis of European sciences and transcendental phenomenology: An introduction to phenomenological philosophy*. Northwestern University Press.

Klimmt, C., Schmid, H., Nosper, A., Hartmann, T., & Vorderer, P. (2006). How players manage moral concerns to make video game violence enjoyable. *Communications: The European Journal of Communication Research, 31*, 309–328.

Leonard, S. P. (2013). Phenomenology of speech in a cold place: The Polar Eskimo language as "lived experience." *International Journal of Language Studies, 7*, 151–174.

MacLean, T. L. (2008). Framing and organizational misconduct: A symbolic interactionist study. *Journal of Business Ethics, 78*, 3–16.

Neuman, W. L. (2011). *Social research methods: Qualitative and quantitative approaches* (7th ed.). Allyn & Bacon.

Waisanen, D. J. (2013). Hermeneutic range in church-state deliberation: Cross meanings in the Los Angeles County Seal controversy. *Western Journal of Communication, 77*, 361–381. https://doi.org/10.1080/10570314.2012.762802

Weber, M. (1991). The nature of social action. In W. G. Runciman (Ed.), *Weber selections in translation* (pp. 7–32). Cambridge UP.

4 The Critical Paradigm

James P. Dimock

Chapter Outline

- Traditional Approaches to the Study of Power
- Rise of Marxism and Critical Theory
- The Postmodern Turn in Criticism
- What Happened?
- What is Postmodernism?
- Conclusion
- Summary
- Key Steps and Questions to Consider
- Discussion Questions
- Activities
- Key Terms

What Will I Learn About Critical Theory?

In the classic Disney-Pixar film *A Bug's Life*, an ant named Flik stands up to the Hopper, the leader of a gang of grasshoppers who tyrannize the ant colony. As winter approaches, however, many of Hopper's gang are not interested in going back to Ant Island to deal with one rebellious ant. Hopper demonstrates the importance of dealing with Flik through a brilliant, if violent, metaphor:

> "Let's pretend this grain is a puny little ant," Hopper says, throwing a few seeds at a couple of reluctant gang members. He asks, "Did that hurt?"
> "Nope," says one gang member.
> "Are you kidding?" laughs another.
> "How about this?" Hopper asks opening a chute and burying them under thousands of seeds. Hopper explains the way the world works to the rest of his gang, "You let one ant stand up to us then they all might stand up. Those 'puny little ants' outnumber us a hundred to one and if they ever figure that out, there goes our way of life. It's not about food. It's about keeping those ants in line. That's why we're going back!"

DOI: 10.4324/9781003109129-5

Hopper's monologue is about power. The grasshoppers' power over the ants isn't physical. One grasshopper is stronger than one ant or even several ants put together, but, if the ants collectively stand up to the grasshoppers, they are physically stronger. The grasshoppers' power is what critical theorists call **ideological**, that is to say, ideological power functions at the level of the ants' thinking about the world, about what they are–and are *not*–capable of doing. Hopper's power is over the ants and his fellow grasshoppers. His companions would have been satisfied living out the winter without going back to Ant Island. Hopper uses both the threat of violence and the use of language to **interpolate** the ideology of power and control in the minds of the grasshoppers. After all, their entire "way of life" is at stake. If the grasshoppers are reluctant to use their power, they may lose everything.

Critical theorists are primarily concerned with power and **oppression**–or the exercise of power by one entity (e.g., a person, group, organization) for its own benefit over another entity. Critical theory is different from other approaches to communication research, since it looks for ways to change the relationships of power and overcome oppression. In this chapter, you will learn about critical methods of research. You may notice this chapter is longer than the other two paradigm chapters (Chapters 2 and 3). By its nature, the critical paradigm is complex, and newcomers often find it convoluted. A number of brief history lessons are needed to understand how the critical paradigm came about. Take your time as you move through the chapter. Let the concepts "percolate" for a while until they reach a nice strong brew. Then you will be ready to take a good long drink and enjoy the critical approach to research methods.

Traditional Approaches to the Study of Power

Power, sometimes called **influence**, has been a subject of interest for social theorists, political scientists, and communication researchers for a long time. In fact, the earliest communication theorists and scholars, the Greek Sophists, were interested in how to use language to influence large groups of people, such as juries and legislative assemblies. Traditionally, power has been understood by communication scholars as the ability to perform an act that will result in a change in someone else (Cartwright & Zander, 1968). For example, Olivia could tell Peter she will beat him up if he does not give her his lunch money. If Peter gives Olivia his lunch money, an act he would not otherwise have done, then we can say Olivia has power over Peter. This type of power is called **coercive power** because it threatens some harm. Olivia could have convinced Peter to give up his lunch money by promising to do his homework for him (**reward power**) or by reminding Peter he had borrowed money from her earlier and promised to pay it back (**legitimate power**). Olivia could have used **persuasive power** by making a compelling argument to turn over the lunch money. Persuasive power is the form of most interest to communication scholars.

A traditional understanding sees power as both a thing (an object that people have and use) and a performance (an action people carry out). This locates power in the consciousness of the person with power (Olivia) and in the consciousness of the person over whom power is exercised (Peter). The idea of power as both a thing and an action influenced Georg Wilhelm Friedrich Hegel (1770-1831), one of the most significant thinkers of the 19th century. Like many philosophers in a dramatic, transformative age, Hegel was interested in change and especially shifts in power and systems of power. The 18th and 19th centuries were a time of great change. Monarchies and religious organizations were losing power as democratic institutions became stronger and economies liberalized and industrialized. Hegel came to believe all of history was the history of change and thus also "the history of thought." For Hegel, as with most critical theorists today, the way we think determines material and historical conditions under which we live.

Hegel's approach is an expression of the scientific and philosophical thinking since the Enlightenment (1685-1815). This rationalist paradigm, first propagated by physicists like Galileo, was rooted in mechanical physics as the master science. They believed the universe and everything in it, including humans and societies, functions much like a pocket watch. The universe is a closed system in which matter in motion causes other matter to move. But rationalism could not explain how things changed. In mechanical physics, change only comes from the outside. As the pocket watch winds down, a force outside the system—a key and a hand to turn it—make the watch go again. However, for mechanical physics, nothing outside of the universe compels the change.

So, what produces change? Hegel believed in dialectic—a tension—between an idea and its contradiction. We tend to think of a contradiction as a thing's opposite. Black is the contradiction of white; yes is the contradiction of no. However, Hegel had a different idea in mind. Gasper (2010) explained contradiction with an example: within every caterpillar lies the potential to become a butterfly. The moment the butterfly comes into existence, the caterpillar ceases to exist. And yet the butterfly does not have the potential to become a caterpillar. Thus, within every caterpillar lies its own negation (the butterfly negates the existence of the caterpillar). If you negate the caterpillar, though, you also negate the butterfly. The important part of the story, for Hegel, is the movement from one to the other—the process of becoming. This Hegel called the **dialectic** or the contradiction within an idea, that an idea contains its own negation.

Hegelian thought is extremely dense and complicated, and we provide only a brief glimpse of his ideas. Suffice to say, for Hegel, a person's place in the universe is determined by thought (the world of ideas). For Hegel, "the sole method by which those who have the good of society at heart can improve society, is to develop in themselves and in others the power of analyzing themselves and their environment" (Berlin, 1963, p. 49). An analysis of self and others is called **critique** (or in the German form *kritik*). Systems of human interaction are systems of the mind; they are ideas and they resist change. However, the ideas contain the elements of their own negation in the same way a butterfly may negate the caterpillar. True change comes from changing ideas or what Hegel called the **Spirit**.

Hegel's philosophy came to dominate the thinking of Europeans, especially Continental philosophers, during the 19th century. In the wake of the French Revolution and the Napoleonic Wars, the thinking took on a decidedly antirevolutionary, or **reactionary**, form. Ideas were understood to be the driving force of history. A nation was the manifestation of a particular idea that cannot simply vanish through revolutionary action or through the efforts of reformers. Only through the nation and the state could a person be what they were supposed to be, and the desire to radically transform the state was self-destructive. Hegel's philosophy elevated intellectuals and idea-shapers such as artists, writers, scientists, and philosophers as the true agents of change.

Let's return to the example of Olivia and Peter. Traditional philosophy could explain why Olivia has power over Peter but not what changed—or might change—that relationship. How could Peter keep his lunch money? Is there a world in which Olivia gives Peter her lunch money? For Hegelians and many critical theorists today, such change begins not in changing actions or behaviors but rather in the ideas that permitted Olivia to believe she had a right to demand Peter's lunch money and Peter believing he must do so.

Rise of Marxism and Critical Theory

Many philosophers embraced the earlier works of Hegel, which stressed the importance of change and freedom, while rejecting his later support of authoritarianism and nationalism. These philosophers were called the Young Hegelians, and they believed ideas are the driving force in history. Others agreed with Hegel's philosophy of change but rejected his idealism. One of the most influential was Karl Marx. (His picture starts out this chapter. Did you think the picture was Flik in his later years?!).

Karl Marx was born in 1818 in the town of Trier in the German Rhineland. He lived in a time of great change. In the years following the French Revolution and the Napoleonic Wars, many Germans hoped the hodgepodge of independent feudal states would be united to form a single nation-state like France or Britain. When Napoleon subjugated the Germans, he imposed a set of laws called **The Napoleonic Code**, which, among other things, lifted many of the prohibitions on Jews entering civil life. Marx's father, Herchel Levi, came from a long line of Rabbis in the Rhineland and took advantage of the code to become a lawyer. The hopes for a liberal Germany were lost following Napoleon's disastrous invasion of Russia in 1812 and his final defeat at Waterloo in 1815. The aristocracy in Germany was restored and promptly reasserted its authority. In 1816, anti-Jewish laws effectively cut off Levi's livelihood. The year before Karl Marx was born, his father converted to Lutheranism and changed his name from Herchel to the more German-sounding Heinrich. Isaiah Berlin (1963) recounts a story of Heinrich giving a speech at a public dinner. Heinrich suggested a wise and benevolent ruler ought to support moderate political and social reform. This mild criticism attracted the attention of the Prussian police, and Marx's father was quick to recant his statements. In Berlin's words:

> It is not improbable this slight but humiliating contretemps [minor dispute], and in particular his father's craven and submissive attitude, made a definite impression on his oldest son Karl Heinrich, then sixteen years old, and left behind it a smoldering sense of resentment, which later events fanned into flames.
>
> (p. 23)

In his adult life, Karl Marx went on to become one of the most insightful and outspoken critics of the new social and political order called capitalism. He remained skeptical of "reformist" approaches to change, tinkering with laws and changing the way things were named and would argue for radical, substantive change in the way people lived their lives and met their daily needs.

Marx was a positivist, a social thinker who believed human behavior was an intelligible, understandable part of the universe. Like Darwin, he saw human beings as part of the natural world. Whatever human beings were, it wasn't a divine force or spirit that made us but the same kind of forces that shaped other social animals, the struggle for survival. For most of human history, we've been driven by the need for food, protection from the elements and from other animals. Humans are, however, different from other animals. Much of philosophy—from Plato and Confucius to the present—is an effort to figure out what makes humans different from other animals. Aristotle, for example, said humans were logical and political animals. Others believe the ability to produce and use tools makes humans unique, while still others have said it is our ability to cry. For Marx, the central and defining aspect of human beings is **labor**. Many creatures transform their environments—birds build nests, and beavers build dams. Yet human labor is fundamentally different. Through labor, human transform their environments and themselves.

Labor power, which for Marx consists of the "aggregate of those mental and physical capabilities existing in a human being, which he exercises whenever he produces a use-value of any description" (p. 336), transformed human beings and forever altered human needs in fundamental ways. What makes human labor different from other animals' labor, the source of its transformative potential, is our ability to divide that labor and to specialize. This is something no other animals do. This is of interest to critical communication researchers because this **division of labor** requires complex and adaptable forms of communication.

As far back as Plato in the 4th century B.C.E., philosophers have talked about this division of labor and its importance in human social evolution. Labor and the division of labor are key concepts in the work of economic philosopher Adam Smith writing in the late 17th century C.E. and early sociologists like Emile Durkheim (1955), who argued the division of labor defined civilization. This division regulates our interactions lest conflicts "incessantly crop out anew" and "mutual obligations had to be fought over entirely anew in each particular instance" (pp. 5-6).

A society without division of labor has each person equally trained and responsible for every task. In such a society, every person is his or her own farmer, blacksmith, police officer, etc. Division of labor maximizes efficiency and permits specialization and innovation. One person specializes in farming, another in breeding oxen for plowing, a third in making plows and farm implements, and a fourth to conduct communication research. (You are now training for the fourth specialization!) Given time to specialize and engage in a craft, each person gets better, recognizes opportunities to improve, and becomes more efficient. Overtime, people identify with the work they perform and take pride and find meaning in their work. The division of labor depends upon fixing social and economic roles. As Marxists understand it, the division of labor is part of a system of **relationships of production** based on social and political classes.

Understanding Class

Many people have trouble understanding class, particularly in places like the United States where class is not something we talk about very often. The U.S. does not have a history of formal nobility, so we don't have many historical or material indicators of class, and those we do are indicators not of *class* but *wealth* (e.g., lower class, middle class, and upper class). Marx understood the relations of production produce two classes, the bourgeoisie (the ruling class) and the proletariat (the working class). A third class, the petite bourgeoise (the middle class), served as coordinators and technicians who administered the rule of the bourgeoise. The petite bourgeoise identified with the ruling class and, in many societies, benefitted from the exploitation of the proletariat. Especially at the upper layers, the petite bourgeoise often has far more resources and access to power than the lower levels and exponentially more than the working class, but, at every layer, the privileges enjoyed by the petite bourgeoise are tied to its support for the ruling class.

The definition of class has little to do with how much money a person has or makes but rather with their relationship to the **means of production**. Every society has means of producing wealth. In an agricultural society, the economic base is land, which is necessary to produce food for humans and animals. In an industrial society, production might be the factories to produce consumer goods. Under capitalism, it is the control of capital. The ruling class controls the capital—the land the factory sits on, the money it needs to buy more raw materials, the shipping lanes to distribute what it makes. The economy depends on what the ruling class controls. Control is what makes them the ruling class. The working class has only their labor to sell. Remember, for Marx, labor is what defines a human being, so selling one's labor is selling one's self. The worker has little choice in what is made, the conditions under which it's made, or to whom it's sold. Of course, a worker can choose to work or to work somewhere else, yet the worker is never in control of those conditions. The factory owner, on the other hand, has all kinds of options. He can choose not to hire anyone, close the factory, move to another city, or make a different product.

In a world in which a person owns his or her own labor, they decide what they will make and when and how it will be used. Let's say a cobbler makes shoes and invents a technique to improve her efficiency and make more shoes in less time. She benefits from her innovation by having extra time to do something else or by making even more shoes and more profit. But if a worker in a shoe factory comes up with the same innovation, the rewards of creativity go to the factory owner. This isn't a hypothetical or historical example. When Jim, who wrote this chapter, worked for a big tech firm, any technological idea he came up with was legally the property of his employer. If he thought of a better way to make computers, that better way was the property of the company who owned his labor, including his intellectual labor.

This separation between the person and the products of their labor was, for Marx, harmful on a social, psychological, and emotional level. In mass production, the worker typically only produces a small part of the final product. This **de-skilling** of labor alienates the worker, reducing one to a tool. The alienation extends to the social system as a whole. Workers see others as competitors with whom they must compete to keep their jobs. Alienation is helped by racial and cultural myths that may further divide workers, preventing them from realizing the power of unification. Alienation **dehumanizes** us. Separating workers from their labor makes them less human in how they relate to one another and how they understand themselves. The ruling class (the bourgeoisie for Marx) is also caught up in the cycle of dehumanization. They are separated from themselves because, while they do not labor the same as workers, they purchase, which furthers an insatiable need to find meaning through consumption.

It is sometimes challenging for people raised in the U.S., where class is very real but often invisible, to think about class, and it is easy to confuse class with money. Rich means ruling class, and poor means working class. That is misleading. Class is defined by a person's relationship to the means of production and their level of ownership over their labor. In order to understand the distinction between classes, let's think of a professional football team. The players—even while many of them make significant amounts of money—are the working class. Their bodies are put on the line suffering damage from being hit over and over again. Their labor produces the game. While we may think of the players as rich and part of the ruling class, they are workers alienated from their labor in many respects. Most have little say in deciding the team they play for and no control over the lineup, the game schedule, or the rules. American football player Colin Kaepernick was driven out of the league not for his inability to play but because he insisted on expressing his political opinions. He could choose to play only if he also chose to abide by rules. Nor could Kaepernick go and play for another team. While the owners may hate things like players' unions and talk about individualism, team owners, like the bourgeoise in Marx's day, often worked together behind the scenes to "blackball" or "lock out" troublesome workers who may have had the right skills but lacked the company attitude. In American football, players need to both have talent and "be grateful" for the opportunity to play. Grateful players do not criticize the system. That's one of the rules, and the rules, both spoken and unspoken, are set by and to benefit the owners in the league. Not the players and not the fans. The issue isn't money, but one's position in the relationships of production, which determines one's class.

Understanding Ideology

Next, we need to understand Marx's distinction between the **base** (also called the **substructure**) and the **superstructure**. Our social world begins with real, material, productive forces and resources. Some communities are built along rivers, which provide transportation or fishing, others on salt flats or grazing lands. The available resources are real material forces that determine the range and scope of economic relationships. In order to live, individuals enter into economic relationships with each other. These material resources and the necessary economic relationships are the base (substructure) of society. Upon this base, the superstructure of the society is built. The superstructure consists of the visible forms of society such as art and culture and institutions like the courts, police, and religion. If the function of the base is production, the function of the superstructure is to reproduce the conditions of production.

In order for the means of production to keep on producing, labor power requires "the material means with which to reproduce itself" (Althusser, 1989, p. 63). These means are wages—the money paid to the worker to purchase housing, food, clothing, and other items to "to present himself at the factory gate" (Althusser, p. 64) each morning, ready to offer his labor power.

But what of the relations of production? At the beginning of this chapter, we looked at an important scene from the movie *A Bug's Life*. The ants, if they gathered together and stood up to the grasshoppers, would surely win. They outnumber the grasshoppers at least a hundred to one! This, Althusser argued, is ideology.

Ideology is a difficult word to understand because many people use the word, and they use it—and even pronounce it—in many different ways. We are going to use the term the way Marx and his co-writer Fredrick Engels (1978) used it in their work *The German Ideology* and how Althusser (1989) used the term in his essay "Ideology and Ideological State Apparatuses." For Marx, Engels, and Althusser, ideology (usually pronounced with a soft *ī*) means a type of false consciousness. An illusion that makes the real world difficult, but not impossible, to see and understand.

Power, from a Marxist perspective, is maintained in two ways. The first is through what Althusser called the **Repressive State Apparatus**. Althusser, like Marx and Engels, did not use the word *state* to refer to a political subdivision (e.g., the State of Illinois, the State of Kansas) but to an independent political entity (e.g., the United States, Great Britain). The state has sovereign power since not subject to any other power. Althusser (1989) described the state as "a 'machine' of repression, which enables the ruling classes to endure their domination over the working class" (p. 68). The state maintains law and order by protecting the established relationships of production. The state makes capitalist exploitation of the working class possible. If the working class refuses to sell their labor or demands a greater share of the profits, the repressive apparatuses kick in—police and national guard to quell riots and imprison (even kill) troublesome radicals. For Kaepernick, that meant no longer working in professional football. For union leaders in some places—even today—it means imprisonment and/or even murder. In a modern, capitalist state, these repressive apparatuses are controlled by—or operate through—the state.

In his 1919 essay "Politics as a Vocation," German sociologist and economist Max Weber (n.d.) defined the state as "a human community that (successfully) claims the *monopoly of the legitimate use of physical force* within a given territory" and "the right to use physical force is ascribed to other institutions or to individuals only to the extent to which the state permits it" (p. 1, emphasis added). Any other use of violence or force is considered criminal. The state is allowed to do things that are illegal for others. The state can declare that a portion of the money you earn belongs to them. The state can tell you what you can, cannot, and must do. If you refuse to accept its rules, the state can fine you or lock you up or even, in extreme circumstances, kill you. The state reserves for itself the exclusive right to the legitimate use of violence. For Althusser (1989), "the Government, the Administration, the Army, the Police, the Courts, the Prisons, etc." are entities that "function by violence" (p. 73).

In a pre-capitalist state, the ruling class has few tools for controlling the masses of laborers, and most of those tools are violent. They are not the only tools, however, and, in a complex economy, we need to understand the second way power is maintained: through what Althusser called the **Ideological State Apparatus**. Ideological apparatuses serve the interests of the state and work hand-in-hand with repressive state apparatuses yet operate on a different level. First, repressive state apparatuses are singular and under public control (we can only have one set of laws, courts, police, and prisons at a time), while ideological state apparatuses are plural (many coming from different directions). Ideological state apparatuses may be held in state hands but more likely under the control of private powers outside the state. Finally, repressive apparatuses work through violence, while ideological state apparatuses operate through **interpellation** by impacting the way we see and understand the world around us. They shape our consciousness in particular ways. Ideological apparatuses include things like:

Religious institutions, which help to explain why some people have power and others don't and provide for an ultimate justice in an afterlife for those who suffer in this one. Religious institutions often teach respect for and obedience to authority as part of a divine and unquestionable plan.

Educational institutions provide for the training of the next generation of workers, making sure we have the right workers in the right proportions to meet our economic needs. Educational institutions provide us with our knowledge of history, science, politics, and other important ideas.

Communication networks such as radio, television, news, and the Internet give us the information we need to make decisions about our lives. They have considerable control over how we understand issues. Audiences rarely get to see news that challenges corporate, economic powers. The institutions that control the media are themselves corporations who are dependent on still other corporations for advertising revenue.

Cultural institutions are an important means of shaping our understanding of the world. Painters have long painted religious scenes and portraits of nobility and the wealthy. Operas and theatres glorify the achievements of great men to whom we should look for our salvation. In our time, the artistic community often appears to be liberal, even radical in their politics. Like the media, television and movies have been advocates of social change including civil rights, women's rights, and rights for lesbian, gay, bisexual, and transgendered persons. Marxists, however, would be skeptical of this support. Media corporations, radio, television, movies, and publishers are part of the corporate power structure.

Althusser (1989) included institutions like legal theory and scholarship, electoral politics, and even political parties and trade unions as ideological state apparatuses. These structures help to create the impression the state is balanced, fair, and responsive to everyone's needs. This is a false consciousness, a vision of the world that does not line up with reality and that obscures reality, making it hard to see and harder to reform.

We need to keep in mind that no hard dividing line exists between repressive state appara- tuses and ideological apparatuses. Courts, for example, rely on legal scholarship and precedent to shape the law, giving courts both ideological power and repressive power. The military fights wars and may suppress an insurrection, yet also trains millions of young men and women, pur- portedly giving them useful skills and indoctrinating certain values and beliefs about the nation and world. These beliefs and values invariably support the status quo, the system as it is now without fundamental changes in the relationships of production.

The Postmodern Turn in Criticism

Marxist criticism is both rationalist and modernist in its outlook and scope. In this sense, criti- cism may be seen as part of the social scientific paradigm described in Chapter 2. Postmodern- ism is an important movement, which some say breaks from Marxism, turning back to a Hegelian idealism, while others argue it is a logical and necessary extension of radical thought going beyond the narrow limitations of Marx's economic determinism. Postmodernism more closely resembles the interpretive paradigm we talked about in Chapter 3.

What Happened?

The world has changed dramatically since the 19th century when Marx was writing. Marx's pro- letariat consisted of German men working in factories or on farms. Since the end of World War II, worldwide movements against colonialism and domestic struggles for civil rights by women, racial minorities, and by lesbian, gay, bisexual, and transgendered persons have radically changed the way we see and think about the world.

The bourgeoise—or ruling class—long recognized the need to use both hard power (repressive apparatuses) and soft power (ideological apparatuses) to control workers. The pyramids could not have been built without both whips and beer. The Romans used their military to control their empire but at home used free food and entertainment (bread and circuses) to control masses of unemployed soldiers. The great trick of modern capitalism was not that it used different tools but its ability to make them seem natural or even not be seen at all.

The rise of reformist movements and the post-war economic boom raised the standard of liv- ing for much of the working class in Europe, North America and parts of Asia, while at the same time the outsourcing of production has pushed many of the problems faced by the 19th century proletariat to the developing world. Because the inequities of capitalism may be harder to see, they are harder to challenge.

Finally, the rise of the world's first communist state, the Soviet Union, beginning with the Russian Revolution in 1917, had an important impact on the development of socialist thought. Led by Vladimir Lenin, the brand of communism pursued by Russians was called Bolshevism and favored a top-down approach to implementing socialism. Once in power, a strong impulse started among radical movements around the world to support the Soviet Union and to model themselves in the Russian model. The Soviets furthered the **Russianization** of leftist move- ments by supporting Bolshevist movements at the expense of other leftist groups such as Trot- skyists and anarchists.

After World War Two, revelations about the crimes of the Soviet leader Stalin and repression of Marxist thought during the Cold War led many leftists to distance themselves from revolu- tionary politics. Marxists became just another political party, joining coalitions with other leftist parties in an effort to legitimize themselves. In the academic world, Marxists retreated to the realm of ideas rather than political reforms.

What Is Postmodernism?

Postmodernism is notoriously difficult to understand and often marked by complex and sometimes mind-numbing language. Lyotard (1993) defined postmodernism as "an incredulity towards metanarratives" (p. xxiv). Lyotard's definition, while a simplification of postmodern thought, highlights a primary assumption of postmodernity and what makes it different from traditional Marxist thought. Marxists understand ideology as a "false consciousness" or a screen between us and reality. Postmodernists do not believe in a definitive Reality or singular Truth, known as the **metanarrative**. Cloud (1994), a communication scholar, argued postmodernism is both idealist (treats ideas as the primary foundation for realities) and relativistic (with rejection of Truth in favor of a plurality of truths and realities). Eagleton (2003), a Marxist critic, defined postmodernism as a "movement of thought which rejects totalities, universal values, grand historical narratives, solid foundations to human existence and the possibility of objective knowledge" (p. 13). So, if they don't believe and study Truth and Reality, what *do* postmodernists believe and study?

Materiality of Discourse

Like Marxists, postmodernists are concerned with the material world, but, unlike Marxists, they define the world very differently. For rationalists, including Marx, language was ephemeral (temporary) and a reflection of the material world. The chair is real. The word "chair" is less real. For postmodernists, **discourse** (the totality of our language use) *is* material in three senses. First, discourse affects the material world. The way we talk about the world shapes our understanding of it and thus how people act in the world. The documentary film *The Ripper* (2020), about a serial killer in Yorkshire, England in the 1970s, gives us a good example. Police, who were overwhelmingly men from rural, middle-class backgrounds, used the word "prostitute" not just to refer to sex workers but to any woman who went to pubs or consumed alcohol publicly without a male family member. Because victims were routinely described and thought of as prostitutes, as opposed to "women," police not only looked for the wrong killer but also sent out the wrong warnings. Women who were not sex workers assumed they had nothing to fear walking home alone, and the public was unwilling to dedicate resources until the murderer began "accidently" killing "innocent women." The word *prostitute* directed thought and impacted behavior. The discourse exercised material force in the world.

Discourse is not just a single word. While some charismatic terms may anchor or orient the discourse, words like *prostitute* create classes and distinctions; they are clustered with other words and include judgments and assumptions about the world.

For Marxists, who are materialists in a more traditional sense, language and the world are separate. Language names—or misnames—the world. For postmodernists, there is no world apart from the names given to it. Language isn't a screen between us and the world. Reality isn't just socially constructed but discursively constructed. All of our relationships, "economic, political, or ideological are symbolic in nature" (Cloud, 1994, p. 142).

Discourse as Performance

In rationalist thought, power has a center. For Marxists, the power center is the means of production. Postmodernists attempt, however, to **de-center** power. Power is not something one *has* but rather something one *does*. Power is discourse performed over and over again, making it possible to do some things and not others. For Michel Foucault (1926-1984), arguably the most important postmodernist, knowledge as a product of discourse is always "controlled, selected, organised and redistributed according to a certain number of procedures, whose role is to avert its powers and its dangers, to cope with chance events, to evade its ponderous and awesome materiality" (Foucault, 1972, p. 216). Separating knowledge and power is impossible. The two are not the same—knowledge is not power and power is not knowledge—yet we always find them together. So, to change the discourse—or what Foucault called the discursive formations—changes the structure of power.

Polysemy

The lack of a metanarrative—no truth existing independently of a person's perspective—means we should not be searching for one singular truth. Representations of discourse such as a conversation, a movie, a book, or a speech are both **fragmentary** (always part of a larger whole) and **intertextual** (comprised of fragments of other texts). The implication is that we cannot find just one truth but are surrounded by many truths and many meanings, what postmodernists call **polysemy**. The idea that communication scholars should be looking at the multiplicity of perspectives has had a significant impact on the field.

Identity

Unlike Marxists, who operate with a simple definition of identity based on class, postmodernists take a much broader view of identity. Like power, identity is not something we have or are born with but something we perform. Because power has no center, postmodernists view the **binary** (a two-part opposition) of bourgeoisie and proletariat or oppressor and oppressed as too simplistic. Because power has many formulations, oppression takes many forms, and postmodernists have looked beyond the class struggle to consider questions of gender, sexuality, and race. Postmodern approaches to criticism recognize that the oppression faced by working-class white men is not the same as faced by Chicano laborers or African American lesbians. If the nature of their oppression is fundamentally different, then we must assume thate the mode of their liberation must also be different.

Conclusion

In the introduction to their work on critical theory, Ingram and Simon-Ingram (1992) wrote:

> Unlike most contemporary theories of society, whose primary aim is to provide the best description and explanation of social phenomena, critical theories are chiefly concerned with evaluating the freedom, justice, and happiness of societies. In their concern with values, they show themselves more akin to moral philosophy than to predictive science.
>
> (p. xx)

Marxism and postmodernism, while different on several key points, are not competing perspectives but two different outlooks within the same overall paradigm. A whole range of thinkers fills the space between Marxism on one end of the spectrum and postmodernism on the other. What unites the researchers is the commitment to using theory and research to bring an end to oppression in whatever form it takes and to maximize human freedom and happiness.

Summary

In this chapter, we explained the critical cultural paradigm, the third of the three research paradigms. This paradigm focuses on various issues, such as the place of power and ideology in society. While each of the three paradigms discussed in section 1 of this textbook approaches research differently, each shares very similar qualities. We will discuss some of those shared qualities in the second section of this textbook, "Research Design."

Key Steps and Questions to Consider

1. Critical theorists are primarily concerned with power and especially with oppression—or the exercise of power.
2. A traditional understanding of power includes influence, coercive power, legitimate power, reward power, and persuasive power.
3. Hegel was concerned with the dialectic—the contradiction between an idea and its negation.
4. An analysis of self and others is now called critique (or spelled in the German form as *kritik*).
5. For Marx, labor is the central defining condition of being human.
6. A Marxist critique focuses on the system of relationships of production based on social and political classes.
7. The substructure, the superstructure, and influences by Repressive State Apparatus and Ideological State Apparatus are key components in the Marxist approach.
8. Postmodernism questions the role and function of a societal metanarrative.
9. Discourse is material within the postmodern perspective.
10. Discourse as performance focuses on power as something one does.
11. Polysemy means discourse is both fragmented and intertextual, allowing for multiple truths, meanings, and realities.

Activities

1. Divide the class into groups. Each group is given a different issue. The issues are slavery, prohibition, women's suffrage, same-sex marriage, and child sex abuse by priests.
   a. How would a Marxist understand the issue?
   b. How would a postmodernist understand the issue?
2. Bring the groups back together and share their insights.
   a. What commonalities emerged from the discussions?
   b. How where the situations different in both a Marxist and Postmodern perspective?
   c. Hang on to your notes from this activity. The notes may come in handy in Chapter 20.

Discussion Questions

1. What types of research questions do critical theorists ask?
2. How do critical methods of research differ from other methods you have studied in this book?
3. How does Marxist criticism differ from postmodern criticism? In what ways are they the same?

Key Terms

Base	Ideological	Polysemy
Binary	Ideological State Apparatus	Postmodernism
Classes	Interpellation	Relationships of Production
Coercive Power	Intertextual	Repressive State Apparatus
Critique	Labor/Division of Labor	Reward Power
De-center	Legitimate	Russianization
Dehumanization	Power	State
De-skilling	Means of Production	Substructure
Dialectic	Metanarrative	Superstructure
Discourse	Oppression	The Napoleonic Codes
Fragmentary	Persuasive Power	

References

Althusser, L. (1989). Ideology and ideological state apparatuses (B. Brewster, Trans.). In D. Latimer (Ed.), *Contemporary critical theory* (pp. 60-102). Harcourt Brace Jovanovich.

Berlin, I. (1963). *Karl Marx: His life and environment*. Time, Inc.

Cartwright, D., & Zander, A. (1968). *Group dynamics: Research and theory*. Harper & Row.

Cloud, D. (1994). The materiality of discourse as oxymoron: A challenge to critical rhetoric. *Western Journal of Communication, 58*, 141-163. https://doi.org/10.1080/10570319409374493

Durkheim, E. (1955/1962). Division of labor. In A. P. Hare, E. F. Borgatta, & R. F. Bales (Eds.), *Small groups: Studies in social interaction* (pp. 5-9). Alfred A. Knopf, Inc. (Original work published 1947).

Eagleton, T. (2003). *After theory*. Penguin Books.

Foucault, M. (1972). *The archaeology of knowledge & the discourse on language*. Pantheon Books.

Gasper, P. (2010). *Marxism and the dialectic*. [Audio File]. wearemany.org.

Lyotard, J. F. (1993). *The postmodern condition: A report on knowledge* (G. Bennington & B. Massumi, Trans.). University of Minnesota Press.

Marx, K., & Engels, F. (1978). The German ideology. In R. C. Tucker (Ed.), *The Marx-Engels reader* (2nd ed., pp. 146-200). Norton.

Vile, J., & Wood, E. (Directors). (2020). *The ripper* [Television series]. Netflix.

Weber, M. (n.d.). *Politics as a vocation*. www.sscnet.ucla.edu/

Section Two
Research Design

5 Data

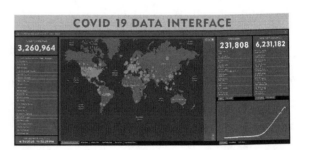

What Will I Learn in This Chapter?

Data is all around us, and it impacts everything we do. In 2020–2021 it was critical for governments to accurately track and report COVID-19 cases. Each day, websites such as the Johns Hopkins Coronavirus Resource Center would update global COVID-19 cases. Without accurate reporting of cases, such data would be impossible. With such resources, governments, resources, medical practitioners, and average people were able to follow the progression of the virus. The previous image is an example of one of these websites, which millions of people visited daily. Information (data) is given to the group who runs this website from a variety of sources; they collate it and then report it visually and numerically for the reader/viewer. Most technological things we do in life function with such matrices behind them: bank transactions, the Internet, phone calls, etc. However, data does not have to just be numeric. Data can also include interview transcripts, observations, paintings, and song lyrics, just to name a few.

Data is an integral aspect of the research process. Without some kind of data, how can research take place? This question brings up other important questions. For example: 1) What is data? 2) How is data collected? 3) Where does data take place? 4) What are the different levels of data? We explore these questions and others in Chapter 5 in our discussion of data.

DOI: 10.4324/9781003109129-7

Data Defined and Sources of Data

When you conduct research, you collect and/or analyze some kind of data. **Data** is information collected in a systematic manner. The information can be numeric (quantitative), or nonnumeric (qualitative, critical, rhetorical). Most communication scholarship comes from one of four kinds of data: 1) texts, 2) observations and/or interviews, 3) self-reports, and/or 4) other-reports.

Texts are written, spoken, performed, or symbolic messages. The texts can be intentional or unintentional (like nonverbals we don't even know we do). If your interest is in written texts, you can choose from a wide range of forms to use in your research project. We discuss in the method chapters later in the book how to analyze such texts. Written texts can be drawn from newspapers, magazines, books, diaries/journals, obituaries, e-mails, maps, photographs, poems, policy statements, chat room logs, bank account records, and the list goes on. Spoken texts include politician inaugural addresses, wedding toasts, concession speeches, acceptance speeches, and so forth. Performed texts can include music, stand-up comedy routines, performance art, a circus routine, mime, etc. Finally, symbolic messages are wide open and can include paintings and other kinds of art, architecture, fashion, jewelry, hair designs, landscaping, tattoo art, etc. If a "text" communicates a message, the "text" can be analyzed from a communicative perspective. The key is to find an effective theoretical and methodological perspective. Many texts are analyzed using methods such as focus groups, interviews, content analysis, rhetorical criticism, or critical/cultural analysis, but other ways exist. For example, Dutta (2020) examined how indigenous villagers in Eastern India negotiated and exerted agency with situated structural absences in day-to-day existence. Using the culture-centered approach, his study examined structural marginalization through the use of focus groups and interviews. We talk more about interviews (Chapter 9) and focus groups (Chapter 10) later in this book. Social scientific, interpretive, and critical scholars all analyze texts.

Observations represent data when you watch human behavior in action. Anthropology has a rich history of this kind of research. Anthropologists such as Margaret Mead (1901–1978) and Franz Boas (1858–1942) spent long periods of time observing groups of individuals. Occasionally, these researchers would break away from the observation of their participants and interact (conduct interviews) with them. Most of Mead's research involved studying the Samoan people, while Boas primarily researched Eskimos of the Canadian Artic and Native Americans in the Pacific. The primary purpose of their research was to watch human behavior in action. This is the main goal: to observe behavior (communication) in action. The data in an observational method is your field notes as you write down what you see occurring. What kind of communicative behavior do you see? What is happening? Why do you think such behaviors are happening? These kinds of questions and many more discussed in Chapter 8 on ethnography comprise observations as data.

Observing can be taken a step further when a researcher decides to interact with the participants by observing and interviewing. In this case, the interview questions become a second form of data that works in conjunction with the observation field notes. With developed interview questions related to the context, a researcher can delve deeper into the behaviors they are interested in studying. We talk more about interviewing in research in Chapter 9. A classic example of observation and interview used by *many* communication instructors is Philipsen's (1976) analysis of "Teamsterville," which is a certain area of Chicago. In the analysis, Philipsen discussed how he observed and interviewed participants in "Teamsterville" to understand the various places for certain kinds of talk. You will find that many social scientists do not use observation and interview data due to its subjective nature. This type of data is generally preferred by interpretive and critical scholars.

A third type of data is self-report data. A **self-report** is when you ask individuals to report about their own behaviors. Typically, this kind of data is quantitative in nature but may be qualitative. Quantitative self-reports are usually closed-ended surveys, such as "on a scale of 1–7, with 1 being *strongly disagree*, and 7 being *strongly agree*, please rate how much you agree with the following statements." You have all seen such questions on a survey before. Qualitative self-reports can include open-ended questions on a survey. For example, you may be asked to "Describe how you felt about Candidate X after watching the debate." The question is asking you to self-report on your feelings about Candidate X. Self-reports are often used in communication research. Self-report data collected in a survey form is a preferred approach for many social scientists. Some statistical problems can emerge, of course, when analyzing self-report data. For example, some scholars argue people taking surveys tend to over- or underestimate their behaviors (Nicotera, 1996; Podsakoff & Organ, 1986). However, in recent analyses of the organizational dissent scale (Croucher et al., 2013) and the argumentativeness scale (Croucher et al., 2017), researchers found only minor to nonsignificant differences between self-reporting and other-reporting. Thus, might fears around self-reporting and the social desirability bias be overblown?

An other-report can be used in conjunction with self-reports to uncover how a communicative act affects a person or to compare the results of a self-versus-other perception. **Other-reports** are when you ask individuals to report on the communicative behavior of another person. In conjunction with self-reports, other-reports can help verify a result. Imagine you are interested in the extent to which people are ethnocentric toward a minority group. You can start off by using self-reports to measure Individual A's self-reported ethnocentrism. For example, you could use Neuliep and McCroskey's (1997) Generalized Ethnocentrism (GENE) scale. A second option is to modify the GENE to ask friends, colleagues, or intimate partners of Individual A to report on the other person's ethnocentrism. You would be modifying the GENE to be an other-report of ethnocentrism. This would only measure what others think about Individual A. Third, you could give a self-report of the GENE to Individual A and another report of the GENE out to those who know Individual A and compare the results to see if any party over-/underestimates Individual A's ethnocentrism. The third approach can be useful to see if people really do know their own behaviors or how others perceive them (Croucher et al., 2013).

Going back to COVID-19 data, there are lots of ways to use data about the virus. Throughout 2020 and at the start of 2021, Stephen and his research team were conducting a variety of research projects on COVID-19. Specifically, they were comparing how minority groups were being blamed for the spread of the virus in different nations. To conduct these analyses, the research team collected data (surveys) in more than 25 nations. The nations were chosen based on the top 15 most infected COVID-19 nations, and 10 of the least per capita infected nations. To make this determination, it was essential for the team to have accurate data from a resource, like the Johns Hopkins Coronavirus Resource Center, to know at a particular date which nations had higher/lower rates of infection. Once the team had this data, they could justify the nations they were analyzing.

Now that we have gone through the four basic kinds of data, the next section describes data sampling.

Data Sampling

Collecting and analyzing all the available evidence when conducting research is not always possible. Let's imagine, for example, you are interested in how fear of contracting COVID-19 relates to willingness to get immunized against COVID-19 among adults in England. Surveying every adult in England is *impossible*. Adults in England is your **population** or the group of cases/units from which you want to collect data. What you need to do is survey a **sample** of adults in England. Essentially, when we sample, we are analyzing a smaller group (sample) we have taken out of a larger group (population) in order to make claims about the larger group (the population). Remember your sample population can provide a wide range of data: textual data, observations/ interview data, self-report data, or other-report data. Many descriptions of samples and populations focus on self-report data, but other forms of data are available.

For social scientific (mainly quantitative) researchers, the purpose of sampling is to create an objective sample that best represents the population so that one can make **generalizations** about the population from the sample. The generalizations are inferences about the behavior of the population one makes from studying the sample (usually statistical for a social scientist). For interpretive, critical, and rhetorical researchers, generalization is not an important issue to consider, as these scholars focus more on subjectivity (think back to Chapters 3 and 4).

Inferences (generalizations) are possible from a sample to a population because of the Central Limit Theorem. The **Central Limit Theorem** states the following. First, under normal conditions, data taken from larger samples will tend to be more normally distributed. Second, as more and more samples are taken from a population, you have a greater chance of having your sample represent the population. Third, random selection is the best way for a sample to represent the population. Fourth, if you are unable to get a random and/or a large sample, you must ascertain the amount of error present in your sample. Based on the Central Limit Theorem and sound methods, we can generalize our findings. **Generalizability** is extending our findings, results, or conclusions from the sample to the population. We will talk more about the Central Limit Theorem and its tenets in Chapter 7 on hypotheses and research questions. For now, it is important to note that the tenets behind the Central Limit Theorem provide mathematical laws for generalizing from a sample to a population.

We see a classic example of population and sampling every four years in election night polling. Take the U.S. as an example. Every four years, many Americans are glued to their televisions and computers watching election results come in and waiting for states to be called for their local, state, and national candidates. Many students have asked us both how a network can call a state for a candidate before all of the votes are counted. The answer is simple—sampling. None of the networks have the entire voting population counted, but they have large enough samples counted to make a generalization (in this case a prediction) about who will win. These samples include the number of votes already counted, exit polls, and other forms of polling. Election-night sampling is an intricate process and does not always work. In 2000 the major television networks called the U.S. state of Florida for U.S. Presidential candidate Al Gore. However, the margin of victory at the time was very slim. The networks had to reverse the calls when it looked like the Gore victory was not a "done deal." In the end, George W. Bush (who became the 43rd president of the U.S.) won the state of Florida after a long legal battle. All in all, social scientists and media networks work hard to avoid the problems that occurred in the 2000 election in Florida. In 2020, the U.S. networks had another issue that delayed their ability to generalize from a sample to the population, mail-in ballots. Millions of Americans voted by mail in 2020, more than ever before. Each state counted these ballots differently, some states counting these ballots before election day and others counting them after all physical ballots were counted. In the end, it took more than a week for some states to officially announce their final results, and news networks did not want to call states like Arizona and Pennsylvania.

Data sampling should be a systematic process, whether you are doing a quantitative or qualitative study. After you have chosen your topic of study and defined your data population, you need to consider whether better to use a random or nonrandom sampling procedure. **Random sampling** is when you choose data in a way that ensures everyone or everything that is part of your data has an equal chance of participation in your study. Random sampling increases your ability to generalize to the overall population. **Nonrandom sampling,** on the other hand, is when not everyone or everything that is part of your data has an equal chance of participation. Therefore, your ability to generalize to the population decreases. We argue random sampling (specifically simple random sampling) is virtually impossible. Here is an example of how one could do a random sample, though.

Let's say your university wants to find out how staff feel about making the COVID-19 vaccine mandatory for all staff. The university has access to the names and contact information of every staff member. A person from the university, let's say Human Resources, could e-mail every staff member's official email account with a survey. With this project, every registered staff member has an equal chance of participating in this study. Such lists often do not exist for many populations, and some populations are just too large for a list. So, in many ways, simple random sampling is impractical but still theoretically possible. In the case of this hypothetical study, if you have the chance to reach *every registered* staff member, you can *honestly* say you have conducted a *random* study on how staff members feel about making a COVID-19 vaccine mandatory.

As random sampling is virtually impossible, and for other reasons outlined later, researchers commonly use four kinds of nonrandom sampling procedures: convenience, snowball, purposive, and quota sampling. You may use nonrandom sampling for a number of reasons. A **convenience sample** is when your data is easily accessible. For example, many quantitative studies published in social sciences (like communication studies) journals have been conducted using surveys of undergraduate communication majors. You may have, in fact, participated in such a research project for a teacher on your campus. Data from convenience samples are easy to collect and generally fairly cheap. Unlike trying to collect random data, which we will talk about shortly, one generally does not need to pay for access to population databases. However, convenience samples have some disadvantages. First, convenience sampling is not random and tends to produce *relatively* nongeneralizable results. Second, some researchers may pick specific people or data samples to further their research agenda. That is to say, they "cherry-pick" their data. Focusing only on college/university students as representative of the U.S. population, for example, has received quite a bit of criticism, but college/university students are rather convenient research participants.

Snowball sampling is particularly relevant to interview data and is similar to convenience sampling. Snowballing can occur when the researcher meets with the first interviewee and the interviewee suggests a second participant. The second interviewee then recommends a third person, and so forth. The sample builds based on participant recommendations. Cheah et al. (2011) used snowball sampling to collect responses from 315 Bosnian refugees regarding their resettlement process. Snowball samples generally start out of convenience, so the same advantages and disadvantages of convenience samples hold for snowball samples. An additional disadvantage can be lack of diversity in the final sample set. For instance, the group of recommended individuals may share common characteristics and lack diversity, thus not resembling the overall population (after all, each interviewee generally knows the person they are recommending as a participant).

Purposive sampling is when the focus of the study is specific groups at the exclusion of other groups. Let's say you are interested in studying the verbal aggressiveness of rugby players. You would only sample rugby players, and not other athletes, thus you exclude other kinds of athletes from your sampling. For example, Kluever Romo and Donovan-Kicken (2012) interviewed 20 vegetarians to uncover communicative dilemmas faced by vegetarians and ways these individuals discuss their lifestyle with others. By focusing solely on vegetarians as their target group, they purposefully excluded individuals who were not vegetarians. The authors located their interviewees using "an online posting on the listservs of two local vegetarian networking groups and through snowball sampling" (Kluever Romo & Donovan-Kicken, 2012, p. 409).

The final kind of nonrandom sampling is quota sampling. **Quota sampling** is where you, as the researcher, predetermine categories and how much data you want in each category. You then collect just enough data to fill each category. In this kind of sampling, you may decide you only want to interview or survey 75 drinkers about how self-disclosure takes place while drinking in a group. With this kind of study design, you have already determined your group, drinkers, and determined the number of drinkers to survey, 75. McMahon et al. (2007) used a quota sample to interview a set number of individuals in different age categories about their feelings on binge drinking.

Three kinds of random-sampling methods are available: simple, systematic, and stratified. **Simple random sampling** is a procedure in which every case in a population has an equal chance of being included in the sample. For instance, say you are interested in securing a random sample of all registered voters in a U.S. county regarding their opinions on the U.S. federal response to COVID-19. County boards have registered voter information on file, but they will be hesitant (if not outright refuse for privacy reasons) to provide the list to anyone (we will talk about this practical aspect shortly). If you had the list, you could generate a representative sample population of registered voters in a county. You could then survey a sample of the voters about their opinions. Since you are working from the official list of registered voters, you have a simple-random-sample.

A systematic sample takes a simple-random-sample a step further. In **systematic sampling**, you randomly choose a starting point in your data and then carefully include every *n*th data point. For example, imagine you are working with the voter list from the county. You start with the fifth name on the list and then mail a survey to every fourth person on the list. All research method texts say the same thing (including the method textbook you are reading right now); a systematic sample and a simple-random-sample are more than likely going to produce similar results.

In a **stratified sampling** strategy, you first identify mutually exclusive categories/groups. Mutually exclusive means an item can appear in only one category/group. Most professional athletes play in only one pro sport—they are mutually exclusive to the one sport (in fact, contracts for most pro athletes prohibit them from playing in multiple sports, professionally or recreationally). However, many high school athletes play in multiple sports—they are *not* mutually exclusive.

Once you have identified your categories/groups, you divide your sample into the categories/groups and then use random selection to select cases/units from each category/group. For voters in the county, you may want to compare registered Republicans and Democrats on their opinions (if they are registered with a political party, then they are mutually exclusive, since someone cannot be registered in both parties at the same time). So, you divide the population into Republican and Democrat and then randomly select Republican and Democrat to receive your survey (you will need to decide if your selection of Republican and Democrat men and women stratifies your sample.)

Random sampling is statistically preferred for generalizability, as it protects our research more from error (we talk more about error in Chapter 7). However, in many cases you may find it difficult (if not entirely impossible) to get a random sample. Getting a random sample may be problematic for the following reasons. First, random samples are expensive, which we have already talked about a little bit. Depending on the population or type of data you are interested in, the cost may be prohibitive for buying a list of individuals or other types of data. Second, negotiating with individuals or groups who may hold access to lists of populations can be time consuming, particularly when working with humans as your population. Third, sometimes a random sample may be theoretically and/or methodologically impossible. In much of Stephen's early work, he was interested in researching how immigrants adapt to a new culture, like the U.S., France, Finland, and Germany. These governments do not have lists of *every* Muslim immigrant within their borders. Thus, a complete list for generating a random sample of Muslim immigrants in these countries is impossible. Fourth, for the interpretive and critical paradigms, generalizability is not of paramount concern. Thus, random sampling is not really an issue. Fifth, your research may adapt based on your findings. If you are conducting an interpretive or critical study, your findings may emerge as you conduct your work. In these cases, random sampling may not work, as you need to be able to identify sources of data and be flexible to change. See Figure 5.1 for a description of the strengths and weaknesses of each of the random and nonrandom sampling methods.

> Over the past year, Stephen and his team have been working with research firms like Survey-Monkey and Qualtrics to "buy" random samples from different countries for their projects. While these samples are closer to random, there are still limits to such samples, as only individuals with access to social media tend to complete the surveys. Thus, not *all* individuals have an equal chance of being reached—not truly random.

Figure 5.1 Advantages and Disadvantages of Sampling Techniques

Sampling Method	Advantages	Disadvantages
Simple random	Most generalizable of all methods.	Hard to do without full list of population. Can be expensive and time-consuming.
Systematic random	Also generalizable. Can be less time-consuming and less expensive than simple random.	What starting point do you choose? Still need a list of the population. More expensive and time-consuming than nonrandom methods.

(Continued)

Figure 5.1 (Continued)

Stratified random	Can be sure specific groups are included by selecting them from the population list. Don't forget, since it's random you have more generalizability.	More complex random method. You must carefully define the groups. Still more expensive and time consuming than nonrandom methods.
Convenience	Inexpensive and easiest way to collect data in general.	Can often be very unrepresentative, not generalizable to the population.
Snowball	Can more easily include members of groups not on lists or people who would not be easily accessible.	How do you know if the sample represents the population? This goes back to a lack of generalizability.
Purposive	Can ensure balance of group sizes when many groups are included.	How do you know if the sample represents the population? This goes back to a lack of generalizability. Research bias and subjectivity can also be issues.
Quota	Can ensure the selection of appropriate numbers of subjects with appropriate characteristics.	How do you know if the sample represents the population? Again, a lack of generalizability.

In Croucher et al.'s (2020) study on prejudice toward Asian Americans in the COVID-19 pandemic, the researchers employed Qualtrics to assist in data collection. Based on a sample of 288 participants who completed a series of Likert-based questions, the researchers found that the more individuals believed their social media to be accurate, the more they believed Asian Americans were a threat to America. In the article, the researchers also report data from other sources, such as Johns Hopkins and the World Health Organization, that discuss the severity of COVID-19. Collectively, different data points are used to demonstrate the severity of COVID-19 and of prejudice toward Asian Americans.

You now have an understanding of the different kinds of data you can collect and the importance of considering the kinds of samples you can collect. The next section briefly discusses the three main places where data collection can take place.

Data Collection Locations

Data collection will usually take place in one of three locations: an archive, the field, or a lab. Where data collection takes place depends on the type of data you are gathering. **Archival research** refers to conducting research in a variety of places including the Internet, a library, a physical archive (many historical archives are available around the world on a variety of subjects), a local town hall of records—basically any place records and documents are stored. The key with archival research is the action of going to a location where you can search for the texts you are interested in analyzing. Since the Internet, archival research has become easier in so many ways, as much of our data (texts) are now online. However, we encourage you, if you are interested in texts, to go to a physical archive and dig into the physical documents. Such an endeavor can be a rewarding experience. Both Dan and Stephen remember, when they went to college/university, spending countless hours scouring physical documents and archives.

The **field** is where communication takes place. Field research means you go out and interview or observe people in their natural habitats. Dutta (2020) went out into the field and met with participants in their natural habitats to better learn about their identities, behaviors, day to day activities, and marginalization. In doing such research, you take risks. Often, you will be out of your comfort zone, as you may not be in your own habitat. You will have to adapt to the environment you are in while conducting your research. Participants, particularly in interpretive and critical studies, are generally more comfortable participating in research when they are in the field, as they are on their own "turf." While you might be out of your element, such research can be very rewarding. You will learn a lot about groups, how they live, and yourself by going into the field and experiencing the life of your participants, even if it is just for a short time. In much of the research conducted today, researchers conduct online surveys using programs like SurveyMonkey or Qualtrics. Thus, researchers are able to send surveys and interview questions out to people via the web and social media. This is a kind of fieldwork that could be considered the "field." We will come back to research in the field in Chapters 8 (Ethnography) and 9 (Interviewing).

The **lab,** on the other hand, is when you, as the researcher, control the setting (environment) in which the study takes place. The lab in this case does not mean a place with science equipment. In lab situations, the research is typically conducted on a college/university campus or in a room at a business or organization where the researcher can control access to the research room (lab), the physical setup of the room, and any other elements they want. A lab setting is a chance for you as the researcher to control many aspects of the data collection setting, unlike the field, where you are at the whim of the environment. If any of you has participated in a study sponsored by your department that has taken place in your building, this is a lab setting. Such a setting is often used by social scientists collecting surveys (Chapters 13-16) or conducting focus groups (Chapter 10).

Definitions and Levels of Measurement

So, now that you have a grasp of the kinds of data you can use, how to sample data, and where to get your data, the next important question to consider is how to define some key terms in your study. The terms we use in our study are important. We need to make sure we are clear in how we define our terms to the reader. Specifically, one should take great care to ensure they have offered concise conceptual and operational definitions of what you want to study before analyzing the data. When you are doing a study, you will need to provide a conceptual definition of the key terms you are studying or testing. **Conceptual definitions** are similar to dictionary definitions of a term. These definitions are based on previous research and used to create an agreed-upon definition for a concept that the author(s) uses in his/her study. For example, Kelly and Kingsley Westerman's (2014) study explored perceived immediacy in workplace communication. In this study, Kelly and Kingsley Westerman provided a review of literature that defined perceived immediacy in workplace communication with a variety of references. This conceptual definition of perceived immediacy makes it clear to the reader exactly what the researchers are studying. Second, one must define to readers how one plans to measure or observe the concept. The purpose of collecting data is to observe, describe, evaluate, or critique a concept. Therefore, you must be clear in your operationalization—how you link your concepts to your method. **Operational definitions** are explanations of the methods, procedures, variables, and instruments you use to measure your concepts. These definitions are in essence the "rules" researchers give themselves for identifying, analyzing, or measuring concepts. Kelly and Kingsley Westerman (2014) (2012) conducted a quantitative analysis using Kelly's (2012) 14-item immediacy scale. The items were adapted into a Likert-type format ranging from 1 (disagree) to 7 (agree). The key is to be clear in your description of your procedures: what method did you use? why did you use the chosen method? and, if it comes from another source, cite it. We talk more about how to select from various methods in Chapters 8-20.

The next few pages focus primarily on operationalization in the social sciences. Knowing these terms is important since they can be used in all research paradigms, appear in journal articles and books, and are fundamental to your basic understanding of the research process. Variables can be measured on four levels: nominal, ordinal, interval, and ratio. Nominal and ordinal level measurements produce categorical level data, which is something social scientists, interpretivists, and critical scholars all use. Interval and ratio level measurements produce continuous data, which are *typically* only used by social scientists. We will now dig a little deeper into each type of measurement.

Nominal variables (or data) are the least precise and the lowest level of measurement.

Data is placed into separate mutually exclusive categories. A classic example of a nominal variable is biological sex (male or female). When an individual on a survey is asked to choose their biological sex, they are often given the choice of male or female. Nominal variables are mutually exclusive categories (categories that do not overlap). Basic demographic questions are nominal data.

Ordinal variables (or data) are rank ordered. Ordinal variables share the same characteristics as nominal variables, plus the categories can be ranked in some way: highest/lowest, least/most, best/worst, etc. An example of ordinal data is Uber rankings. When you take an uber, you have the opportunity after the fact to rate the drive on a scale of 1-5 stars. The driver also can rate you as a passenger. What is the difference, though, between a 4- and a 5-star driver? The problem with ordinal data is that we can't really measure the difference between the stars, we just know that a 5-star driver is ranked/liked better by riders than a 4-star driver, but how much more did the riders really like the driver?

Interval variables (or data) identify a measurable difference between categories and ranks. While an ordinal scale of measurement (like a grading scale) dictates a difference between levels, the difference between 3- and 4-star is not 100% clear. Critics set different standards for what is required to earn stars. Interval level measurements allow us to tell the exact distance between data points. Social scientific research (including communication research) uses two main kinds of interval level scales: Likert scales and semantic differential scales. Most of you have seen a Likert scale before. A **Likert scale** is a form of questioning where individuals are provided with a list of statements that range from (for example) "strongly disagree" to "strongly agree," "exactly like me" to "not at all like me", and "always" to "never." See Figure 5.2 for a typical Likert scale. The example is part of the Patient Self-Advocacy Scale (PSAS) (Brashers et al., 1999). The PSAS is an interval scale measuring the extent to which individuals are advocates for their own health care. It measures three kinds (types) of self-advocacy: illness and treatment education, assertiveness in health care interactions, and potential for nonadherence.

Figure 5.2 Patient Self-Advocacy Scale (PSAS)

Instructions: the following questions ask about your feelings about your health care. For each of the following questions, please indicate your level of agreement with the statement by circling SA for Strongly Agree, A for Agree, N for Neutral, D for Disagree, and SD for Strongly Disagree.

Strongly Agree	Agree	Neutral	Disagree	Strongly Disagree
SA	A	N	D	SD

1. I believe it is important for persons with an illness to learn as much as they can about the disease and treatments.
   SA A   N   D   SD
2. I actively seek out information on my illness when I am sick.
   SA A   N   D   SD
3. I am more educated about my illness than most.
   SA A   N   D   SD
4. I have full knowledge of the problems people have with an illness.
   SA A   N   D   SD
5. I keep notes about my illness and treatment.
   SA A   N   D   SD
6. I research the latest treatments for my illness.
   SA A   N   D   SD
7. I don't get what I need from my physician because I am not assertive enough.
   SA A   N   D   SD
8. I frequently make suggestions to my physician about my healthcare needs.
   SA A   N   D   SD
9. I am more assertive about my healthcare needs than most.
   SA A   N   D   SD
10. If my physician prescribes something I don't understand, I ask questions about it.
    SA A   N   D   SD
11. I ask a lot of questions of my physicians.
    SA A   N   D   SD
12. I frequently offer my physician suggestions about my care and treatment.
    SA A   N   D   SD
13. Sometimes there are good reasons not to follow the advice of a physician.
    SA A   N   D   SD
14. If I am given a treatment by my physician that I don't agree with, I am likely not to take it.
    SA A   N   D   SD
15. I don't always do what my physician or healthcare worker has asked me to do.
    SA A   N   D   SD
16. Sometimes I think I have a better grasp of what I need medically than my physician does.
    SA A   N   D   SD
17. My physician works for me. I would find another physician if I was dissatisfied with my healthcare.
    SA A   N   D   SD
18. I make my own decisions about what treatments I will or will not take, even if my physician prescribes it.
    SA A   N   D   SD

A **semantic differential** indirectly measures thoughts, feelings, or perceptions people have about things using a list of polar opposite adjectives or adverbs. Participants are asked to indicate their feelings by marking a space between one of the opposing adjectives or adverbs. See Figure 5.3 for a semantic differential scale. We will talk more about how to design and use these kinds of surveys in Chapter 13 on Surveys. Palmgreen et al. (2002) provide an example of a semantic differential scale. The scale measures an individual's message sensation and response to messages (advertisements, etc.).

Figure 5.3 Perceived Message Sensation Value (PMSV) Scale (Palmgreen et al., 2002) 17-item scale (We are including the first 6 items only)

Instructions: We would like you to rate the PSA (Ad, message) you just saw on the following scales. For example, on the first pair of adjectives if you thought the ad was very *unique*, give a "1." If you thought it was very *common*, give it a "7." If you thought it was somewhere in between, give it a 2, 3, 4, 5, or 6.

1. Unique	1	2	3	4	5	6	7	Common
2. Powerful impact	1	2	3	4	5	6	7	Weak Impact
3. Didn't give me goose bumps	1	2	3	4	5	6	7	Gave me goose bumps
4. Novel	1	2	3	4	5	6	7	Unemotional
5. Emotional	1	2	3	4	5	6	7	Exciting
6. Boring	1	2	3	4	5	6	7	Weak visuals

For now, there are two key things to understand. First, the scales tap distinct differences between the values. For example, when an individual circles 4 on a scale of 1–5, the researcher has a measurable difference between 1 to 2, 2 to 3, 3 to 4, and 4 to 5. We can do more advanced statistical analyses based on how participants respond to these kinds of scales. Second, interval scales do not have an absolute zero or a complete absence of something. For example, a participant could not score a zero on an IQ test.

A **ratio** variable (data) does the same as an interval variable, except it has a zero point. The presence of a zero point makes it possible to declare relationships in terms of ratios or proportions. For example, you can have $0 in your bank account, you can have zero sexual partners, you may have visited zero overseas nations, or spent zero days in jail. A variable ratio must include a zero for participants to respond.

Researchers from various paradigms prefer to use different kinds of variables. Social scientists will use all the levels of variables. Interpretive and critical scholars will rarely use interval and/or ratio level variables, as these variables lend themselves to higher-level statistical analysis and thus to things like generalization.

Let's go back to the COVID-19 visual at the start of this chapter. Such data provides a lot of information. It showed us where COVID-19 had been (at the time the visual was created and the data collected) and helped us better predict trends in COVID-19 infections and deaths.

In studies published in 2020 and 2021, Stephen and his team used Likert-type data from the U.S., New Zealand, Spain, and Italy to show how majority groups perceive minorities who are stigmatized/blamed for the spread of COVID-19 (Croucher et al., 2020, 2021). In each of these studies the research teams conceptualized prejudice, stigma/blame, and numerous other variables. In addition, the teams operationalized these variables with a series of scales (like the ones in Figures 5.2 and 5.3). Various statistical analyses were conducted and conclusions drawn. Chapters 14–16 in this book demonstrate some of the techniques you can use to conduct statistical analyses.

Summary

In Chapter 5 we discussed the various aspects of "data." Data is information collected in a systematic manner. We described various sampling techniques. We also identified the different places from where you can collect data. The chapter also defined the different levels of measurement. It is imperative to know what "counts" as data, how it can be measured, and what is "good" data. This dialogue continues in Chapter 6 on Evaluating Research.

Key Steps and Questions to Consider

1. Data is information collected in a systematic manner.
2. Data can include texts, observations, interviews, self-reports, and other-reports.
3. Texts are written, spoken, performed, or symbolic messages.
4. Observations are when you watch human behavior in action.
5. A self-report is when you ask people to report about their own behaviors, while an other-report is when you ask someone to report about another person.
6. Data sampling is analyzing a sample we have taken out of a population to make claims about the population.
7. Generalizations are inferences about the behavior of the population one makes from studying the sample.
8. The four kinds of nonrandom sampling procedures commonly used by researchers are: convenience, snowball, purposive, and quota sampling.
9. The three kinds of random sampling methods are: simple, systematic, and stratified.
10. The three data collection locations are: an archive, the field, or the lab.
11. A conceptual definition is when we define our term in a dictionary or scholarly way, while an operational definition is when we define how we are measuring our terms methodologically.
12. The four levels of measurement are: nominal, ordinal, interval, and ratio. Remember that nominal and ordinal focus on categories, while interval and ratio focus on continuous data.
13. Likert scales and semantic differential scales are commonly used to collect interval-level data.

Activities

1. One example we discussed in the chapter was Uber driver ratings. Develop a survey you can distribute to collect data to answer the research question "How do people determine ratings for Uber drivers?" Instead of Uber driver ratings, substitute hotel or restaurant ratings if you are not familiar with or do not use Uber. Remember to determine the type of data, population samples, the data collection methods, levels of measurements, and scales you will use.

2. A number of free online survey tools is available. Try prepping your survey from Activity #1 into an online tool, such as www.SurveyMonkey.com, kwiksurveys.com, and google-forms (just go to googledocs and create a new form). Your instructor may know other survey tools or have a favorite!

3. Distribute your survey. Remember, you will need to follow the research protocols you set for population sampling! What insights can you infer from the data you collected?

Discussion Questions

1. Visit the United States Census Bureau at www.census.gov/aboutus/surveys.html. The Bureau conducts demographic and economic surveys (you will find dozens of surveys across a wide variety of interest areas). Explore a number of the surveys and identify the type of data, population samples, the data collection methods, levels of measurements, and scales used.

2. The American Association of Retired Persons (AARP) also conducts extensive data collection. You can find the AARP surveys at www.aarp.org/research/surveys/. Pick a few surveys and explore the same issues—the type of data, population samples, the data collection methods, levels of measurements, and scales. Can you identify any differences between the U.S. Census Bureau and AARP approaches to data collection and analysis?

Key Terms

Archival Research	Likert Scales	Random Sampling
Central Limit Theorem	Nominal	Ratio
Conceptual Definition	Nonrandom Sampling	Sample
Convenience Sample	Observations	Self-report
Data	Operational	Semantic Differential
Field	Ordinal	Simple random sampling
Generalizations	Population	Snowball Sampling
Interval	Purposive Sampling	Stratified Sampling
Lab	Quota Sampling	Texts

References

Brashers, D. E., Haas, S. M., & Neidig, J. L. (1999). The patient self-advocacy scale: Measuring patient involvement in health care decision-making interactions. *Health Communication, 11,* 97-121. https://doi.org/10.1207/s15327027hc1102_1

Cheah, W. H., Karamehic-Muratovic, A., Matsuo, H., & Poljarevic, A. (2011). The role of language competence, interpersonal relationships, and media use in Bosnian refugees' resettlement process. *Journal of Intercultural Communication Research, 40,* 219-236. https://doi.org/10.1080/17475759.2011.618842

Croucher, S. M., DeMaris, A., Diers-Lawson, A. R., & Roper, S. (2017). Self-reporting and the argumentativeness scale: An empirical examination. *Argumentation, 31,* 23-43. https://doi.org/10.1007/s10503-015-9385-z

Croucher, S. M., Kassing, J. W., & Diers-Lawson, A. (2013). Accuracy, coherence, and discrepancy in self and other reports: Moving toward an interactive perspective of organizational dissent. *Management Communication Quarterly, 27,* 425-442. https://doi.org/10.1177/0893318913476142

Croucher, S. M., Nguyen, T., & Rahmani, D. (2020). Prejudice toward Asian Americans in the COVID-19 pandemic: The effects of social media use in the United States. *Frontiers in Communication.* https://doi.org/10.3389/fcomm.2020.00039

Dutta, U. (2020). Negotiating structural absences: Voices of indigenous subalterns of Eastern India. *Journal of Intercultural Communication Research, 47,* 52-71. https://doi.org/10.1080/17475759.2017.1415952

Kelly, S. (2012). *Examining the role of perceived immediacy as a mediator: Revisiting the relationship among immediate behaviors, liking and disclosure* [Unpublished doctoral dissertation, University of Tennessee]. Knoxville, TN.

Kelly, S., & Kingsley Westerman, C. (2014). Immediacy as an influence on supervisor-subordinate communication. *Communication Research Reports, 31,* 252-261. https://doi.org/10.1080/08824096.2014.924335

Kluever Romo, L., & Donovan-Kicken, E. (2012). "Actually, I don't eat mean": A multiple-goals perspective of communication about vegetarianism. *Communication Studies, 63,* 405-420. https://doi.org/10.1080/10510974.2011.623752

McMahaon, J., McAlaney, J., & Edgar, F. (2007). Binge drinking behavior, attitudes, and beliefs in a UK community sample: An analysis by gender, age, and deprivation. *Drugs, Education: Prevention and Policy, 14,* 289-303. https://doi.org/10.1080/09687630701288461

Neuliep, J. W., & McCroskey, J. C. (1997). Development of a US and generalized ethnocentrism scale. *Communication Research Reports, 14,* 385-398. https://doi.org/10.1080/08824099709388682

Nicotera, A. M. (1996). An assessment of the argumentativeness scale for social desirability bias. *Communication Reports, 9,* 23-25. https://psycnet.apa.org/doi/10.1080/08934219609367632

Palmgreen, P., Stephenson, M. T., Everett, M. W., Baseheart, J. R., & Francies, R. (2002). Perceived message sensation value (PMSV) and the dimensions and validation of a PMSV scale. *Health Communication, 14,* 403-428. https://doi.org/10.1207/s15327027hc1404_1

Philipsen, G. (1976). Places for speaking in Teamsterville. *Quarterly Journal of Speech, 62,* 15-25. https://doi.org/10.1080/00335637609383314

Podsakoff, P. M., & Organ, D. W. (1986). Self-reports in organizational research: Problems and prospects. *Journal of Management, 12,* 531-544. https://doi.org/10.1177%2F014920638601200408

6 Evaluating Research—Warrants

Chapter Outline

- Warrants for Evaluating Social Scientific Research
- Warrants for Evaluating Interpretive Research
- Warrants for Evaluating Critical and Cultural Research
- Summary
- Key Steps and Questions to Consider
- Activity
- Discussion Question
- Key Terms

What Will I Learn About Evaluating Research?

We evaluate almost everything in our lives. Many of you are students in college/university departments that have accreditations. These accreditations are certificates that declare your programs have met a set of standards established by a governing body of some kind. These bodies are set up by a variety of academic, business, and governmental associations/companies. To earn accreditations, a department submits an application that is evaluated. Both Dan and Stephen have gone through these processes and can attest to how time-consuming the process can be. However, such "stamps of approval" are beneficial for departments and colleges/universities because they show that the programs are doing something right, that the programs are meeting some standard(s) critiqued by independent bodies. The statement that we are a reliable investment, academically speaking, from an accreditation agency carries a lot of weight in some circles and can make us feel good.

What does it mean to be reliable? We address this question and many others in this chapter. Researchers strive for reliable methods and results, however, the definition of "reliable" differs considerably depending on a researcher's paradigm (social scientific, interpretive, and/or critical/cultural). Along with having reliable method and results, issues over validity enter the discussion for many researchers. You may be asking yourself the following questions: 1) What is reliability? 2) What is validity? 3) How do these two concepts relate to one another? 4) How do the different paradigms approach these concepts? Some of the concepts we discuss in this

DOI: 10.4324/9781003109129-8

chapter may sound familiar from previous chapters, but a little repetition never hurts. In this chapter, we explore these questions and other aspects of evaluating research. We approach these questions under the umbrella of research warrants. Warrants are assurances of results. In the case of research, warrants allow scholars to state how their data/evidence reliably supports their arguments/claims. You will learn about the different ways in which researchers evaluate/determine what is "good" research.

Warrants for Evaluating Social Scientific Research

You may remember from Chapter 2 on the social scientific paradigm that social scientists approach research from a rationalist approach, emphasizing empiricism and rationalism. When evaluating "good research," social scientists focus on precision, power, parsimony, reliability, and validity.

Precision is how accurate you are at measuring your variables. When a measurement is precise, we know exactly what it is and what it is not. People can agree on a precise measurement. For example, Stephen and his spouse just bought a house in New Zealand. When looking at houses, the two discussed various requirements and requests for the new house: number of rooms, number of bathrooms, should it have a garden (front and back yard), how close should it be to a train station, price, total size, etc. Three key factors ended up being proximity to a train station, price, and if there was a garden or not. Both were able to agree on the following ways to measure these factors. First, it needed a garden, so that was a yes/no question, and "yes" was the answer. Second, both agreed on a maximum price and stated that they could not spend more than $X. Third, they both agreed it needed to be close to a train station, so that was a yes/no question, and "yes" was the answer. However, how close was never specified in meters. Thus, even though they agreed on precise measurements for criteria to choose their new home, there was still room (or variance) for discussion on how far the new house could be from a train station. We will talk later in Chapter 16 about variance.

Power is a multifaceted concept. Conceptual power is the notion that definitions are powerful when they provide broad/detailed insight about a concept instead of niche/specific detail about concepts. Methodological power refers to how it is better for data selection procedures to be as representative of the population as possible, as such samples allow for more powerful generalizations.

Parsimony is the combination of power and precision. A goal of research for social scientists is to be as detailed as possible (cover a broad range of issues) in a succinct way. Researchers strive to use the most powerful and appropriate method(s) for a study. Often researchers may use a variety of advanced statistical analyses to answer research questions.

Reliability, particularly measurement reliability, is an essential warrant to claiming that social scientific research is "good." Your instrument(s) should perform the same way over time, and this is the essence of reliability; a measurement used in 2009 should perform the same way (reasonably so) in 2018. Think of reliability like the clock on your cell phone (since many of you do not use wristwatches anymore). A reliable clock will tell you the precise time, while an unreliable one will tell you it's 4:02 pm when it's really 4:05 pm. Which one do you want? We want the one that correctly tells us the time, consistently.

Unfortunately, our measurements are never 100% reliable. A little bit of error is always involved in our measuring of human behavior. We talk more about error in Chapter 7 on Hypotheses and Research Questions. For now, we want to point out some important points about error. **Measurement errors** are noise or threats to reliability. Three main things cause measurement errors: 1) errors in data entry, 2) instrument confusion, and 3) random human differences. First, people can make mistakes when entering data into a computer program. Stephen and his research teams enter thousands of surveys into a computer program every year, and a survey may be multiple pages long. After data entry, the team goes through and double checks to make sure they did not key in any incorrect numbers. If you consider that they have entered more than a million numbers, it is likely they have entered some incorrect data. For example, instead of entering a 3, they may have keyed in 33. The hope is that they have a limited number of mistakes.

Second, as hard as researchers try, some surveys are not effective. Instructions may not be clear, or questions are worded in ways that confuse or even irritate people. In these cases, the instrument itself can cause a threat to reliability (Croucher & Kelly, 2020).

Third, people complete surveys. People are not perfect; as such their completion of surveys is not perfect. Stephen and his team have seen participants skip pages, resulting in incomplete surveys. People's moods can affect how they answer questions. Finally, some people will agree to answer questions, yet, when they do the survey, they do not take it seriously (put silly or fake answers), randomly answer questions, or put 3 (on a scale of 1 out of 5) for every possible response. In a recent study on COVID-19 in the United States, Stephen and his team were analyzing the results of 650 participants and found that at least 10 participants, when asked to enter in their political affiliation put responses like "None of your business idiot," "Who cares," "Screw you" or an expletive." Such responses, particularly when gathered via a random computer-generated survey, are possible, as respondents are anonymous. Such responses lead to measurement error if not caught. We'll talk later about how to handle such data.

With a basic understanding of error and reliability, the next section defines four ways to determine measurement reliability: 1) intercoder reliability, 2) alternate-forms, 3) test-retest, and 4) internal consistency. **Intercoder reliability** is a statistical analysis of how similar/different coders are in coding data. Neuendorf (2002) stated that intercoder reliability is a "necessary criterion for valid and useful research when human coding is employed" (p. 142). Various statistical measures are available to evaluate intercoder reliability: percent agreement (a basic measure), Cohen's kappa (κ), Spearman's *rho*, Pearson's correlation (*r*), and Krippendorf's *alpha*. For more information on these measures see Neuendorf (2002) or Popping (1988). In most cases, your reliabilities should be at least above .70, if not above .75.

Alternate forms is when you use two or more instruments to measure the same construct/ trait. The objective is to determine the equivalence or similarity of the scores for the participants. For example, instead of giving a participant one measure of motive to communicate, give them two different measures of motive to communicate. With two independent measures we can: 1) better understand individuals' motives to communicate and 2) assert that the measures are reliable measures of the same construct if the results are similar on both tests.

The **test-retest** method for measuring reliability is where you give the same measure(s) to participants at multiple points in time. You are measuring the similarity and stability of results at different points in time. Significant changes in people's scores on a measure may indicate that something has happened since the last time they answered the questions. Researchers have argued that communication traits like argumentativeness do not change much in our lives. While we may become more proficient at arguing as we gain educational levels, our overall tendency to avoid or approach an argument has tended not to change. However, this is not always the case. Using a test-retest method from 2006-2015, Croucher et al. (2018) found that argumentativeness levels did fluctuate over time. In this analysis, the team found that the scores did change over time and that the measure performed the same way over time. Thus, the team was able to establish measurement reliability.

The final way to establish reliability is through measuring internal consistency (sometimes called homogeneity). **Internal consistency** means the items/statements in the measure have generally consistent responses from participants. If you look to Infante and Rancer's Argumentativeness Scale (1982) in Figure 6.1, you see 20 items/statements. Ten of these items/statements measure how likely someone is to approach arguments, while the other 10 measure likelihood to avoid an argument. The 10 approach items and the 10 avoid items are each answered similarly. Answering the items/statements in similar ways shows internal consistency.

Figure 6.1 Argumentativeness Scale–Infante and Rancer (1982)

The following list of questions regards when you argue about controversial issues. Indicate how often each statement is true for you personally by placing the appropriate number in the blank to the left of each item based on the five-point scale. Remember, consider each item in terms of arguing controversial issues.

Almost Never True	Rarely True	Occasionally True	Often True	Almost Always True
1	2	3	4	5

1. While in an argument, I worry the person I am arguing with will form a negative impression of me.
2. Arguing over controversial issues improves my intelligence.
3. I enjoy avoiding arguments.
4. I am energetic and enthusiastic when I argue.
5. Once I finish an argument, I promise myself I will not get into another.
6. Arguing with a person creates more problems for me than it solves.
7. I have a pleasant, good feeling when I win a point in an argument.
8. When I finish arguing with someone, I feel nervous and upset.
9. I enjoy a good argument over a controversial issue.
10. I get an unpleasant feeling when I realize I am about to get into an argument.
11. I enjoy defending my point of view on an issue.
12. I am happy when I keep an argument from happening.
13. I do not like to miss the opportunity to argue a controversial issue.
14. I prefer being with people who rarely disagree with me.
15. I consider an argument an exciting intellectual challenge.
16. I find myself unable to think of effective points during an argument.
17. I feel refreshed and satisfied after an argument on a controversial issue.
18. I have the ability to do well in an argument.
19. I try to avoid getting into arguments.
20. I feel excitement when I expect a conversation I am in is leading to an argument.

Validity is the final key warrant for social scientists in evaluating what is "good" research. When using measures such as surveys, social scientists are interested in the extent to which the test measures what is it supposed to measure (Mason & Bramble, 1989). This is validity. There are three kinds of validity: content, construct, and criterion-related validity.

Content validity is the degree to which a scale, measure, and/or instrument measures *all* aspects of a behavior, trait, or state (Schilling et al., 2007). For example, a researcher claims to have developed a measure of organizational dissent. However, the scale does not include any items regarding dissent from organizational members to other organizational members with power in the organization, what Kassing (1997) called articulated dissent. Let's say the scale only includes dissent among peers (latent dissent) and dissent that an organizational member expresses to those outside of the organization (displaced). The scale will not adequately assess organizational dissent apprehension, because it doesn't measure articulated (or upward) dissent. Thus, this particular scale is limited and has low content validity. To determine the level of content validity, a group of experts in the field (organizational dissent and/or organizational communication) should analyze the scale and determine whether its content is appropriate based on the existing body of literature.

Construct validity is the second type of validity. Construct validity has two parts. First, the construct (a trait, behavior, or communicative state) must be clearly understood and defined. Second, the usefulness in measuring the construct must be established. **Construct validity** focuses on the extent to which the scale, measure, and/or instrument measures the theoretical construct. Let's return to our organizational dissent example—does the scale "really" assess organizational dissent, or does it assess frustration with an organization? The two are similar yet very different concepts. As before, bringing in a group of experts in the field is helpful to assess construct validity.

The third kind of validity is criterion-related validity. A measure, scale, or instrument has **criterion-related validity** when it demonstrates effectiveness in predicting indicators or criterion of a construct (behavior or trait). Concurrent and predictive are the two kinds of criterion-related validity. **Concurrent validity** is when scores are obtained at the same time as the criterion measures. This kind of testing demonstrates that the scores accurately measure an individual's state with regard to the criterion. For example, a self-report of communication apprehension (the test) would have concurrent validity if it could accurately measure the person's levels of apprehension (physical response and emotional response). **Predictive validity** is when the criterion is measured after the test. Career, aptitude tests, and even the SAT, ACT, GRE, LSAT, etc. are helpful in determining how successful people will do in specific occupations or how well they will do in college/university. We can analyze the results people get on these tests and their "success" in their jobs or in college/university to see how valid these career, aptitude, and SAT/ACT/GRE/LSAT tests were.

Warrants for Evaluating Interpretive Research

While social scientists focus on things like objectivity, parsimony, precision, reliability, and validity to determine whether research is "good" or not, interpretivists use very different warrants to evaluate what is "good" research. A fundamental difference between social scientific and interpretive researchers is that social scientists strive for reliable samples that are generalizable. Interpretive researchers do not; instead, they study smaller samples that are, for lack of a better word, in-depth analyses of how groups or case studies understand the world. For a simple and thorough set of evaluative criteria we recommend Tracy (2010). Tracy provided eight "big-tent" criteria for excellent qualitative research. We believe these criteria (warrants) provide a clear understanding of how interpretive researchers evaluate research. The eight warrants for interpretive research are 1) worthy topic, 2) rich rigor, 3) sincerity, 4) credibility, 5) resonance, 6) significant contribution, 7) ethical, and 8) meaningful coherence.

First, the topic under investigation should be a **worthy topic**. The topic should be interesting, significant, timely, and relevant to the discipline and/or society. Some topics get their relevance and interest factors because they may reveal something new or show something researchers have overlooked about a theory or society. Other topics may get their worth because they are personally important to the researcher. The key is that you as the researcher need to justify/explain the topic's worth. Stephen has advised graduate students who have conducted interpretive research on a plethora of topics that are not only personally important to each of them but also worthy topics for their discipline. Ziying (2015) examined intercultural difficulties in flight cockpits. Swarts (2014) explored how professional football players culturally adapt to Finnish culture. Shunyao (2015) looked at gender roles in Japanese anime. Beiroth (2017) analyzed communal traditional values and identity in Basotho.

Second, steps must be taken to make sure the research is done appropriately; this is **rigor**. To determine rigor, ask yourself the following questions taken from Tracy (2010): 1) am I using the most appropriate theory/theories? 2) did I spend enough time in the field (if you collected data in the field)? 3) is my sample the right size, the right data? 4) are my data collection and analysis techniques the correct ones for what I am doing? We talk about methodological rigor in the qualitative method chapters.

The third warrant is sincerity. **Sincerity** is how genuine and vulnerable you are as a researcher. We all make mistakes when we do research, and we should share these mistakes when we write our analysis. Discussion of a study's limitations is imperative to being an open and transparent researcher. Tracy (2010) encourages researchers to openly share their own experiences with their research subjects. The back-and-forth dialogue between researcher and participant creates a more open research environment.

Fourth, you should take steps to establish credibility. **Credibility** is how dependable and trusting you are at conveying the realities expressed to you. You can establish credibility in various ways. We will discuss two ways: thick description and triangulation. When you spend time in the field, particularly doing ethnography, you will learn things about people, groups, and cultures. Your job as the researcher is to convey the details of what you have seen to your readers in the most detailed manner possible. Geertz (1973) said one way is by explaining contextual meanings unique to a cultural group by providing in-depth descriptions of members, activities, and symbols of the culture. An in-depth explanation is called a **thick description**. The richness of your description is important. A thick (rich) description will provide details to the readers of what you as the researcher experienced, which the readers were unable to experience firsthand. **Triangulation** is another way to show credibility. Triangulation is where you use multiple datasets, various methods, various theories, or various researchers all to explore the same phenomenon. The basic idea is that results of a study using triangulation are more credible because the study approaches data collection from various points. Sherlock and Holmes use triangulation when working together to solve mysteries. They are more successful when combining their different approaches than when they work alone.

The fifth warrant is resonance. **Resonance** is using impactful cases or quotations to impact an audience. Tracy (2010) provided various ways resonance could be done, two of which we discuss here: transferability and aesthetic merit. **Transferability** is where readers are able to transfer the results of one study to another context in their life. Stephen has extensively researched immigrants in Europe and the U.S. (Croucher, 2008, 2009a, 2009b; Croucher et al., 2018; Nshom & Croucher, 2018). One way to evaluate research is whether or not these findings resonate with readers' own experiences, particularly if they are immigrants themselves. If another immigrant, Muslim or not, can read the results and relate them to their own life, then the study has resonance. **Aesthetic merit** is where a piece of research is artistically and imaginatively written to the point of affecting the reader(s) (Tracy, 2010). Stephen had a Professor at the University of Oklahoma, Sandra Ragan, who told him a good piece of research is one that reads like a short story. Research should tell an interesting story; one the reader wants to keep reading. This is the essence of aesthetic merit.

As with all research, the work needs to make some kind of contribution to scholarship. Tracy (2010) outlined four kinds of contributions for an interpretive study: theoretical, heuristic, methodological, and/or practical. A study does not need to make each contribution but needs to make at least one. Research makes a theoretical contribution when the study develops, builds on, critiques, or further explains theory. A study could develop a new theoretical line of thinking. For example, Philipsen's (1975) seminal piece on Teamsterville developed codes (theories) of talk based on in-depth ethnographic work. With heuristic contribution, a study piques the interest of readers and calls for further investigations into the same subject. Goffman's work on the presentation of self and interaction (1959, 1961) had significant heuristic merit, as these works and others have inspired countless researchers to explore human encounters. Third, a study can make a methodological contribution. The study could propose a new method of inquiry, like an entirely new way of analyzing qualitative data (Hymes, 1962), or it could merge various interpretive methods not used before (Conquergood, 1992). A methodological contribution can be made in various ways. The final kind of contribution a study can make is to have a practical or applied contribution. A lot of research in health communication, aside from being theoretical, has a very practical/applied side. Such research offers advice to medical practitioners on best practices for better health outcomes.

Seventh, the study should be conducted in an ethical manner. Look back to the section in Chapter 1 on ethics and review the basic ethical procedures present in all research projects. No matter the paradigm, informed consent, doing no harm, avoiding deception, and guaranteeing privacy/confidentiality are essential to a "good" project. In the method section of many studies, you will likely read how the researchers worked to ensure such issues.

Eighth, the study should demonstrate coherence. Tracy (2010) defined **coherence** as how studies should "(a) achieve their stated purpose; (b) accomplish what they espouse to be about; (c) use methods and representation practices that partner well with espoused theories and paradigms; and (d) attentively interconnect literature reviewed with research foci, methods, and findings" (p. 848). Essentially, does a study do what it set out to do, and does it make sense? For example, if you are interested in exploring attachment between intimate partners, you should make sure you are asking about "attachment" and not about "lust," "love," "jealousy," and/or "passion." These are all very different concepts, and you should be careful to be sure you are actually measuring/exploring what you say you are. Ultimately, a coherent study for interpretive scholars shows coherency for the audience through linking their methods with literature and argumentation.

Interpretive researchers strive for high-quality research that can be understood by scholars. By following these eight "big tent" criteria offered by Tracy (2010), your interpretive findings can be better understood and evaluated by your readers.

Warrants for Evaluating Critical and Cultural Research

One of the key issues discussed in Chapter 4 on the Critical Paradigm is how the approach to research emphasizes subjectivity, ideology, critique, and power. Thus, when evaluating research written from this paradigm, many of the same warrants apply as the interpretive paradigm.

Critical researchers are concerned with worthy topics, rich rigor, sincerity, credibility, resonance, significant contributions, ethics, and coherence. Important differences exist, however, between the interpretive and the critical paradigms. As we pointed out earlier, critical research is more like a moral philosophy than a research paradigm in that its principal aim is not "to provide the best description and explanation of social phenomena" but "with evaluating the freedom, justice, and happiness of societies" (Ingram & Simon-Ingram, 1992, p. xx). Thus, unlike interpretivists who are not concerned about generalizability, critical theorists draw broader conclusions about their research.

Critical theorists are often skeptical of social scientific methods of research for various reasons. First, critical theorists contend that social science incorrectly believes that facts exist independent of one's perspective. For a Marxist, the issue is class, while a postmodern theorist will include other aspects of a person such as race, gender, and sexuality. A critical theorist believes that positivistic social scientists, because they attempt to detach research from the material conditions of both the researcher and the subjects of the research, contribute to the alienation of society. Second, because positivistic social science tends to look for regularities (e.g., cause and effect), they may produce a sense of fatalism in readers who believe these things are beyond control and thus not subject to change. Third, scientific approaches to research disempower people who come to believe their conditions are the result of immutable social laws. Finally, critical theories have argued that social scientific research has been used to support "forms of social engineering that enhance the power of those at the top—industrialists, government bureaucrats, and managers—who seek more efficient methods of controlling those at the bottom" (Ingram & Simon-Ingram, 1992, p. xxviii).

At the same time, critical theorists are not satisfied with traditional interpretive approaches to research. While interpretivists acknowledge the perspective of the research and emphasize ethical treatment of research subjects, the interpretivists' emphasis on deep understanding rather than praxis is problematic, particularly for critical theorists influenced by Marx's materialism. An overemphasis on subjectivity means the interpretivist is not able to evaluate communication practices. This form of moral relativism—or the belief that all moral judgments are subjective—makes it impossible to engage in the call for change that is the essence of critical theory. If everyone has his or her own moral code, we have no basis from which we can call one person oppressed and the other an oppressor. The oppressor and the oppressed are moral equals, each acting on their own moral code.

Critical theorists are concerned with the emancipation of their research subjects and their readers. Accomplishing the task requires combining the objective, explanatory methods of social science in order to describe conditions with an "empathic understanding of the subjective attitudes and experiences of actual historical agents" (Ingram & Simon-Ingram, 1992, p. xxix).

The difficulty is knowing when to think like a social scientist, when to think like an interpretivist, and when to think like a critical theorist. The Greek poet Homer told the story of Odysseus, who, at one point on his epic quest, was forced to pilot his ship through a narrow strait with the sea monsters Scylla and Charybdis on either side. The straight was narrow, and, in trying to avoid one monster, the ship and its crew would certainly end up in the clutches of the other. Thus, the expression "between Scylla and Charybdis" means you are caught between two almost impossible dangers. Critical theorists often feel they are between Scylla and Charybdis, always running the risk of being overly objective or being too subjective in their research. So how do we deal with this dilemma?

Reflexivity is the solution for critical theorists. Reflexivity begins with the idea that research must be accountable for itself. For example, a researcher could not conclude that no conclusions are valid. If no conclusion is valid, the conclusion "no conclusions are valid" is not valid. So, some conclusions must be valid. This kind of self-contradiction is important to critical theorists who want to reveal contradictions within systems of thought as a way of destabilizing oppressive ideologies.

Reflexivity goes farther. Reflexivity is the practice of turning criticism back on itself. The critical research invites others to critique their own work. Critical theorists, while they hope the results of their work contribute to emancipation of oppressed persons, do not claim to have produced a final or definitive statement but rather a statement that is itself subject to criticism. Only by turning criticism back on itself, by critiquing the critic, can we be sure we have not been paralyzed by subjectivism or been trapped in an illusion of objectivity.

Historically, reflexivity has been productive in furthering the critical theorists' hopes for liberation. Women made lasting contributions to the feminist movement by critiquing Marxism. They identified Marxism's failure to recognize their unique place within the relations of production. Likewise, oppressed people of color critiqued Marx's colorblindness. While traditional research paradigms attempt to advance our understanding, critical theorists hope to emancipate themselves, their subjects, and their readers by treating emancipation as an ongoing process and not a finished work. Finally, in a peculiar paradox, critical theorists are mindful that their own work may obscure or contribute to other forms of oppression, which other researchers should strive to illuminate.

Summary

In this chapter, we discussed how each of the three research paradigms evaluates and determines what is "good" research. Evaluating research is a critical skill, as it is important for us in our everyday lives to determine "good" from "poor" research. In Chapter 7 we continue this discussion as we explore Hypotheses and Research Questions.

Key Steps and Questions to Consider

1. Precision is how accurate you are at measuring your variables.
2. Conceptual definitions should provide in-depth detail about a concept.
3. Methodological power refers to how it is better for data selection procedures to be as representative of the population as possible.
4. Parsimony is the combination of power and precision.
5. A key difference between social scientists and interpretivists is that social scientists want generalizable samples. Interpretive researchers use smaller samples that are in-depth analyses of how groups or case studies understand the world.
6. Reliability is the requirement that a measurement perform the same way over time.
7. There are three main threats to reliability: 1) errors in data entry, 2) instrument confusion, and 3) random human differences.
8. There are four ways to determine measurement reliability: 1) intercoder reliability, 2) alternate-forms, 3) test-retest, and 4) internal consistency.
9. The extent to which a test (measure, survey, or instrument, for example) measures what it is supposed to measure is validity.
10. There are three kinds of validity: content, construct, and criterion-related validity.

11. The eight criteria for "good" interpretive research are: worthy topic, rich rigor, sincerity, credibility, resonance, significant contribution, ethical, and meaningful coherence.
12. Sincerity is how genuine and vulnerable you are as a researcher.
13. Credibility is how dependable and trusting you are at expressing the words/realities expressed to you.
14. There are two ways you can establish credibility: thick description and triangulation.
15. Resonance is using impactful cases or quotations to impact an audience. Two ways to do this are with transferability and aesthetic merit.
16. A study must make a contribution. The four kinds of contributions are: theoretical, heuristic, methodological, and/or practical.
17. Critical theorists emphasize subjectivity, ideology, critique, power, and emancipation.
18. Critical theorists position themselves in opposition to many of the standards of social science including independent facts, regularities, and causality.
19. The solution for critical theorists is reflexivity in research.

Discussion Question

Communication researchers need to be versed in a wide range of research paradigms and methods. It is also critical as consumers of research that we be able to judge what is good and not good research. Based on what you have read thus far in this book and based on your other coursework, make a list of your criteria for "good" research. Compare your list with the three paradigms from this chapter. Which paradigm do you fit in the most, and why?

Key Terms

Aesthetic merit	Internal Consistency	Sincerity
Alternate forms	Measurement Errors	Test-retest
Coherence	Parsimony	Thick Description
Concurrent Validity	Power	Transferability
Content Validity	Precision	Triangulation
Construct Validity	Predictive Validity	Validity
Criterion-related Validity	Reliability	Worthy Topic
Credibility	Resonance	
Intercoder Reliability	Rigor	

References

Beiroth, A. C. (2017). *Between the old and the new: The impact of communal traditional values and practices on the cultural identity of young and old Basotho* [Unpublished master's thesis, University of Jyväskylä]. Jyväskylä, Finland.

Conquergood, S. (1992). Ethnography, rhetoric, and performance. *Quarterly Journal of Speech*, *78*, 80–97. https://doi.org/10.1080/00335639209383982.

Croucher, S. M. (2008). French-Muslims and the hijab: An analysis of identity and the Islamic veil in France. *Journal of Intercultural Communication Research, 37*, 199–213. https://doi.org/10.1080/17475750903135408.

Croucher, S. M. (2009a). A mixed method analysis of French-Muslims' perceptions of *La Loi 2004–228*. *Journal of International and Intercultural Communication, 2*, 1–15.

Croucher, S. M. (2009b). How limiting linguistic freedoms influences the cultural adaptation process: An analysis of the French-Muslim population. *Communication Quarterly, 57*, 302–318. https://doi.org/10.1080/01463370903109929.

Croucher, S. M., & Kelly, S. (2020). Why care about validity in communication? Special issue introduction. *Annals of the International Communication Association*. https://doi.org/10.1080/23808985.2020.1792788

Croucher, S. M., Kelly, S., Condon, S. M., Campbell, E., Galy-Badenas, F., Rahmani, D., Nshom, E., & Zeng, C. (2018). A longitudinal analysis of the relationship between adaptation and argumentativeness. *International Journal of Conflict Management, 29*, 91–108. https://doi.org/10.1108/IJCMA-0502017-0045

Geertz, C. (1973). *The interpretation of cultures*. Basic Books.

Hymes, D. (1962). Models of the interaction of language and social life. In J. J. Gumperz & D. Hymes (Eds.), *Directions in sociolinguistics* (pp. 35–71). Holt, Rinehart & Winston.

Infante, D. A., & Rancer, A. S. (1982). A conceptualization and measure of argumentativeness. *Journal of Personality Assessment, 46*(1), 72–80.

Ingram, D., & Simon-Ingram, J. (1992). Introduction. In D. Ingram & J. Simon-Ingram (Eds.), *Critical theory: The essential readings* (pp. xix–xxxix). Paragon House.

Kassing, J. W. (1997). Articulating, antagonizing, and displacing: A model of employee dissent. *Communication Studies, 48*, 311–332. https://doi.org/10.1080/10510979709368510

Mason, E. J., & Bramble, W. J. (1989). *Understanding and conducting research: Applications in education and the behavioral sciences*. McGraw Hill.

Neuendorf, K. A. (2002). *The content analysis guidebook*. Sage.

Nshom, E., & Croucher, S. M. (2018). Acculturation preferences towards immigrants: Age and gender differences among Finnish adolescents. *International Journal of Intercultural Relations, 65*, 51–60.

Philipsen, G. (1976). Places for speaking in Teamsterville. *Quarterly Journal of Speech, 62*, 15–25.

Popping, R. (1988). On agreement indices for nominal data. In W. E. Saris & I. N. Gallhofer (Eds.), *Sociometric research: Volume 1, data collection and scaling* (pp. 90–105). St. Martin's.

Schilling, L. S., Dixon, J. K., Knafl, K. A., Grey, M., Ives, B., & Lynn, M. R. (2007). Determining content validity of a self-report instrument for adolescents using a heterogeneous expert panel. *Nursing Research, 56*, 361–366.

Shunyao, Y. (2015). *Japanese anime and women's gender-role changing* [Unpublished master's thesis, University of Jyväskylä]. Jyväskylä, Finland.

Swarts, C. M. (2014). *Adapting to Finland through professional football: Perceptions of players and coaches* [Unpublished master's thesis, University of Jyväskylä]. Jyväskylä, Finland.

Tracy, S. J. (2010). Qualitative quality: Eight "big-tent" criteria for excellent qualitative research. *Qualitative Inquiry, 16*, 837–851.

Ziying, C. (2015). *Intercultural communication difficulties and their effects on flight safety* [Unpublished master's thesis, University of Jyväskylä]. Jyväskylä, Finland.

7 Hypotheses and Research Questions

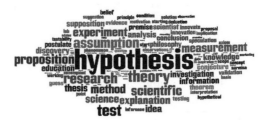

What Will I Learn About Hypothesis and Research Questions in This Chapter?

In the 2016 film, *Arrival*, a dozen alien spacecrafts arrive on Earth. Governments enlist the assistance of scientists to study and learn about the alien spacecrafts. One of the scientists brought on board to assist is linguist Dr. Louise Banks, played by Amy Adams. Dr. Banks, along with a physicist, begins to study the complex circular symbols the aliens use to communicate. As she begins to understand the alien symbols, she begins to realize that how the aliens are communicating is linguistically complex. In a critical point in the movie, Dr. Banks asks the aliens why they are here, and they provide a symbol for her to translate. While many of the other researchers translated this symbol to mean "weapon," Dr. Banks hypothesized it to be "gift." Dr. Banks asserted it was essential to understand how the alien language worked and how they understood concepts. She worked with the aliens to test her hypothesis, showing them other symbols to try to see if they could further explain the difference between "gift" and "weapon". In the end, the aliens gave mankind a "gift" and not a "weapon," and Dr. Banks' hypothesis was correct.

DOI: 10.4324/9781003109129-9

This story is one example of how hypotheses are created and then tested. The process is virtually the same in the social sciences.

The development of and the testing of hypotheses and research questions is critical to the research process. Hypotheses are statements about the relationships between variables, while research questions are questions about proposed relationships between variables. Data is then used to test hypotheses and research questions. To understand the nature of both, we need to know: 1) what are hypotheses and research questions? 2) what do they do? 3) when do we know if our hypothesis or research question is "right"? We explore these questions and others in Chapter 7 in our discussion of Hypotheses and Research Questions.

Types of Hypotheses and Research Questions

A research question is similar to a hypothesis in many ways. A **research question** is the focus of your study and what you are trying to answer. A research question shows some kind of relationship or difference between variables. Research questions can be written to explore processes, understand behaviors, discover meaning, describe experiences, and report stories (Creswell, 2009). We will provide examples later, don't worry.

A **hypothesis** is a testable statement showing how two or more concepts/ideas are related or different in some ways. We develop hypotheses from theoretical propositions, which are statements based in research asserting how concepts/ideas are related. Hypotheses take propositions a step further through empirical testing. Thus, the researcher's focus is to test hypotheses through empirical testing. After empirically testing a hypothesis repeatedly, our confidence increases. You will typically only see hypotheses in quantitative studies and rarely see them in qualitative or critical studies. Hypotheses can be divided into two separate kinds: null and research.

Many social scientists focus on the important work of confirming and disconfirming what we claim to know. This means some researchers are interested in testing the existence of no relationship between variables. A **null hypothesis** states that no relationship exists between variables, or there is no significant effect of an independent variable on a dependent variable. Let's pause here for a moment and define these two key terms—dependent variable and independent variable. In a study or experiment, an **independent variable** is controlled or does not depend on the other variables. A **dependent variable** is being measured/tested in a study or experiment and changes in relation to the values of the independent variable. For example, a researcher is interested in the extent to which political affiliation (conservative, liberal, green, socialist, etc.) influences willingness to get a COVID-19 vaccine. Political affiliation is the independent variable because it stands alone and is not affected by a person's willingness to get a COVID-19 vaccine. On the other hand, the dependent variable is a person's willingness to get a COVID-19 vaccine, as this willingness is influenced by their political affiliation (or at least the research hypothesizes this relationship). A second example is that time spent studying influences test scores. The independent variable is time spent studying, while the dependent variable is a person's test scores.

Returning to the null hypothesis, the null exists for researchers so that we can examine how different our findings are from the null. We compare the null and our results to understand the "importance" or significance of our results. Let's return to the willingness to get a COVID-19 vaccine and political affiliation example; an example of a null hypothesis is:

H_o: There is no relationship between a person's political affiliation and their willingness to get a COVID-19 vaccine.

Your null hypothesis is essentially saying that individuals of different political affiliations do not differ in their willingness to get a COVID-19 vaccine. Participant political affiliation is the independent variable, and how willing they are to get a COVID-19 vaccine is the dependent variable.

A **research hypothesis,** on the other hand, proposes that an independent variable has a significant effect on a dependent variable. A research hypothesis states that a difference/relationship exists. Research hypotheses come in three main forms. The first form is a nondirectional research hypothesis. A **nondirectional hypothesis** states that a difference or relationship exists but does not predict in which direction or magnitude. A researcher's job is to test the significance of the relationship/difference. Nondirectional research questions work in the same way as nondirectional hypotheses. For example, you could propose:

H_1: An individual's willingness to get a COVID-19 vaccine differs based on their political affiliation.

An example of a nondirectional research question could be:

RQ_1: Does willingness to get a COVID-19 vaccine differ between Conservatives and Liberals?

The main difference between the hypothesis and the research question is the depth of previous research. A hypothesis has enough research to propose the hypothesis, and you are trying to *confirm* the difference identified in previous research. With a research question, you have some research *leading* you to think there may be a difference or relationship, but you are not sure. Therefore, you are exploring to see if a difference/relationship exists.

Craig and Wright (2012), in their study of relational development and Facebook, hypothesized "attitude similarity will be predictive of social attraction for Facebook partners" (p. 122). Craig and Wright did not hypothesize "how" predictive attitude similarity would be for social attraction of people on Facebook, just that being more similar in attitude will predict social attraction to others on Facebook.

Craig and Wright (2012) also provided directional hypotheses in their research on relational development and Facebook. A **directional hypothesis** proposes a difference or relationship and states the direction or magnitude (directional research questions work in the same way). Here are some examples of directional hypotheses or research questions:

H_2: Liberals are more likely than Conservatives to get a COVID-19 vaccine.
RQ_2: Will Labor voters be more willing to get a COVID-19 vaccine than National voters in New Zealand?

Unlike nondirectional hypotheses/research questions, directional hypotheses/research questions posit the direction of difference. The researcher has sufficient evidence to put forth a statement of direction or magnitude of difference/relationship.

Let's return to Craig and Wright (2012), who stated, "Individuals who report high levels of social attraction should also report having greater breadth and depth of self-disclosure with their Facebook friends" (p. 122). In this hypothesis, high levels of social attraction are related to greater breadth and depth of social disclosure with Facebook friends; a direct relationship is posited and is one where all variables increase with one another. We will talk more shortly about why you would choose a directional or a nondirectional hypothesis over the other, after we discuss the third kind of research hypothesis, causal.

A **causal hypothesis** proposes a cause-effect relationship between variables. Keep in mind that a true cause-effect relationship is difficult to prove without conducting a true experiment. For the time being, one might propose:

H_3: The more you jog the more weight you lose.
RQ_3: Does jogging lead to weight loss?

The purpose behind the hypothesis and research question is that increased jogging leads to (causes) increased weight loss (the effect). However, without running a "true" experiment we cannot prove this, as there are many external variables to consider: metabolism, food consumption, sleep, etc.

> Going back to *Arrival*, after many attempts to communicate with the aliens, she deduced that she and the other scientists needed to change tactics. She hypothesized that the symbols the aliens were using were indeed a highly developed linguistic structure. Her hypothesis was right, and thanks to her analysis she was able to deduce that the aliens were giving humankind a gift and not a weapon.

What Kind of Hypothesis or Research Question to Use

You may be asking yourself, when should I use a directional, nondirectional, or causal hypothesis or research question? If you want to *test* if a difference or relationship exists between variables, you use a research hypothesis. When you want to *explore* for differences or a relationship, a research hypothesis or research question may be appropriate. These can be directional, nondirectional or causal. When you use a directional hypothesis based on previous research you already know—or at least you think you know—the direction of the relationship/difference between the variables. Thus, you are confirming the relationship or difference. With a directional research question, you have almost enough evidence to pose a hypothesis but are being safe and posing a research question.

A nondirectional hypothesis is still based on previous research but is generally broader, as you may not have enough information to make a specific prediction of the direction of the relationship/difference, or your purpose is just to confirm a difference or relationship between variables (Neuman, 2011; Ragin, 1994). Similarly, a nondirectional research question is more exploratory in nature.

You use a causal hypothesis or research question when you have a significant amount of previous research and evidence to support an argument for a cause-effect relationship between variables. You must take great care to rule out other variables that can influence your proposed relationship. For example, with H_3 and RQ_3, a significant number of other variables could *cause* the effect we were predicting; a few of these were listed. Now that we have defined variables, hypotheses, and research questions, another important issue to consider is: what makes a "good" hypothesis or research question? The next section discusses this important point.

Hypothesis and Research Question Characteristics

You may be asking: what makes a good hypothesis? A well-written hypothesis has five critical elements.

Elements of a "Good" Hypothesis

1. The hypothesis must be a declarative sentence. This means a hypothesis should be a statement and not a question. For example, a hypothesis: "Is there a relationship between organizational identification and burnout?" is not an effective hypothesis because it is a question and not a declarative statement. While an interesting area of research, this is in fact a research question.
2. It posits an expected relationship between variables. The hypothesis: "There is a relationship between organizational identification and burnout" posits an expected relationship.
3. A hypothesis is based on literature. This means that a hypothesis furthers previous research. In the research by Chang (2012) and Craig and Wright (2012), both articles include in-depth reviews of literature that demonstrate relationships between various variables. The hypotheses were put forth to test these relationships.
4. It should not be too long; it should be succinct and to the point. You will find that most hypotheses are only one sentence in length. The Craig and Wright hypotheses are a great example of direct and to the point hypotheses.
5. It must be testable. An example of an untestable hypothesis is: "God exists." The point of this statement is not to criticize faith but to point out that this statement is not testable; one must accept belief in God on faith; you cannot test the existence of a supreme being. Therefore, this hypothesis just does not work. A testable hypothesis related to religion could be: "Individuals with higher religiosity (religious beliefs) are more likely to attend religious services." This is a declarative sentence, posits a relationship between variables, is based in literature, is not too long, and is testable.

So, what makes a good research question? A "good" research question also has five important elements.

Elements of a "Good" Research Question

1. It is in the form of a question. This may seem obvious, but sometimes it is nice to point out the obvious.
2. It tells the focus of your study. While many research questions ask about some relationships or differences between variables, this is not always the case. Exploring relationships between variables and differences between variables is a very social scientific way to look at research questions. Interpretivists and critical scholars use research and research questions. For an interpretive scholar like Miller et al. (2002), exploring European American and Taiwanese mothers' beliefs about childrearing and self-esteem, one research question was: "What are the meanings that European American and Taiwanese mothers associate with the ideas of self-esteem?" (p. 217). A more social scientific take on a research question comes from Croucher et al. (2020) in their study of social media and prejudice toward Chinese Americans during the COVID-19 pandemic: "During the COVID-19 pandemic in the United States, to what extent does social media predict prejudice toward Chinese Americans?"

3. It is based on literature. The Miller et al. (2002), and the Croucher et al. (2020) piece both included extensive reviews of literature that led them to pose their research questions.
4. It is not too long. The Miller et al. (2002) research question is a great example of a succinct question. Two other examples are provided by Eguchi and Starosta (2012): *"RQ1: Are we the model minority? RQ2: Should we perform as if we are the model minority?"* (p. 92). Based on their review of literature related to the model minority image among Asian American professional men, the authors present two direct and simple questions that guide them to an in-depth analysis.
5. It must be something you can research. A bad research question would be: "What is the true meaning of life?" How do you plan on researching that? You could ask: "What do college students believe to be the meaning of life?" Focusing your research on a group and uncovering their meanings of life has made the focus of the study on this group and their interpretations of life, instead of some abstract idea that is impossible to uncover. We discuss in Chapters 8–20 various methods you can use to answer this question and many others in your research.

Testing

Developing a research idea is the first step in the research process. Your research idea will lead to collecting published research articles, which will show up in your literature review (step two). The culmination of your literature review will be a single, multiple, or a combination of hypotheses or research questions (step three). Next, you will need to conduct your research project (step four). In other chapters, we describe various methods you can use to collect data, analyze data, and report data. Each method offers a way for you to test hypotheses or explore research questions, and we offer in-depth discussions of how each method will help you in your research. The fifth and sixth steps (which we will talk about shortly) apply only to the social scientific paradigm and focus on the amount of error involved in your study and whether your results are significant or not, which determines whether you accept or reject your hypothesis. We will now talk about error and significance. The seventh step is to write up your results and conclusions. A discussion of how to do this is included in each of the method chapters.

Error

Two assumptions underlying hypothesis testing and the social scientific paradigm are the Central Limit Theorem and the Bell Curve. As discussed in Chapter 5 on Data, the Central Limit Theorem asserts: 1) under normal situations data taken from larger samples will tend to be normally distributed, 2) as additional samples are taken from a population, you have a greater chance your sample represents the population, 3) random selection is the most preferred selection procedure, and 4) if you can't get a random sample, you must estimate the amount of error present in your sample. The Central Limit Theorem has two important elements we need to discuss at this point. The first is the normal distribution principle.

Statistical distributions can be symmetrical or asymmetrical. An **asymmetrical** distribution is skewed in some way, meaning the majority of scores are shifted either to the right or the left of the distribution's center. A **symmetrical** distribution is a single peak in the distribution at the

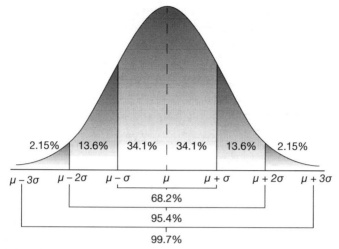

Figure 7.1 Bell Curve

mean, called a **bell curve**. In a bell curve, the dispersion of scores is relatively stable. Figure 7.1 depicts how scores are dispersed within a normal distribution. Under such a distribution, 68% of all scores will fall within +/- 1 standard deviation of the mean, 95% will fall within +/- 2 standard deviations of the mean, and 99% will fall within +/- 3 standard deviations of the mean. Based on this distribution rule, we can test hypotheses and determine scores inside or outside of the normal distribution. Such tests of normality will prove to be an important part of inferential statistics, which we talk about later in this book.

Based on the Central Limit Theorem, the larger your sample and/or the more samples you collect, the more likely you are to have a normal distribution. Normal distributions are likely to occur when a fundamentally random process is at work, but most real-life variables are not random. For example, measures of marital satisfaction are not only nonrandom but generally have a negative skew, because many married couples report high satisfaction. However, real-life distributions are not normal in theory, and we need to test hypotheses and research questions. In every distribution, you will also have an amount of **error** or the degree to which a sample differs from the population. Error is important to consider, since it helps determine the outcome of our hypothesis or research question testing. Let's examine the following case study to better understand error and probability level.

Case Study

Stephen is mainly a cross-cultural researcher. This means most of his research compares phenomena in different cultures. In 2020, his research team embarked on a multi-national analysis of prejudice toward minorities blamed for spreading COVID-19 in more than 20 nations. His research team, based in New Zealand, worked with researchers throughout the world to collect data on prejudice, health attitudes and behaviors, media use, and other communicative constructs. Focusing on the prejudice constructs for the purpose of this case study, as of March 2021 the team had distributed more than 12,000 surveys online. Looking at just data from Brazil, the average age of the participants was 33.26 years old, (*SD* = 11.53 years). The data included 197 females and 213 males. Stephen's research team based their definition of prejudice on Stephan and Stephan's (1996, 2000) integrated threat theory (ITT). ITT proposes that members of a dominant culture perceive members of a minority group to be a threat. These threat perceptions predict prejudicial attitudes and discriminatory attitudes against minority groups. Specifically, two types of threats are prominent: realistic (concerns about the dominant group's existence) and symbolic (threats to morals, values, attitudes, etc.) threats (Croucher, 2013). The research team developed a measure in English and then had it professionally translated into Portuguese, along with many other languages. The final survey that was distributed included measures of ITT, and other measures from health communication, mass communication, interpersonal communication, and demographic questions.

SD = standard deviation. The standard deviation is the average distance between a score (measurement) and the mean. The standard deviation can be negative and or positive. Larger standard deviations (ignoring the sign) represent more variability in the distribution, while smaller standard deviations represent less variability. At this point in time, it is interesting to note that this study had a relatively large *SD* for age, 11.53 years.

Based on current research (AFP, 2020; Caldwell & de Araújo, 2020; Folha de S. Paulo, 2020), the research team contextualized prejudice toward minorities in Brazil during the COVID-19 pandemic. Specifically, the team showed how Brazil's president, Bolsonaro, has called the virus a Chinese virus. A null hypothesis to help frame the research on COVID-19-related prejudice in Brazil could be:

H_0: There is no difference between men and women on COVID-19-related prejudice toward Chinese Brazilians in Brazil.

When comparing COVID-19-related prejudice in Brazil to other nations, such as New Zealand, the team believed a difference existed based on news reports and published evidence. Since the published research did not clearly support a definitive answer, the following research question was most appropriate:

RQ_4: To what extent does COVID-19-related prejudice differ in Brazil and New Zealand?

One particular hypothesis the research team proposed in this study was to explore the link between prejudice and ethnocentrism. There has been extensive research demonstrating a positive relationship between prejudice and ethnocentrism. Essentially, individuals who are more ethnocentric have more prejudice and vice versa (Neuliep, 2017). So, they posed the following directional hypothesis:

H_4: Ethnocentrism is positively related to COVID-19-related prejudice in Brazil and New Zealand.

Now, 410 people is nowhere near the population of Brazil! The research team took a sample of the Brazilian population. Stephen and his team had to be careful of two key things when interpreting their results: error and significance interpretation. Let's answer just one of the questions in this study for now (RQ_4); we will come back to the other ones later. The research team found that Brazilians scored higher on realistic threat (*M* = 4.03; *SD* = 1.30) than New Zealanders (*M* = 3.34, *SD* = 1.17), *t*(1058) = -8.92, *p* < .0001. Brazilians also scored higher on symbolic threat

(*M* = 4.36, *SD* = 1.25) than New Zealanders (*M* = 3.61, *SD* = 1.12), $t(1058) = -10.17$, $p < .0001$. The results represent mean differences between the samples. You may notice a few statistical terms you are not familiar with yet. That is alright; we'll explain one to you now, *p*, which signifies the alpha significance level. When the research team examined prejudice, they ran their results in SPSS, a statistical program we will talk more about in later chapters, and got their results. However, how do we know if the results are statistically significant? In one example, we just said Brazilians scored higher on realistic threat (*M* = 4.03; *SD* = 1.30) than New Zealanders (*M* = 3.34, *SD* = 1.17). What is the real difference between these two means? It's only .69; is that something we should consider *significant?* The statistical results tell the team there is a statistical difference is $p < .0001$ or probability level (*p*).

When conducting statistical research, you must be certain your results are statistically significant before claiming you have found something. Most researchers in the natural sciences and the social sciences rely on the 95% rule, or **confidence interval,** as a minimum standard. This means researchers expect their results to be accurate 95% of the time and allow at the most 5% inaccuracy. Inaccuracy can be attributed to various things such as sampling errors, how people answer questions on a survey, researcher bias, and alternative variables. Ultimately, you want to be sure your results are not by chance, and the data in your sample actually represent the relationship/difference between the variables in the population.

Let's walk through an example. A pharmaceutical company is conducting a clinical trial of a new COVID-19 vaccine. The company is conducting clinical trials on a sample of volunteers (how most clinical trials take place). The company sets a 95% confidence rate ($p < .05$) and finds the vaccine has adverse effects on 5 in 100 people. A rate of 95% is not very good if you consider that 1 billion people could take the vaccine, meaning 50,000,000 people could be hurt. So, what many companies do is raise the confidence interval/rate to 99.9% ($p < .001$). In this case, the company will keep working on the vaccine until only 1 in every 1,000,000 might be hurt by the medication.

The probability level simply helps us determine if our results are statistically significant. Since statistics are related to a sample, the significance of our results tells us how confident we can be that those results represent the population. Figure 7.2 includes some tips to help you determine if a finding is statistically significant.

Figure 7.2 Alpha Significance Levels

$p \geq .05$, there is more than a 5% chance that the null hypothesis is true; there is not a significant statistical finding. We are *not* sure there is something going on.

$p \leq .05$, there is less than a 5% chance that the null hypothesis is true; there is a significant statistical finding. We are 95% sure there is something going on.

$p \leq .01$, there is less than a 1% chance that the null hypothesis is true; there is a significant statistical finding. We are 99% sure there is something going on.

$p \leq .001$, there is a less than .01% chance that the null hypothesis is true; there is a significant statistical finding. We are 99.9% sure that there is something going on.

In the case of prejudice in Brazil and New Zealand, the research team's *p* was rather significant, $p \leq .0001$, and the errors for both conflict styles were very low. The probability level represents the research group being 99.99% sure the results found in their sample would be found in the general population. In fact, due to this high confidence interval, the researchers could confidently say there is a statistical difference between Brazilians and New Zealanders on realistic and symbolic threat (prejudice). Here is another example, to test our null hypothesis: H_0: There is no difference between men and women on COVID-19-related prejudice toward Chinese Brazilians in Brazil. The results reveal: there was not a significant difference between men ($M = 4.40$, $SD = 1.31$) and women ($M = 4.31$, $SD = 1.28$) on realistic threat, $t(408) = .21$, $p = .81$. With this result in mind, we would accept the null hypothesis, as there is no difference between men and women, as hypothesized in the null.

To summarize, here are a few key points about hypothesis testing. Data from a sample will never perfectly reflect what is really the case in the population from which it comes. For that reason, we cannot be sure whether what appears to be a hypothesized difference or relationship in one's sample truly reflects a difference or relationship in the real world. But statistical analysis allows us to estimate the odds. Here is how it all works. First, we defined our independent variables and our dependent variable. Second, we determined the null hypothesis. Third, we use statistics to estimate the likelihood of any difference or relationship in the sample data. Fourth, when the odds are high of no real difference or relationship in the real world, then the research hypothesis is not supported, and the null hypothesis is supported. When the odds are low and we trust that a difference or relationship exists in the real world, then we support the research hypothesis by rejecting the null.

In the movie *Arrival*, Dr. Banks and her colleagues used the scientific method and hypothesizing to solve a linguistic conundrum. It was through data collection and analysis that these scientists were able to solve the alien language and save the planet.

Summary

This chapter was devoted to hypotheses and research questions: what they are, when to use them, what makes a "good" hypothesis and/or research question, and what is the role of error in testing. We see and use hypotheses and research questions all the time; it's important to know how to use them properly. The following chapters, Chapters 8–20, provide how-to guides for various research methods. Next is Chapter 8, with a how-to guide for ethnographic research.

Key Steps and Questions to Consider

1. A hypothesis or research question is the focus of your study; it is what you are trying to answer/explore.
2. An independent variable is the variable that is controlled or does not depend on other variables.
3. A dependent variable is the variable that is being measured/tested in a study/experiment. This variable changes in relation to the values of the independent variable.
4. Hypotheses are testable statements that two or more concepts/ideas are related or differ.
5. The null hypothesis states that there is no difference or relationship between variables.

6. A nondirectional hypothesis states that there is a difference or relationship, but it does not state the direction or magnitude of the difference/relationship.
7. A directional hypothesis states that there is a difference or relationship, and it states the direction or magnitude of the difference/relationship.
8. A causal hypothesis identifies how at least one variable causes a change in at least one other variable. It is extremely difficult to show cause and effect, as you must make sure the effect is caused by your variable of interest and not other variables. We talk more about this in Chapter 15 on Inferential Statistics.
9. Hypotheses should: be declarative statements, state expected relationships, be based on research, be succinct, and be testable.
10. Research questions should: be questions, tell the focus on your research, be based on research, be succinct, and be testable.
11. The Central Limit Theorem is essential to testing hypotheses and exploring research questions because it helps us understand the normal distributions (bell curve) and standard error, which aid us in understanding how similar our similar sample is to the population.
12. The minimum threshold for statistical significance is $p \leq .05$. This means we are 95% sure our results are not by chance.

Activities

Scan through a recent copy of a newspaper. Select an article dealing with communication in some form. Articles dealing with politics or sports are good options. Break the class into groups and have each group:

1. Develop a research question, which helps to shape a potential research project.
2. Turn the research question into a null hypothesis.
3. Turn your null hypothesis into a nondirectional hypothesis. (Assume you have sufficient evidence to support the hypothesis.)
4. Turn the nondirectional hypothesis into a directional hypothesis. (Assume you have compelling evidence to support the hypothesis.)
5. Turn the directional hypothesis into a causal hypothesis.
6. Use the standards in the chapter for a "good research question" and a "good hypothesis" and critique the research questions and hypotheses from the different groups. Notice how the same article (communication issue) can generate multiple different research directions!

Discussion Questions

1. What is the difference between a dependent and independent variable?
2. How does the decision to use a research question or one of the hypothesis forms change the nature of a communication research project?
3. How will the selection of a specific confidence interval change what you can say about your results?
4. What steps can we take to control for error in a communication research project?

Key Terms

Asymmetrical Distribution	Directional Hypothesis	Null Hypothesis
Bell Curve	Error	Research Hypothesis
Causal Hypothesis	Hypothesis	Research Question
Confidence Interval	Independent Variable	Symmetrical Distribution
Dependent Variable	Nondirectional Hypothesis	

References

AFP. (2020, April 6). Brazil minister offends China with racist virus tweet. *AFP Yahoo News.* https://news.yahoo.com/brazil-minister-offends-china-racist-virus-tweet-163351712.html

Caldwell, K. L., & de Araújo, E. M. (2020, June 11). Covid-19 is deadlier for black Brazilians, a legacy of structural racism that dates back to slavery. *The Conversation.* https://the conversation.com/covid-19-is-deadlier-for-black-brazilians-a-legacy-of-structural-racism-that-dates-back-to-slavery-139430

Chang, C. (2012). Ambivalent attitudes in a communication process: An integrated model. *Human Communication Research, 38,* 332–359. https://doi.org/10.1111/j.1468-2958.2012.01429.x

Craig, E., & Wright, K. B. (2012). Computer-mediated relational development and maintenance on Facebook. *Communication Research Reports, 29,* 119–129. https://doi.org/10.1080/0882 4096.2012.667777

Creswell, J. W. (2009). *Research design: Qualitative, quantitative, and mixed methods approaches* (3rd ed.). Sage.

Croucher, S. M. (2013). Integrated threat theory and acceptance of immigrant assimilation: An analysis of Muslim immigration in Western Europe. *Communication Monographs, 80,* 46–62. https://doi.org/10.1080/03637751.2012.739704

Croucher, S. M., Nguyen, T., & Rahmani, D. (2020). Prejudice toward Asian Americans in the COVID-19 pandemic: The effects of social media use in the United States. *Frontiers in Communication.* https://doi.org/10.3389/fcomm.2020.00039

Eguchi, S., & Starosta, W. (2012). Negotiating the model minority image: Performative aspects of college-educated Asian American professional men. *Qualitative Research Reports in Communication, 13,* 88–97.

Folha de S. P. (2020, June 5). Brazil's Education Minister denies discriminating against Asians in pandemic social media post. *Folha de S. Paulo English Version.* https://www1.folha.uol.com.br/internacional/en/brazil/2020/06/brazils-education-minister-denies-discriminating-against-asians-in-pandemic-social-media-post.shtml

Miller, P. J., Wang, S.-H., Sandel, T., & Cho, G. E. (2002). Self-esteem as folk theory: A comparison of European American and Taiwanese mothers' beliefs. *Parenting: Science and Practice, 2*(3), 209–239. https://doi.org/10.1207/S15327922PAR0203_02

Neuliep, J. W. (2017). Ethnocentrism. In Y. Y. Kim (Ed.), *International encyclopedia of intercultural communication.* https://doi.org/10.1002/978111873665.ieicc0030

Neuman, W. L. (2011). *Social research methods: Qualitative and quantitative approaches* (7th ed.). Allyn & Bacon.

Ragin, C. C. (1994). *Constructing social research.* Pine Forge Press.

Stephan, W. G., & Stephan, C. W. (1996). Predicting prejudice. *International Journal of Intercultural Relations, 20,* 409–426.

Stephan, W. G., & Stephan, C. W. (2000). An integrated threat theory of prejudice. In S. Oskamp (Ed.), *Reducing prejudice and discrimination* (pp. 225–246). Lawrence Erlbaum.

Section Three
Research Methods

8 Ethnography

Chapter Outline

- Ethnography Defined
- Approaches to Ethnography
- Ethnographic Claims
- Ethnographic Data
- Ethnographic Data Analysis
- Ethnographic Warrants
- Summary
- Key Steps and Questions to Consider
- Activities
- Discussion Questions
- Key Terms
- Undergraduate Ethnographic Paper

What Will I Learn About Ethnography?

The photo shows the outside of a typical Finnish sauna. The sauna is located in Jyväskylä, Finland. Saunas are an integral part of Finnish culture and a place to socialize as a family, conduct business, and relax. Saunas in Finland date back hundreds of years. The nation has roughly five million people and more than two million saunas, showing just how significant the sauna is for Finnish people. When Stephen first moved to Finland, he had to learn quickly about Finnish sauna culture. Stephen had to adapt culturally to Finnish life. Other scholars have commented on the need to understand and adapt to Finnish sauna life. Edelsward (1991) described how the sauna is an important part of becoming Finnish, learning about Finnish culture, and being accepted by many Finns. Scholars of cultural adaptation (Croucher, 2008; Kim, 2001; Kramer, 2003) have argued important elements of adapting to a new culture include learning about the culture and being accepted by the host culture. When considering the relationship between the Finnish sauna and adapting to Finnish culture, a researcher could ask various questions: 1) how does one learn culturally appropriate communication behaviors related to the Finnish sauna? 2) how does one truly experience a Finnish sauna? (a performance of communication question) 3) how does one experience Finnish culture through a Finnish sauna? Among the methods one could use to approach this research are: interviews, statistics, and content analysis. Ethnography is the method we explore in this chapter.

DOI: 10.4324/9781003109129-11

Ethnography Defined

Ethnography originally comes from cultural anthropology (Malinowski, 1922). Ethnography is the study of, writing about, and/or a description of (*graphy*) people or folk (*ethno*) (Berg, 1998; Spradley, 1979). **Ethnography** is, at its essence, attempting to describe a culture from the viewpoint of a cultural insider (Denzin & Lincoln, 2003). By using ethnography, the researcher describes individuals' behaviors while inferring meaning from those behaviors. The researcher draws inferences from cultural knowledge they have. **Cultural knowledge** includes the explicit and implicit cultural knowledge we have about life. Explicit knowledge includes things we know and can easily talk about.

For example, Stephen used to live in Finland, where saunas are very popular; in fact, saunas are a national pastime. Before moving to Finland, he knew what a sauna was, and he could describe saunas (explicit knowledge). After spending more time in Finland, he learned cultural norms about Finnish saunas (implicit knowledge), including birch boughs to beat oneself for massage and stimulation and that swearing in a sauna is rude. Stephen learned that to be invited to someone's sauna is an honor. The job of the ethnographer is to draw upon explicit and implicit knowledge to provide a thick description of sauna life.

Edelsward (1991) conducted an ethnographic analysis on Finnish saunas. Edelsward described how the sauna is a place for people to come together with nature and culture. Edelsward provided a thick description of sauna life and its relationship to Finnish culture. Geertz (1973) described **thick description** as a detailed explanation of a social setting and lives of the people. Thick description is integral to ethnography. The description is the foundation of an ethnography. The description shows culture in action. We discuss thick description and how to write an ethnography later in this chapter. One can take various ethnographic approaches. We outline three approaches: 1) ethnography of speaking, 2) ethnography of communication, and 3) autoethnography.

Approaches to Ethnography

Ethnography of Speaking

Hymes' (1962) **ethnography of speaking (EOS)** is a method for studying culturally specific communication practices and patterns. EOS is the analysis of factors relevant to understanding how a communication event accomplishes its goals. Philipsen (1992) stated that EOS consists of "hearing and representing distinctive ways of speaking in particular speech communities" (p. 9). Two assumptions are key to the EOS approach. First, speaking differs across cultures. Second, speaking represents social life and, thus, tells us something distinct about the group. Therefore, observing and describing the speech behaviors of a group can tell us a lot about a group. Numerous scholars following an EOS approach have found that our speaking informs us about cultures (Basso, 1970; Croucher, 2008; Engstrom, 2012; Leitner, 1983; Philipsen, 1975; Pratt & Weider, 1993; Zenk, 1988). The acronym **SPEAKING** was developed by Hymes (1962/1974) to explain how to conduct an EOS analysis within a speech community. A **speech community** is a group of individuals who share a common set of norms/rules for interpreting and using speech (Carbaugh, 2005; Philipsen, 1992). The SPEAKING framework is a list of key questions to ask when conducting an EOS analysis. See Figure 8.1 for a description of the SPEAKING framework.

Figure 8.1 Hymes (1974) SPEAKING Framework

S—Setting and Scene. What is the setting—or the time and place of a speech act? What is the scene—or the psychological situation or cultural meaning of a scene?

P—Participants. Who are the people involved (particularly the speaker and the audience)?

E—Ends. What is the purpose or goal of the speech event?

A—Act sequence. What is the order of the event; how does the event progress?

K—Key. What are some hints to help understand the tone or spirit of the speech event?

I—Instrumentalities. What are the forms and styles of speech used by the speaker in the speech event?

N—Norms. What are the social norms that regulate the speech event?

G—Genre. What kind of speech event is taking place? What genre of speech is it?

Ethnography of Communication

Closely linked to Hymes' (1962, 1964, 1974) ethnography of speaking is ethnography of communication. Scholars who conduct **ethnography of communication (EOC)** research focus on the speech acts/events within communities but are more interested in learning and comparing the shared and varied codes of communication among and between groups (Cameron, 2001; Lindlof & Taylor, 2002). Ethnographers recognize that not every social group communicates the same way and are interested in how "shared meaning and coordinated action vary across social groups" (Philipsen, 1989, p. 258). EOC scholars combine linguistic and anthropological approaches to research. Various scholars have approached ethnography from the EOC approach and/or combined the EOC with the EOS approach (Carbaugh, 2005; Croucher, 2006; Croucher & Cronn-Mills, 2011; Katriel, 1990; Katriel & Philipsen, 1981; Philipsen, 1975; Sherzer, 1983).

Here is an example of how Stephen's encounters with Finnish sauna life could be analyzed using SPEAKING (EOS) and the EOC approach:

S—While visiting Oulu, a city 300 miles north of Helsinki, the capital of Finland, Stephen stayed at a hotel in the city center. The event took place in the late summer of 2012. He was still learning about Finland. He decided one night to go to the sauna.

P—Stephen sat in the sauna for about 5 minutes and was joined by a man (mid-30s, like Stephen) and the man's two sons, who were 8 and 10 years old. Nobody else was in the sauna.

E—The father began to speak to Stephen in Finnish (Stephen knew very little Finnish at the time). When Stephen told him in Finnish that he spoke English or French, the man spoke English to him and asked why there was no steam in the sauna. Stephen did not know why. The man explained and showed Stephen how to properly use the empty metal bucket and ladle by their feet to throw water on the hot stones in the corner.

A—He went out of the sauna, filled the bucket with water, and tossed multiple ladles full of water on the hot stones, and, with each ladle, steam arose and filled the sauna. Every few minutes water is thrown on the stones by different individuals (the children included). The sauna participants began to sweat profusely. After 10 minutes, the father instructed his children and Stephen to get out and take a cold shower, then return to the sauna; the shower, he said, helped cleanse and refresh the skin.

K—During the whole process, the children chuckled at how Stephen did not know about Finnish saunas. The father smiled and was happy to help and asked a lot about American culture.

I—The interaction took place in English, and some broken Suomi (Finnish) was thrown in by Stephen to practice the Suomi he learned at school.

N—The four males were nude; in the United States, public saunas generally require bathing suits. You will rarely find a situation in the United States where children are brought to a sauna. Furthermore, if they are brought to a sauna, we doubt you will find them enjoying it to the same level as these 8- and 10-year-olds. To the Finnish, the sauna is a way of life. Stephen also learned norms about throwing water on the stones. There are saunas in the United States that require water in the same way, but here all four people took turns, and there was an unwritten rule as to when water was thrown, something that the father said you just learn as you become one with the Finnish sauna.

G—This was a lesson on Finnish sauna protocol. The experience demonstrated differences between saunas in Finland and the United States.

The job of EOS and EOC scholars is to provide thick description (Geertz, 1973) of the community they are studying. Whether using the SPEAKING framework (EOS) or focusing less specifically on language use (EOC), your study should provide a clear understanding of the phenomena you set out to explore. You need to provide and analyze specific examples to back up your claims (we talk more about this in the Claims section later in the chapter). Examples are your data and can come from a variety of sources (e.g., interviews, observation, media, documents, artifacts), which we outline in detail later. Ethnographies from the EOS and EOC approaches are typically written in the first person since the research is from the interpretive or critical paradigms.

Autoethnography

When a researcher describes and analyzes personal experiences to understand a cultural event, the researcher is conducting an autoethnography (Bruner, 1993; Denzin, 1989; Ellis, 2004; Holman Jones, 2005; Spry, 2001). **Autoethnography** is a combination of ethnography and autobiography. The researcher is describing and analyzing cultural events by reflecting on experiences. The research includes any epiphanies they had during the research process that might influence their lives and the research. Finally, the researcher discusses how experiences and epiphanies come from and/or are possible by being a part of the culture they are studying (Couser, 1997; Denzin, 1989; Goodall, 2006). The key is to integrate theory and method with descriptions of past and current experiences, epiphanies, and cultural descriptions. Autoethnography is usually written in first person (Ellis & Bochner, 2000), and your writing may come in different forms than the EOS or EOC approaches. Many autoethnographies are journals, short stories, poems, personal essays, prose, and any other forms fitting the needs of the authors.

After moving to Finland, Stephen decided to journal his experiences of adjusting to Finnish life. The following excerpt refers to the same night in the sauna in which Stephen met the father and his two sons.

September 7, 2012—I (Stephen) will be the first one to say sitting in a sauna with a man and his two sons completely naked is not something I would normally say is normal for me. I have always been a relatively shy person when it comes to my body. However, I must say I found it very liberating, relaxing, and interesting to sit in the sauna tonight. For someone who studies cultures, or tries to at least because I don't think I can ever truly understand a culture 100%, this was an interesting event. I really did not feel out of place or embarrassed, as the others were in the same position I was. I mean, the father was nude, and so were his sons. It is perfectly normal in Finnish sauna culture to be nude . . . in fact one cannot wear a bathing suit and one should not cover themselves with a towel or they look like a weirdo tourist. For me, this was one of the first times I really felt like I was learning some insider information about Finland from a stranger.

With the knowledge of the different approaches to ethnography, the following section discusses the types of claims used in ethnographic research.

Ethnographic Claims

We now have basic definitions of the three main kinds of ethnography used in communication. The next section describes how claims are supported. Ethnography affords the researcher a chance to make descriptive, interpretive, evaluative, and reformist claims.

Descriptive Claims

Lofland and Lofland (1995) stated that ethnographers typically set out to describe the norms and practices of a group of individuals in a culture. While descriptive claims tend to be the most typical from an EOS or EOC approach, interpretive, evaluative, and reformist claims are possible. Those using an EOS approach are particularly interested in how individuals/groups name and describe their speech events, the parts of those speech events, and the functions of those speech events. Hymes (1962) described how naming and parts of speech events include things like the senders, receivers, and channels. The functions of the speech events are essentially what speech events achieve within a speech community.

Interpretive Claims

Ethnographic methods can aid in furthering interpretive claims about the relationships between communication and culture. An interpretive claim can enhance our understanding of how, for example, communication creates culture and how culture creates communication. In Philipsen's (1975) analysis of Teamsterville, he found the various ways participants in the community spoke like men created a shared sense of identity. This speech community's language created a shared sense of identity that shaped interactions among members and with nonmembers. His EOC approach revealed various elements of life in Teamsterville. An analysis of just some of

Philipsen's work (1975, 1992) shows how he used an EOC and an EOS approach to describe and interpret cultural events/meanings.

Evaluative and Reformist Claims

For example, scholars who use autoethnography may make descriptive, evaluative, and reformist claims. Ethnographies with evaluative and reformist claims are often considered critical ethnographies (Ang, 1990; Conquergood, 1991). Evaluative claims judge the worth or value of the communication you are studying (Denzin & Lincoln, 2003; Lofland & Lofland, 1995). Evaluative claims may advocate for a change in some behavior or practice in a culture. Reformist claims take evaluation a step further and describe negative consequences of a current economic, political, or social system. Therefore, you can approach an ethnography with the intent of describing some behavior or practice and calling for possible change. Patton (2004) described how sexism and racism are often accepted forms of discrimination in higher education.

We can identify two descriptive/interpretive claims about Finnish sauna culture. First, many Finns are happy to help someone learn about saunas. Stephen found himself in many situations where a Finn taught him something new about the sauna. Second, the sauna is a comfortable place for communication. At first, Stephen did not think the sauna—because you are naked—was an appropriate place to talk with people. However, after numerous experiences, it became clear the sauna is a relaxing environment for a conversation. As for an evaluative or reformist claim, Stephen believes the saunas best represent the inclusiveness of the Finnish people. Thus, from an evaluative standpoint, he evaluates the saunas as a positive representation of Finnish society.

Now that we have a grasp of the different approaches to ethnography and ethnographic claims, the following section describes the various kinds of data used in ethnographic research.

Ethnographic Data

An ethnographic research project takes into consideration different types of data. Ethnographic research typically involves conducting participant observations or interviews.

Participant Observation

The backbone of ethnographic research is participant observation. **Participant observation** involves learning by participating in the culture (Briggs, 1986; Warren & Karner, 2005). Your level of participation in the setting can vary from extensive (joining the culture) to minimal (simply observing and not participating). Here are some standards for deciding your level of participation: 1) your comfort level with the setting/participants; 2) the comfort level of the participants with you; 3) how competent are you with the communication of the setting/participants; 4) your purpose in doing the research; 5) how long you can be in the setting (Spradley, 1979).

In Croucher's (2005, 2006, 2008) ethnographic analysis of North African immigrants to France, he used participant observation. Stephen observed the community as a "field researcher" who was not extensively integrated with the community, and his participation was minimal. Other scholars, such as Angrosino, have taken a more active role in their ethnographic studies. Angrosino (1992, 1997, 1998) took on the role of a volunteer with a mental illness community-based agency to better understand the lives of children and adults with an intellectual disability (ID). Both scholars spent a considerable amount of time with their participants but in two different kinds of roles, one as a "researcher" and the other as a "researcher-volunteer."

> Stephen was a participant/researcher in his analysis of saunas. He has never volunteered to work in the saunas.

Interviews

Interviews are an integral part of the ethnographic research process (Babbie, 2002; Briggs, 1986). Interviewing is a question-and-answer process with the participants in your study. Lofland and Lofland (1995) explained how ethnographic interviewing involves conversations and storytelling between researchers and participants. Interviews are often used in conjunction with participant observation to better understand cultural phenomena. Ethnographic interviews have various forms, but generally take one of the following: 1) oral history, 2) personal narrative, or 3) topical interviews (Babbie, 2002; Bernard, 1999; Creswell, 1998). An **oral history** is when participants retell historical moments in their lives. A **personal narrative** is a participant's personal opinion/perspective on an event or experience. A **topical interview** is the participant's opinion or perspective on a subject or topic. Often the three types of interviews overlap, and the interviews can be structured, unstructured, and/or semi-structured. The choice is yours as the researcher to decide what kind of interview(s) you may use depending on the purpose of your project. After you have collected the interviews, you may need to transcribe them to make analysis easier (we talk about analysis shortly). In Croucher's (2006) work with Muslim and Chinese immigrants, he used topical semi-structured interviews to ascertain how the immigrants felt about external pressures to assimilate in France and Canada. In both contexts (France and Canada), the conversations were open but focused on the topic of pressures to assimilate.

> Stephen collected many personal narratives from people he met in the saunas. He had informal conversations with individuals to avoid intruding on their time in the sauna.
>
> When conducting participant observation and interviews, you must keep a few things in mind. First, you must gain access to the community. Will the community allow you to observe and/or participate? Gaining access is one of the hardest steps in ethnography (Patton, 1990). You will find gaining access easier with a community to which you already belong. For example, if you are in a fraternity or sorority, gaining access may be easier for an ethnographic study. However, researchers who are not part of a group often rely on **gatekeepers** or insiders who are willing to facilitate the researcher's entry into the community (Babbie, 2002; Briggs, 1986). In Croucher's (2005, 2006, 2008) research, his gatekeeper was an Imam in Paris who introduced him to numerous Muslim immigrants in France.

> Fortunately, Stephen did not need a gatekeeper for Finnish saunas. He normally went to saunas in hotels for paying guests.

Second, you must strive to establish **rapport** with your participants (Babbie, 2002; Briggs, 1986). Participants must trust you to observe their lives and learn about their culture. So, listen to the participants, do not cut them off in conversation, show empathy for what they are saying, reciprocate in the conversation, and show commonalities when possible (Bernard, 1999; Patton, 1990).

> Stephen spent a great deal of his time listening to the individuals in the saunas talk about sauna culture. Listening is important in rapport building.

Third, you need to be open to change. When you are out in the field, you will find that things do not always go as planned. You may go into a setting expecting one thing and find something else. Unexpected findings and surprises frequently teach us the most about a culture (Babbie, 2002; Croucher, 2008).

> Only men enter a men's sauna in Finland. In Turku, a nude Russian woman walked into the men's sauna and surprised the men. She said she did not understand the written signs. However, stick figures of men are on the wall designating that the sauna was for men only.

Fourth, you need to take detailed notes while in the field. When you are conducting an ethnography, you may be in the field for an extended period of time. You need to write down (log) what you see, hear, smell, taste, etc. in a journal. A journal is an essential tool for remembering what you saw, heard, learned, etc. Take notes about things such as key persons in the field, conversations you hear, actions you see, etc. These types of things are vital in your analysis. Your journal is essential for writing up your final report (Berg, 1998; Creswell, 1998). Date all the entries in your journal—any and every observation could be important in the end. Take notes often in a way comfortable for you. Having more notes than you need is better than coming up short when writing your research paper.

> Stephen put notes on his computer every night after visiting a sauna. Often, the notes were a few pages long and detailed any conversation he had.

Fifth, when done collecting data in the field, you will depart the community. You will reach a data saturation point, a point where you are not learning anything new. The task of leaving the field can be complicated. You have responsibilities to follow when leaving the field. First, do you want to stay in contact with your participants? Staying in contact is a personal choice you need to make based on your research and personal situation. Second, do you plan to share your results with your participants? Various scholars have shared results with their participants (Angrosino, 1998, 1997; Croucher, 2006, 2008; Spencer, 2011). Sharing is a personal choice. The process of sharing results can complete the circle of research, bringing you back to where you started. You may find your research extends in a new direction if the participants read your research and are willing to provide their perspective and insights.

> Stephen is no longer in the field. He will not be able to share his results with his participants because he does not keep their names on file.

Sixth, if you are doing ethnographic work, you will need to work on reflexivity. **Reflexivity** is the ability to reflect on your own experiences to understand how they are a product and producer of a given cultural experience (Ellis, 2004). Look back at experiences in your own life, be retrospective, and see how your experiences are created by and create other cultural experiences. Your experiences in life will influence how you interpret what you encounter in the field. Identifying influences in your life is important and should be reflected in your writing (Alvesson & Skoldberg, 2000).

Now that you have a grasp of the types of data collected for an ethnographic research project, the following section briefly discusses how to analyze ethnographic data.

Ethnographic Data Analysis

Content analysis is often used to analyze ethnographic data. We go into detail on approaches to content analysis in Chapter 11. The process can be used to look for themes in your interview transcripts and to tease out categories from your observation field notes (Bernard, 1999). Scholars also take a symbolic interactionist approach to analyzing ethnographic data. **Symbolic interactionism** is associated with Mead (1934) and Blumer (1969). Shared meanings are created through interactions, and these meanings become reality. Patton (1990) outlined three premises essential to symbolic interactionism: 1) humans act toward things based on predetermined meanings; 2) meanings come from social interactions; 3) meanings are modified as individuals encounter new experiences and individuals.

Here are a few hints about ethnographic data analysis. First, keep in mind the approach to ethnography you are using, which will help determine your approach. If you are using the EOS approach SPEAKING, you will enter the analysis with predetermined categories to guide you. A SPEAKING analysis is different than an EOC analysis when allowing for categories to emerge from the ground up (a form of deductive analysis). Second, be on the lookout for categories and themes in your data. Third, before you enter the setting you will have done a lot of research on the topic. The key is to not allow your previous knowledge of the setting, as opposed to the observations and interview data in front of you, to override your interpretations of the data. Your interpretations must come from what you experienced in the field.

> Stephen's work is mainly from an EOC perspective. Stephen wanted to make sure he allowed his observations and interview data to drive his analysis of Finnish sauna culture and not previous knowledge of the culture.

If you look to the work of scholars who have used the EOS and EOC approaches (Carbaugh, 2005; Croucher, 2008; Katriel, 1990; Philipsen, 1975; Sherzer, 1983), you will find that some have used the SPEAKING framework and some have used content analysis. Autoethnographic scholars have used metaphors (Fox, 2010), grounded theory (McKemmish et al., 2012), and symbolic interactionism (Olson, 2004). So, you have your data and you have some options of how to analyze your data. The next section of the chapter reviews warrants for ethnographic research.

Ethnographic Warrants

Warrants for ethnographic research follow a similar path to interview-based research. Key issues to consider are researcher credibility, adequacy, coherence, and thick description.

Determining researcher credibility has three components: level of training/experience, degree of membership in the social context, and faithfulness. First, how trained is the researcher at conducting interviews and/or observing human interaction? For new researchers, the art of observation and interviews can be somewhat daunting. Ethnography is, like all forms of research, a process one never truly masters. However, you must prepare yourself before you enter the setting by studying the culture to the best of your ability. Many individuals find linking theory to their ethnographies difficult and struggle with writing about their own experiences and then connecting those experiences to other cultural phenomena. Second, you need to determine your level of involvement with the community. Your degree of membership must be made clear to the readers of your research. Are you an emic or etic researcher? Third, you must be detailed in your notetaking and transcriptions. Ask yourself if you have spent enough time in the field—do you have enough interviews, observations, data?

Adequacy and coherence relate to two key issues. First, do you have enough data to make an adequate argument (Patton, 1990)? Have you kept a detailed journal of your thoughts on a particular issue to write up your autoethnography? When Dan did his work among Jehovah's Witnesses in the United States, he had dozens of interviews, he observed their interactions in the Kingdom Hall and at a district convention, and he observed their interactions with family and their congregation. Dan read through thousands of pages of *Watchtower* and *Awake!*, which helped illuminate the interviews and observations. Observing and recording their surroundings helped him better understand their lives as Witnesses. Second, you need to consider whether the results you are presenting provide a coherent argument for the descriptive, interpretive, evaluative, or reformist claims you are making. Look at your examples (observations or interviews), and make sure they back up your claims. Provide more than one example to back up each claim and show readers your evidence. You should strive to vividly describe the examples. The use of thick description (Geertz, 1973) is essential to supporting all types of ethnographic claims.

Stephen wanted to make sure his observations and notes from sauna culture illustrated the various aspects of how Finnish saunas represent Finnish culture. He could discuss how he began to acculturate (Kim, 2001) into Finnish culture through his experience in the saunas.

Summary

This chapter was a how-to guide to ethnographic research. Ethnographic research is generally approached from an interpretive or critical/cultural paradigm. Hopefully after reading the chapter and the accompanying student paper, you feel comfortable enough to conduct your own ethnographic study. Next is Chapter 9, with a how-to guide to interviewing.

Key Steps and Questions to Consider

1. Choose your topic and research it.
2. Choose your population.
3. How will you access the population?
4. Is your project going to be an observation, interview, a mixture of the two, or an autoethnography? Be prepared to justify your choices.
5. If you do an interview-based ethnography, are your questions structured, semi-structured, or unstructured? How many questions are you going to ask? How many people are you going to interview?
6. If your project is a participant-observation, how long will it last?
7. Before you enter the field, did you write, submit, and get approval from your Human Subject Review Board or Institutional Review Board?
8. Will you record the interviews and the observations?
9. Remember you will need to transcribe the interviews (or have someone else do it for you). Transcription takes a lot of time but makes analysis of the interviews so much better.
10. Take good field notes!
11. Be open to change in the setting.
12. Self-reflect on your position as the researcher. Are you a part of the group you are studying or an outsider? Self-reflection is always helpful and aids in uncovering meaning.
13. Remember reflexivity!
14. Look through your transcripts and field notes for either predetermined themes or emergent themes.
15. Support your themes with strong and insightful examples.

Activities

1. Pick a location on campus or in your community and conduct a nonparticipant mini-ethnography. Spend enough time in the location to develop some insight and gather thick description. Focus on one aspect of a communication theory and see what critical or interpretative observations emerge.

2. Visit the same location and switch to a participant observation ethnographic approach. Focus on the same communication theory as the first activity. Again, see what insights emerge from your ethnography.
3. Compare your observations from the nonparticipant and participant observations. How did your thick description change? How did your critical or interpretative insights change?

Discussion Questions

As you read the student paper provided at the end of this chapter, consider the following questions.

1. Using the ethnographic descriptions the student provides, interpret the data in light of different communication theories.
2. Again, using the student descriptions, reanalyze the data using using Hymes' SPEAKING framework described in this chapter.

Key Terms

Autoethnography	Gatekeepers	SPEAKING
Cultural Knowledge	Oral History	Speech Community
Ethnography	Participant Observation	Symbolic Interactionism
Ethnography of Communication	Personal Narrative	Thick Description
	Rapport	Topical Interview
Ethnography of Speaking	Reflexivity	

References

Alvesson, M., & Skoldberg, K. (2000). *Reflexive methodology: New vistas for qualitative research.* Sage.

Ang, I. (1990). Culture and communication: Towards an ethnographic critique of media and consumption in the transnational media system. *European Journal of Communication, 5,* 239-260. https://doi.org/10.1177/0267323190005002006

Angrosino, M. V. (1992). Metaphors of stigma: How deinstitutionalized mentally retarded adults see themselves. *Journal of Contemporary Ethnography, 21,* 171-199. https://doi.org/10.1177/089124192021002002

Angrosino, M. V. (1997). The ethnography of mental retardation: An applied perspective. *Journal of Contemporary Ethnography, 26,* 98-109. https://doi.org/10.1177/089124197026001005

Angrosino, M. V. (1998). *Opportunity house: Ethnographic stories of mental retardation.* AltaMira.

Babbie, E. (2002). *The basics of social research* (2nd ed.). Wadsworth.

Basso, K. (1970). "To give up on words": Silence in western Apache culture. *Southwestern Journal of Anthropology, 26,* 213-230. https://doi.org/10.1086/soutjanth.26.3.3629378

Berg, B. L. (1998). *Qualitative research methods for the social sciences* (3rd ed.). Allyn and Bacon.

Bernard, R. H. (1999). *Social research methods: Qualitative and quantitative approaches*. Sage.

Blumer, H. (1969). *Symbolic interactionism: Perspective and method*. Prentice Hall.

Briggs, C. L. (1986). *Learning how to ask: A sociolinguistic appraisal of the role of the interview in social science research*. Cambridge University Press.

Bruner, J. (1993). The autobiographical process. In R. Folkenfilk (Ed.), *The culture of autobiography: Constructions of self representations* (pp. 38–56). Stanford University Press.

Cameron, D. (2001). *Working with spoken discourse*. Sage.

Carbaugh, D. (2005). *Cultures in conversation*. Lawrence Erlbaum Associates.

Conquergood, D. (1991). Rethinking ethnography: Towards a critical cultural politics. *Communication Monographs, 58*, 179-194.

Couser, G. T. (1997). *Recovering bodies: Illness, disability, and life writing*. University of Wisconsin Press.

Creswell, J. W. (1998). *Qualitative inquiry and research design: Choosing among five traditions*. Sage.

Croucher, S. M. (2005). Cultural adaptation and the situation of French immigrants: A case study analysis of French immigration and cultural adaptation. *International Journal of Communication, 15*, 147-164.

Croucher, S. M. (2006). The impact of external pressures on an ethnic community: The case of Montréal's Quartier Chinois and Muslim-French immigrants. *Journal of Intercultural Communication Research, 35*, 235-251. https://doi.org/10.1080/17475750601027014

Croucher, S. M. (2008). *Looking beyond the hijab*. Hampton Press.

Croucher, S. M., & Cronn-Mills, D. (2011). *Religious misperceptions: The case of Muslims and Christians in France and Britain*. Hampton Press.

Denzin, N. K. (1989). *Interpretive biography*. Sage.

Denzin, N. K., & Lincoln, Y. S. (2003). Introduction: The discipline and practice of qualitative research. In *Collecting and interpreting qualitative methods* (2nd ed., pp. 1-46). Sage.

Edelsward, L. M. (1991). *Sauna as symbol: Society and culture in Finland*. Peter Lang.

Ellis, C. (2004). *The ethnographic I: A methodological novel about autoethnography*. AltaMira Press.

Ellis, C., & Bochner, A. P. (2000). Autoethnography, personal narrative, reflexivity. In N. K. Denzin & Y. S. Lincoln (Eds.), *Handbook of qualitative research* (2nd ed., pp. 733-768). Sage.

Engstrom, C. L. (2012). "Yes . . . , but I was drunk": Alcohol references and the (re)production of masculinity on a college campus. *Communication Quarterly, 60*, 403-423. https://doi.org/10.1080/01463373.2012.688790

Fox, R. (2010). Re-membering daddy: Autoethnographic reflections of my father and Alzheimer's disease. *Text and Performance Quarterly, 30*, 3-20. https://doi.org/10.1080/10462930903366969

Geertz, C. (1973). *The interpretation of cultures*. Basic Books.

Goodall, B. H. L. (2006). *A need to know: The clandestine history of a CIA family*. Left Coast Press.

Holman Jones, S. (2005). Autoethnography: Making the personal political: In N. K. Denzin & Y. S. Lincoln (Eds.), *Handbook of qualitative research* (pp. 763-791). Sage.

Hymes, D. (1962). Models of the interaction of language and social life. In J. J. Gumperz & D. Hymes (Eds.), *Directions in sociolinguistics* (pp. 35-71). Holt, Rinehart & Winston.

Hymes, D. (1964). Introduction: Toward ethnographies of communication. *American Anthropologist, 66*(1), 1-34.

Hymes, D. (1974). *Foundations in sociolinguistics: An ethnographic approach*. University of Pennsylvania Press.

Katriel, T. (1990). "Griping" as a verbal ritual in some Israel discourse. In D. Carbaugh (Ed.), *Cultural communication and intercultural contact* (pp. 99-114). Lawrence Erlbaum Associates.

Katriel, T., & Philipsen, G. (1981). "What we need is communication": "Communication" as a cultural category in some American speech. *Communication Monographs, 48*, 302-317. https://doi.org/10.1080/03637758109376064

Kim, Y. Y. (2001). *Becoming intercultural: An integrative theory of communication andcross-cultural adaptation*. Sage.

Kramer, E. M. (2003). Gaiatsu and the cultural judo. In E. M. Kramer (Ed.), *The emerging mono-culture* (pp. 1–32). Praeger.

Leitner, G. (1983). Indian English: A critique of the ethnography of speaking. *International Journal of the Sociology of Language, 44*, 153–167.

Lindlof, T. R., & Taylor, B. C. (2002). *Qualitative communication research methods* (2nd ed.). Sage.

Lofland, J., & Lofland, L. H. (1995). *Analyzing social settings* (3rd ed.). Wadsworth.

Malinowski, B. (1922). *Argonauts of the western Pacific*. Routledge.

McKemmish, S., Burstein, F., Manaszewicz, R., Fisher, J., & Evans, J. (2012). Inclusive research design: Unravelling the double hermeneutic spiral. *Information, Communication & Society, 15*, 1106–1135. https://doi.org/10.1080/1369118X.2012.707225

Mead, G. H. (1934). *Mind, self, and society*. University of Chicago Press.

Olson, L. N. (2004). The role of voice in the (Re)construction of a battered woman's identity: An autoethnography of one woman's experiences of abuse. *Women's Studies in Communication, 27*, 1–33. https://doi.org/10.1080/07491409.2004.10162464

Patton, M. Q. (1990). *Qualitative evaluation and research methods*. Sage.

Patton, O. (2004). In the guise of civility: The complications of maintenance of inferential forms of sexism and racism in higher education. *Women's Studies in Communication, 27*, 60–87. https://doi.org/10.1080/07491409.2004.10162466

Philipsen, G. (1975). Speaking "like a man" in Teamsterville: Culture patterns of role enactment in an urban neighborhood. *Quarterly Journal of Speech, 61*, 13–22. https://doi.org/10.1080/00335637509383264

Philipsen, G. (1989). An ethnographic approach to communication studies. In B. Dervin, L. Grossberg, B. J. O'Keefe, & E. Wartella (Eds.), *Rethinking communication 2: Paradigm exemplars* (pp. 258–267). Sage.

Philipsen, G. (1992). *Speaking culturally: Explorations in social communication*. State University of New York Press.

Pratt, S., & Weider, L. D. (1993). The case of saying a few words and talking for another among the Osage people: "Public speaking" as an object of ethnography. *Research on Language & Social Interaction, 26*, 353–408. https://doi.org/10.1207/s15327973rlsi2604_1

Sherzer, J. (1983). *Kuna ways of speaking: An ethnographic perspective*. The University of Texas Press.

Spencer, A. T. (2011). Through the linguistic looking glass: An examination of a newspaper as negotiator of hybrid cultural and linguistic spaces. *Speaker & Gavel, 48*, 31–45.

Spradley, J. P. (1979). *Participant observation*. Holt, Rinehart and Winston.

Spry, T. (2001). Performing autoethnography: An embodied methodological praxis. *Qualitative Inquiry, 7*, 706–732. https://doi.org/10.1177/107780040100700605

Warren, C. A. B., & Karner, T. X. (2005). *Discovering qualitative methods: Field research, interviews and analysis*. Roxbury Publishing Company.

Zenk, H. (1988). Chinook jargon in the speech economy of Grand Ronde Reservation, Oregon: An ethnography-of-speaking approach to an historical case of creolization in process. *International Journal of the Sociology of Language, 71*, 107–124.

Undergraduate Student Paper

How does self-disclosure differ in dyadic relationships?

An Authoethnography

Gina Sirico

Communication is a part of our daily lives, and we self-disclose, or voluntarily reveal information, to others in order to create and maintain relationships. Self-disclosure is crucial to maintaining dyadic or interpersonal relationships. Self-disclosure is a way to gain information about another person and learn how they think and feel. Once one person engages in self-disclosure, we expect the other person will self-disclose back in return, which is the act of reciprocity (Borchers, 1999a). Mutual self-disclosure helps relationships become stronger by building trust and understanding for each other.

Depending on the type of relationship and what stage of Knapp's coming together we are in, the amount of self-disclosure varies. Knapp's stages of disclosure are as follows: the initiation stage, experimenting, intensifying, integrating, and bonding (Borchers, 1999b). Initiation is your first impression of the other person, usually within a few seconds of meeting them. In the experimenting stage, questions are asked to each other to determine if you want to continue the relationship. In the intensifying stage, self-disclosure is exchanged and each person is committed to starting a relationship with the other person. In the integrating stage, the individuals become a pair by doing things together and starting to share an identity. The final, or bonding stage is when a couple makes their relationship official (Borchers, 1999b).

Gina has a strong opening by setting up a theory for understanding the focus of her paper. Our one suggestion is to rely on primary sources instead of secondary sources (e.g., read and cite from the original Knapp article instead of relying on Borchers' (1999b) explanation of Knapp).

Studies on self-disclosure are sometimes done by observing other people's relationships. A study can be conducted where the researcher collected surveys from people in different stages of their relationships to analyze their amount of self-disclosure. The participants could be asked by the researcher to do a self-report and disclose their own behaviors of communication to show how they think and feel about their self-disclosure (Merrigan & Huston, 2009). Or an autoethnography can be done by the researcher about one's own self-disclosure.

An autoethnography is a self-narrative that critiques the position of self with others in social contexts (Merrigan & Huston, 2009). Autoethnography is the interpretive or critical analysis of a social setting or situation that connects the "personal to the cultural" (Porter, 2004). Autoethnography relies on systematic gathering and analysis of field data from people involved in genuine life experiences. Written in the first person, autoethnography is based on the interpretive paradigm values of rich description to include one person's multiple realities (Merrigan & Huston, 2009). The writer's focus is on the degree of membership in describing and interpreting one's own sense making in a cultural situation or setting. In this type of research, the key informant is the researcher himself or herself (Merrigan & Huston, 2009).

> Gina has an effective "big picture" explanation of autoethnography but could use more details of the "nuts and bolts" about the steps involved in the process of conducting an autoethnography.

I chose to do an autoethnography for my research about my level of self-disclosure with my boyfriend compared with my roommate. The amount of self-disclosure I engage in is different in each relationship. I looked at how I self-disclose with each person as well as the reasons for my self-disclosure. I discuss why I do and why I do not disclose with each person. I reflect back on my disclosure with each individual during a two-year period (my freshman to sophomore year of college).

> Gina has a good opening for her descriptive section of the research paper.

My relationship with my boyfriend of three years is an integrated relationship. We have passed through all of the stages of coming together that Knapp described. In the Initiating stage, we knew we wanted to continue this relationship based on the visual and auditory cues we gave each other. When I first approached him, his response to my greeting was warm and positive. We exchanged eye contact and smiled, and offered some self-disclosure. I told him our fathers worked together, and it was all a continuous spiral from there. We continued to talk and flirt in our SAT class we had together. We moved on to the experimenting stage, where we continued to share more information with each other, realizing we had similar values and interests. For example, we are both Catholics, and we both previously had our hearts broken. We were each other's sounding boards, and we helped each other cope with the heartbreak, and began to develop a new, better relationship with each other. The experimenting stage lasted a few months, where we dated and went different places together that allowed us to develop our trust, and self-disclose to each other. We began going everywhere together as a couple. In this stage, he was able to self-disclose to me about his parents and their divorce, and I was able to help him deal with this still sensitive situation. In the intensifying stage, we made the commitment to be each other's one and only partner. In this stage, we also began to self-disclose more deeply, and used "we" and "us" instead of "you" and "I". We are currently still in this stage, talking about our future plans together as a couple. We also have more physical interaction, and touch (like holding hands, always being close) is comfortable to us. The integrating stage overlaps with the intensifying stage, where we are starting to take on characteristics of our partner. We smile the same big smile, laugh the same laugh, and have already merged our social circles. Self-disclosure is no longer an issue, and we self-disclose to each other every day. Family and friends are now "ours" and not just "mine". Activities that we care about separately, we now do together. An example is his love of football and my love of dance. We watch football games together, and we took salsa classes together. We are starting to become "one". Our final stage of coming together would be the bonding stage, where we would get married to make our commitment to each other permanent.

> Gina walks us through Knapp's stages but could use more thick description to provide the reader with a commanding picture of the relationship with her boyfriend. More specifics and details will help build a thick description.

The ways in which I self-disclose to my boyfriend are as a means to vent my feelings, clarify my beliefs and opinions, and to get advice and support. I cannot wait to call my boyfriend by the end of the day to self-disclose to him about my day; tell him how I felt about my classes, or if I am stressed. It feels so good to have someone like him to always be there for me, and tell me everything will be okay. He offers me advice on how to help me de-stress. He cares about my opinions and beliefs, and is always there to support me. He listens, which is the most important thing when I feel the need to have someone to talk to. I also self-disclose to him to encourage him to disclose to me.

> Here is an opportunity for Gina to add to a thick description by providing specific instances of venting feelings, sharing opinions, or helping her to destress. The reader needs stories and examples to see her explanation in action and how the actions support her interpretation of the theory.

My boyfriend sometimes has a hard time expressing to me how he feels, so I am sure to encourage him to tell me. He knows I won't tell anyone else, our conversations are between us two only. I have to work on getting him to open up to me more often, because I can tell when something is bothering him, I just have to get him to talk about it with me. Second, I self-disclose because we trust, care and support one another. The most important reason I self-disclose to him is to get his support. I need him to tell me everything will be fine, and know that he believes in me. We are at a point in our relationship where I can self-disclose to him about anything, because we have that trust.

The ways in which I may avoid self-disclosing to my boyfriend are only if I cannot find the opportunity (not the right time or place), or if I cannot think of a way to self-disclose. There are some times when I want to self-disclose, but we will be in a public place, or with other people. I only want to self-disclose to him, I do not want others to hear. A reason for not disclosing is if I can't think of a way to self-disclose; sometimes, I cannot think of the right way to say what I am trying to say. I may also avoid self-disclosing if I feel I do not want to hurt him by saying something wrong that will make him upset with me. If I say something in the wrong way, I may be misunderstood. This has happened before, when I mentioned something that I felt was no big deal, but he took it more seriously, and got mad over it. I try my best to avoid these types of situations, so I am careful as to when and how I self-disclose.

> Again, specific instances and/or examples will help strengthen her thick description. Thick description is critical for any form of ethnography.

Self-disclosure is necessary, and important in order to sustain a healthy, loving, romantic relationship. I self-disclose to my boyfriend as a way to get to know each other better, and as a way to learn about ourselves. We self-disclose to gain each other's trust, the most important aspect in a loving relationship. We gained, and continue to gain trust with one another through self-disclosing often. I self-disclose to my boyfriend as a means of catharsis (get something off my chest), self-clarification, and self-validation. There would be many problems in our relationship if we had problems self-disclosing, because we need to meta-communicate, or communicate back and forth to each other. We must talk to each other, and never run out of things to say in order to maintain our relationship through marriage. The more self-disclosure and meta-communication we have as a couple, the better our marriage will be.

> Gina may have inadvertently provided a level of thick description when she shifted from describing a girlfriend/boyfriend relationship to a married-couple relationship.

My relationship with my roommate is in the initiating/experimenting stages of coming together. We were still getting to know each other freshman year, so our self-disclosure was limited. After two years of knowing each other, we are more comfortable with each other, and self-disclose more often.

> Gina could be clearer with her description of her roommate relationship. We can infer— but not be sure—if they have been roommates for two years since being freshmen.

The most important reason for me to self-disclose to my roommate is to get advice, support, or assistance from her. We both have boyfriends, and that connection makes it easier for me to self-disclose. I can self-disclose with her easily about him and my relationship problems. We both have the same little arguments with our significant others. We are able to give each other advice about how to deal with those problems. We are learning to support each other. I also self-disclose to her as a way to vent my feelings, especially about school. I am able to self-disclose about my course work, as well as my relationship with my boyfriend. Since we are roommates, we share our food and living space.

As a part of the experimenting stage, we go places together, like for meals, and for activities, such as yoga. She is fluent in Spanish, so she is able to help me with my Spanish homework, and is always willing to offer assistance. I am able to help her with her English homework, since I am good at editing papers. Slowly, through self-disclosure, my roommate and I are learning to care about, support, and trust one another.

> The yoga, the Spanish homework, and the English homework help to build thick description and provide insight on their relationship.

My main reason for not self-disclosing to my roommate is because I do not want what I self-disclose to be told to others. I may not self-disclose because I feel I may not get the support I need after I self-disclose to her. I am still afraid of being misunderstood, or hurting her if she herself is in a difficult situation. I do not want to impose on her too much information, where she feels that she can't self-disclose back to me. Sometimes, I cannot find the opportunity to self-disclose because I do not want to "bother" her, or distract her. I want to self-disclose, but feel like I can't when she is preoccupied with homework, her phone, or watching TV.

My relationship with my roommate is still growing, but self-disclosure is important for me to express my feelings, and for us to become trusting of one another. We need to learn to find the right times to continue to self-disclose and become closer friends. I self-disclose to my roommate as a means of impression formation, catharsis, and reciprocity.

> Gina could better integrate how impression formation, catharsis, and reciprocity are defined and evident with her autoethnography. She included the concepts but could provide more guidance to the reader regarding how they are apparent within her analysis.

In conclusion, self-disclosure is important in building and maintaining relationships. I see this importance through my romantic relationship with my boyfriend and through my friendship with my roommate. I have to self-disclose, and we have to self-disclose with each other to get to know one another and grow together. The reasons I self-disclose in each relationship differ. Self-disclosure brings two people closer together and creates trust, which is important in a dyadic relationship.

References

Anderson, L. (2006). Analytic autoethnography. *Journal of Contemporary Ethnography*, *35*, 373–395. https://doi.org/10.1177/0891241605280449

Borchers, T. (1999a). *Interpersonal communication, self-disclosure*. www.abacon.com/commstudies/interpersonal/indisclosure.html

Borchers, T. (1999b). *Interpersonal communication, relationship development*. www.abacon.com/commstudies/interpersonal/indevelop.html

Merrigan, G., & Hutson, C. L. (2009). *Communication research methods*. University Press.

Porter, N. (2004). *CMA methodology, autoethnography*. http://anthropology.usf.edu/cma/CMAmethodology-ae.htm

9 Interviewing

What Will I Learn About Interviewing?

This is a photo (2009) of Stephen in Kolkota, India. Stephen was attending Durga Puja festivities. Durga Puja is an annual Hindu festival celebrating the Hindu Goddess Durga. For many Hindus, particularly those in West Bengal, this is the biggest festival and cultural event of the year. Durga Puja celebrations are held around the world as Indians migrate from India to multiple corners of the world. The festival takes place during a six-day period, during which large pandals, or temporary structures made of bamboo and cloth, are made. Some of these pandals are very simple, while some are extremely elaborate. The purpose of the pandals is to house the stage where the Durga idol stands; the idols are almost entirely made of clay and paint. During the festival, worshipers enter the pandals and worship the idols. At the end of the festival, the idols are taken to a local river and "given" back to the river. As a communication researcher and as someone who greatly admires Indian cultures, the celebration of Durga Puja has always fascinated Stephen. Stephen learned that, for some Indians, celebrating Durga (the Goddess) enhanced their sense of "Indianness," (a chance to celebrate culture, history, and being Indian), while for others the celebration is just a chance to drink and be merry with friends. A communication scholar might approach Durga Puja and look at how this celebration relates to an individual's identity (Collier & Thomas, 1988; Cupach & Imahori, 1993; Ting-Toomey, 1993, 1999). The scholar could ask if the celebration of holidays and identity are related to one another. In fact, Noth (1995) argued that the two are related. Such a relationship could be explored through a variety of research methods (e.g., ethnography, focus groups, and statistics). The method we explore in Chapter 9 is in-depth interviewing.

Approaches to Interviewing

Interviews are widely used in communication, the social sciences, the humanities, business, and other fields of inquiry to gain an understanding of cultural, sociological, psychological, linguistic, and consumer behaviors (Briggs, 1986; Giles et al., 1977; Hall, 1989; Neuman, 2011). The purpose of **interviewing** is to ask questions and get answers from the participants involved in your study in order to gather data. Interviewing has three traditional approaches: structured, semi-structured, and unstructured. No matter which approach a researcher may choose, using interviews as a data collection method should be guided in some way by theoretical inquiry (see Chapters 2–4 if you need a refresher on the relationship between theory and method).

Structured Interviews

A **structured interview** is *very structured*, hence its name. With this type of interview protocol, the interviewer: 1) prepares all the questions ahead of time (called an **interview guide**); 2) asks each participant the exact same questions in the exact same order; 3) has few if any open-ended questions in the interview guide (such questions allow participants too much room for variation from an interviewer's script); 4) does not use personal opinions as possible responses during the interview (e.g., by agreeing/disagreeing with a response).

> "How do I prepare questions?" is a common concern for many students using interviews for data collection. We recommend the following. First, you should have some understanding of a theory or context you are interested in studying. Second, think of key issues you are interested in studying. Third, ask yourself "what questions will help me better understand my area of interest?" Fourth, write down your questions. Fifth, check the number of questions. Participants may not join the study if it will take too much of their time. Sixth, write your questions in a conversational style (we will talk about how an interview is a conversation shortly). Stephen's Durga Puja project involved extensive reading on identity, religious holidays, and India. Two of Stephen's questions included: 1) how is Durga Puja part of being Bengali? 2) is it important to celebrate Durga Puja? These easy to understand and very open-ended questions helped Stephen better understand the holiday, identity, and India.

Self-administered questionnaires (self-reports where people write down their answers) are a type of structured interview (Kvale, 1996). Other typical types of structured interviews include telephone interviews where the interviewer fills in the participants' responses and online interviews with closed-ended options (a popular one is Survey Monkey). A medical interview is a type of structured interview many of us have experienced. Health professionals have a set list of questions asked in a specific order. The benefits of structured interviews are: 1) the individuals conducting these kinds of interviews only need to be trained to follow basic data collection instructions; 2) less of a relationship is generally developed between the interviewer and participants; 3) data collected is considered by many who conduct this type of research to be more reliable (Patton, 1990; Warren & Karner, 2005).

Semi-Structured and Unstructured Interviews

Semi-structured and **unstructured interviews** are similar in many ways. First, the interviewer and participant have a formal interview where they meet and chat about a specific topic. The interview is more of a conversation than a one-way process like a structured interview. Semi-structured and unstructured interviews include narrative interviews where you are collecting a person's life stories. The selection of where to conduct an interview is often agreed upon by the interviewer and the interviewee including over the phone or online (e.g., by Zoom or Skype). Agreeing upon a location for an interview makes participants feel more comfortable about the entire interview process (Patton, 1990). Dan had a graduate student who was planning to interview participants at high school speech tournaments during breaks in the schedule . . . then the COVID-19 pandemic struck. Speech tournaments were cancelled. Her research might have been delayed for months (or even years). Instead she shifted her location from tournaments to Zoom. Here interviews continued as planned, and her research was back on track.

Second, semi-structured and unstructured interviews are similar since the interviewer has developed an understanding of the setting/context to allow most of the questions to be open-ended in nature. The questions are written to allow participants to answer in a variety of ways. You might, for example, ask few questions requiring a "yes" or a "no" response. Then the similarities end.

Researchers who conduct semi-structured interviews combine techniques of structured and unstructured interviews. You will prepare a flexible interview guide to help guide the conversation with your participants. The guide (or list of questions) is flexible, so you can follow the flow and adapt as the conversation progresses (e.g., if something is important to the participant, you can spend more time on the subject than something else on the guide).

Unstructured interviews generally do not have an interview guide (a prepared series of questions). You will instead spend time building rapport and allowing each participant to shape how they want to talk about the subject of the study (Briggs, 1986).

Patton (1990) said building **rapport** during the interview process is important. He defined rapport as showing "respect [for] the people being interviewed, so that what they say is important because of who is saying it" (p. 317). The building of rapport can be done in many ways. When Stephen was conducting research in Montreal among Chinese shopkeepers, he spent great deal of time browsing the participants' shops before he began the interviews (Croucher, 2003, 2008). Stephen used the information he gained from browsing to establish rapport during the interviews. Asking the interviewees about their business showed he was interested in their stories as immigrants and shopkeepers and in their business. Stephen focused on being professional but not too formal, which may have intimidated his interviewees.

Most researchers start their research among people they know—such as family and friends—or rely on student samples. If you are conducting your research among family and friends, you should already have rapport. If you are conducting your research among students, you will need to take some steps to establish rapport; however, students often are given an incentive to be involved in the interview, and so establishment of rapport should be relatively easy. If your interview involves individuals you do not have previous contact with, you must take steps to show them you are interested in their stories . . . or else why should they share the stories with you?

Figure 9.1 Comparing Interview Types

Structured	Semi-Structured	Unstructured
Questions are prepared ahead of time	A main set of questions is prepared	No pre-prepared questions
Each participant asked the same set of questions	Follow-up questions are flexible and may not be asked of each participant	Questions may change for each participant
Questions asked in the same order	Question order may change as interview progresses	No specific order to questions asked in the interview
No variation from the interview script	Interview script is flexible	No interview script is used
Uses mostly closed-ended questions	May use a mix of closed-ended and open-ended questions	More a discussion than a series of questions
Participants have limited range of responses	Participants have a variety of response options	Participants have maximum range of responses available
Data is straightforward to analyze	Data is a mix of responses and will require careful analysis	Data can get messy and difficult to analyze

Semi-structured interviews are typically used 1) when interviewers only have one chance to meet with a participant(s) in the field and 2) ethnographic observation can precede the interviews (Bernard, 1999). Unstructured interviews, on the other hand, are often employed when researchers: 1) plan to revisit the same participants on multiple occasions and 2) are open to having the participants influence their understanding/approach to the subject/context (Briggs, 1986). Generally, researchers will ask participants if they can audio record or video record semi-structured and unstructured interviews. In-depth notetaking is always a good idea during interviews, even when permission to record is granted. A researcher can jot down observations and insights, which may not be as apparent on a recording. Notes are also your backup in case the recording files are damaged.

Both semi-structured and unstructured interviews offer participants a chance to openly express their opinions. The open expression of views provides what Geertz (1973) called **thick description.** Thick description is an in-depth understanding of a culture or setting provided by the members of the culture and captured by others (researchers and journalists). Semi-structured interviews offer interviewers the opportunity to prepare a flexible guide before the interview, which can make the interview process a lot easier. Do you remember Dan's work with Jehovah's Witnesses from the chapter on ethnography? Dan's transcribed interviews produced approximately 300 pages of interview data, which provided a thick description for the study. Now, don't freak out. Dan's work was intensive, taking months of data collection. Your own research can produce a thick description in less time and fewer pages of transcribed interviews.

Now that you understand the different approaches to interviewing, the next section of the chapter discusses the types of data typically used in interview projects.

Data in Interviews

When planning to use structured, semi-structured, or unstructured interviews, you must ask: what is your data? Your data—what you are analyzing—will likely be spoken or written words. If you are conducting semi-structured and unstructured interviews, the data is almost always the spoken word. Structured interviews might use the written word if the participants completed a questionnaire or survey. You will need permission from your participants to audio record or video record the interviews. Your data consists of the transcripts of the interviews and any notes you take during the interviews.

Transcription of interviews is a very individualized process—meaning everyone does it differently. Here are some tips to help make the process easier. First, if audio recording your interviews, various software programs can make transcribing a lot easier (e.g., Interact-AS, NCH Software, Nuance, Vocapia, VoiceBase). If you don't want to or can't buy one of these programs, you can still transcribe while listening to an audio file. You will need to do a lot of stopping and starting to make sure you write down what your participants say. Second, we have found it beneficial to transcribe interviews shortly after they are conducted. In our opinion, transcribing interviews while fresh is the best option. Third, insert notes in the margins of the transcription describing what you remember happening during the interview. Trust us, you will forget a lot about the interviews in the future. Transcribing is a time-consuming process, but you must get your interview data into textual form to fully analyze it.

Sampling is important in interviewing (so you may want to review your notes on random and nonrandom sampling). Depending on your population, a random sample may prove difficult (if not impossible), thus necessitating a nonrandom sample. In fact, nonrandom sampling is necessary and useful in interviewing. Stephen regularly interviews Muslim immigrants in France (Croucher, 2006, 2008). Stephen found that a random sample is nearly impossible in any nation that does not keep records based on religious affiliation (including France). Even when governments track religious affiliation, many individuals are undocumented and other variables make a random sample difficult. Stephen has found convenience and/or snowball sampling appropriate for his research.

Next, how many interview participants do you need? The question is not easy to answer. **Data saturation**—or the point at which no new data emerges—is a matter of judgment. As you conduct more qualitative research, such as interviewing and ethnography, you will develop the skills to evaluate what you have collected and tell yourself: "I have enough information because my participants keep repeating the same information and I'm not learning anything new."

Thinking back to the relationship between identity and Durga Puja, we must decide what structure of interview to use since 1) we have a fairly strong grasp of identity theories, 2) we may only be able to talk to people once, maybe twice, and 3) we are open to revising or altering our theoretical ideas of the relationship between Durga Puja and identity. So, we might go for semi-structured interviews. Our next step is to look at the data, claims, and warrants for the interview.

With an understanding of the various approaches to interviews and the types of data used in interviews, the following section discusses the types of claims used in interview research.

Claims in Interviews

The key for researchers using interviews (and any other method) is the claims they are trying to make. Two different claims are primarily associated with interviewing as a method—descriptive and interpretive. Granted, other claims can be associated with interviews (evaluative and reformist), and these are discussed at length in the chapter focusing on critical/cultural studies. Remember, claims can define what is occurring and reveal individual meaningful structures within society.

Journalists, for example, continuously ask questions to find out what is happening about daily events. These descriptive tales of what is happening are the backbone of journalism. From local to national to international events, personal accounts told to journalists in the field add thick description to what is occurring. Along with describing events, journalists often add what we call the "human element" to the story. Interviewing individuals on the street and getting their point of view on an issue and how an issue affects them helps the reader better understand how those affected by the issue understand it.

As we write this chapter, protests are happening around the world in response to the murder of George Floyd in Minneapolis, Minnesota. The protests spread to more than 2,000 cities in all 50 of the United States and in 60 other countries. Journalists from around the world were reporting on the protests, on damage to property and looting in Minneapolis, on police response, on political response, and on the social justice group Black Lives Matter (defining what is occurring). Journalists also collected individual stories from protesters in cities large and small including St. Peter (MN), New York City, Barcelona, Melbourne, Cape Town, London, and Tel Aviv (revealing individual meanings). In fact, according to the *New York Times*, the death of George Floyd may have triggered the largest social movement in U.S. history (Buchanan et al., 2020). Research will be conducted on the movement for many years to come. You might decide to join in, from your own interests, the research on this social movement.

Communication researchers use interviews to define what is occurring in a setting and to reveal individual meanings. Philipsen (1992, 1997), in an in-depth analysis, explored being a member of Teamsterville, a neighborhood just outside of Chicago. Through in-depth semi-structured and unstructured interviews, Philipsen was able to define specific characteristics of masculinity/femininity in Teamsterville. For example, the front porch is for women, the bar is for men, and conflicts were not settled through talking but fighting (defining what is occurring). He learned by interviewing various individuals why certain rules existed for specific behaviors in Teamsterville. The collective reason for these behaviors came down to what the participants understood to be a "code of honor" (revealing individual meanings).

As we prepare to conduct our semi-structured interviews, we ask if the participants will let us video record the interviews. The recordings, our interview notes, and a transcription of the interviews are our data.

As with all research, warrants are necessary; therefore, the following section describes the warrants used to evaluate research using interviews.

Warrants in Interviews

The standards used to judge whether the data supports your claims in an interview-based project/study are subjective, especially since most researchers using interviews subscribe to the interpretivist approach. As the purpose of interviews is generally to define what is occurring and to illuminate meanings, warrants for interviews address the ability of the researcher to describe multiple realities. Therefore, issues of researcher credibility, adequacy, and coherence are key issues (Lindlof, 1995; Miles & Huberman, 1994; Strauss & Corbin, 1998). Your credibility as a researcher is an important standard by which interpretive research is judged because the researcher is the instrument through which interpretations and meanings are made (Patton, 1990). Components used to determine researcher credibility include level of researcher training/experience, the researcher's degree of membership in the social context, faithfulness/coherence, and reflexivity.

Training and Experience

Unlike research conducted through a discovery approach where issues of reliability and validity are paramount to determine the effectiveness of an instrument and/or experiment, the researcher is the instrument in the interpretive approach. Therefore, one's level of experience in interviewing is important. Researchers conducting and analyzing interviews will with experience develop techniques to observe and analyze the experience of their participants. If one is aware of what should happen, we all learn some things while in the field. For example, when Stephen first went into the field as a master's student to interview shopkeepers in Montreal, he did not have much experience. However, he was aware of what he should be doing. He had taken research method courses as an undergraduate and graduate student (just as you are doing). Such courses prepared him for the task. Stephen learned that some things he was taught (in books like this) were spot-on accurate. Unfortunately, some things were not as quite as clear. Stephen realized the difficulty of taking notes while conducting interviews. Some of his participants found his notetaking rude, and the textbooks did not prepare him for the reaction. So, Stephen combined what he learned in the field with what he learned from his classes and textbooks. Stephen is now theory aware *and* field aware . . . his training and experience developed in tandem. To this day, he is continually expanding his training and experience.

Degree of Membership

When conducting an interview-based project, an integral warrant is your degree of membership. Fitch (1994) stated that researchers should be "deeply involved and closely connected to the scene, activity, or group being studied," while at the same time "achieve enough distance from the phenomenon to allow for recording of action and interactions relatively uncolored by what [you] might have had at stake" (p. 36). The two statements create a difficult balancing act. Interpretive researchers involved and connected with the social context are better equipped to interpret participants' statements and look for individual meanings in their statements, while researchers involved in and connected with the social context better understand the participants' lives. However, a researcher who is *too* involved may lack the distance and affect their interpretation of the data. Much of the difficulty goes back to our emic vs. etic discussion.

In his study of the *Tico Times*, an English-language newspaper in Costa Rica, Spencer (2011) argued "English-language media outlets could and should be viewed as minority-language media outlets as they are cultural negotiators for tourists, sojourners and other transnational migrants" (p. 31). Spencer spent months observing and interviewing staff members at the newspaper for the project. He is fluent in Spanish and spent years traveling and living in Latin and South America. In this study and in his other work, Spencer makes every effort to be deeply involved with his participants and the phenomenon, while at the same time not becoming too involved to potentially alter his perceptions.

Faithfulness

Morse (1998) described faithful researchers as "meticulous about their documentation," and to "file methodically, and keep notes up-to-date" (p. 67). Simply put, faithfulness means being detailed. When a researcher is in the field conducting interviews, they should consider: have I spent enough time in the field, have I interviewed enough people, have I gone over my notes and transcripts enough, and have I conducted enough research to support my findings (Lofland & Lofland, 1995; Patton, 1990)? Answering such questions will help ensure research is thorough and faithful.

Coherence

Think of coherence as logic and internal validity. When conducting an interpretive study using interviews, a researcher must ask if the results logically support the claims they are making. When our examples are coherent, we can relate our findings to similar social situations (Fitch, 1994). In a classic example, Philipsen's (1976, 1992) analysis of Teamsterville discussed the importance of place and what it meant to be a man. Philipsen provided a plethora of interview examples to illustrate each of his arguments. The arguments emerged from his analysis of the interview transcripts and ethnographic observations. Each of the examples supported the points Philipsen was illustrating. For example, when Philipsen (1976) discussed the issues of inclusion in Teamsterville, he described how:

> Once a stranger is located, talk might be relatively free, depending on the kind of person he is. "The hillbillies" and "the Mexicans" live within the neighborhood boundaries but do not, in the eyes of the long-term white residents really "belong" there.

> (p. 17)

The example of "Hillbillies" and "Mexicans" not belonging in Teamsterville clearly illustrates the point Phillipsen was making about who is and who is not a member of this community, thus adding coherence to his arguments.

Reflexivity

When we reflect on the research process, we are considering the research process and our place within it. Different theoretical approaches, values, and interests may affect the research process. As a researcher, you should consider your position in relation to what you are studying. For example, how can your education, socio-economic standing, religious beliefs, age, gender, sex, sexual orientation, political views, and personal experiences affect what you pay attention to the most during an interview? How do these aspects impact what questions you are interested in asking? You should personally reflect on and be cognizant of these factors while conducting your interviews and later when analyzing them.

The purpose of our interviews with Indians is to describe how Durga Puja relates to Indian identity. We hope that during our interviews participants will discuss Durga Puja, their identities, the festival, and how the Goddess affects them. We recognize that our participants will be just a small sample of Indians ... many others think like them and others think nothing like them. This is part of the interpretivist paradigm.

The following section describes how to analyze your interview data.

Analysis of Interview Transcripts

A researcher can use various methods to analyze interview transcripts from an interpretive approach. Researchers can conduct a content analysis of their interview transcripts, approach the project and the analysis from a critical/cultural perspective, conduct a content analysis, conduct a grounded theory analysis, or perform a rhetorical criticism. Grounded theory is one of the more popular forms of qualitative data analysis. Glaser and Strauss (1967) defined grounded theory as "the process of breaking down, examining, comparing, conceptualizing, and categorizing data" (p. 61). Through the process of inductive coding, themes or "salient categories of information supported by the text" (p. 22) "emerge" from the analysis of texts, instead of being pre-chosen by the researcher. Glaser and Strauss (1967) claimed researchers conducting a grounded theory analysis should follow four steps:

While Stephen has a strong grasp of Indian culture, he is not Indian. Thus, any of his attempts to understand Indian culture, identity, and Durga Puja are those of an outsider (etic research). We want to be meticulous in our research, so we will make sure we take a lot of notes and spend plenty of time trying to understand our participants to make sure our representation is faithful. Finally, we will use clear and concise examples to support our claims to make sure our analysis is coherent.

After the four stages are finished, researchers sort their memos into broad theoretical categories, which Strauss and Corbin (1991) claimed facilitate making theoretical arguments and conclusions.

---

1. Collect data from participants (conduct interviews).
2. Take detailed notes during each interaction (the interviews).
3. Code (write) in the margins of transcripts of interviews the central theme or purpose of each line or passage of an interview. Bernard (1999) recommended using a highlighter to differentiate ideas (themes) that are similar within transcripts and from one interviewee to another. The coding stage allows themes to naturally "emerge."
4. Memo—or write down generalized links between what is coded and established theory. The researcher will pull out quotations they have identified from their coding (step 3) to support specific theoretical arguments in the literature.

Stephen will want to make sure he uses clear examples from his interviews to illustrate the different ways Durga Puja relates to identity. After sifting through the transcripts, some themes may emerge that relate to Collier and Thomas' (1988) or Ting-Toomey's (1993, 1999) conceptions of identity. Stephen's job is to use examples that coherently relate to theory.

Summary

This chapter was a how-to guide to interviewing as a research method. As seen in the chapter, interviewing is generally approached from the interpretive or critical/cultural paradigm. We hope that, after reading the chapter and the accompanying student paper, you have enough knowhow to conduct your own study using interviews.

Key Steps and Questions to Consider

1.   Choose your topic and research it.
2.   Choose your population.
3.   How will you access this population?
4.   Are you doing a random or nonrandom sampling?
5.   Is your questioning going to be structured, semi-structured, or unstructured?
6.   How many questions are you going to ask?
7.   How many people are you going to interview? This is a hard question to answer. There is no magic number of interviews you need to do to reach data saturation.
8.   Before you enter the field, did you write, submit, and get approval from your Human Subject Review Board or Institutional Review Board?
9.   Remember rapport!
10. To tape/video record the interviews or not?
11. Remember you will need to transcribe the interviews (or have someone else do it for you) . . . this takes a lot of time, but it makes analysis of the interviews so much better as you will better know what you have in your data!
12. Self-reflect on your position as the researcher. Are you a part of the group you are studying or an outsider? This self-reflection is always helpful as it aids in uncovering meaning.
13. Look through your transcripts for either pre-determined themes or emergent themes. Your grounded theory analysis.
14. Support these themes with coherent examples. Continuation of your grounded theory analysis.
15. Throughout this whole process you may have already been writing some of your research paper (analysis of literature, for example), if not, start.

Activities

Activity 1: Identifying Interview Questions. Type "interview questions" into an Internet search. You will get millions of results Pick a "top 10" or "top 100" list of interview questions. Work through the list and identify which questions work best with a structured, semi-structured or unstructured interview. You can divide the class into groups with each group working through different lists (and, with millions of hits, you will have no shortage of lists available!).

Activity 2: Practice Interviewing. Divide the class into pairs. Have students interview each other using a few of the interview questions from Activity 1. The students can conduct brief interviews rotating to a new partner every 5–10 minutes (and switching between being interviewee and interviewer). How did the students establish rapport in each interview? What do the results from the interviews reveal?

Activity 3: Analyzing Interview Data. Pick a "riveting talk" from TED.com. Select a communication theory that relates to the TED talk. Treat the TED talk as interview data. Conduct a grounded-theory analysis. See what themes and patterns "emerge" from the talk. For a challenge, try transcribing the TED talk! Try dividing the class into groups with each group analyzing a different TED talk.

Discussion Questions

1. How will the student's data and analysis change if switched from Likert-scale questions to open-ended questions?
2. Discuss how different sampling approaches will affect the student's data and results.
3. Discuss possible communication theories, which may tie in with the student's paper. How will the inclusion of theory/theories into the study make the research stronger?

Key Terms

Data Saturation	Rapport	Unstructured
Grounded Theory	Semi-structured	Sampling
Interview Guide	Thick Description	
Interviewing	Structured	

References

Bernard, R. H. (1999). *Social research methods: Qualitative and quantitative approaches*. Sage.

Briggs, C. L. (1986). *Learning how to ask: A sociolinguistic appraisal of the role of the interview in social science research*. Cambridge University Press.

Buchanan, L., Bui, Q., & Patel, J. K. (2020, July 3). Black Lives Matter may be the largest movement in U.S. history. *New York Times*. www.nytimes.com/interactive/2020/07/03/us/george-floyd-protests-crowd-size.html

Collier, M. J., & Thomas, M. (1988). Cultural identity. In Y. Y. Kim & W. B. Gudykunst (Eds.), *Theories in intercultural communication* (pp. 99–120). Sage.

Croucher, S. M. (2003). *A threatened dragon: An analysis of the perceptions of Chinese shopkeepers in Montréal's Quartier Chinois toward La Loi 101, a linguistic law mandating the supremacy of the French language in Québec* [Unpublished thesis]. Mankato, MN.

Croucher, S. M. (2006). The impact of external pressures on an ethnic community: The case of Montréal's Quartier Chinois and Muslim-French immigrants. *Journal of Intercultural Communication Research, 35*, 235–251. https://doi.org/10.1080/17475750601027014

Croucher, S. M. (2008). *Looking beyond the hijab*. Hampton Press.

Cupach, W. R., & Imahori, T. (1993). Identity management theory. In R. L. Wiseman & J. Koester (Eds.), *Intercultural communication competence* (pp. 112–131). Sage.

Fitch, K. L. (1994). Criteria for evidence in qualitative research. *Western Journal of Communication, 58*, 32–38. https://doi.org/10.1080/10570319409374481

Geertz, C. (1973). *The interpretation of cultures*. Basic Books.

Giles, H., Bourhis, R. Y., & Taylor, D. M. (1977). Towards a theory of language in ethnic group relations. In H. Giles (Ed.), *Language, ethnicity and intergroup relations* (pp. 307–343). Academic Press.

Glaser, B. G., & Strauss, A. L. (1967). *Discovery of grounded theory: Strategies for qualitative research*. Aldine.

Hall, E. T. (1989). *Beyond culture*. Anchor Books.

Kvale, S. (1996). *InterViews: An introduction to qualitative research interviewing*. Sage.

Lindlof, T. R. (1995). *Qualitative communication research methods*. Sage.

Lofland, J., & Lofland, L. H. (1995). *Analyzing social settings* (3rd ed.). Wadsworth.

Miles, M. B., & Huberman, A. M. (1994). *Qualitative data analysis: An expanded sourcebook* (2nd ed.). Sage.

Morse, J. M. (1998). Designing funded qualitative research. In N. Denzin & Y. Lincoln (Eds.), *Strategies of qualitative inquiry* (pp. 56–85). Sage.

Neuman, W. L. (2011). *Social research methods: Qualitative and quantitative approaches* (7th ed.). Allyn & Bacon.

Noth, W. (1995). *Handbook of semiotics*. Indiana University Press.

Patton, M. Q. (1990). *Qualitative evaluation and research methods*. Sage.

Philipsen, G. (1976). Places for speaking in Teamsterville. *Quarterly Journal of Speech, 62*, 15–25. https://doi.org/10.1080/00335637609383314

Philipsen, G. (1992). *Speaking culturally: Explorations in social communication*. State University of New York Press.

Philipsen, G. (1997). A theory of speech codes. In G. Philipsen & T. Albrecht (Eds.), *Handbook of international and intercultural communication* (pp. 51–67). Sage.

Spencer, A. T. (2011). Through the linguistic looking glass: An examination of a newspaper as negotiator of hybrid cultural and linguistic spaces. *Speaker & Gavel, 48*, 31–45.

Strauss, A., & Corbin, J. (1991). *Basics of qualitative research: Grounded theory procedure and techniques*. Sage.

Strauss, A., & Corbin, J. (1998). Grounded theory methodology: An overview. In N. K. Denzin & Y. Lincoln (Eds.), *Strategies of qualitative inquiry* (pp. 158–183). Sage.

Ting-Toomey, S. (1993). Communicative resourcefulness: An identity negotiation theory. In R. L. Wiseman & J. Koester (Eds.), *Intercultural communication competence* (pp. 72–111). Sage.

Ting-Toomey, S. (1999). *Communication across cultures*. Guilford.

Warren, C. A. B., & Karner, T. X. (2005). *Discovering qualitative methods: Field research, interviews and analysis*. Roxbury Publishing Company.

Undergraduate Student Paper

No Matter the Letter, We're All Greek Together

Heather Kerr

Freshman year of college is an exhilarating, one of a kind experience for students. Most freshmen are 17 or 18 years old living on their own for the first time. This major life change usually leads to students reevaluating and reworking their social identity. Some students may rely on behavior that has worked for them in the past. Others may emulate behavior they have seen work for others in high school. Still more seek social acceptance and validation from their peers by joining clubs and organizations. Perhaps the organizations with the worst reputation in many colleges are the fraternities and sororities. Despite years of negative media portrayal and assorted hazing scandals across the country, thousands of students continue to pledge their lifelong loyalty and define their social identity with them every year.

> Heather has started with a strong introduction, which sets the context for her study.

I am on my journey to understand the broad correlation between Greek life and social identity and how wearing letters (clothing usually t-shirts with the Greek letters of an organization) affect one's sense of social identity. I decided the best way to understand this would be to go directly to the source. My study consisted of eight willing participants from three different organizations. Four participants were boys and four were girls. They ranged in age from 18 to 21. Every grade was represented with one freshman, four sophomores, two juniors, and one senior. I met with each participant at their convenience for an interview. Each interview lasted between 10 and 15 minutes. I had a list of approximately eight questions but went in with an open mind and asked follow up questions whenever I deemed necessary depending on participants' answers. Instead of recording the interviews, I went with a pen and paper to take notes. After my final interview was completed, I had nearly six pages front and back of notes. Each participant chose an alias and all information pertaining to this study were kept in a private location accessible only to myself.

> Heather is not clear if she belongs to a Greek organization. The reader does not know her *degree of membership* within the organizations she is studying. Heather provides good demographic information on the people she interviewed but is less clear how the participants were selected for the study. Standards for selecting interviewees are best if set before the interview process begins. Sometimes the selection process needs to be adjusted as the selection process proceeds, in which case the researcher acknowledges the variation that occurred and why it was implemented. It appears from her description that Heather is using a semi-structured approach. She can strengthen her paper by stating the approach she is using instead of leaving it up to a reader to infer the interview protocols. Finally, Heather clearly states her method of data collection (pen and paper).

The theory I was interested in testing was Social Identity Theory. Social Identity Theory was developed in the late 1970s by Tajfel and Turner (Mcleod, 2008). Tajfel and Turner proposed a system of three mental processes involved in determining whether a person is part of the "in" group or "out" group (Mcleod, 2008). These groups are extremely important because they give the people who belong to them a sense of pride and self-esteem. They also provide a sense of belonging and contribute greatly to social identity. People divide the world into groups of "us" vs. "them" because it helps us understand things better. By enhancing the status of our own group and diminishing the status of opposing groups, we increase our own sense of self-worth (Mcleod, 2008). This division into groups of "us" vs. "them" is the first step in Social Identity Theory, also known as categorization.

The second stage is social identification. In this stage, people adopt the traits and behaviors they attribute to their selected group (Mcleod, 2008). For example, a new member or pledge of a Greek organization who knows nothing of Greek life aside from what he or she has seen in *Animal House* or *Van Wilder* movies would most likely drink heavily and engage in risky behavior at parties or other social events. This type of behavior may not be the norm for all Greek organizations but because the new member may not know otherwise, they choose to act this way in an attempt to fit in. If this is not the way the rest of the group behaves, the individual will usually catch on quickly and adapt his or her behavior again to better match the rest of the members.

The third and final stage of social identity theory is social comparison. Now that the member has identified and begun to act similarly to the rest of the organization, he or she starts comparing his or her group to other groups (Mcleod, 2008). Since people's measure of self-worth relies so heavily on how their group compares to other groups, competition and prejudices arise (Mcleod, 2008). It is extremely important to be aware that once groups have been labeled rivals their standing is critical for its members' self-esteem (Mcleod, 2008). These rivalries tend to become exacerbated during the spring semester when many colleges including Marist hold their annual Greek Week challenges. Greek Week at Marist College is a week of events such as a belly flop contest, relay races, pop tab collection, a talent show performance promoting Greek unity, as well as other events organizations can use for winning points. At the end of the week, the fraternity and sorority with the most points are dubbed Greek Week Champions and the prize is bragging rights for the next year.

> Heather provides a strong explanation with appropriate examples of the theory she is using to understand her interest between Greek life and one's social identity. However, a reader is not provided an explanation of how Heather plans to process her interview data. A reader is not sure if she is using grounded theory or a different interview analysis approach.

When asked to describe their respective organization in three adjectives, members of the same organization had similar results. The brothers of Alpha Phi Delta, the Delta Theta chapter I interviewed all thought their organization was hardworking, welcoming, and motivated, or used close variations of those adjectives (Chaz, Chunk, Fink, personal communications, 2011). The sisters of Kappa Kappa Gamma, Zeta Chi chapter generally thought their organization was intelligent, classy, and supportive (Cookie, Forge, Luce, Procs, personal communications, 2011).

A reader does not know if Heather is using her participants' real names or if she is using pseudonyms. Confidentiality and anonymity are an integral part of the research process. Use of pseudonyms is the appropriate approach, and Heather could acknowledge their use in the paper.

Six out of eight participants reported major positive changes in their self-image and self-worth since joining their respective organizations. Girls were more likely to admit to deeper emotional connections and reported feeling "lost," "having trouble finding people [they] clicked with," and unsure of "having a group of friends that would be with [them] forever" without their organizations (Cookie, Procs, personal communications, 2011). Boys, on the other hand, were more likely to feel "like any other kid" (Fink, personal communication, 2011) and be less emotional about Greek life giving them "more of a sense of purpose and belonging" (Chunk, personal communication, 2011). Only one participant reported Greek life "has not had any impact on [her] self-image" (Forge, personal communication, 2011).

Heather is effectively using *thick description* to support her analysis of the interview data.

Every participant reported wearing their letters at least once a week (Chaz, Chunk, Cookie, Fink, Forge, Luce, Procs, Turtle, personal communications, 2011). One participant reported wearing letters "as often as possible" (Chaz, personal communication, 2011) and another reported carrying a tote bag with the letters of her sorority on it every day (Luce, personal communication, 2011).

Despite the obvious pride in one's organization, there was no evidence of blatant dislike for members of other Greek organizations or non-Greek students. One participant claimed to not have an opinion because she did not feel everyone had to be involved in Greek life (Forge, personal communication, 8 December 2011) but the general consensus was pity when non-Greeks miss out on opportunities Greeks may experience:

I certainly don't think anything negative about people outside of Greek life. I think they're missing out on some absolutely wonderful aspects and everybody could benefit [from it] but I also understand why people are hesitant to join after the way [Greek life] is portrayed in the media . . . it looks like drinking, hazing, and being [sexually promiscuous] but it's really so much more than that. (Procs, personal communication, 2011)

Even the rivalries between organizations seem relaxed. "I feel connected [to members of other Greek organizations] because they are part of a sisterhood as well" (Cookie, personal communication, 2011). I believe the attitudes come from the idea of Greeks wearing their letters 24/7. "I'm still a brother and as long as I am I will represent [my organization] as best I can" (Fink, personal communication, 2011). The negative stigma against Greek life, especially fraternities, makes students even more conscientious of their behavior and determined to turn opponents into advocates:

> Not all Greeks are the same. We are as diverse as the population, so one bad experience does not represent all of us. That would be like saying that all lacrosse players are rapists because a few Duke Lacrosse players were accused of it.
>
> (Chaz, personal communication, 2011)

My research concludes little correlation between physically wearing the letters ΚΚΓ, ΑΦΔ, or ΤΔΧ across one's chest and social identity. The members of these organizations all seem to realize, especially at a school as small as Marist College, they must be conscientious and responsible for their words and actions at all times. They work hard to maintain and protect their own reputation and to build up Greeks collectively.

Heather has a brief yet effective interpretation of what her analysis means for social identity—at least on the Marist College campus. Interview data/analysis can be limited to the context in which the interviews occurred. Extrapolating to other campuses is problematic. However, exploring the issue on other campuses opens up opportunities to engage in additional communication research!

References

Chaz, Personal Communication, 5 December 2011.
Chunk, Personal Communication, 5 December 2011.
Cookie, Personal Communication, 4 December 2011.
Fink, Personal Communication, 5 December 2011.
Forge, Personal Communication, 8 December 2011.
Luce, Personal Communication, 8 December 2011.
Mcleod, S. (2008). Social identity theory. *Simply Psychology*. www.simplypsychology.org/social-identity-theory.html
Procs, Personal Communication, 7 December 2011.
Turtle, Personal Communication, 7 December 2011.

10 Focus Groups

What Will I Learn About Focus Groups?

During every election season, the news channels (e.g., CNN, Fox, MSNBC) use focus groups of voters discussing the candidates before, during, and after any candidate debates. A moderator was in the room while participants watched the debate. The moderator asked questions about the issues and the candidates. The questions helped the news channels make claims about the candidates, including who "won" the debate and what issues we care about.

While the news channels were running focus groups, the candidates were running their own focus groups. All major candidates have consultants who develop campaign materials (e.g., slogans, advertisements, and even campaign colors). Campaign materials are generally pretested on focus groups. The campaign materials are tested by consultants using focus groups, making alterations, and then releasing the materials to the general public. Focus groups are standard practice in advertising and filmmaking (Morrison, 1998). Communication scholars can easily employ focus groups to study a variety of theories and/or communication situations. For example, a researcher could use focus groups to look at different ways candidates persuade voters using theory of planned action (Ajzen, 1985), social judgment theory (Sherif et al., 1965), elaboration likelihood model (Petty & Cacioppo, 1983), or inoculation theory (McGuire, 1964: Pfau, 1992). In this chapter, you will learn how to use focus groups to gather data for your research projects.

DOI: 10.4324/9781003109129-13

What Is a Focus Group and Why Use One?

A **focus group** is a research data collection method where people are interviewed about a specific topic. Focus groups can range from formal, to informal, to brainstorming, to interviews in the field (Lindlof & Taylor, 2002). Like interviews and ethnography, focus groups typically fall under the interpretive or the critical/cultural paradigms. However, social scientists have been known to use focus groups. As with the previously discussed qualitative methods, two claims are generally associated with focus groups: descriptive and interpretive. Focus groups are led by a **moderator** (also called a facilitator). The moderator leads the discussion among the participants in the group. We talk more about the role of the moderator in a bit.

Focus groups are used extensively in mass communication and advertising (Lindlof & Taylor, 2002), and have gained prominence in the social sciences (Berg, 2009). By broadly exploring the thoughts of a group of people on a specific subject of interest, focus groups identify "general background information about a topic of interest" (Stewart et al., 2006, p. 15). Today, researchers use focus groups for a variety of research projects.

Peterson et al. (2012) explored how "successfully home stable individuals" help them remain home stable and factors that could challenge their stability. Their study brought identified numerous thoughts about what individuals think causes homelessness. Sanders and Anderson (2010) analyzed the conflicts between faculty and students over disappointing college/university grades. The results revealed the discussions could be uncomfortable, yet also positive and constructive.

Focus groups explore general information about topics for a variety of reasons. First, moderators in focus groups usually have a list of questions to guide the group. The questions help the moderator elicit information from the participants. Since numerous participants are in the group, numerous points of view should emerge during the discussion. Second, the moderator's questions are a starting point. Focus groups generally take on a life of their own (when guided by the moderator).

Sometimes focus groups can be used to help "generate important insights into topics that [are] not well understood" (Berg, 2009, p. 165). Often with qualitative methods like interviews and ethnography, researchers are trying to learn more about constructs and how they occur in real life. Researchers tap what Carey (1994) called the **group effect**. When group members interact, new data and insights emerge that previously, on individual levels, may have been less accessible. Group interaction can lead to more in-depth understandings of communication phenomena.

A focus on diversity, equity, and inclusion are critical factors to consider as you prepare to collect data through focus groups. Rodriquez et al. (2011) address the issue through what they describe as culturally responsive focus groups (CRFGs). Drawing on feminism and critical race theory, their framework provides an approach to collect culturally authentic data when a moderator is working with participants from traditionally marginalized populations. CRFGs have six primary elements. The researcher is socially conscious; the researcher seeks to understand participants' context and stories for better understanding how they know and live in the world; the researcher wants a comfortable focus group so all participants can share; the researcher is aware of the participants' social identities and how they shape the data gathered from the focus group; the researcher is aware how their own stories may influence understanding the participant' stories; the researcher uses time in the focus group to guide the co-construction of knowledge among the participants.

The following is an example of how focus groups can tap a variety of opinions. Shyles and Hocking (1990) found United States Army troops were not all fond of the U.S. Army's "Be All you Can Be" campaign. Using 12 focus groups, Shyles and Hocking demonstrated how active members of the Army saw the campaign in a negative light and may have lowered troop morale. After Shyles and Hocking completed their data analysis, the advertising firm that developed the ads were not pleased with their results. Shyles and Hocking discussed the data with the firm and "went so far as to offer to conduct one of these replications at the ad agency's expense. The conversation ended abruptly, and not only were Shyles and Hocking not sued, neither researcher ever again received a communication from the advertising agency" (Hocking et al., 2003, p. 402). A few years later, after new ads were aired with "Be All You Can Be," the ads were modified; the modifications fit the issues noted by Shyles and Hocking.

How to Prepare for a Focus Group

A researcher must prepare a well-designed focus group. One must consider six important components. First, as with all the other forms of research discussed in this textbook, you need to be sure you have a research agenda for your study. Second, determine if a focus group design is appropriate for your study. For example, while a focus group could be used to collect data on people's public behaviors, ask individuals about their self-disclosures, or study how conflict styles differ across age groups, other methods may produce more fruitful findings.

Let's say you want to explore the effectiveness of a new campaign slogan developed for a political candidate. A survey will only take a snapshot of people's feelings at one point in time. An ethnographic approach could work, but observing people watching the slogan or reading it really will not provide you with much information about how potential voters feel about the slogan. Individual interviews will lack interaction between potential voters. A focus group is really the best method for the study. A focus group has the voters talk to each other, and you—as the researcher—will use their interactions as data.

Second, once you have decided on the focus-group approach, you need to determine how many focus groups you will conduct and how many people you will have in each group. Debates happen over both questions. Here's the rule on the minimum number of focus groups: never settle on just one focus group. You need more than one focus group so that you can compare the results from the groups. You can see emerging trends in your data when you conduct multiple focus groups. Let's return to our political campaigns scenario. You may see participants consistently pointing out strengths and weaknesses in a political slogan. Lindlof and Taylor (2002) argued that a sound study should have a minimum of two or three focus groups.

You want 3-15 people in each focus group. When you have only three people in a group, you have less chance of seeing the group effect (Carey, 1994). However, a group that is too big can become hard to handle, and you may see participants splintering off into subgroups, which can make data collection difficult. We talk more about this later. Many researchers who use focus groups typically want 6–12 people (Lindlof & Taylor, 2002). Just like interviewing and ethnography, you need to find your participants. Do you post flyers in significant places, work your gatekeepers, use e-mail lists, use social media. . . ? Use the best means available to locate your participants. One of the things we talk about later is how, often, your participant selection for a focus group is nonrandom, including convenience or purposive sampling. In a study using a focus group, try to include people with a variety of opinions to generate the true group effect.

So, set up two or more groups with 6–12 potential voters, and ask them to look over the new slogan for the candidate. One common technique in focus groups is to show some sort of stimulus material and ask participants to respond. In the case of the slogan, you could show the group the statement and record their opinions. In each group, try to have voters who are from a broad range of the political continuum. Seek a broad range of gender identities in your group to see how they respond to the slogan. Strive for people from different ethnic/racial backgrounds. The more diversity in your group, the better chance of learning how the general public responds to the slogan.

Third, are you going to pay your group members for their participation? In a research project using focus-group interviews, the participant is actively engaging and spending valuable time with the researcher. Thus, in some cases, researchers may offer participants compensation for their time, including financial or other incentives (e.g., food, extra credit). **Incentives for participation** are paid or unpaid ways of encouraging people to participate in a study. The type of incentive will depend on your population. Some focus groups can range from 30–90 minutes (and sometimes longer); a researcher is taking time from the participants. At the University of Jyväskylä, where Stephen previously taught, some departments offered movie tickets to research participants. Some universities permit offering students extra credit for participation. In advertising research, for example, firms may pay or provide free products for participation. You need to be upfront with your participants in the informed consent form if offering incentives. You should also identify any incentives in your write-up of the study.

Since you are using your participants' time, you might offer an incentive for participation. Since the individuals are not undergraduate students, extra credit in a class is not appropriate. Maybe provide lunch, movie tickets, a gift certificate for coffee, or something similar.

Fourth, determine where the focus group will take place. Unlike ethnographies, which take place in the natural setting of the participants and interviews, which can take place in the natural setting or in a lab, focus groups almost always take place in a controlled environment. You, as the researcher, determine the place and time for the group to meet. Hocking et al. (2003) listed a few conditions that explain why focus-group locations are predetermined by the researcher:

Most focus groups are run at night, with one group following a second by 10-to-15 minutes. Because of the interaction required, most groups run between one and two hours, with at least one refreshment and bathroom break included. Some research companies have two-way mirrored and electronically monitored rooms that you can rent. You need a room that is conducive to communication and not too formal. Preferably you want your participants to face each other, perhaps in a circle around a table.

(p. 205)

These conditions make clear why a researcher wants a focus group to meet in a predetermined, controlled location—too many variables cannot be controlled in a natural environment.

Choose a location that suits your needs. Some university departments have focus group or laboratory rooms you can use. Many advertising firms and other corporations have specially designed rooms for focus groups. The key is to have a plan for where you will hold your focus groups, keeping in mind: 1) how many people will be in each group? 2) how long will each group last? 3) are you recording the groups? (4) how is the room setup? 5) are restroom facilities nearby? 6) is the location easy for the participants to find?

Fifth, as discussed in the chapter on interviewing, recording interviews can make data analysis a whole lot easier. With focus groups, your data will involve *what* people say and *how* they say it. So, you will need to decide if you are going to audio or video record the groups. You will, of course, need to get permission from the participants to record. We recommend you record the focus groups and then transcribe the data as soon as possible after conducting each group. Numerous software programs can make transcribing easier (e.g., Interact-AS, NCH Software, Nuance, Vocapia, VoiceBase). Remember, you should still take notes during a focus group even if recording. Taking notes will add to your understanding when you analyze the transcripts because you can jot down insights during the focus group sessions.

You decide that you are only interested in what the participants say about the slogan. In this case, it is only necessary to audio record the focus group. Make sure to get permission from all the participants before recording the focus groups.

The sixth element, and one of the most important, is preparing a moderator. The moderator is the one who leads the focus group and makes sure the discussion guide is followed. A **discussion guide** is the program for the focus group. The guide includes your opening and closing statements and the questions for the group. The moderator uses the discussion guide as a roadmap for leading the group. The questions in the guide are based on the main purposes of the study. Figure 10.1 is an example discussion guide. The questions in the guide are only as successful as the moderator. Morgan (1988) described how a moderator should be a good interviewer and must be a good listener. A moderator should be prepared to adapt questions if participants do not respond to some questions. "Moderators try to achieve a fine balance between enfranchising individuals to speak out and promoting good group feelings" (Lindlof & Taylor, 2002, p. 183). A good moderator has a knack for bringing in quiet participants and politely silencing aggressive or overly talkative participants. Many advertising firms hire moderators with strong communication skills to lead focus groups. Hocking et al. (2003) strongly urged researchers *not* to serve as moderators for their own focus groups. Hocking et al. urged researchers to hire professional moderators whenever possible. Of course, few student-researchers can afford to hire a professional moderator, so be prepared to moderate your own focus groups.

Figure 10.1 Sample Discussion Guide for Study on Political Slogan Effectiveness

PARTICIPANT INTRODUCTION

Hello, my name is [name here] and I have been asked to lead a discussion today about a new slogan Candidate X is developing for his/her election campaign. What we are going to do today is watch his/her new advertisement, which includes the new slogan, and then I am going to ask you some questions. There are no right or wrong answers. I am just interested in what you think about the slogan and the advertisement.

Everything you say here will be kept completely confidential. We will be audio recording the focus group today and then transcribing the session. The transcripts from the group will be summarized and presented in such a way that no individual could be identified in the future.

What I am passing out to each of you now is an informed-consent form. This form outlines everything that you will be doing today, all of your duties and responsibilities. This form also explains the benefits of this study and how to contact the researchers in case you have any questions or concerns about the study. The form also notes that for participating in this study, which should take about 60 minutes, you will receive a $10 Starbucks gift card. However, if you stop your participation before completion of the study, which is your right, you will not receive the gift card.

One last thing before we get started. I would like each of you to take a nametag and put your first name on it. It can be your real first name or a fictitious one; it is up to you, whatever you feel comfortable with. Can everyone now take a couple of minutes and read over the informed consent, ask any questions you might have, and, if it okay, sign it? Let me know when you have signed it and I will collect it.

Has everyone signed the forms? Okay, let's get started. I am going to turn on the audio recorder now. Can I have each of you say your name for the group and introduce yourself? [THIS IS A GREAT WAY TO GET EVERYONE'S NAMES ON THE RECORDER]

FROM THIS POINT, THERE IS A LOT OF VARIABILITY IN WHAT YOU CAN DO

I would like you all to watch the following new advertisement that was just developed by Candidate X's team—[play advertisement].

FOCUS GROUP QUESTIONS

Okay, now that you have seen the new ad, I have some questions for us to think about. (HERE THE QUESTIONS ARE GUIDED BY THE FOCUS OF THE STUDY; WE WILL LIST TWO

SAMPLE QUESTIONS. DEPENDING ON HOW LONG THE GROUP IS, REMEMBER TO BREAK FOR BATHROOM ☺

1. What did you like and what did you dislike about the advertisement?
2. Candidate X in this advertisement is trying to persuade you that he/she is the best candidate for President. How does he/she do that?

THE GROUP COULD CONTINUE WITH MORE QUESTIONS ABOUT THE ADVERTISEMENT UNTIL THE MODERATOR IS READY TO WRAP UP THE GROUP.

Well I would like to thank you for your participation in this discussion today. I think we have really uncovered some interesting insight into (name the advertisement). As I said at the start, if you have any questions about the study, feel free to contact us via the information provided on the forms. Now, I think it's time to pass out some coffee gift cards. Thanks again.

How to Conduct a Focus Group

If you have taken the proper steps to prepare, then conducting the group is systematic. You have your questions designed, your number of groups and participants are set, incentives for participation are offered, the location is reserved, your recording equipment is prepped, and you've chosen a moderator. When you conduct a focus group you need to: 1) make sure the location is functional, 2) double-check the recording device(s), 3) conduct the discussion using the guide, and 4) analyze the results. First, while you may have a location set for the group, always make sure the location is ready before the participants arrive. This may sound silly, but Dan and Stephen have been involved in research projects (as researchers and participants) where we have arrived and things are not ready. Remember, you are asking for your participants' precious time, and watching a researcher run around in circles setting up the room is wasting their time. Second, since you will likely be recording, check the equipment before the group begins. What a shame if your participants are ready and the tech is not.

Third, use your discussion guide to conduct the focus groups. The discussion guide helps the moderator(s) facilitate the focus group. If you look at Figure 10.1, this kind of guide can be modified in many ways to help a well-trained moderator lead a discussion. The moderator is looking for the participants to answer specific questions pertinent to the research. However, the moderator does not give the participants answers. Thus, the moderator needs to be open to the participants providing a variety of expected and unexpected answers. This is one reason why the discussion guide needs to be flexible. Like open-ended interviews, discussion guides should be flexible. The moderator (and the discussion guide) work to remain on the same research theme while allowing participants to talk about issues important to them and relevant to the group's subject.

Fourth, once a focus group is complete, you need to analyze the transcripts (your data). You can analyze qualitative data in numerous ways. For example, you could conduct a grounded theory analysis (Glaser & Strauss, 1967; Strauss & Corbin, 1991), a metaphoric analysis (Gill, 1994), a conversation or discourse analysis, or a content analysis. We talk more in depth about some of these methods in later chapters in this text. The notes and observations are an important part of your analysis. A well-trained moderator should be versed in taking good notes and understanding human behavior. Talk to the moderator(s) and find out what they thought about the groups and use their insight as additional data to help your analysis.

With our advertisement for Candidate X, we decide on our day for the first focus group, we recruited our participants, we have our discussion guide and moderator, we have our coffee gift cards, and we have the recording device all ready. We (the advertising firm) show up an hour beforehand with the moderator to make sure the location is set up and ready for the session. We do a test run of the audio recorder (it works great!). Then the participants arrive. The moderator reads the introduction and goes through the script on the guide. After the session, which was a lively discussion about the advertisement, by the way, we go back to our firm and get a debriefing from the moderator on their thought about the participants and the session. We add their notes and thoughts (as data) to our transcripts. We are still debating whether we will analyze our data using a content analytic approach or a discourse analytic approach, but we will decide that soon. Tomorrow, we have another session, our second of six focus groups.

Advantages and Limitations of Focus Groups

Focus groups have numerous advantages and a few limitations. The five main advantages to focus groups are: 1) cost, 2) speed, 3) quantity of participants, 4) ability to reach sensitive populations, and 5) the group effect. The first three advantages of a focus group are closely linked to one another: cost, speed, and quantity of participants (Berg, 2009; Lindlof & Taylor, 2002). Focus groups often provide an inexpensive and quick way to gather data from participants. If one conducts three focus groups with 7 people in each group, this means the person has collected responses from 21 people at 3 points in time. Consider the alternative of conducting 21 individual open-ended interviews on 21 separate occasions. The data for the three focus groups will likely take less time to collect. The cost of data collection (e.g., transportation, recording, incentives for participation) may end up being less for 3 focus groups than for 21 individual interviews. The fourth advantage of focus groups is the ability to reach sensitive populations. In many situations, you may want to investigate a sensitive topic, such as sexual abuse. In such studies, participants may not feel as comfortable discussing the issue one-on-one. However, people are more likely to be open about sensitive topics when in the presence of other individuals who have similar experiences (Morgan, 1988). Finally, as previously mentioned, focus groups allow us to tap the group effect (Carey, 1994). When people are together with others discussing an issue, they are likely to bounce ideas off one another and feed from each other. These group interactions produce more insights into the communication phenomena under investigation.

Focus groups have two limitations to keep in mind: 1) the moderator(s) and 2) the participants. While the moderator is necessary to facilitate a successful focus group, you must make sure the moderator is well trained. If the moderator is not well trained and is unable to successfully manage the group, then the focus group could fail. The discussion could stagnate, some participants may monopolize the conversation, or, (worst-case scenario) the moderator may monopolize the conversation. The role of the moderator really is integral to the success of the focus group. Second, the participants themselves can make or break a focus group.

Participants are volunteers. Like Forrest Gump said, "Life is like a box of chocolates, you never know what you're gonna get." Well, participants are like that; you never know what you're gonna get.

> Based on the participants in our focus groups to discuss Candidate X's advertisement, we should learn some things about how average voters think about the advertisement. If we have been careful in our development of the discussion guide – particularly in the questions – and chosen a good moderator or moderators, our job should be a success. Focus groups are increasingly used by advertisers and also by researchers in communication. This qualitative method, if executed properly, can be an effective tool to analyze how groups perceive messages and how groups interact.

Summary

This chapter was a how-to guide for focus groups. As discussed in the chapter, focus groups are generally approached from the interpretive or critical/cultural paradigms. Hopefully, after reading this chapter and the accompanying student paper using focus groups, you feel comfortable enough to use focus groups for your own research project.

Key Steps and Questions to Consider

1. A focus group is a research method where a group of people are interviewed about a specific topic.
2. The types of focus groups range from formal group interviews, to informal group interviews, to brainstorming sessions, to group interviews in the field.
3. Focus groups are led by a moderator (sometimes called a facilitator), an individual who leads the discussion that takes place among the participants in the group. Typically, the moderator is not the researcher in charge of the project.
4. The group effect is when a researcher is able to tap a multitude of opinions because a group is responding to one another's ideas and opinions in a group setting.
5. You should try to conduct at least two or three focus groups, if not more.
6. A focus group generally has between 6-12 people.
7. Some researchers will provide incentives to participate in focus groups.
8. Focus groups typically take place in a "lab" setting and not in the natural environment.
9. Audio or video recording focus groups is a best practice.
10. The discussion guide is a tool used by the moderator(s) to lead the focus group through a series of questions.
11. Like most qualitative research methods, researchers have many options for analyzing focus group data.
12. Two different claims are associated with focus groups as a method: descriptive and interpretive.
13. Researcher credibility, adequacy, and coherence are key issues to consider regarding warrants in focus group research.

Activities

1. Try a series of practice focus-group sessions. Divide the class into groups of 5-15 students. Each group will select a communication issue and develop a short discussion guide of 3-5 questions. Once the guide is ready, each group exchanges their discussion guide with another group. Each group selects a moderator and, using the discussion guide from the other group, holds a focus group. The process continues with the group exchanging discussion guides until every group has held a focus group with each guide.

2. The class as a whole can use the data from the practice group sessions and try a practice analysis of the data. What themes emerged from the data collected from each discussion guide?

3. Run a web search for "focus group advertising." Compare how the websites explain focus groups with what you've learned in this chapter. What differences emerge between academic research focus groups and corporate focus groups?

Discussion Questions

1. What types of research questions can be answered with data collection through focus groups?
2. When should a researcher avoid using a focus group for data collection?
3. What limitations should be taken into consideration with focus-group data?
4. What approaches can you take for analyzing data from focus groups?

Key Terms

Discussion Guide	Group Effect	Moderator
Focus Group	Incentives for Participation	

References

Ajzen, I. (1985). From intentions to actions: A theory of planned behavior. In J. Kuhland & J. Beckman (Eds.), *Action-control: From cognitions to behavior* (pp. 11-39). Springer.

Berg, B. L. (2009). *Qualitative research methods for the social sciences* (7th ed.). Allyn & Bacon.

Carey, M. A. (1994). The group effect in focus groups: Planning, implementing and interpreting focus group research. In J. Morse (Ed.), *Critical issues in qualitative research methods* (pp. 225-241). Sage.

Gill, A. (1994). *Rhetoric and human understanding*. Waveland Press.

Glaser, B. G., & Strauss, A. L. (1967). *Discovery of grounded theory: Strategies for qualitative research*. Aldine.

Hocking, J. E., Stacks, D. W., & McDermott, S. T. (2003). *Communication research* (3rd ed.). Allyn & Bacon.

Lindlof, T. R., & Taylor, B. C. (2002). *Qualitative communication research methods* (2nd ed.). Sage.

McGuire, W. J. (1964). Inducing resistance to persuasion. Some contemporary approaches. In L. Berkowitz (Ed.), *Advances in experimental social psychology* (Vol. 1, pp. 191-220). Academic.

Morgan, D. L. (1988). *Focus groups as qualitative research*. Sage.

Morrison, D. E. (1998). *The search for a method: Focus groups and the development of mass communication research*. University of Luton Press.

Peterson, J. C., Anthony, M. G., & Thomas, R. J. (2012). "This right here is all about living": Communicating the "Common sense" about home stability through CBPR and photovoice. *Journal of Applied Communication Research, 40*, 247-270.

Petty, R. E., & Cacioppo, J. T. (1983). Central and peripheral routes to persuasion: Application to advertising. In L. Percy & A. Woodside (Eds.), *Advertising and consumer psychology* (pp. 3-23). Heath.

Pfau, M. (1992). The potential of inoculation in promoting resistance to the effectiveness of comparative advertising messages. *Communication Quarterly, 40*, 26-44. https://doi.org/10.1080/01463379209369818

Rodriguez, K. L., Schwartz, J. L., Lahman, M. K. E., & Geist, M. R. (2011). Culturally responsive focus groups: Reframing the research experience to focus on participants. *International Journal of Qualitative Methods, 10*, 400-417. https://doi.org/10.1177/160940691101000407

Sanders, M. L., & Anderson, S. (2010). The dilemma of grades: Reconciling disappointing grades with feelings of personal success. *Qualitative Research Reports in Communication, 11*, 51-56.

Sherif, C. W., Sherif, M., & Nebergall, R. E. (1965). *Attitude and attitude change*. Saunders.

Shyles, L., & Hocking, J. E. (1990). The Army's "Be all you can be campaign." *Armed Forces and Society, 16*(3), 369-383.

Stewart, D. W., Shamdasani, P. M., & Rook, D. W. (2006). *Focus groups: Theory and practice* (2nd ed.). Sage.

Strauss, A., & Corbin, J. (1991). *Basics of qualitative research: Grounded theory procedure and techniques*. Sage.

Undergraduate Student Paper

Communicating Emotions through Visual Framing and Influence

Rebecca Rachel Engels

Each individual expresses, processes and interprets emotions differently. My research is constructed around the notion in which we each interpret artwork differently, mainly shocking photographic images by the use of visual framing. I am also interested in the message the photographer is attempting to communicate through their artwork, as well as how our personal interpretations may be influenced by others, especially those who tend to dominate the conversation. According to Rodriguez and Dimitrova (2011), "Many consider audience frames as mental maps people form to cope with the flood of information to which they are subjected everyday. Audiences actively classify and organize their life experiences to make sense of them. These "schemata of interpretation" or "frames" that enable individuals to "locate, perceive, identify, and label" the world around them" (p. 49). This statement reaffirms my thesis: each individual has their own unique framework for interpretation. Although individuals may possess their own opinions and emotions regarding a specific text, photograph or work, their initial response may fluctuate due to the strong opinions of others. I've found dominant individuals or people in a position of power have a profound impact on the views of others. The influential factor some individuals' possess allow them capable of manipulating the perception of other viewers, possibly because of advanced knowledge, intimidation, or ulterior motives.

My research consisted of six photographs, each photograph aiming towards a specific basic human emotion. I had two photographs for death, one for happiness, loneliness, fear, and love. I set up two focus groups from 11 beginner and advanced photography students. I posed two questions regarding each image; what emotions does this image evoke and what emotions do you feel the photographer was trying to induce? Participants were asked to provide answers to said questions by writing down an immediate response, I was able to get the participants initial response to the image without manipulation by others during the conversation regarding the image. After participants gave their initial written response, I conducted an engaging and open discussion regarding each image shown. By doing so, I was able to observe if the conversation was being steered in a certain direction or potentially opinions changing due to the power structure of the discussion. By taking detailed notes throughout the discussion, returning back to them later and comparing them to the participants written answers, I was capable of obtaining honest results from the students both verbally and nonverbally.

> Rebecca sets up an intriguing question in her introduction. She has merged multiple areas of communication—textual, visual, and verbal—into her study. Her use of focus groups to explore the question should produce interesting results.

Literature Review

While initially researching prior work similar to my study, I found minimal research, which was like mine. According to Rodriguez and Dimitrova (2011), "One of the main reasons why there are relatively few studies that employ visual framing compared to textual framing is that there is a great deal of confusion as to how visual frames are supposed to be identified in the first place. To this day, identifying visual frames remains a challenge; the methods of doing so cover the gamut" (pp. 50–51). Because of our high functioning society and advancing technology, the general population has grown accustomed to images, which have been manipulated and stray away from reality. Which makes it difficult for viewers to see an image and question whether the image is depicting reality or fantasy. According to Brantner et al. (2009), "frames can be described as interpretation patterns which serve to classify information for handling it efficiently" (p. 524). Each individual establishes meaning for a certain image, how we organize information stems from life experience and general knowledge.

Brantner et al. (2009) highlighted the importance and significance of powerful imagery in association with our perception and interpretation of the image at hand. I agree with the notion emotions are easily portrayed through visual stimuli rather than words, although words are arbitrary.

Another interpretation is from Rodriguez and Dimitrova (2011) regarding visual framing. Although images may show reality, certain horrific aspects of reality are not seen by everyone, even attempted to be hidden from society, a dead body for example. A portrait of nightmarish qualities is not something an ordinary photographer would try to capture, unless they were attempting to expose a hidden reality.

The literature review provides sufficient background to understand the nature of research conducted in her area of interest. However, be careful of using an article-by-article approach. Look for themes that permeate across the journal articles and then organize the review around the themes. Otherwise, you are counting on your readers to figure out how the articles interact.

Methods/Procedures

My method for collecting data is two focus groups. I expect to find each subject's written reaction to each photograph will be similar to his or her verbal reaction to the image. I am curious to determine whether subjects who are knowledgeable about photography will produce significantly different opinions regarding each image compared to those whom are not as knowledgeable. I will have a threefold analysis of my observations: First, what the subjects initial written reactions were in both groups. Second, the subjects' verbal and nonverbal communication styles when discussing each image. Finally, initial reactions compared to verbal reactions with both groups.

The participants were aged roughly 18 to 24 years old, upper-level digital photography students, and basic photography students. The first focus group included the advanced photography students with three white/Caucasian females and one Hispanic male. Students participated at their own will; it was remarkable how much effort the advanced students put forth towards the research. Each student involved provided detailed responses and actively participated in the group discussion administered honest opinions and were incredibly respectful towards one another.

The participants in the second focus group, the beginner students were ages 18 to 21 and had little to no knowledge regarding photography. Most, if not all were freshmen varying in educational backgrounds, majors and belief systems. I decided to incorporate the beginner photography students to obtain a variety of results pertaining to each image. Also, to establish if more influence during the discussion occurred in the beginner students versus advanced students. I anticipated the beginner students would produce original, potentially vague ideas and bring new emotions to the table.

> The method section is fairly clear. Rebecca provides justification for the selection of participants in each focus group. The threefold analysis is well designed and easy to follow. One could replicate the study following Rebecca's procedures. Rebecca could provide more insight with the specific processes used during each focus group discussion. Did she use a structured, semi-structured, or unstructured format? How long was planned for each focus group? And were participants informed that they could leave anytime during the focus group, if so desired?

Results

The results I obtained were slightly skewed, but helped me comprehend the significance of an educational background on such a subject versus having none whatsoever. During the first focus group, throughout our discussion each participant derived their own set of unique meanings from each photograph. My method for collecting data consisted of observing the conversation and its progression by taking detailed notes, as well as analyzing the written answers provided by participants.

Photograph number portrayed happiness. Female participants brought up the idea of skin cancer. The male participant thought the girl in the photograph was shy. He noted the light and colors portray sunshine, or happiness.

The second photograph was the first of two images portraying death. The photograph was taken in the Japanese wilderness of a dead body found, possibly a suicide. The male student was already aware of Japanese suicide phenomenon in the woods, something I had not anticipated. He pointed out the sadness of dying alone, a melancholy aspect of this image, an emotion many attempt to regress. The female participants expressed an extreme depression while viewing this saddening illustration of a human who died alone in the woods.

The third photograph is a bearded man who sits alone naked on a chair in front of a small audience. A female participant verbally expressed the emotion of feeling awkward; she also found the image to be humorous.

The fourth photograph portraying love, did not communicate the emotion of love very clearly I realized. During the discussion, a female participant voiced her opinion of the feeling of betrayal or possibly adultery. The male participant thought the man in the photograph was a customer and the woman was a prostitute because of a half-hearted embrace. Another female participant brought up the notion of despair or potentially false love or mental illness.

The second photograph depicting death was a Vietnamese man about to be shot in the head. The discussion proved to be interesting because many of the students did not initially respond to the photograph with the idea of death. The male student voiced his opinion of possible fear, power, or even control. He had been exposed to the video of the same man getting shot in the head, although did not bring up the notion of death. The female participants felt the photograph was attempting to communicate the idea of war, potentially anger. After allowing participants to express themselves, I quoted the photographer of this image, Eddie Adams, "two people died in that photograph: the recipient of the bullet and General Nguyen Ngoc Loan." After using the word *death* many of the students agreed this image was trying to portray death in its most obvious form, a photograph of a man moments before his death.

The final photograph portrayed loneliness. Not one student voiced an opinion on loneliness throughout the discussion. The female participant brought up the idea of the old woman being desperate. Another female participant found herself coming to the conclusion the woman was suffering, possibly because of a mental illness or a brain disorder.

The beginner students were different from the advanced students in a few ways. There were two males and three females; all students were ages 18 to 21. The beginner students were profoundly more shocked and/or confused when viewing the images in comparison to the advanced students. The written answers proved very useful for the beginner group because answers differed from the group discussion, many words were misspelled, and the responses were much more naive than the advanced participants' written responses.

The first photograph was happiness. All of participants wrote down happy/happiness, three out of five wrote down sunshine or warmth and one male wrote down perhaps the woman in the photograph was sending or receiving a text message. The text message notion was surprising, but after thinking critically for a moment, perhaps this emotion is a reflection of the dominance technology has on our modern society. All of the participants verbally expressed sunshine and/or happiness and agreed the photographer was attempting to communicate the allure of happiness, warmth and sunshine.

The second photograph was the dead body in the Japanese woods, portraying death. Four out of five participants wrote down death or tragedy. One participant wrote down war and murder. All the students were silent at the beginning. None of the participants quite knew what exactly the image was or how they should feel about it. At first, one of the female students began giggling nervously when this particular image was presented. Perhaps the photograph was slightly too intense for the demographic.

The third photograph depicted fear. Most, if not all of the students could not contain their laughter for this image. I understand the fact the man was nude and slightly uncomfortable looking. All of the participants written answers differed, as well as their verbal discussion. One male participant wrote down, "sad because he is frail" for his response to the image. Perhaps the controversy surrounding this shocking image was too much for young minds to bear.

The fourth photograph depicting love did not generate such a response from the beginner group. Only one male student wrote down love, but did not express such an emotion verbally. Each participant wrote down "awkward" or "disgusting." One female student wrote down she believed the photographer was attempting to communicate the vulnerability of love.

The fifth photograph attempting to communicate death was the image of the man getting shot in the head. All of the students wrote down sadness/oppression/suffering. Two of the female students had a similar idea, which the photographer was attempting to communicate the notion of the things happening in other areas of the world. None of the students saw death in the image. Each student seemed unable to associate the idea of death because the man was still alive in the photograph, Since he was Vietnamese it was difficult for the younger minds to find a common ground with the image. To them it seemed he was just a man in a country, which they did not have any prior knowledge of, therefore could not come to terms with a set emotion other than war and oppression.

The sixth photograph was the old woman clutching the doll in the hospital or nursing home showing loneliness. Each participant expressed on paper the emotion of being lonely, feeling bad for the woman, the aspect of old age, etc. The male students wrote down for the image, "confusion" and "bliss". Perhaps participants wrote these emotions down because the image is very haunting, a true reality of what lies ahead for every human being. All participants agreed the old woman was clearly depicted loneliness in the most obvious form. The discussion continued to a deeper level, one female student expressed seeing her grandmother in the nursing home suffering from memory loss. She disclosed with me how this image reminded her of her grandmother, making her feel sad and empathetic towards the matter.

> The results are interesting, but the picture-by-picture approach through each focus group may make tracking the results awkward. Rebecca can strengthen the results by identifying themes in the results and then writing up the themes. Some of the results may be better laid out in one or more tables. Tables make comparing the results quick and efficient, especially when multiple datasets are involved (e.g., two focus groups).

Interpretation

Through the research, many aspects I did not anticipate surfaced through the discussion portion; the written answers disclosed significantly more personal emotions. While I was initially constructing my project, I was quite convinced the advanced photography students would produce a specific set of results because of their knowledge regarding photography. I assumed some, if not all, would have already been exposed to at least one of the images. I was correct in such a sense, the male participant in the advanced focus group recognized two of the images but derived different meanings than the ones I had established for each one. The emotional responses provided by the advanced students proved very intriguing, participants brought up specific emotions I had not recognized, adding weight to the notion of visual framing differing from each individual.

The results I did find were fairly accurate to the information I anticipated to gain. I understood not all students, especially the beginner ones, would be able to grasp the concept I had assigned to each photograph. Often times, the answers provided by the beginner students differed tremendously from the verbal answers, also something I had expected. Younger minds are more susceptible to influence and peer pressure, maturity only comes with age, knowledge and cohesiveness. I gathered, through my research the idea which we each construct our own meanings for images based on a general knowledge and the aspects of life which we have been exposed.

> Rebecca provides good interpretation of her results. She draws some insights from the results of her study.

Implications and Conclusions

The participants may have kept certain emotions to themselves for a variety of reasons, perhaps embarrassment or uncertainty of how to process such strong emotions with each image. The scope for my focus groups could have been larger, involving more participants to produce more results and emotions. I feel as though if the groups had been larger, the discussions would have been longer and perhaps a bit more in depth because more opinions would have surfaced. If I were to involve more participants in focus groups, instead of simply gathering more photography or art students, I would involve students who had absolutely no background in the field of art or communication. I feel this additional aspect to my research could have added more weight to my thesis, involving a variety of students rather than such a narrow scope for my research.

It would have been interesting to merge the two focus groups into one large group, to gather more data regarding influence factor of the research. Perhaps the advanced students would have a profound impact on the views of the beginner students because of their knowledge and age difference. Reasoning for not merging the groups came from potentially anticipated discomfort deriving from both parties, if the group became one not all the participants would be acquainted with one another and potentially hold back from expressing themselves to their full potential.

I expected to find a substantial distinction between the beginner and advanced students. Although the two groups produced entirely different results, there were some similarities such as overall confusion for the image depicting fear, and uncertainty regarding the image portraying death, particularity the man getting shot in the head. Perhaps the confusion circulating around these two images in particular stem from discomfort while viewing the photographs. I believe my research is additional to the field of communication because although prior research exists involving the analysis of visual framing, the research does not include the aspect of shocking images, or influence. My research may be similar to certain studies but is unique in its own.

Larger focus groups or combining the focus groups may not provide the additional insight Rebecca believes they will. Larger groups tend to fragment into mini-groups, and the researcher can lose track of the multiple discussions going on. Expanding beyond photography to other students' interpretations of the images might add an interesting dimension. Finally, Rebecca found that initial selection of the images is a critical component of her study.

References

Adams, E. (Photographer). (1968). *General Nguyen Ngoc Loan killing Viet Cong operative Nguyen Van Lem* [Print Photo]. www.famouspictures.org/mag/index.php?title=Vietnam_Execution

Arbus, D. (Photographer). (1970). *Dominatrix embracing her client*. [Print Photo]. http://diane-arbus-photography.com/

Brantner, C., Lobinger, K., & Wetzstein, I. (2009). Effects of visual framing on emotional responses and evaluations of news stories about the Gaza conflict 2009. *Journalism & Mass Communication Quarterly, 88*(3), 523–540.

Haggblom, K. (Photographer). (2012). www.kristianhaggblom.com/public/jukai.html

Hill, S. (Photographer). (n.d.). *Ron mueck exhibition at the ngv*. [Print Photo]. http://xtremeprints.com/stock/

Johnson, M. (1993). (Re)framing the photograph. *Word & Image*, *9*(3), 245–251.

Macdonald, I. (Photographer). (2011). *The greatest*. [Print Photo]. http://noneedforalarm.wordpress.com/page/5

Rodriguez, L., & Dimitrova, D. (2011). The levels of visual framing. *Journal of Visual Literacy*, *30*(1), 48–65.

Stevens, C. (Photographer). (2008). *Victoria, nursing home resident*. [Print Photo]. http://vervephoto.wordpress.com/category/ohio-university/page/2/

Stifano, S. (2009). *Movies, meaning and social influence: A developmental-interactionist theory of film communication*. Paper presented at the International Communication Association.

11 Content Analysis

Chapter Outline

- Data in a Quantitative Content Analysis
- Units of Analysis
- Coding Schedule, Pilot Testing, and Intercoder Reliability
- Analyzing and Reporting Data in a Quantitative CA
- Summary
- Key Steps and Questions to Consider
- Activities
- Discussion Questions
- Key Terms
- Undergraduate Content Analysis Paper

What Will I Learn About Content Analysis?

What you see to open the chapter are two very different images. One is President Trump and former Vice President Biden as they competed during the 2020 presidential election. The second image is two people exploring online dating. One image represents a competition; the other represents cooperation. One shows the public sphere of U.S. politics. The other shows the intimate nature of dating. While very different contexts and types of people, both are open to research using content analysis. We will use both scenarios to explore the wide-ranging world of content analysis from a quantitative and qualitative approach.

Content Analysis (CA) is a long-standing and well-respected method for conducting communication research. In 1952, Berelson described CA as a technique for an objective and systematic description of communication. Cole (1988) stated that the method is a way to analyze written, verbal, or visual messages. Neuman (1997) defined CA as a method for gathering and analyzing the content of text. A "text" for Neuman is anything written, visual, or spoken. In other words,

DOI: 10.4324/9781003109129-14

CA is a research method for systematically describing, categorizing, and/or making inferences about communication. The claims we make vary depending on whether we are using a quantitative or qualitative CA. We start with exploring all the pieces and how to conduct a quantitative CA. Then we tackle the complexities of a qualitative CA.

Data in a Quantitative Content Analysis

The data for a quantitative CA depends on what you want to study. Before collecting your data, you should have a clear objective and research question(s) or hypotheses. Once you have the foundation, you can be more certain your data and analysis are relevant for the research. Remember, a CA systematically describes, categorizes, and makes inferences about the communication.

In Waters and Lo's (2012) study of nonprofit organizations' use of Facebook, the data was 225 random Facebook pages. Their sample was random, and the three nations (75 Facebook pages per nation) were chosen based on previously studied cultural differences between the nations. Therefore, their choice of content and sample was purposeful. Garner et al. (2012) studied dissent on television by sampling "two weeks of primetime programming, defined as 8:00 p.m. to 11:00 p.m., on CBS, ABC, NBC, FOX, and CW. We recorded three hours of programming on five channels for 14 days, giving a sample of 210 hours of television" (p. 614). The networks were appropriate since they represent large segments of American primetime viewing. Two weeks gives the researchers sufficient time to measure regular television programming.

Let's say we want to conduct a study comparing television advertising from the Trump and Biden campaigns and by PACs during the presidential election. This kind of CA is using archival data. Remember to save all the ads you find on YouTube or other search engines. You do not want to lose your data! Next, we describe the process of categorizing quantitative data.

Categories in a Quantitative Content Analysis

Categories are areas, themes, groupings, classes, or types with explicit parameters for coding the data. Content categories develop from the following question: what content categories produce the data needed to answer the objectives of the research? Remember to first conduct a thorough review of the literature to determine what categories researchers have used. Conducting a CA using categories based on previous research is called a **deductive CA**. For example, you want to explore political beliefs presidential candidates express during elections. Scholars have already developed categories for such an analysis, so looking to their work is to your benefit (Benoit, 1999; Benoit & Glantz, 2012; Dover, 2006). Creating your own categories is an **inductive CA**.

The categories in a CA need to be **mutually exclusive**. Basically, mutually exclusive means that something cannot be counted in more than one category. For example, if you are conducting a CA on the beliefs of presidential candidates as displayed in PAC vs. candidate advertising, you should focus your study on their advertisements and the different beliefs depicted in the ads. The different beliefs should not overlap but should be mutually exclusive.

Overlapping categories make it difficult to distinguish differences or infer anything about the communication.

Now that we have discussed data and the basics of content categories, next we define units of analysis and explain how to count units of analysis.

Units of Analysis

We should consider two issues when determining units of analysis. First, in every CA, choose the scale of the content you are going to code. Second, think about how you are going to count the units. The objectives of a study determine the scale of the content. In our study of presidential advertising, we have many options. Do we want to analyze individual words, whole sentences, symbols, themes, or each ad as a whole? The **unit of analysis** is the specific parameters you are analyzing. Let's say we decide to code sentences as our unit. Next, we have to consider the recording units and context units of analysis.

A **recording unit of analysis** focuses on the content. In our presidential election study, individual sentences in every ad are the recording units. We count sentences and separate sentences into different categories. We might analyze the sentences in the ads using the categories defined by Benoit (1999). If a sentence does not fit one of the categories, we can create a miscellaneous category. Remember to avoid overlapping categories. We want the categories to be mutually exclusive.

The **context unit of analysis** means we consider the context surrounding the content (the recording unit). For example, a sentence from a Trump ad may say, "Biden is a leader." However, the next sentence says, "A sleepy FAILED leader with BAD ratings." Looking at the context surrounding the initial recording unit is essential to make sure you do not code a sentence into the wrong category.

Next, how do you count your data? You can count data three ways in quantitative CA: 1) frequency, 2) space and time, and 3) intensity or direction. **Frequency** is the number of times a unit is recorded. **Space** is the amount of coverage devoted to a message (e.g., number of words, number of paragraphs, column inches in a newspaper, seconds/minutes in a video).

While quantitative and qualitative content analysts will often count data in similar ways, their coding schedule, pilot testing, and analysis may differ. The following section discusses how to prepare a coding schedule, how to pilot test a CA, and how to check for intercoder reliability.

> In our study of campaign ads, we are focusing on each sentence in the ads. Thus, the sentences are the units of analysis. We need to look at the context in which the sentence is placed to make sure a sentence is in the correct category. We decide to count the frequency of categories so we can state how often a particular category or function of a political campaign ad is used.

Coding Schedule, Pilot Testing, and Intercoder Reliability

You will need to systematically code the data to find your recording units of analysis. Creating a coding schedule or a coding sheet is helpful. A **coding schedule** tracks, records, and categorizes the communication. Figure 11.1 is an example of a simplified coding sheet to analyze presidential campaign ads.

Figure 11.1 Sample Coding Sheet for Presidential Campaign Commercials

---

Name of Coder: _____

Advertisement Number (Number each ad for tracking): _____

Sponsor: _____

Dates Advertisement Aired: _____

Sentence (unit of analysis)   **Category**

1.   __ Acclaim/Praise
                                                    __ Criticize/Attack
                                                    __ Respond/Defend
                                                    __ Miscellaneous
2.   __ Acclaim/Praise
                                                    __ Criticize/Attack
                                                    __ Respond/Defend
                                                    __ Miscellaneous
3.   __ Acclaim/Praise
                                                    __ Criticize/Attack
                                                    __ Respond/Defend
                                                    __ Miscellaneous

---

We recommend first conducting a pilot study with a portion of your data. A **pilot study** is a trial run. For example, we collect 120 ads from presidential campaigns and conduct a preliminary CA on 10% of the ads. The pilot study checks the coding process and identifies potential problems. We will talk about this in a moment.

Next, how many people will be coding data? More than one coder means determining the level of agreement between the coders. **Intercoder reliability** is a statistical means for establishing the degree of agreement. Various statistical measures are available for intercoder reliability: a simple percentage of agreement, Cohen's kappa (κ), Spearman's *rho*, Pearson's correlation (*r*), and Krippendorf's *alpha*. For more information on these measures, see Neuendorf (2002) or Popping (1988). In most cases, your reliabilities should be above .75. The next section outlines how we can report our results.

Analyzing and Reporting Data in a Quantitative CA

Computer programs such as SPSS have made quantitative analysis easier to conduct. The analysis could start at a basic level with the percentage or number of times a particular category occurs. You can take quantitative analysis a step further by comparing the categories using a chi-square to determine which category has statistical significance. Beniot and Glantz (2012) used chi-squares in their study of 2008 general election presidential TV ads. Beniot and Glantz found that television ads contained more attacks (65%) than acclaims (34%), and stressed policy (58%) more than character (42%). Hop over to the chapter on inferential statistics for an explanation about conducting a chi-square.

Our coding sheet is set up to conduct a quantitative analysis of presidential campaign ads. We decided to watch 120 ads from each campaign and code them (*N* = 240) based on the functional theory by Benoit (1999). We could break down the frequencies for how often ads used acclaimed/praised, criticized/attacked, responded/defended for a candidate. We place each ad in one category. We then organize the results into a table like Figure 11.2 (a hypothetical table, not a real analysis of presidential ads).

Figure 11.2 Frequency Distribution of the Function of Presidential Television Ads

Candidate	Acclaim/Praise	Criticize/Attack	Respond/Defend	Misc.
Biden (120)	65 (54.16%)	30 (25%)	25 (20.84%)	0
Trump (120)	45 (37.5%)	55 (45.83%)	20 (16.67%)	0
N = 240	110 (45.83%)	85 (35.42%)	45 (18.75%)	0

CA is a useful method for analyzing large bodies of data. However, CA does have its limits. CA does not address causality. While CA can point out changing trends or identify categories/themes, the method cannot answer *why* these categories or themes emerged. You should be cautious not to overestimate your results when conducting a CA.

What Distinguishes Qualitative From Quantitative?

You will notice certain similarities between qualitative CA and quantitative CA. Both approaches have been around for quite a while. In fact, Berelson (1952) was among the first to separate CA into qualitative and quantitative approaches.

Both use a systematic approach to sorting data. Both use a series of defined steps to sort data. Both make use of a coding frame. However, Schreier (2013) identified three characteristics between qualitative and quantitative CA. First, in a qualitative CA the coding frame and coding process may adapt during the analysis. The coding frame for a qualitative analysis is more flexible than the quantitative approach. Second, a qualitative study considers the coding frame as part of the analysis. The analysis starts to emerge during the coding. However, a quantitative study considers coding only as data collection with the analysis occurring later through rigorous statistical analysis. Finally, Graneheim and Lundman (2003) contended that qualitative CA focuses on explicit content and latent content. **Latent content** is not stated directly in the data but is inferred from the overall content and context of the data.

You can identify a qualitative CA by three characteristics: 1) the process reduces and streamlines the data into manageable segments, 2) the process is systematic for placing data into the coding frame, and 3) the process remains flexible to provide the best insights of your data. Finally, qualitative CA involves three elements: codes, categories, and themes. We discuss each of these three elements later in the chapter.

Three Approaches to a Qualitative Content Analysis

Qualitative CA has three distinct approaches: conventional, directive, and summative (Hsieh & Shannon, 2005). We draw on Hsieh and Shannon to describe the three approaches.

A **conventional** approach describes a communication event. The approach works best when limited research has been done and existing theories do not fit. Conducting the analysis means allowing codes to emerge from the data. The approach is inductive since no preset codes, standards, or expectations are used. A conventional approach provides an intimate connection with the data since outside influences do not alter the process. The disadvantages include missing key codes or categories providing an incomplete picture of the data. The issue becomes one of internal validity—does the analysis hold true to the full dataset? Finally, it's frequently confused with the grounded theory approach to qualitative analysis. When you move onto a graduate program in communication studies, we recommend reading Cho and Lee's (2014) interesting read detailing the differences between qualitative CA and grounded theory.

Sharabi and Dykstra-DeVette (2019) conducted a conventional qualitative CA. They were interested in how relationships develop from a first email to a first date from 105 participants. Allowing the themes to emerge from the data, Sharabi and Dykstra-DeVette identified 7 primary categories with 18 subcategories. The results demonstrated strategies adapted based on gender, opening lines, and preferences in a mate.

A **directive** qualitative CA draws on existing theory and research to help guide the coding process. The directed approach extends and deepens (or challenges) previous research. The previous studies may focus your research question(s), assist in identifying important concepts, and provide direction for developing your coding frame. Where (or when) the existing research falls short, you can continue the analysis using emergent process from the conventional approach. The use of existing research is the primary advantage of the directed approach. You're not starting with the blank page of the conventional approach. The directed approach provides some existing structure for understanding the data. Researcher bias is the main limitation to the directed approach. The existing work may influence your data collection and analysis. You might miss key themes in the data because they were filtered out by the approach.

An effective directive qualitative CA was conducted by Pujazon-Zazik et al. (2012) when they investigated how teenagers engaged in self-presentation on dating websites. The researchers conducted a content analysis using established parameters for risky behavior (e.g., sex, alcohol, drugs, violence). Analyzing both text and images from 752 public profiles, Pujazon-Zazik et al. discovered that females were more likely include risky behaviors in their dating profiles.

A **summative** qualitative CA starts in a similar fashion to a quantitative CA counting specific unit(s). A summative approach uses the count to demonstrate repetition and intensity of certain word(s) in the data, then goes one more step by including latent analysis as part of the process. Latent analysis involves interpreting underlying meaning. For an example, let's return to your online dating study. You conduct a word count for "relationship." A latent analysis might expand the word search to include "hooking up" and "FWB" (friends with benefits). Then you carefully study the surrounding content and context when each word/phrase appears. Looking at the "big picture" turns your initial word counting into a summative qualitative CA. An advantage is a richer understanding of when and how different terms are used. The disadvantage is an overreliance on researcher credibility. The readers are placing trust in the researcher for making connections between the content, context, analysis, and interpretation.

Gathering and Organizing the Data

In qualitative CA, your data should consider both content meaning and contextual meaning. You are closely examining the communication in order to classify large amounts of data into an efficient number of codes, categories, and themes representing similar meanings within the text (Weber, 1990). Qualitative CA focuses on careful scrutiny of the data and organizing the data into meaningful groups in order to understand what is occurring in the communication. The groups are referred to as codes, categories, and themes.

Codes are basic labels you assign to a phrase or segment of text. For example, let's say you interviewed people for their perceptions about online dating sites. Your basic codes might include "single," "divorced," "straight," "gay," or "long-term relationship." Codes identify key points in the data. You might notice new codes jumping out from the interviews. Such codes are the basic level of your CA. Developing your codes can be done in three ways—open coding, theoretical coding, and axial coding.

The first approach is **open coding**. LaRosa (2005) defined open coding as breaking data apart to identify concepts or categories in the data (themes). In open coding, written data is reviewed line by line. Everything in the transcripts is coded to get an understanding of what is occurring. A researcher typically compares emergent codes to support identifying additional emerging codes. This is known as the **constant comparison** approach and is a great way for researchers to identify similarities and differences in the data.

The second approach is **theoretical coding**. The data is coded using a theoretical lens. For example, if you are interested in cultural identity in dating, you look for data specifically addressing the development, management, and other aspects of identity. The selective sampling means you may overlook some of the data since your focus is from a specific theoretical perspective (Glaser, 1978).

The third approach is axial coding. **Axial coding** is an inductive and deductive process for relating codes and creating categories (Charmaz, 1994). In axial coding, you reread your data with your open or theoretical codes in mind. You are working to confirm your data is correctly represented in the coding process or to make sure something vital was not overlooked. You want to make sure, just as with a puzzle, that all the pieces fit together.

Your coding process will develop into a coding frame. The **coding frame** is a critical component of a successful qualitative CA (Schreier, 2013). The coding frame must be constructed, described, and maintained throughout your study. The coding frame is the centerpiece of your study. A poorly developed coding frame will result in weak research. Do your study justice and take the time (and effort) to build a strong coding frame. As we noted earlier, the coding frame will adapt and flex as the study progresses. A good way to start may be with a few preset codes based on your research question(s). Then use open coding to allow additional codes to emerge as your study progresses and you dig into the data.

Categories are broad groups of codes used to structure your analysis. Developing categories helps to reduce the number of codes used to classify your data. Let's return to your online dating example. You may identify a series of codes grouped together as "companionship," "affection," or "romance."

Themes are high-level clusters of your categories. Themes identify major elements in your data and are usually a limited number (usually four to five max for a major study). Developing metaphors or analogies is often an effective way to cluster categories into themes. For example, your online dating themes may include "long-term relationship," "lifetime commitment," or "just for fun." Developing themes takes time and patience. If you find the concept of thematic development of high-level interest, we recommend Ryan and Bernard (2003) on techniques for identifying themes. The themes help us make sense of the world and play a critical role in your interpretation of the data.

Steps for a Qualitative CA

Conducting a qualitative CA involves seven main steps.

1. Review existing literature connected to your research questions. Let's say you are interested in how people form and shape their cultural identities. You review previously published studies by researchers like Collier (1998, 2005) and Collier and Thomas (1988) to gain an understanding of how cultural identity is formed.
2. Collect your qualitative data using one or more the approaches we've discussed in other chapters, including interviews, ethnographic field notes, and focus groups.
3. Prepare your data for analysis. Qualitative data is easier to analyze if in a tangible form, such as a transcript. We highly recommend you transcribe focus-group and open-ended interviews. Ethnographic field notes may also serve as tangible data.
4. Start the coding process. Depending on your approach (conventional, directive, summative), use the appropriate coding techniques (open, theoretical, axial).
5. Use a coding process to develop your coding framework. The coding framework will guide the identification of categories and themes.
6. Identify the categories and themes that emerge from your coding of the data.
7. Finally, move into the interpretation phase by reviewing your codes, categories, and themes. What is the data telling us about the communication phenomenon you have been researching? Make sure to connect your interpretation back to your research question(s). The entire research project should develop into a strong study worthy of sharing with your scholarly colleagues.

Summary

This chapter is a how-to guide for conducting a content analysis. A CA can be social scientific, interpretive, and critical/cultural. CA is a multifaceted method. After reading the chapter and the student paper, you should feel comfortable to try your own CA. The key is to find one that fits your research question(s).

Key Steps and Questions to Consider

1. Qualitative CA and quantitative CA share certain qualities yet are distinct in how they approach data analysis.
2. In a quantitative CA, you can be identify and count the recording unit of analysis. For example, we can count sentences and we can separate sentences into different categories.
3. A pilot study is a trial run of your CA where you work out any potential kinks in your process and procedures.
4. Intercoder reliability is a statistical analysis of how similar/different coders are in coding content categories. You can use percent agreement (a basic measure), Cohen's kappa (κ), Spearman's *rho*, Pearson's correlation (*r*), or Krippendorf's *alpha* to test reliability. Your reliabilities should be above .75.
5. Conventional, directive, and summative are three approaches for conducting a qualitative CA.
6. You can use open coding, theoretical coding, and/or axial coding to organize your data.
7. Concepts, categories, and themes help to organize and illuminate your data.
8. Remember, a CA does not show causality.

Activities

1. Divide the class into groups. Have each group watch the same episode (or multiple episodes) of a television sitcom (e.g., *Game of Thrones*, *The Big Bang Theory*, *Mad Men*, *Family Guy*, *The Simpsons*). The assignment for each group is to code the humor in the episode(s) using a quantitative approach. Group 1 is tasked with finding and using pre-existing humor categories (a deductive CA). Group 2 will develop their own categories (an inductive CA). Group 3 will let the categories emerge from the data. Compare the results from the three groups. What differences are evident in the results? How did the different approaches influence the results?
2. Using the results from Activity 1, have each group run intercoder reliability on their results.
3. Conduct a qualitative CA of research articles. First, go to Google Scholar at https://scholar.google.com/. Google Scholar is a specialized area of the Google search engine focused on scholarly literature from dozens of disciplines. So, let's give Google Scholar a try.
4. Type "online dating" into the Google Scholar search engine. Copy the titles for the first 50 scholarly articles you find. Use seven-step process detailed in the chapter to analyze the articles (data). Try developing codes, categories, and themes. What are the final themes that emerge from your analysis?
5. Repeat the process but use the terms "online dating" and "communication studies." What different themes emerged when your dataset is narrowed?

Discussion Questions

1. How can the context unit of analysis influence our understanding of the data in the content unit of analysis?
2. What role does the unit of analysis play in a CA? Why should a researcher be concerned with the unit of analysis?
3. Debate the differences between the three approaches to a qualitative CA (conventional, theoretical, and summative). Based on the debate, which is the strongest approach?
4. How might a quantitative researcher and a qualitative researcher approach the same CA study differently? What aspects of content analysis may change between quantitative and qualitative?

Key Terms

Axial Coding
Categories
Codes
Coding Frames
Coding Schedule
Constant Comparison
Content Analysis (CA)
Content Categories

Context Unit of Analysis
Conventional Approach
Deductive Content Analysis
Directive Approach
Inductive Content Analysis
Intercoder Reliability
Latent Content
Latent Meaning
Manifest Meaning

Mutually Exclusive
Open Coding
Pilot Study
Recording Unit of Analysis
Summative Approach
Themes
Theoretical Coding
Units of Analysis

References

Benoit, W. L. (1999). *Seeing spots: A functional analysis of Presidential advertisements, 1952–1996*. Praeger.

Benoit, W. L., & Glantz, M. (2012). A functional analysis of 2008 general election presidential TV spots. *Speaker & Gavel, 49*, 1–19.

Berelson, B. (1952). *Content analysis in communication research*. Free Press.

Charmaz, M. A. (1994). *Constructing grounded theory: A practical guide through qualitative analysis*. Sage.

Cho, J. Y., & Lee, E. (2014). Reducing confusion about grounded theory and qualitative content analysis: Similarities and differences. *The Qualitative Report, 19*(32), 1–20. https://doi.org/10.46743/2160-3715/2014.1028

Collier, M. J. (1998). Researching cultural identity: Reconciling interpretive and post-colonial perspectives. In D. V. Tanno & A. Gonzales (Eds.), *International and intercultural annual: Vol. 21. Communication and identity across cultures* (pp. 121–147). Sage.

Collier, M. J. (2005). Theorizing cultural identifications: Critical updates and continuing evolution. In W. B. Gudykunst (Ed.), *Theorizing about intercultural communication* (pp. 235–256). Sage.

Collier, M. J., & Thomas, M. (1988). Cultural identity. In Y. Y. Kim & W. B. Gudykunst (Eds.), *Theories in intercultural communication* (pp. 99–120). Sage.

Dover, E. D. (2006). *Images, issues, and attacks: Television advertising by incumbents and chal-lengers in presidential elections*. Rowman & Littlefield.

Garner, J. T., Kinsky, E. S., Duta, A. C., & Danker, J. (2012). Deviating from the script: A content analysis of organizational dissent as portrayed on primetime television. *Communication Quarterly, 60*, 608–624. https://doi.org/10.1080/01463373.2012.725001

Glaser, B. G. (1978). *Theoretical sensitivity: Advances in the methodology of grounded theory*. Sociology Press.

Graneheim, U. H., & Lundman, B. (2004). Qualitative content analysis in nursing research: Con-cepts, procedures and measures to achieve trustworthiness. *Nurse Education Today, 24*, 105–112. https://doi.org/10.1016/j.nedt.2003.10.001

Hsieh, H.-F., & Shannon, S. E. (2005). Three approaches to qualitative content analysis. *Qualita-tive Health Research, 15*, 1277–1288. https://doi.org/10.1177%2F1049732305276687

LaRosa, R. (2005). Ground theory methods and qualitative family research. *Journal of Family and Marriage, 67*, 837–857. https://doi.org/10.1111/j.1741-3737.2005.00179.x

Neuendorf, K. A. (2002). *The content analysis guidebook*. Sage.

Neuman, W. (1997). *Social research methods: Qualitative and quantitative approaches*. Allyn & Bacon.

Pujazon-Zazik, M. A., Manasseb, S. M., & Orrell-Valente, J. K. (2012). Adolescents' self-presentation on a teen dating website: A risk-content analysis. *Journal of Adolescent Health, 50*, 517–520. https://doi.org/10.1016/j.jadohealth.2011.11.015

Ryan, G. W., & Bernard, H. R. (2003). Techniques to identify themes. *Field Methods, 15*(1), 85–109. https://doi.org/10.1177%2F1525822X02239569

Schreier, M. (2013). Qualitative content analysis. In E. Flick (Ed.), *The Sage handbook of qualita-tive data analysis* (pp. 170–183). Sage.

Sharabi, L. L., & Dykstra-DeVette, T. A. (2019). From first email to first date: Strategies for initiat-ing relationships in online dating. *Journal of Social and Personal Relationships, 36*, 3389–3407. https://doi.org/10.1177%2F0265407518822780

Waters, R. D., & Lo, K. D. (2012). Exploring the impact of culture in the social media sphere: A con-tent analysis of nonprofit organizations' use of Facebook. *Journal of Intercultural Commu-nication Research, 41*, 297–319. https://doi.org/10.1080/17475759.2012.728772

Weber, R. P. (1990). *Basic content analysis*. Sage.

Quantitative CA: Undergraduate Student Paper

Good Housekeeping and Negative Social Comparison

Benjamin Smith

In our society, body image has become very important to most people to various extents. Women are constantly bombarded through the media with what the ideal figure is etc . . . which inevitably leads to many problems. I will use content analysis to analyze the magazine *Good Housekeeping*, which has an audience of 23,916,000, to see the breakdown of what they focus on in terms of body image for women, the target market of the magazine (Hearst Women's Network, Good Housekeeping Demographic Profile, n.d.). Obviously, there are different aspects to achieving a healthy body image, such as exercise, eating healthy and the way you present yourself (appearance). I believe an analysis of the contents of *Good Housekeeping* will show that there is an uneven distribution in the various aspects in achieving a healthy body image, which is detrimental to the self-esteem and over all well-being of woman in society.

> Benjamin has an effective opening to his paper. He sets up the reason for his content analysis (body image), why the reason is relevant to society, and the primary source of his content (*Good Housekeeping*).

Method

To conduct my analysis of *Good Housekeeping* I will be using content analysis. I have obtained the June 2011 issue of *Good Housekeeping* and picked three categories to look at as targets. The first category is food. This category is looking at any pages that target health foods, healthy options, and diet foods to target weight loss and healthy habits. The second category I am looking for is body appearance, which includes pages/articles that deal with the woman's appearance, such a slimming outfits and styles/make-up that are looking to make you appear younger, healthier and thinner. The last category I am looking at is actual exercise for weight loss and healthy living.

> First, Benjamin may find that one issue of a magazine is insufficient for his content analysis. The articles and ads in one issue may not represent the normal content of the magazine. A random selection of multiple issues spanning a year (or even multiple years) may provide stronger results.

My research question: Is there an uneven distribution in body image factors in the media targeting women? I predict an uneven distribution in the three categories that are vital to achieve healthy living, weight loss, and an overall body image as described above. After sorting through the pages of *Good Housekeeping* and categorizing the pages that fit into one of the three categories, I will analyze them and look at the prevalence of each to see if there is an even distribution or if more emphasis is put on certain categories which will cause the women to be ineffective in their pursuit of the overall healthy body image, weight and healthy lifestyle.

Benjamin should be cautious in laying out his research question. He sets up a null statement (he does not take a position on how he thinks the data will play out in the research question). But then he shifts and let his personal opinions drift in the research. One must always be cautious in social scientific research to avoid the issue of bias. His prediction of an uneven distribution could be interpreted as bias and could influence the coding process.

Theory

Social Comparison Theory

Social Comparison Theory deals with how individuals compare themselves with others in our society. As we experience and see others, we continuously compare ourselves to others making either positive or negative comparisons based on how we feel about ourselves (Schwartz & Andsager, 2011). Generally, the media portrays body images that are nearly impossible to achieve, which undoubtedly leads to frustration and lower dissatisfaction among the individuals making the comparisons. The media no longer portrays just body images, but also ways to achieve a better body image. If there is a skewed coverage of how to achieve a better body image, by this I mean more emphasis put on one aspect instead of the many aspects needed, then there will not be success in achieving the desired outcome. This, as part of the social comparison theory, will lead to increased dissatisfaction among viewers of the media because there will be lower self-esteem as they make their comparisons. This will occur because the ways to achieve the ideal body image are supposedly given to you in the media, but you are still unable to achieve the outcome even when you are told directly how to. This whole process can repeat itself leading to women actually going the opposite way of what they are trying to achieve, which is a better body image. The media will therefore be causing more harm with regards to the social comparison theory then they would if they gave an even distribution of the categories needed to achieve a healthy body image and overall lifestyle.

Benjamin has integrated theory providing a strong foundation for the study. Social Comparison Theory is useful for understanding the content of his analysis. He can strengthen the section by providing evidence and source support for many of the claims he makes. For example, he states "The media no longer portrays just body images, but also ways to achieve a better body image," yet no documentation is provided to prove the statement.

Results

Good Housekeeping breaks down their publication into the categories they cover and the percentage of which they cover. Of the three categories I am looking at, their relating categories are Food & Nutrition, Health (Exercise/Wellbeing) and Beauty/Grooming (Hearst Women's Network, Good Housekeeping Editorial Coverage, n.d.). Food & Nutrition are said to account for 20.2% of their publication, Health for 7.5% and Beauty/Grooming for 6.2% (Hearst Women's Network, Good Housekeeping Editorial Coverage). After looking through the June 2011 issue, I found 39 of the 202 pages were targeting health food/nutrition, 21 pages targeting Beauty, which deals with body image appearance, and 1 instance targeting exercise for healthy living/weight loss. Therefore, my percentages are the following, Food/Nutrition are 19.3%, Beauty/Grooming is 10.4% and Health is ½%. Food/Nutrition is close to what *Good Housekeeping* reports (20.2% reported compared to 19.3% found); Beauty/Grooming is fairly close to the reported value (6.2% reported compared to 10.4% found). The last finding is the health, which is reported at 7.5% and found at ½%. Although *Good Housekeeping* openly reports what the magazine breakdown is, and that the focus is not evenly distributed, the actual distribution is skewed a lot more than reported which may have drastic impacts on women's self-esteem. *Good Housekeeping* magazine touts itself as being the most trusted source for advice about food, diet, beauty, health, family and home (Hearst Women's Network, About Good Housekeeping Magazine). The fact that there is not an even distribution in their coverage of these three categories can lead to more harm to the women they are serving, as all three categories are necessary to achieve the outcome these women are presented with in the magazines.

Benjamin can strengthen his results section in a number of ways. First, he can move the data provided by the Hearst Women's Network from Results to the end of his Introduction section. A reader assumes any results in the Results section are from the current study, not from a previous study.

Second, a reader can get lost wading through all the categories and percentages. A table (or a series of tables) can better a reader with such data. The write up can then be focused on the highs and lows of the data.

Finally, Benjamin could move the comparison of his results with Hearst Women's Network's information and interpretation of the results to a new Comparison & Interpretation section or to the Conclusion section of his paper.

Conclusion

With the combination of media influences and various theories, such as the Social Comparison Theory, it becomes clear that what articles and topics that are targeted towards women could potentially have a profound impact on their health and self-esteem. To have a healthy lifestyle and better body image, it is important to not only eat right, as 19.3% of *Good Housekeeping* covered, but there also needs to be an equal amount of exercise and even appearance that plays a key role in a healthy body image. When one of these is focused on more than others, it can lead to false perceptions of what needs to be done. If a woman believes eating healthy meals is all that is needed to have a more positive body image and slim down, then if the food alone does not accomplish that, then there is a higher likelihood that she will have more negative comparisons about herself. It is for this reason that media such as *Good Housekeeping*, who have a reputation as a trustworthy source for women, need to portray a fuller picture for the women they are targeting in order to actually improve their self-image, instead of possibly making problems worse

References

Hearst Women's Network. (n.d.). About Good Housekeeping magazine. *Good Housekeeping*.

Hearst Women's Network. (n.d.). Good Housekeeping demographic profile. *Good Housekeeping Media Kit*. www.ghmediakit.com/r5/home.asp

Hearst Women's Network. (n.d.). Good Housekeeping Editorial coverage. *Good Housekeeping Media Kit*. www.ghmediakit.com/r5/home.asp

Schwartz, J., & Andsager, J. L. (2011). Four decades of images in gay male-targeted magazines. *Journalism & Mass Communication Quarterly, 88*, 76–78.

12 Discourse Analysis

Margarethe Olbertz-Siitonen

Chapter Outline

- Why Study Discourse?
- What Is Discourse Analysis?
- What Kinds of Data Are Needed?
- How to Transcribe
- How to Conduct a Discourse Analytic Study
- Summary
- Key Steps and Questions to Consider
- Activities
- Discussion Questions
- Key Terms
- Undergraduate Student Paper

What Will I Learn About Discourse Analysis?

Discourse is an everyday aspect of human life and includes conversations, debates, theatre plays, news interviews, speeches, chat logs, blog entries, newspaper articles, e-mails, or official documents. Every day you follow or engage in discourse. As you start reading this text, you are participating in discourse. Discourse is "what people say or write" (Antaki, 2008, p. 431). Analyzing talk or texts from a discourse-analytic perspective means determining what is achieved through their production.

This chapter discusses why discourse is a worthwhile object of research in communication studies. You will learn what discourse analysis represents and what different discourse-analytic approaches have in common. This chapter provides you with information on aspects of data collection and data processing critical for conducting consistent and reliable discourse-analytic work. The chapter will introduce important principles and practical advice on analyzing discourse. Discourse analysis is a broad field of inquiry and involves a number of points to consider for your research project.

Why Study Discourse?

Let's explore some reasons to study discourse. Analyzing discourse has the advantage of working with first-order data, which means you observe and discover authentic practices and real-life concerns. Talk and texts provide you with insight into the ways people construct and account

DOI: 10.4324/9781003109129-15

for social reality and the nature of social action. By studying discourse, we uncover what people actually do by means of certain lexical choices, rhetorical formats, a particular line of argument, and so on. In the case of spoken discourse, also *how* something is said can be important. For example, you might find seemingly random or irrelevant details—such as hesitations, pauses, or speech volume—meaningful resources in social conduct.

What you discover when studying discourse can have all sorts of practical, political, and societal implications. This is because discourse is a locus of social interaction. What happens in society largely happens through discourse. Findings on discursive practices can increase public awareness of how gender inequalities, power, or culture and cultural differences are our doing and as social constructs inextricably tied to discourse. Piller (2012) argued, "we do not have culture but . . . we construct culture discursively" (p. 5). Observations on the discursive construction of culture might encourage treating people as individuals whose activities are situated rather than determined by group membership. On a smaller scale, insights into conversational structures can help facilitate effective communication in institutional settings. Understanding how a single word is enough to change the course and outcome of talk is relevant for personnel in-service encounters, such as interactions between doctor and patient or clerk and customer (see Stokoe, 2014). In fact, the Conversation Analytic Role-Play Method (CARM), which is a communication skills training program developed by Stokoe (2014), builds on research within a larger framework of discourse studies.

Discourse runs through all aspects of human life. Analyzing discourse or "what people do" (Potter, 2016, p. 190) can tackle a number of different communication research problems. Whether your research questions are open ended (e.g., how discourse is organized and what is achieved through that organization) or directed at a specific social fact (e.g., how group membership is constructed), employing discourse analysis will enable you to shed light on core characteristics of the issue at hand. Let's take a closer look at basic premises and principles of discourse analysis (DA). Over the next sections, you will find answers to the following questions: What is discourse analysis? What kinds of data are needed? How do I transcribe data? How do I conduct a discourse analytic study?

What Is Discourse Analysis?

DA really is an umbrella term describing a field of study. DA is not a single method but includes a number of different approaches. These approaches can be distinguished by research interests, underlying theoretical or philosophical considerations, the kind of data utilized, and analytical procedures. In a more traditional sense, **DA** stands for the study of texts and talk, focusing on language use and on language as a means of social action (Antaki, 2008; Potter & Hepburn, 2008; Silverman, 2011).

A comprehensive definition of DA

In their anthology *Discourse Analytic Research: Repertoires and Readings of Texts in Action*, Burman and Parker (2017) bring together a selection of various discourse studies. Burman and Parker consider what the collected contributions have in common, providing a comprehensive and far-reaching definition of discourse analysis.

According to Burman and Parker (2017), the studies share a concern with the ways language produces and constrains meaning, where meaning does not—or does not only— reside within individuals' heads and where social conditions give rise to the forms of talk available. In its various forms, discourse analysis offers a social account of subjectivity by attending to the linguistic resources by which the sociopolitical realm is produced and reproduced. (p. 3).

Burman and Parker (2017) continue by underlining how "all involve an attention to the ways in which language (as with other representational systems) does more than reflect what it represents, with the corresponding implication that meanings are multiple and shifting, rather than unitary and fixed" (p. 3).

Table 12.1 Discourse analytic methods and data according to researchers' interests (Antaki, 2008, p. 432).

What actions to be revealed	Candidate theory/method	Typical data
Personal meaning-making	Narrative Analysis, Interpretative Phenomenological Analysis	Interviews, diaries, autobiographies, stories
Imposing and managing frames of meaning and identities	Interactional Sociolinguistics, Ethnography of Speaking	Audio and video recordings, ethnographic observations
Accomplishing interactional life in real time	Conversation Analysis	Audio and video recordings
Displaying and deploying psychological states, describing the world and promoting interests	Discursive Psychology	Audio and video recordings, texts
Constituting and representing culture and society	[Generic] Discourse Analysis	Texts, interviews
Constituting and regulating the social and the political world, the operation of power	Critical Discourse Analysis	Official and unofficial texts, speeches, media accounts and representations, interviews

DA is characterized by its commitment to **social constructionism** (Potter & Hepburn, 2008). What we say and write are not approached as objective accounts of social facts but as constructions that accomplish "versions of the world, of society, events and inner psychological worlds" (Potter, 2016, p. 190). Within this broad framework, various theoretical perspectives guide research on discourse, and you can choose among a number of methods. In Table 12.1, you find an overview of the most common approaches, their scopes, and typical data compiled by Antaki (2008).

Antaki's (2008) table shows how approaches range from **micro-** to **macro-level** phenomena. While **conversation analysis** is concerned with the stepwise organization of talk and the accomplishment of mutual understanding, studies in **critical discourse analysis** take a political stance and examine discourse contributing to the construction and reproduction of power. Of course, the multitude and diversity of approaches somewhat blur the scale of DA. However, according to Antaki (2008), any discourse analytic work is characterized by four key features: 1) a focus on natural talk or texts, 2) an appreciation of words as embedded in their co-text and wider context, 3) a sensitivity toward the nonliteral meaning of words, and 4) special attention to the social actions achieved through language use. The four points outline the frame of DA and provide valuable benchmarks for your own analysis.

In recent years, DA has seen a shift toward **multimodality** (Jones, 2012). Across approaches, scholars have started to focus on language use as one out of many equally relevant resources (or **modes**) of communication. Beside language, modes include gestures, gaze, body orientation, or the design and layout of documents. *"Multi*modality" from this perspective is approached holistically with no mode treated by the analyst as more important than the other.

Work conducted within the framework of DA typically follows a qualitative, inductive, and data-driven line of inquiry. Common aims of discourse studies are to uncover the underlying patterns and structures of **meaning-making** in spoken and written discourse and to trace the ways social reality is produced, negotiated, and reinforced in everyday discursive practices (Keller, 2013).

What Kinds of Data Are Needed?

What kind of discursive material you should collect is informed by your research interests and by the approach you have chosen. For example, if you like to study how immigrants reflect on their experiences living abroad and organize these experiences into individual storylines, your approach likely will be **narrative analysis** (Antaki, 2008). Your study will use data containing personal accounts of immigration, such as open-ended interviews, blog entries, articles, journal entries, or even autobiographies. On the other hand, a research project can develop in reverse order, with data informing your research interests and approach. This is the case when you are allowed access to an existing set of data or you simply come across an interesting phenomenon you would like to study.

As mentioned earlier, one unifying feature of most DA approaches is their concern with natural texts and talk. In other words, the study relies on **naturally occurring data**. If you are uncertain whether the data can be considered natural, a memorable rule is Potter's (2002) "dead social scientist's test" (p. 541): data is naturally occurring when the recorded situation would have taken place despite the researcher's existence. The Potter rule clearly excludes social experiments conducted in controlled laboratory settings and surveys and questions the applicability of interviews or focus groups. Such modes of data collection yield **biased** material, since it is influenced and shaped by the researcher's informed decisions.

However, qualitative interviews and focus groups are often justified by approaching them as social constructs themselves, for example "interviews *as* discourse data" (Nikander, 2012, p. 397; emphasis added). This means the data is seen within the context of their production: what participants tell and how they tell it is tied to the circumstances of being interviewed. Participants' answers should not be taken as factual information. Second, researchers may place emphasis on the role of the interviewer in their analysis (e.g., Nikander, 2012). Focus groups and interviews as discourse data include the option of studying interviews and focus groups entirely in their own right. For example, exploring the activities involved in the mutual organization of research interviews can help unveil underlying expectations about participating in these kinds of data collection. Similar to the service encounters mentioned earlier (Stokoe, 2014), such analysis has the potential to further demonstrate how one word can change the outcome of an interview.

Puchta and Potter (1999), in a discursive psychological study on question formats in market research focus groups organized in Germany, discovered that moderators use extended or elaborate questions to ensure interviewees' participation and "guide the responses made by participants" (p. 332). Such findings demonstrate how moderators or interviewers are crucially involved in the production of answers.

An ongoing debate is whether data containing mundane conversations or institutional talk can ever be completely free of researchers' interference. The recording of natural interactions involves setting up and operating a video camera, microphones, or audio recorders and keeping field notes (Silverman, 2011). **Labov's Observer's Paradox** (1972) identifies the problem: "the aim of linguistic research in the community must be to find out how people talk when they are not being systematically observed; yet we can only obtain this data by systematic observation" (p. 209).

On the other hand, many forms of written language are produced and archived irrespective of academic interests, satisfying the requirement of authenticity particularly well. Even certain audio/visual recordings may be considered truly natural, including TV interviews, moderated talk shows, vlogs, and so on. The recordings were produced for larger audiences and are an essential part of their construction. Social media brings with it the added advantage of allowing unobtrusive collection of data. For example, the camera is an essential element of video-mediated talk. Automated chat logs are another source of genuine discursive data made available by everyday technology.

Considering research ethics

As with any kind of study involving humans, you have to follow the principles of ethical conduct in research, such as getting **informed consent** from your research participants. However, keeping participants' integrity in mind is particularly important with naturally occurring data. Authentic data gives you access to people's real-life concerns and may contain sensitive information that should not be traceable to any particular person. Protecting your participants' identity is important.

How to Transcribe

The process of data collection often includes preparing and organizing the material for later analysis. In the case of spoken discourse, you are required to **transcribe** your data (transfer recorded interaction word by word into written form). We recommend you start rough drafts of **transcripts** during the process of gathering research material, allowing you to get acquainted with the details of the recordings, which may help build research questions and focus any additional data collection.

Transcripts are important to DA for four reasons. First, transcripts are a way to handle the transient characteristics of talk, which would otherwise be difficult to trace or inaccessible. Fixed in written form, spoken discourse becomes available for thorough and recurrent examination. Second, transcripts have the practical advantage of allowing quick access to keywords with the help of a search function. Third, the process of transcribing compels repeated review of the data, providing insight and forming an initial picture of participants' practices. Transcriptions are considered the first step of analysis or a "major 'noticing device'" (ten Have, 2007, p. 95). Finally, any kind of DA study needs to be open to scrutiny based on the "'validity through transparency and access' principle" (Nikander, 2008, p. 227) of qualitative research. You are expected to make the analysis available to your readers and to demonstrate what exactly your observations and reflections are based on. By including in your research report transcripts of analyzed extracts, you establish reference points and ensure that others can follow your analytical argument.

When you transcribe you can follow specific **transcription conventions** (rules developed to mark temporal and prosodic features of talk including pauses, intonation contours, stress, and volume). The conventions you choose depend on your approach. Kowal and O'Connell (2014) provide an overview of four notation systems commonly utilized in DA. Transcripts usually consist of three columns including line numbers, the current speaker or speakers (using masked initials or pseudonyms), and a written version of their talk. The rough scheme in Figure 12.2 gives you an idea of the prevailing form of transcripts:

Figure 12.2

Line Number	Speaker(s)	Communication
1	name1	talk
2		talk
3		talk
4	name2	talk
5	name1	talk
6	name3	talk
7		talk
8	name2	talk

We highly recommend numbering each line of the transcript, even if the turn of one participant stretches over several lines. Line numbering ensures the discourse in your analysis can be traced back to the transcript with little difficulty. Second, use a monospaced font—such as Courier New—to produce a clean and aligned transcript. A monospaced font allows you to precisely mark, for example, overlapping talk (see example (2) lines 02-03) in Figure 12.3.

Figure 12.3 Two examples of transcripts

```
(1)
(from Wells, 2011, p. 443)
 1. I: Um-hum.
 2. R: Yeah. I do . . . my daughter was about ten then. And
```

```
 3. That's where I got something like a little gap
 4. Because I think I end up leaving her then for a year or two.
 5. But . . . and because I know when I would
 6. Come to my mother's just to leave her, it would
 7. Almost be just antagonizing, you know, all the
 8. Screaming and pulling on me and, you know,
 9. Because she wanted me . . . she wanted to be with me.
10. I: Um-hum.
11. R: She wanted to stay with me. She wondered 'Why
12. you going and I'm not going?'
13. I: Um-hum.
14. R: And, ah, and it got to really be [] real strenuous on me and
15. my daughter

(2)
Ava and Bee (from Sidnell, 2010, pp. 52-53)

01 Ava: I'm so:: ti:yid. I j's played ba:ske'ball t'day since the
02 firs' time since I wz a freshm'n in hi:ghsch[ool.]

ii
iii(h)[(°Whe(h)re.)
05 Ava:  [Yeah fuh like an hour enna ha:[lf.]
06 Bee:       [.hh] Where
07 didju play ba:sk[etbaw. ]
08 Ann:     [(The) gy]:m.
09 Bee: In the gy:m? [(hh)
```

As can be seen in the two examples, transcripts of talk differ remarkably in their level of detail. How thorough you need to be is informed by your research interests. The first case stems from a study exploring a mother who had temporarily lost the custody of her children giving her account of maternal identity (Wells, 2011). Focusing only on the wording of her narrative is sufficient for the study. The second transcript, on the other hand, has a conversation analytic background and relies on the precise notation of stretches and overlaps. The detailed transcript allows for a fine-grained analysis of the organization of talk, such as the mutual accomplishment of **turn-taking** (Sidnell, 2010). A multimodal approach to interaction further calls for transcripts that take account of all relevant modalities. Multimodal transcripts include notations of verbal activities and prosodic features, gestures, gaze, and bodily orientations and their exact timing and progression (see Mondada, 2007). Often such transcripts are enriched with schematic pictures or–depending on participants' permissions–photographs. However, even the most detailed transcript constitutes a work in progress and may be adjusted later on. As you proceed with your analysis you might hear things differently, or maybe your focus changes and requires you to add more details.

Translating data

If you are analyzing discourse produced in a foreign language, you might be required to enclose translations into your research report. In the case of written discourse, placing a translation directly beneath the original is often sufficient. When representing translated talk, on the other hand, you have several options: (1) you can provide a translation below the original transcript, (2) include the translation line by line into the transcript or (3) choose a parallel format where original and translation are side-by-side (Nikander, 2008).

How to Conduct a Discourse Analytic Study

While transcripts are essential, analysis of spoken discourse always includes the original recordings. When transcribing, you have to make certain choices, since details might be difficult to mark down or vocal features can be heard differently and so on. A transcript is a selective **interpretation**. This is why discourse analysts usually rely on a combination of recording *and* transcripts.

Analyzing discourse is more of a back-and-forth procedure than a linear process. Indeed, no clear-cut, step-by-step guidelines exist for conducting any kind of DA study, but you are expected to make your own methodological choices in accordance with your data, research interests, and theoretical grounds. DA work has been compared, in fact, to a skill requiring experience, a certain mentality, and creativity (Keller, 2013; Potter, 2016). Of course, discourse studies are not free of methodological commitments, and you have to be clear about your decisions and remember to justify them well. However, approaching your data with as little provision as possible can facilitate the discovery of phenomena that a rule-governed analysis might overlook. To get a better picture of conducting a DA, Rapley (2007) recommends reading other people's work. Academic journals in the field, such as *Discourse Studies*, *Text & Talk*, and *Discourse & Society*, are useful for studying others' methodological approaches. Your department/school might organize regular data sessions where you can improve your skills by analyzing data together with experts.

"There are no hard-and-fast answers or solutions to any of the debates and dilemmas you will face when undertaking work on conversations and texts. It often depends on what you read, how you read it, and what just makes sense to you in the context of your own work. Above all, I would suggest going and reading examples of as many people's empirical work as you have time for, to get a sense about the practical decisions they made and the practical solutions they employed" (Rapley, 2007, p. 109).

As DA generally aims at discovering patterns and recurrent structures of meaning-making, one way to begin tackling your data is by identifying themes and by organizing them into a collection of different categories. This kind of **coding** is done through careful examination and re-examination of your material (for more on coding practices, see Keller, 2013): once you come across something interesting, mark it down and label it using a descriptive phrase or a keyword. See if you can find similar instances in the data, and refine your initial tag or classification with what the occurrences have in common. You might be required to add subcategories or expand existing codes in order to catch nuances and distinguish certain formats from others. During this process, you may come across a number of interesting phenomena. However, we advise limiting your focus and keeping track of how single categories and subcategories relate to each other and the main theme of your study. While coding can help you create and manage an archive, coding is not always necessary or a sufficient step. As Potter (2004) puts it: "Part of DA may involve coding a set of materials, but this is an analytic preliminary used to make the quantity of materials more manageable rather than a procedure that performs the analysis itself" (p. 216).

Analyzing, then, means to explore and explain what is going on in your data. While coding involves finding and categorizing interesting passages, analysis is more about figuring out what exactly makes these passages interesting. Remember that, in the process of conducting a discourse analytic study, you cannot necessarily follow a straight path. Data collection, transcribing, coding, and analysis often overlap.

Whatever your approach—conversation analysis, narrative analysis, critical discourse analysis, discursive psychology—try to keep the four key features of DA in mind (see Antaki, 2008). While DA provides no fixed instructions on how to analyze your data, the key features reveal underlying principles and can assist you in navigating your analysis. First, avoid repeating or paraphrasing what participants say, but rather try to make sense of people's activities and provide a profound and clear account of what you think they are doing. This is based on the assumption that what people say or write constitutes versions of reality that cannot be approached as simple facts or truths. You should always demonstrate how you arrived at a certain understanding. According to Rapley (2007),

> your job is to convince others that your claims, your interpretations, are both credible and plausible, that you are not just making this up from thin air or this is just your vague hunch, but that your argument is based on the materials from your archive.

(pp. 128-129)

This goes hand in hand with an appreciation and discussion of previous work on the subject. DA's views on social reality have further analytical consequences. For example, from a discourse analytic perspective status, gender or cultural membership is only achieved through discourse. Rather than referring to such attributes as an explanation for certain behavior or using them as a starting point for your research, the idea is to explore how, for what purposes, and under which circumstances they are brought up in discourse. Finally, treat single contributions in relation to their placement by considering what preceded a certain expression or a word and what it leads to next.

Summary

This chapter provided you with some basic insights into the broad area of discourse analysis. As is often the case with such introductions, this text constitutes more of a starting point—but one that hopefully inspires you to learn more about this field and maybe even a certain approach in particular. In general terms, DA allows us to recognize the ways people (together) create meaning and social facts. Although analyzing discourse is a skill requiring learning by doing, the chapter should help guide you in the process.

Key Steps and Questions to Consider

1. DA describes a field of study, encompassing a number of different approaches.
2. Conducting a discourse analytic study often includes recurrent and overlapping steps.
3. Usually discourse analytic work means studying naturally occurring data.
4. In the case of spoken discourse, data collection involves the recording of suitable situations, which means setting up cameras and audio recorders beforehand.
5. Recording and using naturally occurring data entail specific demands with regard to research ethics.
6. Recorded data should roughly be transcribed to allow for a better overview. The notation of single passages that become relevant for analysis can be refined later on using an established transcription system.
7. The data may be organized by categorizing interesting phenomena. However, while coding sometimes includes analytical elements, analysis does not stop there.
8. Analyzing means exploring and explaining what is going on in the data.
9. Analysis generally aims at discovering patterns and structures of meaning-making. The main focus is on how people constitute social facts through discursive practices.
10. A multimodal approach to discourse does not favor language over other modes of communication.
11. The research report should demonstrate clearly how presented findings have evolved and follow the "'validity through transparency and access' principle" (Nikander, 2008, p. 227).

Activities

1. Find an online TV or radio interview. Transcribe a short passage of the talk from the interview (approximately one page). Prepare a rough transcript. Then go into details by marking the pauses, overlaps, stresses, and so on. For an example, see Puchta and Potter (1999, especially p. 333).
2. Practice coding. Using the interview you found online, label interesting instances and organize them into categories and subcategories. Focus on the different ways the interviewer addresses the interviewee.
3. Pick one instance from your interview for closer inspection. What is happening? How can this be explained? Try to trace and reconstruct what the interviewer is doing by addressing their interview partner in a certain way.

Discussion Questions

1. What kinds of discourse do you come across on a daily basis? What makes them interesting for closer inspection? How could they be approached analytically?
2. Under which circumstances could discursive data that stem from experiments in laboratory settings be considered naturally occurring? What questions could be directed at such materials from a DA perspective?

3. If you are working in groups or pairs, agree on a talk for activity 1, and decide which part of that talk should be transcribed. Everyone transcribes the passage on their own and then compares their notations. In which ways do they match? What differences do you find? What implications do these similarities and differences have for possible analysis?

Key Terms

Bias	Macro-Level	Social Constructionism
Coding	Meaning-Making	Transcribe
Conversation Analysis	Micro-Level	Transcription Conventions
Critical Discourse Analysis	Modes	Transcripts
Discourse Analysis (DA)	Multimodality	Turn-Taking
Interpretation	Narrative Analysis	
Labov's Observer's Paradox	Naturally Occurring Data	

References

Antaki, C. (2008). Discourse analysis and conversation analysis. In P. Alasuutari, L. Bickman, & J. Brannan (Eds.), *The Sage handbook of social research methods* (pp. 431–446). Sage.

Burman, E., & Parker, I. (2017). Introduction–discourse analysis: The turn to the text. In E. Burman & I. Partker (Eds.), *Discourse analytic research: Repertoires and readings of texts in action* (pp. 1–13). Routledge.

Jones, R. H. (2012). Multimodal discourse analysis. In C. Chapelle (Ed.), *The encyclopedia of applied linguistics*. Wiley. http://onlinelibrary.wiley.com/doi/10.1002/9781405198431.wbeal0813/pdf

Keller, R. (2013). *Doing discourse research: An introduction for social scientists*. Sage.

Kowal, S., & O'Connell, D. (2014). Transcription as a crucial step of data analysis. In U. Flick (Ed.), *The Sage handbook of qualitative data analysis* (pp. 64–78). Sage.

Labov, W. (1972). *Sociolinguistic patterns*. University of Pennsylvania Press.

Mondada, L. (2007). Multimodal resources for turn-taking: Pointing and the emergence of possible next speakers. *Discourse Studies, 9*, 194–225. https://doi.org/10.1177%2F1461445607075346

Nikander, P. (2008). Working with transcripts and translated data. *Qualitative Research in Psychology, 5*, 225–231. https://doi.org/10.1080/14780880802314346

Nikander, P. (2012). Interviews as discourse data. In J. F. Gubrium (Ed.), *The Sage handbook of interview research: The complexity of the craft* (pp. 397–413). Sage.

Piller, I. (2012). Intercultural communication: An overview. In C. B. Paulston, S. F. Kiesling, & E. S. Rangel (Eds.), *The handbook of intercultural discourse and communication* (pp. 3–18). Wiley-Blackwell.

Potter, J. (2002). Two kinds of natural. *Discourse Studies, 4*, 539–542. https://doi.org/10.1177%2F1461445602004004901

Potter, J. (2004). Discourse analysis as a way of analysing naturally occurring talk. In D. Silverman (Ed.), *Qualitative research: Theory, method and practice* (pp. 200–221). Sage.

Potter, J. (2016). Discursive psychology and the study of naturally occurring talk. In D. Silverman (Ed.), *Qualitative research* (4th ed., pp. 189–206). Sage.

Potter, J., & Hepburn, A. (2008). Discursive constructionism. In J. A. Holstein & J. F. Gubrium (Eds.), *Handbook of constructionist research* (pp. 275–293). Guilford Press.

Puchta, C., & Potter, J. (1999). Asking elaborate questions: Focus groups and the management of spontaneity. *Journal of Sociolinguistics, 3*, 314–335. https://doi.org/10.1111/1467-9481.00081

Rapley, T. (2007). *Doing conversation, discourse and document analysis*. Sage.

Sidnell, J. (2010). *Conversation analysis: An introduction*. Wiley-Blackwell.

Silverman, D. (2011). *Interpreting qualitative data*. Sage.

Stokoe, E. (2014). The conversation analytic role-play method (CARM): A method for training communication skills as an alternative to simulated role-play. *Research on Language and Social Interaction, 47*, 255-265. https://doi.org/10.1080/08351813.2014.925663

ten Have, P. (2007). *Doing conversation analysis*. Sage.

Wells, K. (2011). A narrative analysis of one mother's story of child custody loss and regain. *Children and Youth Services Review, 33*, 439-447. www.researchgate.net/deref/http%3A%2F%2Fdx.doi.org%2F10.1016%2Fj.childyouth.2010.06.019

Undergraduate Student Paper

The gradual production of a humorous event in a Finnish talk show (translated from Finnish)

Saara Vilokkinen

Saara has prepared a very detailed transcript, which depicts all the features relevant for her conversation analysis. The transcript shows, for example, overlaps, stresses, intonation, and pauses as well as in-breaths.

1	Host	*kenen idea oli laittaa laura räty (0.5) ministeriksi.* whose idea was it to select laura räty (0.5) as secretary.
2	Guest	*.hh aika harvat asiat on niinku kenenkään* *yksittäisten* .hh quite few things are the ideas of
3		*ihm[isten ideoita]* a [single person alone]
4	Host	*[mut se oli sun idea,]* [but it was your idea,]
5		(0.5)
6	Guest	*mut mä olin siinä <u>mu</u>kana* but I was inv<u>o</u>lved in this
7		*kun sitä [kehiteltiin (sitä)]* when this [was developed (this)]
8	Host	*[se oli <u>sun</u> <u>idea</u>¿]* [it was <u>your</u> <u>idea</u>¿]
9		(.)
10	Guest	*.h mä olin* .h I was
11		*<u>mu:</u>[kana siinä kun sitä kehiteltiin sitä ideaa?* *]* in[vo:<u>l</u>ved in this when this was developed this idea?]
12	Host	*[.h ((naurahtaa))* *<SE] oli* [.h ((laughs)) <IT] was
13		*[SUN <u>IDEA</u>>* [YOUR <u>IDEA</u>>

```
14   Guest   [mä olin MUKANA SIINÄ?
             [I was INVOLVED IN THIS?

             (.)

15   Host    mä satun tietään et se oli sun idea,
             I happen to know that it was your idea,

16           ((naurahtaa)) oliko?
             ((laughs)) was it?
```

(for transcription conventions see Sidnell, 2010)

This passage is taken from a Finnish talk show ("Hjallis") that was broadcasted on MTV3, a Finnish TV-channel, on the 10th of October 2014. The guest of this show was Taru Tujunen, the former party secretary of a large Finnish party. I chose this data, because I remembered seeing the show on television and noticing that the talk was intense and possibly interesting to analyze from a conversation analytic perspective. Of course I attempted to watch the conversation again without presuming too much beforehand. However, this 15 second-long stretch of talk which takes place two minutes after the beginning drew my attention and I decided to focus my analysis on this particular passage. In principle, the extract could have also been longer for the analysis of this case, but I believe that within these 15 seconds one can already identify a certain phenomenon using conversation analysis.

It is sometimes important to include (preceding) talk if it becomes relevant in the course of a certain passage. However, in this case Saara's choice to keep the extract at 15 secondsisgment derable to is passage. 15 seconds, does not ons that humor.or exa,pleion analysis. The transcript shows, for example, is justified–no more insight is needed to analyze this segment (and to be able to follow as a reader without difficulty).

In the beginning of the passage Hjallis, the host, asks his guest whose idea it was to select Laura Räty as secretary. Hjallis poses his question quite calmly with falling intonation, but as can be seen in the transcript he makes a clear pause of half a second after mentioning the name of Laura Räty (line 1). Also his guest, Tujunen, begins to speak with a rather calm and continuing intonation, responding that ".*hh quite few things are the ideas of a single person alone*" (lines 2–3), until Hjallis cuts in at the end of her reply. Hjallis clearly takes on the role of the interviewer by dramatizing and by answering in overlap in his guest's stead: "*but it was your idea,*" (line 4). After a very short pause, Tujunen answers emphatically: "*I was invo̲lved in this when this was developed (this)*" (lines 6–7), clearly stressing the word 'involved', but again Hjallis cuts in, using more emphasis himself: "*it was your̲ idea̲¿*" (line 8). Until this point Hjallis has been physically oriented towards his guest, and he reinforced his interruptions through intensive eye contact with Tujunen.

After a micro pause, Tujunen repeats her answer with yet more weight: ".*h I was invo̲:lved in this when this was developed this idea?*" (lines 10–11). Again Hjallis interferes towards the end of her sentence, now almost shouting with very strong emphasis: "<*IT was YOUR*

IDEA>" (lines 12–13). At the same time Hjallis shakes his finger at her thereby still intensifying his exclamation. Partly in overlap with this, now Tujunen herself shouts back: "*I was INVOLVED IN THIS?*" (line 14) and in turn shakes her finger at Hjallis. At lines 16–17 Hjallis continues a little quieter, but still with clear accentuation: "*I happen to know that it was your idea, ((laughs)) was it?*".

> Saara reproduces the course of this talk with great care, and she pays attention to non-verbal activities. It is easy to follow how the passage slowly builds up.

From my point of view, this conversation is quite a typical example of talk shows that strive to entertain, such as "Hjallis". Hjallis takes a rather authoritative interviewer role by interrupting his interviewee—in this case Tujunen—with his assumptions, which he readily presents as truths. However, he nevertheless ends this passage by saying "*I happen to know that it was your idea, ((laughs)) was it?*". In the beginning he does not hesitate to make claims of truth while his interviewee is still speaking, and he even says that he knows the story. Yet, in the end, by asking "was it?" (line 17), he still indicates that his assumptions are not necessarily reliable. I think that this is a clear device for dramatizing and making the talk more exciting and thus more entertaining for the audience, by grilling the interviewee, so to speak. This might even be exactly "Hjallis'" trademark in general.

Tujunen starts out answering Hallis' question calmly and professionally, with level intonation, but she clearly reacts to his accentuated interruptions by intensifying her own intonation and stressing words she wants to highlight. Tujunen also accelerates her speech rate and increases the volume of her talk in reaction to Hjallis' progressively emphasized and louder interruptions. However, it is noteworthy that between these gradually pronounced turns there is also continuous laughter, and as they produce those turns both parties are smiling at each other increasingly. The debate in this situation is clearly not conducted in a hostile spirit, but takes a rather humorous turn. Clearly, the parties react to one another's turns by precisely responding themselves still a bit louder and with still some more emphasis after the other has done the same, as well as by increasing their laughter and smiles. It is also notable how Hjallis reinforces his most prominent turn by shaking his finger and how immediately after this Tujunen does the same in her own turn. The parties therefore clearly build on each other's activities in this conversation, together producing this humorous passage.

> In her conclusions Saara reflects on her observations. She makes some important points here: for example, her analysis of this passage demonstrates how the participants interactively achieve humor and how both speakers orient to the presence of an audience (i.e. using resources of entertaining).

Reference

Sidnell, J. (2010). *Conversation analysis: An introduction*. Wiley-Blackwell.

13 Surveys

Chapter Outline

- Why Use Surveys?
- How to Create a Survey
- How to Administer a Survey
- How to Analyze Survey Data
- Advantages and Disadvantages of Surveys
- Summary
- Key Steps and Questions to Consider
- Activities
- Discussion Questions
- Key Terms
- Undergraduate Survey Paper

What Will I Learn About Surveys in This Chapter?

Most of us have taken a survey of some kind. Many of us, in fact, have more than likely taken a customer satisfaction survey. These surveys measure our level of satisfaction with an organization and its services. You may have been asked how satisfied you were with service at a fast-food restaurant, at a hotel, or with a recent purchase. These surveys used to be mailed to people's homes (some still are). Most surveys are now distributed online. A second kind of survey you may have taken is a questionnaire in one of your classes where you answered different questions about communicative, sociological, or psychological processes/behaviors. Students regularly fill out these kinds of surveys on college/university campuses.

Surveys have a long history in social scientific research, government, and economics. When William the Conqueror ruled England, he had a census collected (1085-1086), which was called the *Domesday Book* (Miller, 1983; Neuman, 2011). After this census, the gathering of population data became common government practice, which continues today in just about every nation. Researchers also began to collect survey data on how people lived. Henry Mayhew, for example, chronicled urban life in London from 1851-1864. DuBois (1899) detailed urban conditions among African Americans in his text, *Philadelphia Negro*. After Cattell (1890) proposed the idea of empirically measuring mental and emotional processes, surveys became a regular part of social scientific research. In Chapter 13 you will learn all about surveys.

DOI: 10.4324/9781003109129-16

Why Use Surveys?

A **survey** is a social scientific research instrument in which respondents are asked questions about their own or other individuals' attitudes, behaviors, beliefs, perceptions, and/or values. While many of these categories overlap, differences exist depending on how a researcher approaches a study. Figure 13.1 shows some basic examples of things you can focus on in a survey.

Figure 13.1 Some Things You Can Ask About in a Survey

1. Attitudes/Beliefs and Opinions—What type of job is the prime minister doing? Do you believe television news is fair and balanced?
2. Perceptions—To what extent does the media present things fairly?
3. Values—To what extent do you care for your family, even when you have to sacrifice what you want?
4. Behaviors—How many hours a week do you spend on Facebook?
5. Numerous other aspects of human life can be explored using surveys, such as: demographic characteristics (sex, age, and religious identification), expectations (do you plan on going to college in the future?), and knowledge (who is the prime minister of Canada?).

While surveys are useful for data collection, they are not always the most appropriate method. Surveys are most appropriate for use in the following situations: when you need new data and when people are best at providing the data about what you are studying.

First, use a survey to collect new data on some phenomenon. For example, you cannot use a survey if you are interested in studying the social identities of Spartan and Athenian soldiers during the Peloponnesian War. You are unable to collect surveys since the soldiers are long dead; the war took place between 431–404 BCE. Instead, you will need to look through historical documents and read the accounts of soldiers, look through newspaper articles, and the like. The fact that you can't access the population is important. If you can't access the population, you can't collect the data. So, ask yourself the following key questions: 1) are you able to collect the data and 2) do you need to collect the data using a survey?

A second reason to use a survey is because people are best at providing the data about what you are studying. One fundamental purpose of a survey is to measure an individual's own perceptions of their attitudes, behaviors, beliefs, perceptions, and/or values. If you are interested in studying public opinion on how New Zealand's Prime Minister and her government handled the COVID-19 lockdown, a survey may be appropriate. You could measure individuals' personal opinions on the government's decision and about the prime minister, Jacinda Ardern. Since taking office in 2017, numerous polls have evaluated the decisions made by the prime minister and her Labour Government. Such public opinion polls are a standard survey form.

Another standard survey form is a communication or psychological self-report, like the Personal Report of Communication Apprehension (McCroskey, 1982). Using this survey, a researcher can measure an individual's level of communication apprehension. When the respondent fills out the survey, they are reporting their personal perception of how much communication apprehension they have. If you think back to Chapter 5, some researchers criticize self-reports because respondents can over- or underestimate their attitudes, behaviors, beliefs, perceptions, and/or values (Fisher, 1993; Oetzel, 1998). To correct for an over-/underestimation, researchers encourage the use of other-report surveys (Croucher et al., 2019; Podsakoff & Organ, 1986). We will talk more about self- and other-report surveys later in this chapter. For now, just remember, self-report surveys give the subjects a chance to answer questions about themselves, which can provide in-depth information about phenomena.

Video cameras and clerks in stores can tell a lot about how "satisfied" we may be about our shopping experiences at different shopping locales. However, we as shoppers are the most qualified to judge our overall shopping satisfaction. This is why we are often asked to fill out customer service questionnaires/surveys. The same can be said about opinion polls during elections. News networks and companies like Gallup rely on surveys or polls to evaluate public opinion. Such polls are not perfect, which we will talk more about shortly.

How to Create a Survey

As discussed in Chapter 5 on Data, Chapter 6 on Evaluating Research, and Chapter 7 on Hypotheses and Research Questions, one of the purposes of research from a social scientific approach is to measure variables and test hypotheses and research questions. This is facilitated using well-designed surveys. Creating a survey for distribution to participants involves three macro-steps. The steps are detailed in Figure 13.2.

Figure 13.2 Steps in Survey Creation

Step 1. Theoretical

1. Choose a theoretical framework(s) that will guide the study.
2. From your theoretical framework(s), develop hypotheses or research questions that the survey will help you test.

Step 2. Structural

1. Create new survey questions and response categories or use preexisting survey instruments.
2. Choose a type of survey (mail, online, paper, etc.).
3. Be sure the survey is clearly laid out with easy-to-follow instructions.

Step 3. Logistical

1. Decide on how you want to collect and store the data.
2. Pilot-test the survey instrument.

Choose a Theoretical Framework and Develop Hypotheses/ Research Questions

The first step in creating a survey is to choose your theoretical framework(s) that will guide the study. Ask yourself, what are you studying? What phenomena are you interested in testing/

exploring with your survey? You will have a hard time coming up with any kind of survey instrument if you cannot answer these questions. Second, you should develop research questions(s) and/or hypothesis/hypotheses for your study. Survey research is **deductive research**. With this kind of research, you begin with a theory of interest and then propose hypotheses/research questions. Your hypotheses/research questions are statements of how variables are related to one another. Your survey is designed to measure the variables and, thus, test the hypotheses/research questions, which help you arrive at conclusions about the theory.

> Let's say we are interested in testing whether WeChat users get the same gratifications they seek from using WeChat. An extensive body of literature exists on gratifications sought and obtained (Boyd & Ellison, 2007; Chen, 2011; Gan & Li, 2018; Herzog, 1940; Katz et al., 1974; McQuail, 2005; Ruggiero, 2000). Research has shown, for example, that users of sites such as Facebook seek out friends and believe they get friends from these sites (Raacke & Bonds-Raacke, 2008). Users of WeChat in China, for example, tend to use it for technological, social, utilitarian, and hedonistic gratifications (Gan & Li, 2018). Hypotheses or research questions could be derived from previously written research to better understand WeChat and the gratifications sought and obtained. Once the hypotheses and/or research questions are generated, the next step is to either create an entirely new survey or to use a preexisting survey instrument.

Once you have decided on the focus of your study, you need to consider the following issues: 1) whether you want to create a new survey or use a preexisting one, 2) the type of survey you want to use, and 3) how to make sure your survey is easy to use. A big decision you need to make, one Stephen and his research team have grappled with in the past, is whether you use preexisting scales or if you create an entirely new scale to measure a particular phenomenon. There are pros and cons with both approaches. Researchers may find using a preexisting measure helpful because one does not have to generate a lot of questions. Creating a new instrument to measure a phenomenon involves quite a bit of statistical analysis, since you must demonstrate that the instrument is both statistically valid and reliable. If you want to create your own survey, you will need to conduct multiple pilot tests and run the questions through numerous statistical tests (exploratory and confirmatory factor analyses, for example). Such analyses are well beyond the scope of this text. Therefore, we recommend that you use preexisting scales whenever possible.[1] We recommend the use of preexisting scales with caution. One of the things Stephen and Dan have seen is students choosing random measures and deciding to use them for their research. Your theoretical framework(s) must guide your measure selection. Choose a measure or measures that help you address your hypotheses/research questions. For example, imagine collecting 100 surveys on communication apprehension when the real purpose of your study is to explore jealousy. You will have just collected 100 surveys and spent the time and energy to do this, and in the end your data will not help you achieve your goal to understand jealousy.

Survey Questions and Response Categories

However, for argument's sake, let's say you want to create your own survey instrument, or you have an assignment requiring you to create survey questions. Consider the following questions when you design your survey:

1. What kinds of questions and levels of questions should you include in a survey?
2. How do you make sure the questions you include are valid and reliable?
3. How can you avoid confusing questions?
4. To what extent should you consider the perspective of the participants when writing the questions?
5. Are you leaving anything out of the survey?

These are just a few of the many questions you need to ask when designing and/or choosing your survey questions. Multiple checklists and various suggestions are available to help you create surveys (Hocking et al., 2003; Neuman, 2011; Wrench et al., 2008). The following in Figure 13.3 are some recommendations to help you create a well-constructed survey.

Figure 13.3 Elements of Well-Constructed Survey Questions

1. Try to use multiple levels of questions.
2. Be cautious of the language you use in the survey.
3. Avoid double-barreled questions.
4. Avoid leading questions.
5. Avoid double negatives.
6. Avoid overlapping or unbalanced response categories in questions.
7. Be sure the survey is well organized.

Multiple Levels of Questions

Most surveys will include nominal, ordinal, and interval-level questions (think back to Chapter 5 on Data). Some surveys will include ratio-level and open-ended questions. Examples of nominal-level questions include demographic questions (e.g., sex, political affiliation, and educational level). You should include such questions when they are important to your topic of study. If political affiliation (like other variables) is not important to your subject, then you may not need to ask about it.

Ordinal-level questions are also often used in surveys. Such questions could, for example, ask people about their income level or educational level. If you decide to include these types of questions (and maybe nominal-level ones as well), you need to plan what kinds of statistical tests you will use to analyze the data. We will talk more about data analysis in the following chapters.

Interval-level are the most common type of questions you will find on surveys. Interval-level variables are typically Likert and semantic differential/bipolar adjective questions. Much social scientific research relies on interval-level questions to measure human behavior. Look back to Example 5.7 (Patient Self-Advocacy Scale [PSAS]) for an example of Likert-type questions that are typical for a communication survey.

Another kind of question you can include on your survey is an open-ended question. While most survey questions limit a respondent's choices (answers), open-ended questions allow respondents to answer any way they want. Here's an example of an open-ended question: "Describe the feelings you have about President Joe Biden." The question allows respondents to open up about their feelings with a variety of statements, words, drawings, or whatever they want. Open-ended questions can be helpful for researchers since they provide information you do not expect with Likert-type questions. You can analyze open-ended questions statistically using methods such as content analysis (which we talked about in Chapter 11). A combination of various question types can make any survey "better." Different levels of measurement (nominal, ordinal, interval, ratio, and open-ended) allow researchers to analyze data using varied methods and approach a phenomenon from a variety of angles.

> In a recent survey, Stephen and his research team included a variety of questions to investigate likelihood of people in the U.S. to wear masks and wash hands to combat the spread of COVID-19. Their survey included various demographic questions, such as: "What is your highest educational level?" Response options included: high school, two years of college/university, completed college/university, MA or equivalent, doctorate or equivalent. Ordinal level questions were also included. One example included, "How many people do you know who have contracted COVID-19?" Response options ranged from: zero, 1-2, 3-5, 6-10, 11-15, more than 15. An example of a Likert-type question was: "Based on this 5-point scale: (1 = strongly disagree to 5 = strongly agree), Wearing a mask in public protects me from contracting COVID-19." An example of an open-ended question is: "What is your religion? (please write in your religion. If you do not have one, please write that down)."

Survey Language

The language choices we make when writing survey questions can have a tremendous effect on how participants understand and answer questions. When writing survey questions or instructions, try to avoid jargon, slang, and abbreviations. **Jargon** is language specific to a particular group, profession, or trade. For example, communication, like all disciplines, has a lot of jargon. Let's say you are interested in how social media use differs between the U.S. and Nicaragua (Spencer et al., 2012). You might want to explore teledensity—or the number of media (Internet) connections per person—and its effects on media use. If you ask respondents about teledensity, many will not understand the question. "What is teledensity?" might be the first question people ask you, because this is not a common word for people to use in everyday conversation.

You should also avoid **slang**, or nonstandard vocabulary made up of informal words. Unlike jargon, slang does not have to be associated with a particular group. Slang varies based on an individual's language. Seemingly simple words have taken on new meanings with the growth of the Internet. "Friend" and "unfriend" take on entirely new meanings with Facebook users. When Stephen moved to Finland in 2011, he found many of the English words he used had different meanings to English-speaking Finns. He was in a meeting and said he went somewhere that was an armpit of a town. People did not understand him, because it is not common outside of the U.S., Canada, and maybe the UK to call a place an armpit. The word *armpit* is slang for an undesirable place. So, be cautious of using slang in surveys, as it can confuse respondents.

Abbreviations can cause problems with survey collection as well. If we were to create a survey asking students their thoughts on the viability of a new committee in the WCA to measure the effectiveness of offering more sessions at the biannual conference, would you understand what we are talking about? Chances are slim. The WCA is the World Communication Association. Every other year the conference has sessions (meeting times) where communication researchers share their research.

Double-Barreled Questions

A **double-barreled question** contains two or more questions. For example, if you are conducting an airline quality survey, you might ask: "Do you like the seating and meal options provided onboard?" Respondents may want to answer both yes *and* no to the question because they may like the meal options but not like the seating options. For example, the airline may have great meal options in their economy cabin but have really uncomfortable seats. The question is not meant to confuse the respondents, yet it is asking two separate things. A better way to ask about meal and seating options is to ask two separate questions: "Do you like the meal options on onboard?" and "Do you like the seating options onboard?"

Leading Questions

A second kind of question you should avoid in a survey is a leading question. A **leading question** directs respondents toward one answer over another. Avoid questions such as: "You agree with the prime minister's recent decision to close the borders during the COVID-19 pandemic, don't you?" This wording tells the respondent you assume the prime minister made a good decision and the respondents should too. When conducting a survey, you want respondents to believe all of their responses are equally valid; leading questions do not portray a sense of respecting respondents' opinions.

Double Negatives

A third kind of question to avoid is the double negative. Basic grammar rules tell us this is a poor sentence: "I have never played no musical instruments." In fact, grammatically and logically the sentence means one has played musical instruments. We should avoid double negatives in survey questions. An example of a double negative survey question is: "Do you agree politicians should not be required to have term limits?" The question is confusing. A good rule is to just keep the questions simple: "Politicians should be required to have term limits (agree or disagree)."

Overlapping/Unbalanced Categories

When respondents answer questions on a survey, their options need to be mutually exclusive, exhaustive, and balanced. **Mutually exclusive categories** means the response options do not overlap. Take, for example, a question about television viewing: "How many hours a day do you watch television?" with the response categories: 1-4, 4-8, 8-12, 12-16, 16-20, 20-24. The problem is that the categories overlap. Here's a better way to list the categories: 1-4, 5-9, 10-13, 14-17, 18-21, 22-24. Now, the hours do not overlap and are mutually exclusive.

Exhaustive categories mean everyone has a category to choose. In previous research, Stephen's research team regularly asked respondents about their marital status. Response options included: Single, Married, Divorced, Widowed, Partnered. Stephen's research team determined the options were exhaustive. The team added "Partnered" to the survey since in Finland (where the research team started) many individuals are legally and informally "Partnered." Everyone taking the survey should have had an option that suited them.

Balanced categories provide participants a balance of opinion options. A typical Likert-type question may have responses ranging from "strongly agree" to "strongly disagree" or "very unlikely" to "very likely". The continuum provides balanced categories. The two polar opposites provide a balance of opinions. If you provide only "strongly agree" and "agree," you are providing leading categories for your respondents. Semantic differentials often have adjectives pairs such as honest/dishonest, cheap/expensive, kind/mean, etc.

Organization of the Survey

The organization of a survey is of key importance. The structure of a survey, particularly the order in which you put your questions, is often based on researcher preference. However, you should follow some norms. When including interval or ratio-level questions, here are a few things you should think about. First, try to put all of the questions with the same type of responses (answers) together. For example, put all of the questions that range from *strongly agree* to *strongly disagree* together and all of the questions that range from *very unsatisfied* to *very satisfied* together. Clustering these kinds of questions together will generally make it easier for your respondents to answer questions with less confusion.

Second, most surveys tend to keep together the questions that focus on the same context. Many surveys will focus on multiple issues, and each issue might include more than one measure. You will commonly see all measures that focus on one issue clustered together (pages 1–2, for example) and then the measures that focus on another issue clustered together (pages 3–4, for example). This can help your participants remain in the same mindset while they answer questions on each separate issue.

Third, you need to consider where you place nominal-level questions; should they be at the start or the end of the survey? This really is a personal preference of the researcher. Stephen and Dan have both seen surveys with the demographic (nominal-level) questions at the end and at the beginning. The key is to keep the questions together, as you do not want to disrupt the rhythm of the respondents. Once respondents begin answering demographic or other nominal questions, it may seem odd to have more at a later stage. The same can be said about open-ended questions. Once respondents switch into an open-ended mindset, it can be difficult to get them back into a closed-ended mindset. Remember, the responses for open-ended questions can take up space on the survey. Thus, these kinds of questions are generally placed at the end of surveys.

Fourth, any sensitive questions should be placed at the end of the survey. Let's say you are doing a survey on musical festival attendance, and one of your variables you want to correlate is drug use. You may want to start by asking about music festival attendance using Likert-type items, then ask demographic questions, and finally ask about possible drug use. You do not want to ask about drug use first because the questions could embarrass, anger, or lead respondents to start answering in either socially desirable or dishonest ways.

Types of Surveys

We would like to describe two types of surveys. Each type has advantages and disadvantages. The first kind is a paper-based survey. **Paper-based surveys** are just what they sound like—the survey is printed on paper and provided to participants. The survey is usually given to participants in one of four ways: face-to-face, take-home, in the mail, or over the telephone. With face-to-face surveys, the respondents fill out the survey with the researcher present. Many of you may have participated in research where you take a paper survey for extra credit in a lab or classroom; this kind of research is a paper-based, face-to-face survey. If you are allowed to take the paper-based survey home and turn it in later, then you have a take-home survey. Sometimes researchers will mail surveys to potential respondents. Mailing surveys to respondents can help broaden the reach of a study. Typically, the researcher will include a self-addressed, stamped return envelope with the survey. The final delivery method for paper-based surveys is over the telephone. Researchers will call respondents and conduct surveys over the phone. Using this method, the researcher will ask the respondent the survey questions and then record the answers on the survey.

Web-based surveys are becoming the most popular kind of survey. **Web-based surveys** are presented and collected entirely online. As people increasingly use the Internet, it is no surprise that researchers have turned to the net as a way to collect data. Companies like Qualtrics, SurveyMonkey, and MTurk are an easy way to distribute surveys. Once the surveys are online, invitations are sent to people to fill out the surveys. A researcher can then export the collected data into a statistical software package and analyze the results. Figure 13.4 shows the advantages and disadvantages of paper and web-based surveys. Based on these advantages and disadvantages, you can choose whether paper or web-based surveys are the most appropriate for you.

Figure 13.4 Advantages and Disadvantages of Paper and Web-Based Surveys

Survey Issue	Face to Face	Take Home	Mail	Web-Based
Cost	Highest	High	Medium	Depends*
Delivery Speed	High	Medium	Slowest	Fastest
Possible Length of Survey	Longest	Same	Same	Shortest
Response Rate	Highest	High	Lowest	Medium
Ability to Ask				
Probing Questions	Yes	No	No	No
Open-Ended Questions	Yes	Limited	Limited	Limited
Sensitive Questions	Limited	Limited	Yes	Yes
Ability to Use Visual Aids	Yes	Limited	Limited	Yes
Social Desirability Bias	Highest	High	Lowest	Medium
Interviewer Bias	Highest	High	None	None

We put a * next to "Depends" under Web-Based cost. There are a couple of reasons for this. Web-based surveys have expanded significantly in the past five years. Researchers can distribute their own web-based survey, which is really cheap. In this case, you as the researcher put the survey online and send the link out yourself. However, researchers also can work with a firm like Qualtrics or others and have the firm distribute the link/survey for them. In this case, the company locates the participants. Such a data collection technique is much more expensive. However, in such a situation, the company will work with a researcher to set up specific population/sample parameters where you as the researcher determine exactly who you want taking your study. The more parameters you have, the more expensive the data collection. The more participants you want, the more expensive the data collection, because the company pays each participant a small amount of money to take your survey. The more questions you have, the more money it costs as well. Such datasets are increasingly common.

Clear Instructions

Have you ever tried putting together a complex piece of furniture (like Ikea), had a hard time programming electronics, or been confused by a school assignment? Clear instructions are a plus in all facets of life. We should also remember Murphy's Law: if something can go wrong, it probably will. Easy-to-follow instructions are important in order to facilitate smooth completion of a survey. Easy-to-follow instructions = more participants completing the survey.

   Stephen has been asked many clarifying questions by participants taking his surveys. Here's an example of survey instructions and questions participants have asked. "Please indicate in the space provided the degree to which each statement applies to you by marking whether you (1) strongly agree, (2) agree, (3) are undecided, (4) disagree, or (5) strongly disagree with each statement. There are no right or wrong answers." Participants have asked: do I use numbers, or should I use roman numerals? Can I use pen or pencil? If I write in an answer, can I erase it before I turn in the survey? The key is to preempt as many questions as possible and to make your survey easy to follow.

To prepare for such questions, Stephen and his team try to make sure participants know how to answer each set of questions. The consent document given to participants contains the following statement: "Please be sure to follow all instructions as closely as possible. Also, you may use pencil or pen to complete this survey. You may also change your answers for any question, as long as you do so before you turn in the survey." Stephen's team is sure more things still need to be added to the statement; those additions will come in time.

Logistical Concerns

Once the survey is written, you need to think about two logistical concerns. First, you need to think about how you are going to collect and store the data, and second you need to think about pilot-testing the survey. The decision about collecting and storing the data is likely guided by the type of survey you are using. If you are web-based, the survey data will be collected and stored online. If you are paper-based, you need to think about how you will collect and where you will store the surveys. We will talk more about collection in a moment. How long you must store survey data depends on your college/university; some Institutional Review Boards (IRBs)/Human Subject Review Boards (HSRBs) require you store data for two to five years.

   Pilot testing is always a good idea. A pilot test allows you to check your survey instructions and questions with a representative sample population. Pilot testing is a way to test how well your survey will function among your real sample. We will not discuss here how many participants are needed for a pilot, since that is determined by how many questions you have. (A power analysis can help you determine this. Look online for power analyses if you are interested in this.) For now, just know that we strongly encourage you to pilot test any survey instrument.

How to Administer a Survey

The administration/data collection stage is when you are ready to go out into the field and collect your data. This can be a very exciting process. We identify three key things you must consider: 1) who are the participants? 2) how are you collecting the data? 3) is your survey a one-shot or a longitudinal design? Whenever you design a new survey or use a preexisting survey, a question that should guide you is: To what population do you intend to generalize? Once you have determined your intended population, you need to decide on your sample and how you will locate that sample (think back to Chapters 5–7). Nordin and Broeckelman-Post (2020) were interested in demographic differences in student mindset in introductory communication courses. College students were the population for his study. The sample for the study was 1,524 university students recruited from communication courses at a large mid-Atlantic university in the United States.

For Nordin and Broeckelman-Post (2020), collecting data was relatively easy since the sample was easily accessible: university students. University students are easy to find and are generally used to filling out surveys. The researchers had students fill out a survey as a homework assignment. If your sample is harder to reach, finding the sample population and collecting the survey may not be easy. In Croucher et al. (2012), the researchers' population was average citizens in India (n = 657), Ireland (n = 311), Thailand (n = 232), and the U.S. (n = 592). The total sample (n = 1,792) was located via various social networks, religious organizations, and universities/colleges.

For Croucher et al. (2012), the survey was what we call a one-shot survey, or a **cross-sectional** design. This means that the team collected the surveys at one point in time. The results of the survey reveal what the respondents feel about the phenomena at that given moment when they completed the surveys. While this tells us a lot about the respondents and their feelings, it does not tell us anything about how their feelings may change over time. If other researchers wanted to measure how perceptions, traits, or behaviors change over time, they would need to conduct a **longitudinal design**. In this type of surveying, respondents are given the same questions over a period of time to track changes in perception, traits, or behaviors. If changes occur, researchers attribute those changes to some variable within the study. Nordin and Broeckelman-Post (2020) conducted such a study. All in all, how you administer a survey depends largely on the population to which you are generalizing.

How to Analyze Survey Data

The data-analysis stage follows survey administration. Analyzing survey data is a four-part process: 1) check the surveys for errors, 2) enter the data, 3) double-check what you entered, and 4) analyze the data. The first thing you should do after you get your data collected is go through it and see if you have any errors. Errors can be lots of things. You might have returned paper-based surveys with lots of unanswered questions. What you do depends on the number of unanswered questions. For example, you have 100 survey questions and two unanswered questions. Statistical solutions are available to "fix" the survey. Talk with your instructor about how you can replace missing values with means and the ethics of such a decision. Another issue you may encounter is when a participant answers every question with the same value. Sometimes you will get people who do not really care about your research and simply circle the same answers for every question. In these cases, you need to decide whether you keep or discard their survey data. Stephen often discards these surveys and puts a note in his final manuscript about how: "'X' many surveys were discarded because they were incomplete or improperly completed."

Second, you need to enter your data. Entering data can be time consuming, especially if you use paper-based surveys. You need to type every answer into some kind of computer program. If you use a web-based survey, a lot of time can be saved because you can export/import the data into a computer program for data analysis. Web-based programs like Survey Monkey allow you to distribute a survey and then import the data into excel or SPSS (Statistical Package for Social Sciences), one of the most used statistics programs. Other statistical software programs include SAS, XLSTAT, R, or MATLAB. Check with your instructor on which statistical programs are available on your campus and which one the instructor prefers.

No matter what program you use to enter your data (particularly if you enter data by hand from paper-based surveys), you must make sure you double-check the numbers. As you go through your surveys, you are likely to make mistakes. Over time, you will enter a lot of data. In 2013, Stephen's research team hand-entered 1,200 surveys. Each survey had 115 questions for a total of 138,000 responses. The team was bound to enter a few of wrong numbers (e.g., a 3 instead of a 2 for a question, a 4 instead of a 5). Go through and double-check your data! In 2020, the research team worked mainly with Qualtrics, so the team did not have to hand-enter data. However, the team still went through and made sure people didn't put the same answer for every question. For example, some participants put "3" for every answer. When checking data, it's essential to flag such participants and not to include them in your analysis.

Finally, you need to analyze the data. Chapter 14 on Descriptive Statistics and Chapter 15 on Inferential Statistics outline ways in which you can analyze quantitative survey questions. Chapter 11 on Content Analysis offers ways you can analyze open-ended survey questions. The type of analysis you use depends on the type of questions and variables you have on the survey.

Advantages and Disadvantages of Surveys

Survey research has numerous advantages and some limitations. The seven main advantages to survey research are: 1) cost, 2) speed, 3) quantity of participants, 4) ability to distribute in a variety of places and methods, 5) ability to ask a lot of standardized questions, 6) standardization of questions can lead to more reliable results, and 7) surveys can lead to more generalizable results. Surveys provide researchers a relatively cheap and fast way to garner responses from a lot of participants in a variety of places using lots of means (Neuman, 2011). With surveys, unlike other methods, researchers are able to ask standardized questions. Standardized questions are the same for each participant, without deviation. Asking such questions provides reliable results, as a researcher can argue that each participant was asked the same *exact* questions. While many qualitative methods may have strict interview or focus groups scripts, deviations from the script can occur, which makes it impossible to state that *all* participants are asked the exact same questions. Standardization is one of the reasons surveys lead to generalizable statistical findings.

Survey research has four main limitations: 1) surveys do not focus on context, 2) a survey is an inflexible instrument, 3) surveys generally need a large number of participants to be reliable, and 4) self-report surveys may trigger a social desirability bias. The first disadvantage of survey research is that surveys do not focus on context. Researchers who use surveys generally are not researching context. By nature, a method of research emphasizing standardization is not going to also focus on context. Thus, contextual cues and issues of subjective nature will be lost. Second, a survey is an inflexible instrument/document. Part of the standardization aspect of surveys is that, aside from open-ended questions, surveys do not leave room for free expression. Participants are asked to circle or mark how they feel about various things/issues. There is *very* little room for open expression of feelings, aside from the numbers provided on most surveys. Third, surveys, unlike qualitative research, need a large number of participants to be statistically reliable. This requirement can be difficult for many researchers, particularly those taking a class like yours where you have limited time and resources. Fourth, some participants may answer questions in ways to make themselves look better; this is considered the social desirability effect (Fisher, 1993). If a researcher is interested in how often people express jealousy, it can be difficult to get honest answers from some participants, because jealousy is perceived as a negative behavior. People do not want to be seen negatively, so they are more likely not to answer questions honestly and instead to portray themselves positively. Ultimately, the researcher must weigh the advantages and disadvantages of surveys, along with their needs, when determining whether surveys are the right method for them.

Summary

This chapter was a how-to guide to surveys. Surveys are conducted by social scientific researchers but can also be conducted by interpretive and critical/cultural researchers, depending on the focus of the questions/survey. Hopefully, after reading the chapter and the accompanying student paper, you feel comfortable enough to go out there and conduct your own survey. Next is Chapter 14. with a how-to guide to descriptive statistics.

Key Steps and Questions to Consider

1. A survey is a social scientific research method in which respondents are asked questions about their own or other individuals' attitudes, behaviors, beliefs, perceptions, and/or values.
2. Surveys have a storied history/tradition. The first "surveys" date back to the 11th century.
3. Two reasons to use surveys are because you want or need to collect new data and because the people you are surveying are best at providing/answering the questions you are asking.
4. Be sure your survey is based on some theoretical framework.
5. Survey research is deductive research.
6. Avoid jargon and slang in survey questions.
7. Avoid double-barreled and leading questions on surveys, as well as double negatives.
8. Try to have mutually exclusive, exhaustive, and balanced response categories for survey answer option.
9. Try your best to have an organized survey. If the survey is not easy to follow, people will get confused and not do the survey or will do it incorrectly. The same is true for easy-to-understand instructions. Make the instructions as easy to understand as possible!
10. There are two main kinds of surveys: paper or web-based. Paper-based surveys are on paper and are given to participants. The survey is given to participants in one of four ways: face-to-face, take-home, in the mail, or over the telephone. Web-based surveys are presented and collected entirely online.
11. When you administer the survey, consider two things: 1) who are the participants, and 2) how are you collecting the data?
12. Analyzing survey data has four parts: 1) check the surveys for errors, 2) enter the data, 3) double-check what you entered, and 4) analyze the data.
13. Seven advantages to survey research: 1) cost, 2) speed, 3) quantity of participants, 4) ability to distribute in a variety of places and methods, 5) ability to ask a lot of

standardized questions, 6) standardization of questions can lead to more reliable results, and 7) surveys can lead to more generalizable results.

14. Four limitations to survey research: 1) surveys do not focus on context, 2) a survey is an inflexible instrument, 3) surveys generally need a large number of participants to be reliable, and 4) there is a possible social desirability bias with self-report surveys.

Activities

1. Team Task 1: Find the Flaws: Your instructor will divide the class into teams and assign an online survey to each team. The *Washington Post* has a site of surveys (www.washingtonpost.com/politics/polling) useful for the task. Each team is tasked with finding as many flaws as possible in their assigned survey. The flaws must meet the standards established in this chapter.

2. Team Task 2: Build a Survey. (Each team will need access to a computer.) Each team will develop a brief survey (20-25 questions) on a communication research question of their choice. The questions will be in a variety of formats (e.g., Likert scale, yes/no, open-ended). Each team will be assigned a different online survey instrument (e.g., SurveyMonkey, KwikSurveys, Zoomerang, ESurveysPro, SurveyPlanet) and then build their survey. Teams will keep detailed notes on satisfaction/frustration levels in using the site to create their survey. Teams will share both their completed surveys and their detailed survey-construction notes.

Discussion Questions

1. Think back on your personal experience with starting a survey but not completing the task. What about the survey made you quit? The length of the survey? The type of questions asked on the survey? The format of the survey? Share and compare your experience with others. Use the information to help guide construction of your own research surveys!

2. Think about your own communication research interests. Will a survey be an effective method for collecting data to answer your research questions? What limitations might you face? Share your thoughts with your classmates. Did they have similar/different limitations? Would those limitations also affect your study?

Key Terms

Balanced Categories	Jargon	Paper-Based Survey
Cross-Sectional Design	Leading Question	Pilot Testing
Deductive Research	Longitudinal Design	Slang
Double-Barreled Question	Mutually Exclusive	Survey
Exhaustive Categories	Categories	Web-Based Survey

References

Boyd, D. M., & Ellison, N. B. (2007). Social network sites: Definition, history, and scholarship. *Journal of Computer-Mediated Communication, 13*, 210-230. https://doi.org/10.1111/j.1083-6101.2007.00393.x

Cattell, J. M. (1890). Mental tests and measurements. *Mind, 15*, 373-381.

Chen, G. M. (2011). Tweet this: A uses and gratifications perspective on how active Twitter use gratifies a need to connect with others. *Computers in Human Behavior, 27*, 755-762. https://doi.org/10.1016/j.chb.2010.10.023

Croucher, S. M., Homsey, D., Guarino, L., Bohlin, B., Trumpetto, J., Izzo, A., Huy, A., & Sykes, T. (2012). Jealousy in four nations: A cross-cultural analysis. *Communication Research Reports, 29*, 353-360.

Croucher, S. M., Nshom, E., Zeng, C., & Rahmani, D. (2019). Social desirability among prejudice scales: An integrated threat theory analysis. *Journal of Intercultural Communication, 50*.

DuBois, W. E. B. (1899). *The Philadelphia Negro*. Benjamin Bloom.

Field, A. (2009). *Discovering statistics using SPSS* (3rd ed.). Sage.

Fisher, R. J. (1993). Social desirability bias and the validity of indirect questioning. *Journal of Consumer Research, 20*, 303-315. https://doi.org/10.1086/209351

Gan, C., & Li, H. (2018). Understanding the effects of gratifications on the continuance intention to use WeChat in China: A perspective on uses and gratifications. *Computers in Human Behavior, 78*, 306-315. https://doi.org/10.1016/j.chb.2017.10.003

Herzog, H. (1940). Professor quiz: A gratification study. In P. F. Lazarfel (Ed.), *Radio and the printed page* (pp. 64-93). Duell, Sloan, and Pearce.

Hocking, J. E., Stacks, D. W., & McDermott, S. T. (2003). *Communication research* (3rd ed.). Allyn & Bacon.

Katz, E., Blumler, J. G., & Gurevitch, M. (1974). Uses and gratifications research. *The Public Opinion Quarterly, 37*, 509-523. https://psycnet.apa.org/doi/10.1086/268109

Levine, T. R., Bresnahan, M. J., Park, H. S., Knight Lapinski, M., Lee, T. S., & Lee, D. W. (2003). The (in)validity of self-construal scales revisited. *Human Communication Research, 29*, 291-308.

McCroskey, J. C. (1982). *An introduction to rhetorical communication* (4th ed.). Prentice Hall.

McQuail, D. (2005). McQuail's mass communication theory (5th ed.). Sage.

Miller, W. L. (1983). *The survey method in the social and political sciences: Achievements, failures, and prospects*. Frances Pinter.

Neuman, W. L. (2011). *Social research methods: Qualitative and quantitative approaches* (7th ed.). Allyn & Bacon.

Nordin, K., & Broeckelman-Post, M. A. (2020). Surviving or thriving? Demographic differences in mindset across the introductory communication course. *Communication Education, 69*(1), 85-104. https://doi.org/10.1080/03634523.2019.1679379

Oetzel, J. G. (1998). The effects of self-construals and ethnicity on self-reported conflict styles. *Communication Reports, 11*, 133-144. https://psycnet.apa.org/doi/10.1080/08934219809367695

Pedhazur, E. J. (1997). *Multiple regression in behavioral research: Explanation and prediction* (3rd ed.). Wadsworth.

Podsakoff, P. M., & Organ, D. W. (1986). Self-reports in organizational research: Problems and prospects. *Journal of Management, 12*, 531-544. https://doi.org/10.1177%2F014920638601200408

Raacke, J., & Bonds-Raacke, J. (2008). MySpace and Facebook: Applying the uses and gratifications theory to exploring friend-networking sites. *CyberPsychology & Behavior, 11*, 169-174. https://doi.org/10.1089/cpb.2007.0056

Ruggiero, T. E. (2000). Uses and gratifications theory in the 21st century. *Mass Communication & Society, 3*, 3-37. https://doi.org/10.1207/S15327825MCS0301_02

Spencer, A. T., Croucher, S. M., & Hoelscher, C. S. (2012). Uses and gratifications meets the Internet: A cross-cultural comparison of U.S. and Nicaraguan new media usage. *Human Communication, 15*, 228-239.

Wrench, J. S., Thomas-Maddox, C., Richmond, V. P., & McCroskey, J. C. (2008). *Quantitative research methods for communication: A hands-on approach*. Oxford University Press.

Undergraduate Student Paper

Social and Gender Theory in the Cinema

Michael J. Caiola

For my paper, I decided to study the relationship between social activities and gender roles. I found little research on this topic and thought it would be interesting to dwell more into this topic. This topic is vast so I decided to boil the question into one concise problem.

Do "female" students have a better and more interactive social life?

> The opening to the paper may create a few confusions for the reader. First, the title mentions cinema, yet the introduction talks about social activities, not cinema. Second, the title and introduction refer to gender, yet the research question uses the term *female*. *Female* identifies a person's sex, not one's gender. Ask your instructor to discuss the differences between sex and gender. The two terms are routinely conflated in survey research. Finally, a reader may be confused why *female* is in quotation marks in the research question. Stephen and Dan are not really sure why the student chose to place the word in quotation marks. Remember, your goal is clarity for your readers.

Method

I used the survey method to collect data for this project. I decided to collect from just students in college as they seemed the most likely to be in social situations. With the vast amount of people at college and the college lifestyle, social interactions are plentiful. This limited my distribution to a non-random sample. I also did not want just my friends and people I associate with to give me my data so I decided to make an online survey.

> The student clearly identifies the sample population as nonrandom but could provide more clarity by discussing if she is going to include all college students or is limited to a specific group of college students (e.g., traditional, nontraditional, first-year, seniors). The student could also identify which online survey website was used. Not all online survey websites are created equal (as you hopefully discovered from the Team Task 2: Build a Survey activity).

Using this online survey and Facebook, I was able to limit my pool to just students at my college (on the college Facebook network). Using this network, I began to distribute this online survey to students and get the responses organized in a spreadsheet form. In addition, the online form was anonymous and there was no way to obtain any information on the identity of the participant. This allowed the participant to keep his/her identity safe while answering the questions truthfully. This fact is important, as I did not want male students to embellish how masculine they are or for females to embellish how feminine they are.

The survey itself consisted of nine questions. Four questions were about movie choices, four were about social interactions, and one question asked what gender the participant associates. The gender question allows us to group the data into two sections: male and female. The movie questions rank the preference of the movie genres thriller and chick-flick on a Likert 10-point scale. First, we asked the participant to rank preferences of thrillers, then preference of chick-flicks and then which one was enjoyed the most. In addition, I asked an interval question to see how many movies the participant saw in the last year. I figured a low score on this question might not make them acceptable for this survey. We then asked four ratio questions about the participants' social life. The first asked the participant to estimate how many friends were at the college. The next two asked how many friends the participant normally talks to each week and how many did he actually talk to the previous week. Then we asked one more question, how many friends the participant talked to earlier today. This last questions, allowed us to decide if the data we were getting was accurate. If it was too large of a number, we felt the data was corrupt and omitted it from our research.

> Any confusion between wording in the title and the introduction starts to clear up as more details are provided about the organization of the survey. A paper title and introduction should, however, provide a reader with a strong understanding of the content of the paper. How could the student have rewritten the title and introduction to avoid any confusion?
>
> The student repeats the sex/gender conflation. A gender question will not necessarily provide sufficient data for sorting into male and female.
>
> The student does an excellent job of identifying the justification for the different types of questions (Likert, interval, ratio). Concluding with a check for data corruption is a strong choice.

Theory

The theory I studied was actually a combination of two theories. The first theory was social theory. Social theory is a large and vast theory that incorporates anything that has to do with or interprets social phenomena. Usually this is shown by networking charts or some sort of graph theory. We took a more liberal approach and combined it with Gender Role Theory. Gender Role Theory focuses on how different sexes represent themselves in the real world. According the World Health Organization, "'sex' refers to the biological and physiological characteristics that define men and women. [While] 'Gender' refers to the socially constructed roles, behaviors, activities, and attributes that a given society considers appropriate for men and women" (WHO, 2011).

> The student provides a strong description here of the distinction between gender and sex. An overview of this distinction in the introduction may have helped clear points of confusion earlier in the paper.
>
> The theory explanation is a little thin and could use more development to see better how the research question is being addressed by the theories.

Using this, we decided to select one or two attributes that can distinguish someone as masculine or feminine or for lack of better words: male or female. To do this we chose two different movie genres: thrillers and chick-flicks. The thriller genre signifies a more masculine choice as it usually utilizes action, suspense and male-lead getting a pretty girl. The chick-flick genre signifies a more feminine choice as this genre usually involves attractive young men being the object of affection. In addition, chick-flicks usually allow an outlet for emotion. This could be done through crying, sadness, happiness, or even joy. This study does not cover individual actions but instead groups these emotions all under chick-flicks.

> The study could be strengthened by using established definitions for thriller and chick-flick (supported, of course, with source citations).

For the purposes of this study, we shall define a chick-flick to be any movie that fits the description above. That movie has a main demographic of women, allows for an outlet for emotion, features attractive men, or is a romantic movie. Keep in mind several movies overlap genres and themes but thrillers and chick-flicks seem to be on the opposite sides of the scale. Originally, we were going to use action movies, but there has been a trend in the last decade to make action movies have a steady romantic B-plot. Although these plots are not always well developed, we decided that thriller we satisfy the same requirements with less hassle.

> Review the section earlier in the chapter on mutually exclusive categories. Is the student going to run into data-collection issues when the movie genres may overlap?

Data

After sifting through our data and picking out the participants that corrupted data or filled out the form incorrectly. This left us with 19 participants—11 males and nine females. The data can be seen in Table 1. Looking at the data we could see that, on average, men chose thrillers over chick-flicks, while females chose chick-flicks over thrillers. This is good and means we were correct with our first assumptions and the questions are modeled correctly. To be more formal we ran a one-sample test (Table 2) on the entire sample—nothing jumped up as significant so we continued onto the main data.

> The Table 1 raw data is normally not expected to be included in the write-up of a study. However, the instructor may have required inclusion as part of the assignment.

However, this does not tell us anything about the connection between male and female genre choices and social interactions. First, we did an ANOVA to see if we have correlation between thriller preferences, Chick-Flick preferences, and the comparison preference with total amount of friends (See Table 3). As the table shows, there is no significant correlation between them. If Sig. < .05 then we would have a significant correlation. Nevertheless, that does not mean we do not have a result, in fact using our data we can say there is definitely no correlation between gender roles and total amount of friends.

As mentioned above we want to know the role of gender on a greater and more interactive social life. If we take the total number of friends to satisfy how great a social life is, we still need to look into interactive social life. We looked at our data in an ANOVA again but this time over friends talked to during a normal week (See Figure 4). This data seems even more random, getting nowhere near .005. So once again, we can conclude, that gender roles have no correlation with the amount of friends one interacts with on a regular basis.

Although two null hypotheses were not the main intention of this paper, all is not lost. With a sample of only 19 people, we cannot really say if we fully represented the population. With more data, there is a chance that we could have a correlation. In fact, playing with some of our data we see that there seems to be a significant correlation between those who are more feminine and to the amount of people one talks to in a single day (See Figure 5). We believe that this is purely a coincidence although it is statically significant.

The student ran a number of different statistical tests and produced some interesting results. However, normally the details about the planned statistical packages are explained and justified in the method section of the paper showing that the study has been carefully planned.

Our next step would be to collect more data and from a bigger population. Then we could recalculate these statistical tests and see if we have additional correlations and if our only significant correlation still holds. However, optimally we should shoot for more than 19 participants in a sample, so that we know our results hold some merit. In addition, we could look into the emotions a movie evokes and add additional gender role questions.

In conclusion, we tried to find a correlation between gender roles and social interactions. We defined gender roles simply by movie choice and we defined social interaction with amount of people talked to. To improve upon this we could get more data and more detailed questioning. Our results we found this time showed no significant correlation but we believe they may be one with more data points.

Table 13.1

Gender	Past Year	Thriller	Chick-Flicks	Between	Estimate	Normally in a week	Previous Week	Today
Male	10	8	6	3	40	30	30	10
Male	5	9	6	2	205	60	65	23
Male	5	10	10	3	30	15	10	8
Male	10	1	2	5	40	15	20	9
Male	10	8	4	2	80	40	30	10
Female	10	1	8	10	15	5	4	6
Female	10	7	10	5	50	15	20	8
Female	5	4	8	7	25	12	25	8
Male	5	8	3	2	30	5	7	3
Female	5	1	8	10	26	15	20	8
Female	5	6	5	5	8	7	6	3
Female	5	4	8	8	6	10	16	12

(Continued)

Table 13.1 (Continued)

Gender	Past Year	Thriller	Chick-Flicks	Between	Estimate	Normally in a week	Previous Week	Today
Female	5	6	6	5	0	5	7	3
Male	10	7	5	4	50	25	25	10
Male	10	6	6	5	100	40	50	20
Male	10	7	7	4	57	23	9	14
Female	10	7	4	4	40	20	15	15
Male	10	8	7	3	30	20	30	15
Male	10	8	2	2	15	5	20	1

Table 13.2 One Sample Test

					95% Confidence Interval of the Difference	
			Test Value = 0			
	t	df	Sig. (2-tailed)	Mean Difference	Lower	Upper
Thriller	9.835	18	.000	6.10526	4.8011	7.4094
Chick	11.141	18	.000	6.05263	4.9112	7.1940
Compared	8.182	18	.000	4.68421	3.4814	5.8871
Friends	4.214	18	.001	44.57895	22.3557	66.8022
Normal Week	5.751	18	.000	19.31579	12.2594	26.3722
Last Week	6.083	18	.000	21.52632	14.0917	28.9609
Today	7.396	18	.000	9.78947	7.0087	12.5703

Table 13.3 ANOVA

		Sum of Squares	df	Mean Square	F	Sig.
Thriller	Between Groups	96.000	8	12.000		
	Within Groups	55.833	6	9.306		
	Total	131.789	18			
Chick	Between Groups	37.781	12	3.148	.299	.964
	Within Groups	63.167	6	10.528		
	Total	100.947	18			
Compared	Between Groups	76.939	12	6.412	1.094	.483
	Within Groups	35.167	6	5.861		
	Total	112.105	18			

Table 13.4 ANOVA

		Sum of Squares	df	Mean Square	F	Sig.
Thriller	Between Groups	35.789	10	3.579	.298	.961
	Within Groups	96.000	8	12.000		
	Total	131.789	18			
Chick	Between Groups	28.697	10	2.870	.318	.953
	Within Groups	72.250	8	9.031		
	Total	100.947	18			
Compared	Between Groups	37.605	10	3.761	.404	.910
	Within Groups	74.500	8	9.313		
	Total	112.105	18			

Table 13.5 ANOVA

		Sum of Squares	df	Mean Square	F	Sig.
Thriller	Between Groups	82.956	10	8.296	1.359	.339
	Within Groups	48.833	8	6.104		
	Total	131.789	18			
Chick	Between Groups	85.781	10	8.578	4.525	.021
	Within Groups	15.167	8	1.896		
	Total	100.947	18			
Compared	Between Groups	76.855	10	7.686	1.744	.221
	Within Groups	35.250	8	4.406		
	Total	112.105	18			

Note

1. Instructors will sometimes encourage students to create their own scales and use them for assignments. Such assignments are perfectly acceptable as these assignments push students to develop questions and explore phenomena. However, such measures are not statistically valid and/or reliable unless rigorously tested. For more information on statistical tests like factor analyses and on how to statistically test the validity and reliability of surveys, see: (Field, 2009; Levine et al., 2003; Pedhazur, 1997; Podsakoff & Organ, 1986).

Reference

World Health Organization (WHO). 2011. www.who.int/gender/whatisgender/en/index.html

14 Descriptive Statistics

Chapter Outline

- Representations of Data
- Measures of Central Tendency
- Variability
- Distribution Shapes
- Summary
- Key Steps and Things to Consider
- Activities
- Discussion Questions
- Key Terms
- Undergraduate Descriptive Statistics Paper

What Will I Learn About Descriptive Statistics?

Stephen is not a baseball fan, but one thing that interests him about baseball is the statistics. Baseball is filled with so many acronyms to describe a variety of statistics about the game: BA (batting average), EQA (equivalent average), FC (fielder's choice), LOB (left on base), RISP (runner in scoring position), SB (Stolen base), BS (blown save), GF (games finished), HRA (home runs allowed), TC (total chances), VORP (value over replacement player), and GB (games behind), to name a few. Two of the most known statistics are ERA (earned run average) and RBI (run batted in). Each are descriptive statistics outlining the effectiveness/ability of a pitcher, batter, or runner.

ERA represents the mean (average) of earned runs given up by a pitcher per nine innings, which is the normal time of a baseball game. The statistic is calculated by dividing the number of earned runs by the number of innings pitched and then multiplying by nine. Historically, Ed Walsh, who played from 1904-1917, had the best ERA in history of 1.82, meaning 1.82 earned runs allowed per nine innings. Of active players in 2021, Clayton Kershaw, who plays for the LA Dodgers (2008-), has an ERA of 2.43.

RBI is a descriptive statistic representing the number of times a batter makes a play that allows a run to be score. Essentially, each time a batter hits the ball and any player scores, the result goes into their RBI. Hank Aaron is the all-time career leader in RBI with 2,297. Of active players in 2021, Albert Pujols, who plays for the Los Angeles Angels, is currently the all-time leader in RBIs among active players with 2,100.

DOI: 10.4324/9781003109129-17

Both the ERA and RBI statistic and many others tell baseball fans a lot about the game and their favorite players. A lower ERA means the pitcher is doing a better job, while a higher RBI describes a more successful batter. In Chapter 14 you will learn about descriptive statistics. Before we move on, you should have a definition of statistics and descriptive statistics. **Statistics** is a way of organizing, describing, and making inferences from data. Statistical methods are used in the natural, physical, and social sciences (communication). **Descriptive statistics** show how sample data appear in numerical and visual terms. In this chapter, we talk more about the language of statistical methods and how to apply these methods.

Representations of Data

We cannot recall how many students have asked us for tips on how better to understand quantitative research. We both admit quantitative methods, like other methods, may not be the easiest method to grasp, but a step-by-step approach can simplify the process. Stephen and Dan recommend that the first step when doing quantitative research is to find some way to look at your data in picture form. Representations of data can be very helpful in showing us what we have to work with and what we don't. Various kinds of tables, charts, graphs, and other representations show data in a nonnumeric form. The choice of form comes down to the type of data or variables in your study.

If you are working with nominal and/or ordinal data, pie and/or bar charts are the most appropriate choices to represent your data. A **pie chart** is a circle divided into proportional parts representing statistical data. Each part of the circle represents a specific category. You may have seen, for example, pie charts in newspapers or magazines representing "male" and "female." Figure 14.1 is based on a sample of individuals who completed the Intergroup Anxiety Scale (Stephan & Stephan, 1985) (*n* = 1481). The pie chart visually represents the difference in number between men and women in the sample. A quick glance at the pie chart reveals that the sample has slightly more females than males. The pie chart shows how visualization can be helpful when you begin your data analysis by showing what is going on with your data. While pie charts are

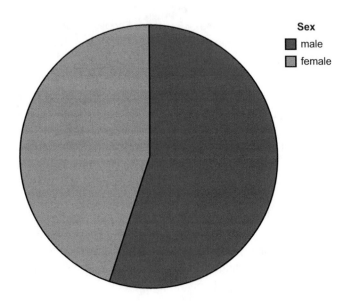

Figure 14.1

a good first step, they are rarely used in research papers and articles since they do not offer sophisticated insight about data distribution.

A more advanced option is the bar chart. A **bar chart** displays the category (variable) on the horizontal axis of the chart and the numeric value of the variable on the vertical axis. Therefore, in the case of males and females in the same organizational dissent study, a bar chart looks like Figure 14.2.

In this case, the horizontal axis (*x*-axis or abscissa) defines the variables, while the vertical axis (*y*-axis or ordinate) lists the mean of the variables. Bar charts can be taken a step further. With a bar chart, you can compare multiple groups on various categories/variables. One of the variables of interest in anxiety research is educational level. With a bar chart, you show the relationship between sex and educational level (Figure 14.3). A quick glance at the table shows males with only high-school education with higher levels of intergroup anxiety than other groups.

If you are working with interval and/or ratio data, a histogram is the most common visual representation for your data. However, you will rarely see a graph/representation reported in research papers or journals. Just like pie charts and bar charts, histograms are most often used to help researchers understand their data during preliminary analysis.

A **histogram** is similar to a bar chart. However, in this case, continuous data is represented on the *x*-axis, unlike nominal or ordinal data with a bar chart. A second difference you will notice with a histogram is how the bars are generally connected on a histogram (unless there is a gap in values), while the bars are never connected on a bar chart. The example in Figure 14.4 is taken from a study on attitudes toward health and COVID-19. Look back to Chapter 5 and example 5.7. The survey from Brashers et al. (1999) measures individuals' patient self-advocacy. One aspect of this scale is an individual's tendency to be an assertive patient in health-care interactions. The values in the following histogram represent the mean scores of 337 individuals.

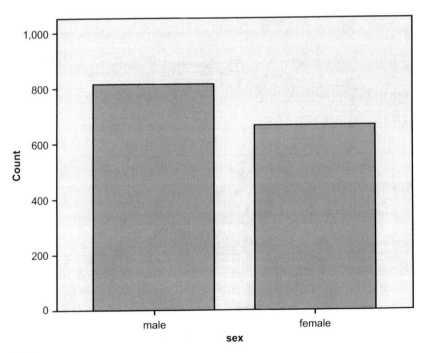

Figure 14.2

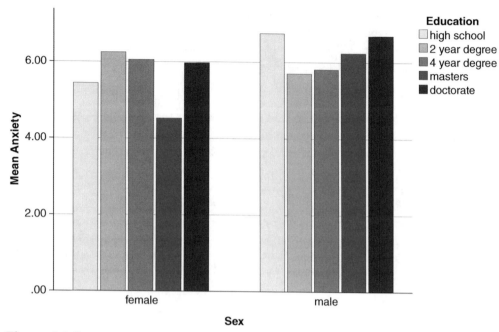

Figure 14.3

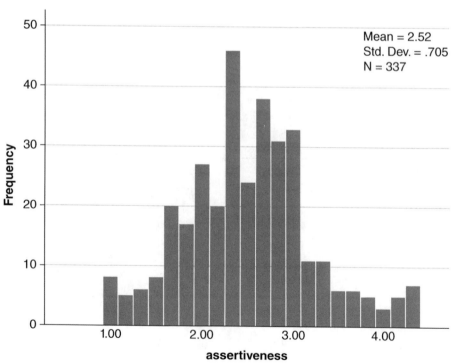

Figure 14.4

Statistical programs such as SPSS and SAS make the creation of visual representations fairly simple. Once you have data entered into one of the programs, a visual representation is just a few clicks away. However, just because we can create visuals does not mean we need to make them for everything. A key question to consider regarding visual representations is: do I need it? If you can describe the data easily with a visual, then make one; if not, then don't.

What kind of visual representation could you use to explain ERAs or RBIs? You could use a pie chart to show which teams reach different statistical thresholds. Such a chart would show any trends among different teams. A histogram could track the mean RBI in the league over time to show any potential trends. The key is that you can visually represent any statistical measure.

Measures of Central Tendency

Measures of central tendency reduce data down to a single descriptive statistic. Various measures of central tendency are available, and each differs in how it defines typical or average.

The mode is the most basic and most frequently occurring measure of central tendency. Consider the following (hypothetical) example about the home-nation of tourists who visit Wellington, New Zealand, where Stephen lives, in one month.

Data 14.1

500 Australians	100 Indonesians	30 Italians
900 Chinese	65 Swedes	90 Brits
200 Americans	150 Indians	15 Mexicans
200 Japanese	55 Brazilians	
125 Fijians	180 Germans	

What is the mode for tourists visiting Wellington? The most frequently occurring nationality is Australian ($n = 500$). This is a case of a unimodal sample (one mode). A sample with two modes is bimodal and three modes is trimodal. A sample with four or more modes is not desirable (we will talk more about this a little later in the chapter). Modes are rarely used in communication research. Modes by themselves are not really meaningful. However, shortly we will discuss some exceptions.

The **median** is the midpoint of a distribution, with 50% of the scores above and 50% below the midpoint. Consider the following fictitious example of yearly salaries for an academic department.

Data 14.2

Faculty Member #1 – $145,456
Faculty Member #2 – $35,500
Faculty Member #3 – $42,456
Faculty Member #4 – $64,365
Faculty Member #5 – $47,668

What is the median yearly income in this department? When you sort the data from highest to lowest:

$35,500 $42,456 $47,668 $64,365 $145,456

The middle score–$47,668–is the median. However, the procedure only works if you have an odd number of scores. If you have an even number, there is no middle score. Add a sixth person to the department (Faculty Member #6 – $54,500). The sorted data now looks like this:

$35,500 $42,456 $47,668 $54,500 $64,365 $145,456

Since the data has no one middle score, you need to calculate the sum of the two middle scores ($54,500 and $47,688) and divide by 2 ($54,500+$47,688/2 = $51,094). The median can some-times be a nice measure to get a rough estimate of the middle of a distribution, but it is not the average–or the most exact measurement of the center of a distribution. We will discuss this more later in the chapter. You should not stress about calculating the median by hand; statistical computer programs do it for us! (But we should still know what the software is doing.)

The third kind measure of central tendency is the **mean,** which is an average of the scores. The mean is the most commonly reported measure of central tendency. A mean is the sum of the data divided by the number of cases making up the sum. We're going to present you with a couple of equa-tions. Don't get scared by the equations. Look for the "big picture," and all the pieces will fit together. Remember, we have computers to help with the calculations. The formula for the mean requires taking all the scores, adding them together, then dividing by the number of scores (Equation 14.1).

$$\bar{X} = \frac{\Sigma X}{n}$$

In this formula the Mean, Σ, is the symbol to add up the values of your variable (X) and then divide by the number of cases (n). Here is an example for you to try on the following set of numbers, which represents the number of vacation days people take to visit Wellington per year (n = 30).

Data 14.3

1, 2, 3, 3, 4, 4, 5, 5, 6, 6, 7, 8, 8, 9, 9, 10, 10, 11, 15, 15, 17, 18, 18, 19, 20, 22, 23, 25, 30, 30

$$\bar{X} = \frac{363}{30}$$

Therefore, $\bar{X}$ = 12. In case you were wondering, the median (9+10/2) = 9.5, and the data distri-bution has *many* modes (3, 4, 5, 6, 8, 9, 10, 15, 18, 30).

Now, we have three measures of central tendency–mode, median, and mean. The question is: when do I use which one? We offer three "rules" to follow.

When to Use Which Measure of Central Tendency

Rule 1: If your data is nominal, you should use the mode to report the data. For example, if you are reporting data about the most common hair color on campus, the mode is the most appropriate measure.

Rule 2: If you are reporting ordinal, interval and/or ratio data, you should use the mean, as these types of variables lend themselves to having an average (mean).

Rule 3: Keep in mind that the mean can be sensitive to extreme scores. Therefore, when you have extreme scores and the data is skewed (we will talk more specifically about skew in a minute), you should use the median. Go back to Example 14.2 with the faculty data. The median is $47,668, while the mean is $67,089. The mean is quite a bit higher than the median. (Almost $20,000 higher!) This difference is due in large part to the $145,456 salary. So, remember, the mean is sensitive to extreme scores.

Variability

While you will typically find the mean reported in most research articles (or another measure of central tendency), another statistic often indicates how the data is dispersed/varied. You should know about three main kinds of variability: range, standard deviation, and variance. The simplest kind of variability is **range**, which you find by subtracting the lowest score from the highest score in a distribution ($r = h-l$).

Let's look at the set of scores in Data 14.3. The range is equal to (30-1)−or 29. The range simply tells us the difference between the highest and the lowest numbers in a set of scores. The range does not tell us anything about the frequency of scores, since we could have multiple 30s in a distribution and few of anything else. The range only tells us the distance between scores.

A second kind of variability is the **variance** (s^2), which is a measure of how much distribution exists around a single point in a distribution, typically the mean. To calculate the variance, you first need to know the deviation (d) scores, which are found by subtracting every x score from the mean ($d = x-mean$). Once you have the deviation scores, you can compute the formula for the variance; see the following (Equation 46.2):

$$s^2 = \frac{\Sigma d^2}{n-1}$$

The variance from 14.3 is:

$$s^2 = \frac{4^2}{30-1} = \frac{16}{29} = .55$$

The variance is rarely reported in scholarly research, since it is difficult to subtract every score from the mean. However, squaring the values changes how the values were originally entered and measured. Thus, most researchers take the square root of the variance for a more parsimonious measure of variability; this is called the standard deviation.

The **standard deviation** (represented by the symbol sigma, σ), shows how much statistical variation exists from the mean and is the square root of the variance. For the data in Data 14.3, the σ = .74. The standard deviation is the average distance between a score (measurement) and the mean. Larger standard deviations (ignoring the sign) represent more variability in the distribution, while smaller standard deviations represent less variability. So, in our number of vacation days example (46.3), the standard deviation is .74. This means the average difference between any person's number of vacation days and the mean is .74 days. The formula for the standard deviation is as follows (Equation 16.3):

$$\sigma^2 = \sqrt{\frac{\sum(X - Mean)^2}{n-1}}$$

The standard deviation tells us how far scores "deviate" or differ from the mean. The standard deviation is helpful for research involving hypothesis testing and inferential statistics. For now, know that as you read communication journal articles you will find that the two most often used descriptive statistics are the mean and the standard deviation. Bolkan et al. (2020) studied student interest in instructor narratives. They reported the means and standard deviations of various measures, which helped illustrate how students respond to instructor narratives. For example, student interest was measured on a scale of 1–5. The mean (*M*) was 3.35, and the standard deviation (*SD*) was .91. The reporting of such descriptive statistics is standard practice for researchers in communication and other scholarly disciplines.

As with the creation of visual representations, statistical programs such as SPSS and SAS can easily compute central tendency and variability. You don't have to compute the mean, standard deviation, and variance by hand, but it's good to know *how* the formulas work. Once you know how to use a statistical program, you enter the data, click a few buttons, and, presto, you have your results.

If you are working for a baseball team's Marketing or Advertising branch, the uses of central tendency and variability are endless. Such statistics such as the RBI can be big money. Whenever a player is close to breaking any baseball record, teams promote such races, like the 1998 homerun race between Mark McGwire and Sammy Sosa. In the end, both broke a previous single-season record held by Roger Maris, and increased interest and ticket sales. On a down note, both players have now been linked to/or admitted to taking steroids during the season.

Distribution Shapes

Now that you have an understanding of visual representations of data, central tendency, and variability, we can discuss how these elements can affect the shape of your data distribution. Visual representations such as a histogram can show the shape of a distribution. A distribution has four key characteristics: symmetry, skew, modality, and kurtosis.

Your data distribution can be **symmetrical** or **asymmetrical.** Imagine you have a histogram. Now draw a line down the center. If the left and the right sides of the distribution are identical (or fairly close to identical), then the distribution is **symmetrical.** If the two sides are not identical, then the distribution is **asymmetrical**. A symmetrical distribution will have an identical mean, median, and mode in a bell curve. A perfect bell curve is hard to come by, but Figure 14.5 shows a hypothetical distribution of how many hundreds of New Zealand dollars the average tourist spends per visit in Wellington. You will notice the distribution is symmetrical and bell shaped. A symmetrical distribution is what we call a normal distribution. Symmetrical distributions have specific aspects that allow higher-level statistical testing than extremely asymmetrical distributions.

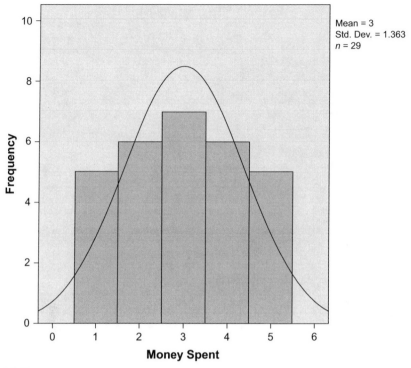

Figure 14.5

An asymmetrical distribution, however, indicates a high probability that the data is skewed in one direction. **Skew** means that the majority of scores are shifted to the right or left of a distribution's center. A way to understand skew is to look at the "tail" of a distribution. People's income is a classic example of how a distribution can be skewed. Most people's income is skewed to the lower end of the pay scale, while only a few people make a lot of money. This is an example of **positive skew**, where the majority of the scores shift to the left of the distribution (lower end), and the tail of the distribution points out to the higher numbers. A distribution can also be negatively skewed. A **negative skew** is when the majority of the scores shift to the right of the distribution (higher end), and the tail of the distribution points to the lower numbers. An example is retirement age. More people retire when they are 65 or older than when they are 50 or younger. Skewed distribution points to a random or constant error in the data.

Figure 14.6 depicts a positive skew. This data explores the extent to which registered Republicans in the U.S. after the 2020 presidential election are willing to get vaccinated against COVID-19; higher scores show more willingness. In Figure 14.6, you can see that most of the data is on the left-hand side of the histogram. Figure 14.7 shows a negatively skewed distribution. This data shows the extent to which registered Democrats in the U.S. after the 2020 presidential election are willing to wear face masks to combat the spread of COVID-19; higher scores show more willingness. In Figure 14.7, you can see that most of the data is on the right-hand side of the histogram.

Skewed data can lead to misleading statistics, as skewed distributions can push up or pull down the mean. Consider salaries again. A company may say their average (mean) salary is relatively good.

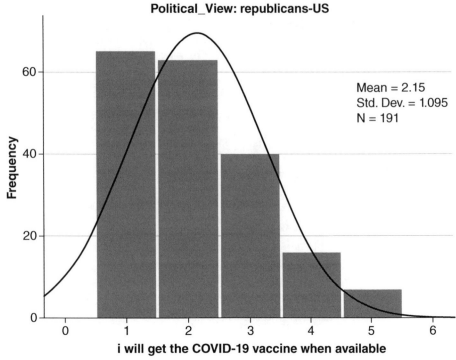

Figure 14.6

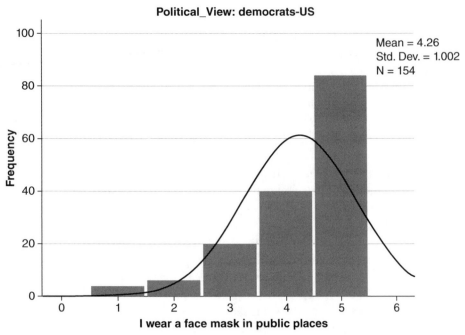

Figure 14.7

Unfortunately, the mean may be pulled up by a select few very high-paid employees, which skew the mean. While knowing in which direction, if at all, your distribution is skewed, the modality of your distribution is also important. **Modality** refers to the number of peaks in your distribution. A distribution can be unimodal with one peak or noticeable "hill" in the distribution. A distribution can also be bimodal (two peaks) or multimodal (multiple peaks). Imagine we were to ask 100 people about their communication apprehension (CA). Fifty of those people have never taken a speech class before and fifty of the people are on their college speech and debate team. Chances are we will have two very separate kinds of scores in this distribution; one group will likely have lower CA than the other group. The difference between the two groups will probably create a bimodal distribution like the one displayed in Figure 14.8. The distribution clearly shows two distinct groups of individuals.

The final way to describe your distribution is by analyzing its kurtosis. **Kurtosis** measures how peaked your distribution is. The more peaked the distribution, the more kurtosis it has; a distribution with high kurtosis is considered **leptokurtic** (leaping). This type of distribution does not have a lot of variance, and most of the scores are similar. A leptokurtic result may occur because individuals in a culture may tend to answer questions similarly.

On the other hand, a distribution with little kurtosis is considered **platykurtic** (plateau or flat). A platykurtic result generally means that each score is happening with almost the same amount of frequency. Playtkurtic distributions typically have multiple modes, like the distribution in Data 14.3. The multiple modes could be attributed to a variety of factors: the instrument you are using could be unreliable/invalid, or you might have a constant or random error. Figure 14.9 depicts a leptokurtic distribution and 14.10 a platykurtic distribution. When you compare the two pictures,

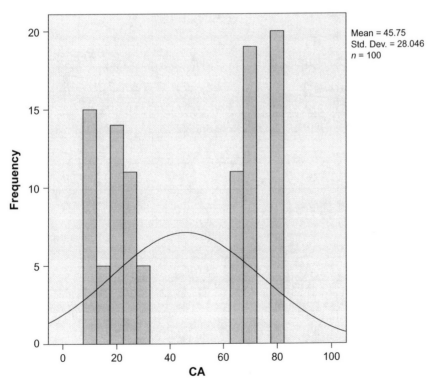

Figure 14.8

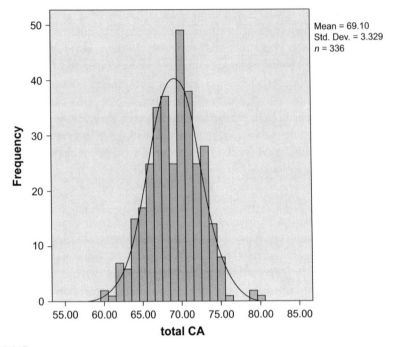

Figure 14.9

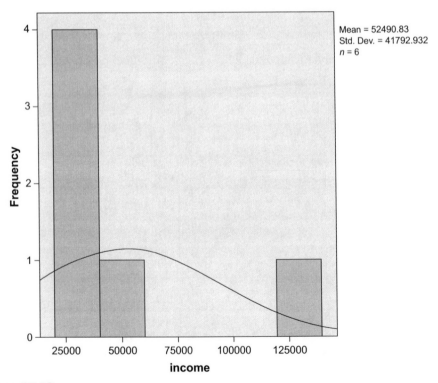

Figure 14.10

you can see how the data is distributed differently. In 14.9 the data lumps together in the middle, while in 14.10 the data does not cluster together.

The level of skewness and kurtosis is relatively easy to compute in your data since SPSS and SAS can compute the figures for you. Is there a threshold for skewness and kurtosis? No official cutoff criteria exist for determining when skewness or kurtosis is *too* large, and your data is *too* asymmetrical, thus nonnormal. Some statisticians will get concerned about skewness and kurtosis at -1/1, while others will not be bothered at -7/7 (Burdenski, 2000; Curran et al., 1996; Looney, 1995).

While a high RBI is assumed to represent a successful batter, this might not always be the case. The statistic has faced some criticism. Some baseball commentators and historians have argued that the statistic is biased, as it rewards a batter's position in the batting order; essentially, batters who bat after others who get on base are rewarded for the efforts of previous successful batters. Thus, RBI results may be skewed due to "good" batters batting for average teams, and other "average" batters hitting after "better" batters. The point is that a statistic requires understanding the context around it.

Summary

This chapter was a how-to guide to descriptive statistics. Generally, statistics are used by social scientific researchers, but they can sometimes be used by interpretive and critical/cultural researchers, depending on the focus of the study. Hopefully, after reading the chapter and the accompanying student paper, you feel comfortable enough to try and use some descriptive statistics. The next chapter is a how-to guide to inferential statistics.

Key Steps and Things to Consider

Here are some key things to remember as you compute descriptive statistics or prepare visual representations of data.

1. Descriptive statistics describe data.
2. Pie and bar charts predominantly show frequencies of categories, while histograms display continuous data.
3. Ask yourself if visually representing your data will be helpful to the reader before you produce a visual representation.
4. Mode, median, and mean are different. Remember why we use and report each in certain circumstances.
5. Range, variance, and standard deviation are different. Remember why we use and report each in certain circumstances as well.
6. Data distributions can be—and often are— shaped in different ways. This is attributed to things like skewness and kurtosis. Know what these things are and what they mean to your data.

Activities

1. Read the example student paper at the end of the chapter. Using the data from the student paper, try to construct a pie chart, bar chart, and histogram.
2. Using the data from the student paper, prepare tables of data in APA style.
3. Compare the charts from Activity 2 with the Tables from Activity 3. Which set of data representation is appropriate for the data? Which set of data representation best informs the reader?

Discussion Questions

1. Read the example student paper at the end of the chapter. The student drifted from a communication focus in the study. In Figure 14.6, you can see that most of the data is on the left-hand side of the histogram How could you fix the research to pull the focus back to communication studies?
2. What data could be collected that keeps a research focus on communication studies?
3. What descriptive statistics are appropriate for the data you have collected?

Key Terms

Asymmetrical	Leptokurtic	Range
Bar Chart	Mean	Skewness
Descriptive Statistics	Median	Standard Deviation
Histogram	Modality	Statistics
Kurtosis	Mode	Symmetrical
Measures of Central	Pie Chart	
Tendency	Platykurtic	

References

Bolkan, S., Goodboy, A. K., & Kromka, S. M. (2020). Student assessment of narrative: Telling stories in the classroom. *Communication Education, 69*(1), 48–69. https://doi.org/10.1080/03634523.2019.1622751

Brashers, D. E., Haas, S. M., & Neidig, J. L. (1999). The patient self-advocacy scale: Measuring patient involvement in health care decision-making interactions. *Health Communication, 11,* 97–121. https://doi.org/10.1207/s15327027hc1102_1

Burdenski, T. (2000). Evaluating univariate, bivariate, and multivariate normality using graphical and statistical procedures. *Multiple Linear Regression Viewpoints, 26*(2), 15–28.

Curran, P. J., West, S. G., & Finch, J. F. (1996). The robustness of test statistics to nonnormality and specification error in confirmatory factor analysis. *Psychological Methods, 1*(1), 16–29. https://psycnet.apa.org/doi/10.1037/1082-989X.1.1.16

Looney, S. W. (1995). How to use tests for univarite normaility to assess multivariate normality. *American Statistician, 49*(1), 64–70.

Stephan, W. G., & Stephan, C. W. (1985). Intergroup anxiety. *Journal of Social Issues, 41,* 157–175. https://doi.org/10.1111/j.1540-4560.1985.tb01134.x.

Undergraduate Student Paper

The Role of Sex in Automobile Accident & Violation History

Daniel Allen

In society today there are many stereotypes. This is true of driving habits, where there are stereotypes of the ways men and women drive. These stereotypes include the idea that men are competent, if aggressive, drivers, while women are incompetent drivers (James, 2007). These stereotypes, often seen as false in nature, are advocated by some as being definitively true in both the cases of males and female drivers. However, studies have shown that males are statistically worse drivers, with insurance premiums higher for male drivers due to an increased risk of accidents, tickets, and other automobile related issues; male drivers are in fact 3.41 times more likely to be charged with reckless driving than females (Tannert, 2009). This is one of many statistics that support the idea that men are careless drivers in comparison to women. Thus, in an attempt to find proof either proving or disproving these stereotypes, this study compares the driving history and habits of male drivers to female drivers. Both sexes were asked to complete the same survey about their legal driving history, involving accidents, tickets or other legal issues, and even simple driving habits.

> The student has made a "classic" mistake. He forgot to keep his research centered in the discipline. Communication studies overlaps and draws from a significant number of other disciplines—sociology, psychology, English, philosophy, women's studies, gender studies, ethnic studies, and business, to name just a few. Interesting questions may emerge worthy of research, but we need to make sure and always double-check the foundation for the research. The student in this paper starts with some nice premises focusing on stereotypes of driving habits. Stereotypes are a legitimate communication question. But the actual thesis of the research sidesteps the communication issues.

To test this, the questionnaire was distributed to an equal number of male and female participants, all of college ages (18–22). Of the potential participants, it was required that the person possess a driver's license and also have an automobile on campus to eliminate any bias caused by students who very rarely or did not drive a vehicle.

> The age of participants and status as college students may create statistical anomalies. Driving habits may change throughout life, so how someone 18-22 years old drives may not reflect how someone 30-45 years old drives. College students may have different driving habits than alums.

In total, 80 participants completed the questionnaire. By choosing upper-classmen houses at random on the Marist College campus, a similar, yet random, selection of both males and females was completed. The 12-question survey included sections on frequency of driving activities and what kind of driving, accident history and whether the participant was found at fault for any accidents, legal history, and common driving habits such as violation of laws and mobile device use. The last question asked the participants to rank their driving abilities on a Likert scale of 1 to 10, with 10 being the optimal driving ability. Participants were unaware of the comparison between sexes in the questionnaire in an attempt to limit any possible bias. The major areas analyzed in the results of the questionnaire were the frequency of accidents, the frequency of being caught during a traffic violation, the frequency of bad driving habits and traffic violations, and an in-depth analysis of the self-evaluation of driving abilities.

> The student does a nice job of describing the process for participant selection. The student describes the questionnaire in clear and precise language, including steps taken to limit bias.

One very interesting statistic arising from the questionnaire involved the amount of time spent driving by participants. Of the 40 male participants, 32 (80%) answered they drove daily or almost daily—four to six times per week—with only eight answering they drove less than four times per week. Among the female participants, 21 (52.5%) answered they drove the same amount, nearly a 30% difference. This number could prove difficult in analyzing the remainder of statistics, as this would indicate male drivers spend much more time behind the wheel of a motor vehicle. The results of the questionnaire show similar results for men and women in the section regarding accident history. Of the 80 participants, only three reported having been involved in an accident, two men and one woman, and none of the three reported they were found at fault for the incident.

> The student makes a potential inaccuracy about the data. The student assumes that the number of times someone drives equates with time spent driving. Consider this scenario: person A drives every day Monday through Friday for 10 minutes each day (5 days * 10 minutes = 50 minutes/week). Person B drives two days a week for 45 minutes (90 minutes/week). Using the framework established by the student researcher, Person A drives more than twice as much as Person B. However, Person B actually spends more than twice the time driving.
>
> The student researcher could have collected data on multiple levels: 1) number of times one drives a week; 2) number of minutes/hours one drives a week; 3) number of miles one drives a week. The researcher could have taken the data to even more levels by inquiring about where the driving occurred (e.g., metro, suburban, rural), if driving alone or with others, and what type of vehicle was driven. The additional levels of data may help better address the research question.
>
> A key point to remember in data collection: easier to collect data you may not use than to find out later you really need data you did not collect.

The number of traffic violations differed highly between male and female drivers, with 22 (55%) male drivers reporting that they had received a ticket for a traffic violation while only eight (20%) female drivers reported the same. Of these violations, nearly all violations were speeding tickets, with one male reporting a reckless driving charge, one male reporting cell phone violations, two males reporting seatbelt violations, three females reporting cell phone violations, and one female reporting seatbelt violations. Of these four male drivers who received tickets other than speeding, all but one reported having also received speeding tickets. Of these four female drivers, only two reported they had received speeding tickets. Therefore, whereas male drivers are about 50% certain to receive a speeding ticket, female drivers are only about 15% certain to receive a similar ticket—a large difference. Altogether, male drivers were 35 percent more likely to receive a ticket from a police officer.

The rundown of the results can get awkward to follow. The student can streamline the presentation of the results with visual representation of data. A simple table with male/female on the vertical and type of violation across the top will simplify review of the results for the reader.

A table can help both research and reader. The table easily displays the results and allows the researcher to unpack and explain the most salient points in the text instead of writing up every point of data in the text.

Another major difference was the use a cellular device during operation of a motor vehicle. Of the 40 male drivers, 16 (40%) answered they would answer a call or text while driving, with eight answering only voice use, six answering only texting, and an additional two answering they did both. The female statistic for use of a cell phone, and in particular texting while driving, was much higher than the 40% of males who used a phone and 20% who would text while driving. Of the female drivers, 33 (82.5%) answered they would answer a call or text while driving, with five answering only voice use, two answering only texting, and 26 answering they did both. This means 70% of the female participants would text while operating a motor vehicle, a full 50% higher than male participants. This illustrates a trend of women tending to communicate via cell phone much more than men, and especially through texting since in total 77.5% of female drivers would at least use calling capabilities during driving. Of the 80 participants of the survey, not a single participant, male or female, indicated that they had a hands-free device for their cell phones when asked.

A second table laying out the results for cellular device use will again help to streamline presentation of the results. Remember to refer to the APA style manual when prepping a table.

Whereas the results of the two previous sections showed clear differences between male and female drivers, the driving habit section showed little difference, if only supporting the trend that male drivers commit more traffic violations than women. Of the male participants,

27 (67.5%) reported they regularly speed while driving, and two of the 27 male drivers reported they not use blinkers often. Of the female participants, 24 (60%) reported they regularly speed, with 7 of the female drivers also reporting they do not use blinkers regularly. This does indicate male drivers are slightly more prone to speeding, yet also indicates female drivers are more than three times to neglect using blinkers while driving. Altogether, male and female drivers were not very different in reporting instances of unlawful driving habits.

Another section where male and female drivers differed tremendously was in the self-evaluation at the end. Male drivers tended to score themselves much better than women, with the male average slightly below 8 out of 10, whereas the female average was only about 6.5 out of 10. Male scores ranged from 4 to 10 and female scores from 5 to 9, given male drivers a larger range of scores. The median for male drivers was an 8 and for female drivers a 6, indicating a difference between male and female drivers. The mode for male drivers was an 8, with 19 (47.5%) males, and the mode for female drivers was a 6, with 20 (50%) females, indicating that the results across the board showed a much higher self-reporting of driving ability in males. Although this does not indicate actual driving ability, it does indicate how each sex sees themselves behind the wheel—very likely indicating who is more comfortable operating a motor vehicle.

The student provides the mode and median scores for the self-evaluation but does not provide a good explanation of why the mode and median are appropriate or insightful for the study. His professor simply may have required all three measures of central tendency be included in the paper.

The student explains that the mode and median scores may demonstrate comfort with a motor vehicle. However, the scores may also reflect respondent bias. The participants may "buy in" to a degree the very stereotypes the student is researching. For example, a male respondent may accept the stereotypes and, therefore, self-report strong driving abilities.

The stereotypes of male and female drivers persist regardless of statistical evidence to the contrary of commonly held beliefs. Other statistical studies have shown male drivers are much more likely to be caught violating traffic laws, yet the typical stereotype of women drivers remains that women are unable to operate a motor vehicle competently. The findings of this study shows men are more likely to commit traffic violations and be caught in the process of doing so, yet women are more likely to have bad driving habits such as cellular phone use while driving, however it should be noted that in most states cellular phone use during operation of a motor vehicle is illegal. Overall, the males rated their driving abilities very highly, while women tended to rate their driving abilities dramatically lower, indicating possibly a lack of self-esteem in female drivers. Even how comfortable behind the driver's wheel could be a factor in driving ability, and female drivers in this survey indicate an extreme difference from male drivers in this regard.

The student provides strong interpretation of the data. However, descriptive statistics only show comparisons of the data, not the strength of relationships between the data. The student is overstating his results with *"very* highly," *"dramatically lower,"* and *"extreme* difference." Chapter 16 explains inferential statistics, which you can use to test and make such statements.

According to these results, the theory that men are more likely to commit traffic violations is upheld, although it must be questioned whether men are more focused than women when driving due to very high rate of cell phone usage by women drivers. A very high percentage of traffic violations by men were speeding, rather than more egregious violations, and men also reported more extensive driving than women. With this information, the theory that men are more dangerous drivers must be questioned, although the practice of charging higher premiums to male drivers at the same time seems practical due to the higher infraction rate and similar accident rate.

Remember our opening question about whether the research has a communication focus. Review the final paragraph of the paper and re-ask the question. The study is interesting, but what is the connection to communication studies? Conducting communication research requires careful attention to the question. Stephen and Dan have seen many a promising start to a research project wander and drift off course when the student did not keep their own discipline central to the study.

References

James, L. (2007). *Principles of driving psychology.* Message posted to www.drdrving.org/
Tannert, C. (2009, May 4). *Who are better drivers: Men or women?* Message posted to editorials.auto. msn.com

15 Inferential Statistics

Chapter Outline

- What Is Inferential Statistics?
- Tests of Relationships and Prediction
- Summary
- Key Steps and Questions to Consider
- Activities
- Discussion Questions
- Key Terms
- Undergraduate Inferential Regression Paper

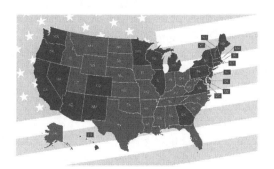

What Will I Learn About Inferential Statistics in This Chapter?

On November 3, 2020, voters in the U.S. participated in federal, state, and local elections. In terms of the presidential election, more than 81 million cast a ballot on election day or cast a mail-in ballot. In the weeks leading up to the election, political commentators, politicians, and average citizens could not predict who would win the presidential election, incumbent President Donald Trump or challenger Joseph Biden. Polls conducted in various states showed close races in states such as Arizona, Florida, Wisconsin, Michigan, Georgia, Pennsylvania, Nevada, and even Texas. Going into election night, it was hard to predict the outcome.

Predicting the results of elections is not an easy task. In 2000, the United States suffered an executive and judicial fiasco when news agencies prematurely "called" the state of Florida for Democratic presidential candidate Al Gore, when in fact Republican candidate George W. Bush won the state (debate still rages over who actually won Florida). In the end, Bush won Florida and the presidential election. In 2016, many political polls had Democratic candidate Hillary Clinton beating Republican Donald Trump by a sizeable vote and state count. An important note–in the United States electoral system, a candidate wins states and is not elected by a majority of the people. However, on election night, Trump, not Clinton, won a majority of the states (57% of the electoral votes), while Clinton beat Trump in the popular vote (48.2% to 46.1%). Many of the pollsters were baffled by the result. In 2020, another baffling scenario unfolded. On election night, Trump had "won" more states, as many states were not officially done counting ballots,

DOI: 10.4324/9781003109129-18

with many absentee/mail-in ballots still being counted. However, as more states counted their mail-in/absentee ballots, Biden won many of these preliminarily undecided states. Eventually, he surpassed the 270 Electoral votes needed to win the U.S. presidency, as per the U.S. Constitution. After weeks of legal challenges, political posturing, protesting, and, unfortunately, some violence, Biden was inaugurated President of the U.S. on January 20, 2021.

Political polling is based on the bell curve, sampling, error, and inferential statistics. While pollsters often get it "right," there are many examples of when the polls are simply nowhere close to the final result. Predicting who will win a presidential election or how a population will vote has many variables. The job of a good pollster is to take many variables into consideration when making prediction(s). In this chapter, we explore such questions and other aspects of inferential statistics. In the previous chapter, we defined statistics as a way of organizing, describing, and making inferences from data. **Inferential statistics** allow us to make conclusions (inferences) from a sample to a population.

What Is Inferential Statistics?

In other chapters, we talked about the Central Limit Theorem and how you can make inferences or estimations about a population from your sample. Don't worry, we will talk more about this process throughout the chapter. The process of inference is the key to inferential statistics. Through the process of inferential statistics, you are able to statistically test what you think you know about the population based on your sample. Inferential statistics has two main families of tests you can use: tests of difference and tests of relationship/prediction. We will describe each family and explain how you can conduct various tests. The first section discusses test of differences, while the second section is a description of relationships and prediction.

Tests of Difference

If you are interested in comparing differences between men and women on the amount of self-disclosure on Facebook using a Likert scale, this would be a test of difference (an independent samples *t*-test). If you want to compare differences between freshmen, sophomores, juniors, and seniors at your school on willingness to communicate (WTC) interval data, this would be a test of difference (a one-way analysis of variance ANOVA). If you are interested in analyzing how FOX, CNN, and MSNBC cover the presidential debates, this would be a test of difference (a Chi^2-test). Each of these proposed studies has numerous differences between the statistics you would use. Let's discuss the properties of each, how to do each statistical analysis, and how they differ.

t-Test

A *t*-test is a multipurpose statistic used when you are comparing two group means. With a *t*-test, your dependent variable must be continuous (interval or ratio-level data), and the independent variable, which is called the grouping variable, is a nominal or ordinal variable. *T*-tests can be used in regression analyses but are most often associated with testing differences between two group means. For example, you could use a *t*-test to explore whether males or females have higher GPAs on your campus, whether New Zealanders or South Africans like rugby more (we could measure affection toward the game), whether winter temperatures are colder on average in January in Finland or Sweden, and whether your understanding of research methods improved from the start to the end of your class. *T*-tests can do all of this. There are two kinds of *t*-tests: an independent samples *t*-test and a dependent (paired) samples *t*-test. An **independent samples *t*-test** compares the means of two groups that are not the same (e.g., male and female GPA). A **dependent samples** or **paired samples *t*-test** is used when you are comparing the means of two groups matched in some way, such as when someone takes a test at the start of the semester and then the same test at the end of the semester and you compare the results. You should know some basic principles of the *t*-test.

Principles of a *t*-test

1. The dependent variable must be an interval or ratio-level variable.
2. The independent variable must be nominal or ordinal-level variables.
3. The dependent variable should be normally distributed, meaning there should not be a high skewness or kurtosis.
4. The larger the sample, the less likely the difference between the two means analyzed is created by sampling error. We discussed sampling error in Chapters 7 and 15.
5. The further apart the means, the less likely the difference was created by sampling error.
6. The more homogeneous the sample, the less likely the difference between the two means was created by sampling error.
7. *T*-tests evaluate the extent to which data distributions do not overlap. Overlap is smaller to the extent that the difference between means of two distributions is large and/or the SDs are small.

Dependent Samples *t*-test. The purpose of a dependent samples *t*-test is to compare the mean score at one point to the mean score at a second point. For example, Stephen consistently gives his students in Research Methods/Statistics 101 the final exam on the first day of class and then the same exam during the final exam period. He would compare their scores from the first day to the last day to see how each student's scores differed. This pretest and posttest format is the essence of a dependent-samples *t*-test. Stephen is able to compare individual results and the class average from the pretest to the final test. He hopes, of course, that the students improve their knowledge of statistics.

Conducting a dependent samples *t*-test is relatively easy in SPSS, one of the most used and easiest to use statistical software programs. Stephen and his team have regularly used longitudinal research to explore potential change in attitude and/or behavior (Croucher et al., 2018, 2020). In a recent study, his team explored the extent to which registered Democrats and Republicans were likely to wear masks to combat the spread of COVID-19 before and after the 2020 U.S. presidential election. Respondents were provided with a question that asked them how often they wear a mask in public to protect themselves from COVID-19. Respondents answered this question, along with a series of other questions, in September 2020 and then again in December 2020. Stephen and his team were interested in whether the political situation around the election would change people's likelihood of wearing a mask. The study called for a dependent samples *t*-test (the grouping variable is the same person with two different means). To conduct the test, SPSS has a few simple steps.

Steps to Conducting a Dependent Samples t-test in SPSS

1. Go to "Analyze" and choose "Compare Means."
2. Within "Choose Means" select "Paired-Samples *t*-test."
3. Once you click on "Paired-Samples *t*-test," a new box will open. You will see the following buttons: "Options" "Bootstrap," "Reset," "Paste," "Cancel," and "OK."
4. At this point in your studies, you do not need to be concerned with "Options" and "Bootstrap." "Reset" will reset everything you have done. "Paste" will allow you to paste things in. "Cancel" closes the box, and "OK" runs the *t*-test.
5. Scroll down your list of variables to select the pair of variables you want.
6. You need to choose the first one and then hold down the Ctrl key on your keyboard and then select the second variable you want.
7. Then click on the arrow to transfer this pair over for analysis. You can conduct more than one analysis at a time, just repeat this process.
8. Then press the "OK" button and your analysis will be conducted.

In Stephen's data on mask wearing, he selected his two variables and pressed "OK." The following three outputs (Outputs 15.1–15.3) show the results of the dependent samples *t*-tests for registered Republicans and Democrats:

The first output, Output 15.1, shows the means, standard deviations, and standard error of the mean before and after the election for both Republicans and Democrats. The second output, Output 15.2, shows the correlation between the pre- and the posttest. In this case, the likelihood of wearing a mask is highly correlated between September and December 2020 for Democrats ($r = .346, p < .001$) and for Republicans ($r = .412, p < .001$). We will talk more about correlations in a few short pages. The third output, 15.3, is the important one showing if a significant difference exists between the two means. In this case, a significant difference does exist in willingness to mask for both Democrats and Republicans. Reporting the results of the test is relatively simple; let's write up the results for Democrats:

> Democrats likelihood to wear a mask to combat COVID-19 before ($M = 2.86, SD = 1.35, SE = .11$) the 2020 U.S. presidential election significantly increased after the election ($M = 4.26, SD = 1.00, SE = .08$), $t(153) = -12.61, p < .001, r = .35$).

Paired Samples Statistics

Political_View			Mean	N	Std. Deviation	Std. Error Mean
democrats-US	Pair 1	I wear a face mask in public places	2.86	154	1.348	.109
		I wear a face mask in public places	4.26	154	1.002	.081
republicans-US	Pair 1	I wear a face mask in public places	3.39	191	1.413	.102
		I wear a face mask in public places	2.47	191	1.439	.104

Output 15.1

Paired Samples Correlations

Political_View			N	Correlation	Sig.
democrats-US	Pair 1	I wear a face mask in public places & I wear a face mask in public places	154	.346	<.001
republicans-US	Pair 1	I wear a face mask in public places & I wear a face mask in public places	191	.412	<.001

Output 15.2

Paired Samples Test

Political_View			Paired Differences					t	df	Sig. (2-tailed)
			Mean	Std. Deviation	Std. Error Mean	95% Confidence Interval of the Difference				
						Lower	Upper			
democrats-US	Pair 1	I wear a face mask in public places - I wear a face mask in public places	-1.396	1.374	.111	-1.615	-1.177	-12.609	153	<.001
republicans-US	Pair 1	I wear a face mask in public places - I wear a face mask in public places	.916	1.547	.112	.695	1.137	8.186	190	<.001

Output 15.3

Let's break down the statement:

1. "Democrats' likelihood to wear a mask to combat COVID-19 before (*M* = 2.86, *SD* = 1.35, *SE* = .11) the 2020 U.S. presidential election significantly increased after the election (*M* = 4.26, *SD* = 1.00, *SE* = .08)," is showing the reader the mean differences before and after the election.

2. "*t*(153) = -12.61, *p* < .001, *r* = .35" represents the following: "*t* = -12.61" is your *t* value (rounded up from -12.609). Your *t* value is an arbitrary number telling a reader the chance the two means are different from one another. We need more information to determine whether or not the *t* value is significant.

3. "(159)" is the degrees of freedom in the study. **Degrees of freedom** or *df* is the number of independent values in any given calculation minus the number of estimated parameters. Basically, the *df* is the number of values that can vary in a calculation. The *df* formula and the amount it varies is represented by *n* -1. In this case, the *df* equals 154 (the sample size) minus 1 or 153.

4. "*p* < .0001" is the alpha level significance for the *t*-test. The *p* level tells you if the test is significant (remember, to be significant the *p* must be less than .05) and if you should reject the null. In this case, there is a significant difference, so the two means are significantly different from one another, and we should reject the null.

5. "*r* = .35" is the correlation between the value in September and December (rounded up from .346). We will talk more about this shortly.

Independent samples *t*-test. Independent samples *t*-tests are used when you are comparing the means of two groups not the same. For example, you could compare the amount of self-disclosure between men and women in an intimate relationship. Like a dependent samples *t*-test, conducting an independent samples *t*-test is relatively easy in SPSS. Part of the new research into COVID-19 was also exploring vaccine hesitancy. Republicans and Democrats were asked how likely they were to get a vaccine when available. This analysis calls for an independent samples *t*-test, as the grouping variable is two different groups (Republicans and Democrats) with mean scores on likelihood of getting a vaccination. Conducting the test involves just a few simple steps in SPSS.

Steps to Conducting an Independent Samples t-test in SPSS

1. Go to "Analyze" and choose "Compare Means."
2. Within "Choose Means," select "Independent Samples t-test."
3. Once you click on "Independent-Samples *t*-test," a new box will open. You will see the following buttons: "Options" "Bootstrap," "Reset," "Paste," "Cancel," and "OK."
4. Just like with the dependent samples *t*-test, choose your dependent variable. In this case, you only choose one and not two.
5. Highlight it and click the arrow to move it over to the "Test Variable(s)" Box. In Stephen's analysis of vaccine hesitancy, this variable is named "vaccine1." You then need to choose your grouping variable; this is your independent variable. Stephen wanted to compare Republicans and Democrats, "Grouping Variable."
6. You need to tell the computer which groups to analyze (Define groups), Stephen coded Democrats as 0 and Republicans as 1 in his SPSS file.
7. As with the dependent samples *t*-test, you can run one or multiple tests at once.
8. Press the "OK" button and your analysis will be conducted.

The following two outputs, Outputs 15.4-15.5, show the results of the independent-samples *t*-tests for Republicans and Democrats:

Output 15.4 shows how many Republicans and Democrats are in the sample, the mean, the standard deviation, and the standard error of willingness to get vaccinated for each group. Output 15.5 is the independent samples test table from SPSS. First, you may notice two *t* values and something called "Levene's Test for Equality." Levene's test is exploring whether the variances between the two groups are equal. If the Levene's test is nonsignificant, then equal variances between the two groups can be assumed, and you report the numbers on the top row of the table. If Levene's test is significant, we can assume that equal variance between groups cannot be assumed. Thus, our *t*-test has to be statistically altered; this is most evident in the *df* and sometimes in the significance of (*p*) values. In such cases, you will report the values on the bottom, "Equal variances not assumed." In the case of this particular *t*-test, Levene's test is significant and equal variances cannot assumed, so we report the values on the bottom row. The results are:

Democrats (*M* = 4.53; *SD* = .88) have significantly higher likelihood of getting vaccinated than Republicans (*M* = 2.55; *SD* = 1.15), $t(342.09) = 18.14$, $p < .0001$.

T-tests are widely used in communication research. Ivanov et al. (2012) used dependent-samples *t*-tests to explore the effects of attitudinal attacks on attitude change. Ivanov et al. found that

Group Statistics

	Political_View	N	Mean	Std. Deviation	Std. Error Mean
I will get the COVID-19 vaccine when available	democrats-US	154	4.53	.879	.071
	republicans-US	191	2.55	1.150	.083

Output 15.4

Independent Samples Test

		Levene's Test for Equality of Variances		t-test for Equality of Means					95% Confidence Interval of the Difference	
		F	Sig.	t	df	Sig. (2-tailed)	Mean Difference	Std. Error Difference	Lower	Upper
I will get the COVID-19 vaccine when available	Equal variances assumed	24.212	<.001	17.636	343	<.001	1.983	.112	1.762	2.204
	Equal variances not assumed			18.140	342.089	<.001	1.983	.109	1.768	2.198

Output 15.5

some inoculation messages could generate resistance to persuasive messages, while other messages would not. Yun et al. (2012) used independent samples t-tests to check the effects of a public speaking course on writing skills. Yun et al. found that students who take a public speaking course have better writing structure and syntax.

In the 2020 election, commentators talked a lot about how African American voters were more likely to have a favorable opinion of Joe Biden, while Caucasian/white voters were more likely to have a favorable opinion of Donald Trump. The commentators were more than likely getting this information from a t-test or a more advanced statistical test that was operating like a t-test. What they were doing was asking likely voters how they felt about the candidates and their likelihood of voting for each candidate. This kind of information is important for candidates and their teams, as it can help them know how to tailor their messages and campaigns.

One-Way Analysis of Variance (ANOVA)

A **one-way analysis of variance (ANOVA)** has many characteristics similar to a t-test. The test is a way to compare more than two groups (such as ethnicity, religious identification, level in school) on an interval or ratio-level variable. For example, you could use ANOVA to examine 1) how individuals based on their academic year at your school (e.g., freshman, sophomore, junior, and senior) differ on job satisfaction, 2) how years working for a company potentially affect an individual's willingness to dissent about organizational decisions, and 3) how people from different nations (more than two) differ on their tendency to approach arguments. Each of these questions can be addressed by ANOVA. Some basic principles of ANOVA are similar to the t-test. In the case of ANOVA, the result is the F-test.

Principles of a One-Way ANOVA

1. The dependent variable must be an interval or ratio-level variable.
2. The independent variable must be a nominal or ordinal-level variable.
3. The dependent variable should be normally distributed; there should not be high levels of skewness or kurtosis.
4. The larger the sample, the less likely the difference between the means is created by sampling error.
5. The further apart the means, the less likely the difference was created by sampling error.
6. The more homogeneous the sample, the less likely the difference between the means was created by sampling error.
7. ANOVAs evaluate the extent to which multiple distributions do not overlap. Overlap is smaller to the extent that the difference between means of multiple distributions are large and/or the SDs are small.

While calculating the *F* in an ANOVA is a complex process, we thankfully have programs like SPSS to help us. Conducting ANOVA is an easy process. For this example, we are going to return to the COVID-19 data. Specifically, we are going to compare how much Americans perceive Asians as a realistic threat to U.S. society based on how many people they know who have had COVID-19. SPSS has a few simple steps.

Steps to Conducting a One-Way ANOVA in SPSS

1. Go to "Analyze" and choose "Compare Means."
2. Within "Choose Means" select "One-Way ANOVA."
3. Once you click on "One-Way ANOVA" a new box will open. You will see the following buttons: "Contrasts," "Post Hoc," "Options," "Bootstrap," "OK," "Paste," "Reset," "Cancel," and "Help."
4. Choose your dependent variable(s), the one(s) you want to analyze. Highlight it and click the arrow to move it over to the "Dependent List" box. You can analyze multiple variables if you want, but let's focus on one for now. In Stephen's analysis of mask wearing, he named his variable "realistic2." So, you click on "realistic2" and then click the arrow to move it over to the "Dependent List."
5. As we are interested in how people with different levels of acquaintances with COVID-19 differ in "realistic2", our factor (independent variable) is "knowncovidpatients". So, click on "knowncovidpatients" and move it to "Factor."
6. Click on "Options" and then click the "Descriptive" and the "Means plot boxes." The Descriptive box will provide you with descriptive statistics, and Means plot will visually show you your data. Then press "Continue."
7. Click "Post Hoc," choose "Tukey," "Scheffé," and "Games-Howell," click "Continue" and then "OK." The ANOVA will then run. See Outputs 15.6–15.10.
8. To compute the η^2, click on "Analyze," "Compare Means," and then "Means." Highlight "realistic2" and click the arrow to move it to the dependent list. Highlight highest "knowncovidpatients" and click the arrow to move it to the independent list. Click "Options" and then click "Anova table and eta". Click "Continue". Click "OK."

Descriptives

realistic2

	N	Mean	Std. Deviation	Std. Error	95% Confidence Interval for Mean		Minimum	Maximum
					Lower Bound	Upper Bound		
0 people	177	2.9642	.61595	.04630	2.8728	3.0556	1.33	5.00
1-3 people	74	3.1577	.70705	.08219	2.9938	3.3215	1.33	4.00
4-6 people	55	3.4000	.77619	.10466	3.1902	3.6098	1.33	4.00
7 or more people	39	3.5214	.52312	.08377	3.3518	3.6909	1.67	4.00
Total	345	3.1382	.68429	.03684	3.0657	3.2106	1.33	5.00

Output 15.6

ANOVA

realistic2

	Sum of Squares	df	Mean Square	F	Sig.
Between Groups	14.881	3	4.960	11.570	<.001
Within Groups	146.200	341	.429		
Total	161.081	344			

Output 15.7

Output 15.6 shows descriptive statistics for each group. In this case, participants were able to choose that they knew 0 people, 1-3 people, 4-6 people, or 7 or more people who had COVID-19. Looking at Output 15.6, individuals who knew 4-6 people with COVID-19 on a scale of 1-5 had a mean of 3.40, compared to a mean of 2.96 for those individuals who knew nobody with COVID-19.

Output 15.7 is the ANOVA output. In the ANOVA output, you have the F value (11.57), numerator df (3), denominator df (344), SS_b (4.96), SS_w (.429, round it to .423), and significance level p (<.001). This table tells us if ANOVA is significant or not, so do we have difference? Based on this table, ANOVA is significant ($p < .001$). Therefore, there is a significant difference in perception that Asians are a realistic threat to the U.S. during the COVID-19 pandemic based on how many people someone knows who has had COVID-19.

Output 15.9 is a line plot of the data. While outputs tell us a lot, what is missing is a direct comparison between each level of knowing COVID patients. We may see a steady increase in perception of threat from knowing zero people to knowing one to three people to seven or more people, but is it significant? The picture would lead us to think we have significance, but we can't be sure. This is where the post hoc comparisons come in (see Output 15.8).

If we look back to our ANOVA table in Output 15.7, we know our ANOVA is significant, but what groups differ? This is where we need to compare our groups to one another. **Post hoc comparisons** are follow-up tests to determine whether all groups or certain pairs of group means are significantly different from one another. You can choose from numerous post-hocs. The most commonly used ones are Tukey's and the Scheffé test. **Tukey's** should be used when you have an equal number of participants/items in your independent categories/groups. The **Scheffé test** can be used when you have an unequal number of participants/items in your independent categories/groups. The Scheffé test is more conservative, which means the criteria for statistical significance is stricter than Tukey's. Both the Tukey's and the Scheffé test assume equal variances. If equal variances are not assumed, a good option is the Games Howell test. This post-hoc operates much like the other post-hocs but does not assume equal variances. In the case of this

Multiple Comparisons

Dependent Variable: realistic2

	(I) KnowCovidPatients	(J) KnowCovidPatients	Mean Difference (I–J)	Std. Error	Sig.	95% Confidence Interval Lower Bound	95% Confidence Interval Upper Bound
Tukey HSD	0 people	1–3 people	−.19344	.09064	.144	−.4275	.0406
		4–6 people	−.43578*	.10108	<.001	−.6967	−.1748
		7 or more people	−.55715*	.11583	<.001	−.8562	−.2581
	1–3 people	0 people	.19344	.09064	.144	−.0406	.4275
		4–6 people	−.24234	.11657	.162	−.5433	.0586
		7 or more people	−.36371*	.12956	.027	−.6982	−.0292
	4–6 people	0 people	.43578*	.10108	<.001	.1748	.6967
		1–3 people	.24234	.11657	.162	−.0586	.5433
		7 or more people	−.12137	.13707	.812	−.4753	.2325
	7 or more people	0 people	.55715*	.11583	<.001	.2581	.8562
		1–3 people	.36371*	.12956	.027	.0292	.6982
		4–6 people	.12137	.13707	.812	−.2325	.4753
Scheffe	0 people	1–3 people	−.19344	.09064	.210	−.4481	.0612
		4–6 people	−.43578*	.10108	<.001	−.7198	−.1518
		7 or more people	−.55715*	.11583	<.001	−.8826	−.2317
	1–3 people	0 people	.19344	.09064	.210	−.0612	.4481
		4–6 people	−.24234	.11657	.231	−.5699	.0852
		7 or more people	−.36371	.12956	.050	−.7277	.0003
	4–6 people	0 people	.43578*	.10108	<.001	.1518	.7198
		1–3 people	.24234	.11657	.231	−.0852	.5699
		7 or more people	−.12137	.13707	.853	−.5065	.2637
	7 or more people	0 people	.55715*	.11583	<.001	.2317	.8826
		1–3 people	.36371	.12956	.050	−.0003	.7277
		4–6 people	.12137	.13707	.853	−.2637	.5065
Games–Howell	0 people	1–3 people	−.19344	.09434	.175	−.4392	.0523
		4–6 people	−.43578*	.11444	.002	−.7364	−.1352
		7 or more people	−.55715*	.09571	<.001	−.8097	−.3046
	1–3 people	0 people	.19344	.09434	.175	−.0523	.4392
		4–6 people	−.24234	.13308	.269	−.5895	.1048
		7 or more people	−.36371*	.11736	.013	−.6704	−.0570
	4–6 people	0 people	.43578*	.11444	.002	.1352	.7364
		1–3 people	.24234	.13308	.269	−.1048	.5895
		7 or more people	−.12137	.13406	.802	−.4722	.2294
	7 or more people	0 people	.55715*	.09571	<.001	.3046	.8097
		1–3 people	.36371*	.11736	.013	.0570	.6704
		4–6 people	.12137	.13406	.802	−.2294	.4722

*. The mean difference is significant at the 0.05 level.

Output 15.8

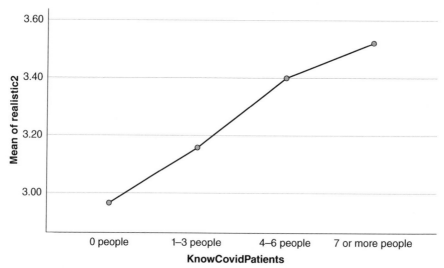

Output 15.9

Measures of Association

	Eta	Eta Squared
realistic2 * KnowCovidPatients	.304	.092

Output 15.10

particular ANOVA, if you look at Output 15.6, you will see each group has a different number of participants. Thus, equal variances should not be assumed. Therefore, we look to the Games Howell's test.

Output 15.8 (Multiple Comparisons) shows direct mean comparisons between each educational level on argumentativeness. Based on the Games Howell comparison, you can see individuals with who know 1–3 people scored .19 higher than those who know 0 people. Those who know 7 or more people scored .557 higher than those who know 0 people. The (*) in the figure means the difference is statistically significant ($p < .05$) between the two groups. These comparisons are helpful in better understanding specific differences between groups.

Output 15.10 shows the η^2 or the eta squared result. This statistic tells you the strength of association between your independent and dependent variables. It explains the amount of variation in the dependent variable shared with the grouping variable. A higher value represents a stronger relationship, effect.

Writing up ANOVA results look like this:

A one-way ANOVA was conducted using how many individuals a person knows who has had COVID-19 as the independent variable and realistic threat perception from Asians in the U.S. during the COVID-19 pandemic as the dependent variable. A significant difference was found: $F(3, 344) = 11.57$, $p < .001$, $\eta^2 = .09$. A Games Howell post-hoc comparison was conducted, which indicated individuals with more acquaintances who had COVID-19 tended to have higher levels of realistic threat.

The write-up has a few important points. "$F(3, 344)$" is showing the reader the different degrees of freedom in the study, 34 is the numerator *df*, and 344 is the denominator *df*. "11.57" is the *F* value for the ANOVA, which we know is significant because of the *p* value, "$p < .001$." The final element is "$\eta^2 = .09$." This is eta squared for the ANOVA. Eta squared represents the effect size for the difference in the ANOVA test. An eta squared can range from zero to one. A small eta squared means no difference, while a large eta squared indicates a difference between the groups. A small effect size ranges from .01–.05; a medium effect size ranges from .06–.13, while a large effect size ranges from .14 and above. All in all, ANOVA is a helpful method for exploring differences between more than two groups on a continuous variable.

In the 2020 U.S. election, commentators talked a lot about educational divides and regional differences in how people would vote. Both sides were competing for different geographic regions and for different educational groups. When the dust settled after the vote, there were clear regional differences in how people voted (rural vs. urban). People in more urban areas tended to vote for Biden, while rural voters tended to vote for Trump.

Chi-Square

The third test of difference is not like the ANOVA or *t*-tests. Remember, ANOVAs and *t*-tests assume that the population you are generalizing to and the samples you are working with are normally distributed. These types of tests (and correlation and regression) are called **parametric** tests. A **nonparametric** test is used when you are unable to make assumptions about how data in the population are distributed, your sample may not represent the population, and the data you are working with is categorical (ordinal or nominal). A **Chi-square** is a nonparametric test used to compare the observed frequencies of a variable against the expected frequencies to see if a statistical difference exists between the two. A basic principle underlying the Chi-square is that a sample will break down into equal groups. For example, if you have 250 dogs and divide them into 5 breeds, statistically you should expect to have 50 of each breed. However, rarely does a sample break down into equal groups. What we observe can be rather different than what is statistically expected. A Chi-square has some required elements.

Principles of a Chi-Square

1.   All of the variables under analysis must be nominal variables.
2.   Larger samples are more representative of the population.

Let's look to the 2020 U.S. presidential election. In the election, pollsters regularly asked men and women (nominal variable) whom they were going to vote for (nominal variable). This is a classic question and could be analyzed using a Chi-square. If a pollster samples 100 people and asked them if they were going to vote for Trump or Clinton, statistically each candidate should get 50 votes. A perfect distribution does not happen very often. A Chi-square can help us. To conduct this particular Chi-square using SPSS is easy (see next box "Steps to Conducting a Chi-Square in SPSS").

Steps to Conducting a Chi-Square in SPSS

1. Go to "Analyze," choose "Descriptive Statistics," and then choose "Crosstabs."
2. Once there you will find a box with: "Exact," "Statistics," "Cells," "Format," "Bootstrap," "Row(s)," "Column(s)," "Layer 1 of 1," "OK," "Paste," "Reset," "Cancel," and "Help."
3. If we are interested in how the sexes differ in their preference for a political candidate, our two variables are sex and presidential preference. In a simple Chi-square we are comparing how groups (rows) compare on a particular variable (column). In this case, you will click on "sex" and move it over to "Row(s)" and move *prespreference* (what we named presidential preference) over to column(s).
4. You need to tell SPSS to run a Chi-square. Click on "Statistics" and click the box for "Chi-square" and then click "Continue."
5. Click "Cells," make sure "Observed" and "Expected" are clicked, and press "Continue." Then press "OK."
6. You should get something like Outputs 15.11–15.13:

Output 15.11

Case Processing Summary

	Cases					
	Valid		Missing		Total	
	N	Percent	N	Percent	N	Percent
sex * prespreference	100	100,0%	0	0,0%	100	100,0%

Output 15.12

- sex * prespreference Crosstabulation

			Prespreference		Total
			Biden	Trump	
sex	male	Count	20	30	50
		Expected Count	26,5	23,5	50,0
	Female	Count	33	17	50
		Expected Count	26,5	23,5	50,0
Total		Count	53	47	100
		Expected Count	53,0	47,0	100,0

Output 15.13

Chi-Square Tests

	Value	df	Asymp. Sig. (2-sided)	Exact Sig. (2-sided)	Exact Sig. (1-sided)
Pearson Chi-Square	6,784[a]	1	,009		
Continuity Correction[b]	5,781	1	,016		
Likelihood Ratio	6,865	1	,009		
Fisher's Exact Test				,016	,008
Linear-by-Linear Association	6,717	1	,010		
N of Valid Cases	100				

a. 0 cells (0,0%) have expected count less than 5. The minimum expected count is 23,50.

b. Computed only for a 2x2 table

We can see many things when we look at these figures. First, Output 15.11 shows that all 100 cases (people) answered the question. Output 15.12 shows how many of each sex preferred each candidate. You can see more men preferred Trump, while more women preferred Biden. The count is observed in the data, while the expected count is the statistical expectation for each sex and their presidential preference when the null hypothesis is true. Figure 15.2 is the result of the Chi-square test. The Chi-square result is: $\chi^2 = 6.784$, $p = .009$, which is indeed significant. The Chi-square shows a significant difference between what was expected and what was observed. The result of the test is written as:

> The results show a significant association between a voter's sex and their preference for president, χ^2 (1) = 6.784, p = .009. Based on the results, men prefer Donald Trump, while women prefer Joe Biden.

Chi-squares are regularly used in communication research and in business, advertising and marketing. Steimel (2012) used Chi-square to explore memorable messages volunteers receive from the organizations they serve and how these messages relate to the volunteer experience. In advertising and marketing, Chi-square is prominent is in taste-testing. We have all heard "two out of three people prefer" one beverage, or toothpaste, or insurance company. Stop and think about it, and you will realize this is a simple Chi-square analysis. One of the activities at the end of this chapter is to conduct a taste test and analyze the data using Chi-square.

In the 2020 U.S. Presidential election, Americans often heard news reports about how men were more likely to vote for Trump over Biden. A simple Chi-square analysis could produce such a result.

Tests of Relationship and Prediction

While some statistical tests are helpful in comparing data, other tests can help us understand relationships between variables and predict how variables will affect other variables.

Correlation

When Stephen was nine, he wanted to play tennis with his friends. His mom got him a tennis racquet, and he went out to play. He had never played before and was horrible. He came home and put the racquet away. His mom told him that the more you practice, the better you will be. He picked up the racket and kept practicing, and today he is a pretty good player. Stephen's tennis ability and the amount he practices can be related in three ways: 1) positively related, which means the more he practiced the better he got; 2) negatively related, which means the more he practiced the worse he got; or, 3) not related at all, meaning as he practiced his playing abilities remained the same. These three relationships are the fundamental principles of a correlation. A **correlation** is a statistical measure of the degree to which two or more variables (interval or ratio) in a sample are related to one another. The statistical term for correlation is the Pearson product-moment correlation coefficient represented by (r). Correlations range from -1.00 to +1.00. A 0.00 correlation represents no relationship between the variables. A correlation (r) of .00 to .25 is a weak correlation, .26 to .50 is a moderate correlation, while .51 and above is a strong correlation. Correlations of -.55 and +.55 have the same magnitude, just different directions (one is positive and the other is negative). We will talk in a moment about direction of correlations.

You can have four types of correlations (relationships): positive, negative, curvilinear, and no relationship. In the following paragraphs, we provide examples of each by focusing on just two variables for each relationship. Please keep in mind that with correlations you can correlate multiple variables with one another at the same time; however, for simplicity we are focusing on just two variables at a time.

A positive correlation is when both variables move in the same direction. As one variable increases in value, the other increases (+/+), and as one variable decreases in value, the other decreases (-/-). Here is an example write-up of a positive correlation (r = .107, p < .001). Figure 15.1

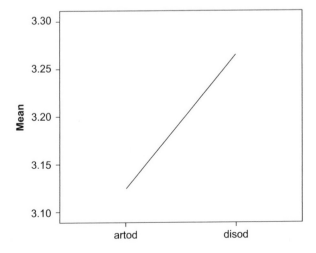

Figure 15.1

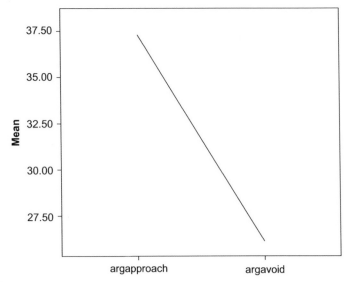

Figure 15.2

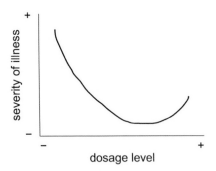

Figure 15.3

shows that the more someone is willing to express articulated dissent in an organization, the more they are willing to express displaced dissent regarding an organization (Kassing, 1998).

In Figure 15.2, you can see a negative correlation. A negative relationship means that as one variable increases in value, the other decreases (+/-), and as one variable decreases in value, the other increases (-/+). In this correlation, the more someone is willing to approach an argument, the less willing they are to avoid an argument (r = -.35, p < .001).

A curvilinear relationship is positive or negative when it begins but then switches directions. Take, for example, the severity of an illness and medication dosage. The more medication you take, the better you generally feel (+/+). However, eventually you can take too much medication, and your body may start to reject and get sick from the medication (+/-). Figure 15.3 is an example of this kind of relationship.

The final kind of relationship is no relationship. Sometimes variables simply are not related to each other. Argumentativeness, for example, is more than likely not related to how much a person likes country music. This relationship should more than likely be nonexistent, so we are not even going to try to create a figure for it. ☺

Principles of Correlations

1. The variables you are correlating must be interval or ratio-level variables.
2. Work for a large sample, as larger samples are more representative of the population.
3. Try to have fairly similar sample sizes for each of your variables. If one variable has 200 responses and the other has 50, this can lead to sampling error issues.
4. A correlation does not mean one variable causes another variable to change. Correlations do not equal causality!
5. Correlations can be one- or two-tailed. If you have a directional hypothesis or research question, you have an idea of the relationship between the variables, so you should explore that particular relationship (one-tailed). If your hypothesis/research question is nondirectional, you have less certainty of the relationship, thus a two-tailed correlation is used to explore the relationship.

Conducting the correlation analysis is actually one of the easiest tests in SPSS, compared to the other statistical tests. We are going to look at some more of the COVID-19 data. Looking back to example 5.7 on patient self-advocacy, Stephen and his team asked people in the U.S. about their own self-advocacy during the COVID-19 pandemic. Specifically, let's look at two constructs, how much information a person seeks out about their illness and how assertive a person is about their health care. Brashers et al. (1999) argue that these two behaviors are positively related/correlated. Stephen and his research team collected data on this construct among more than 335 participants in the U.S. during the COVID-19 pandemic. Conducting a study on this relationship calls for a one-tailed correlation, as research has shown that the constructs should be positively correlated. To see how these two constructs are correlated is a simple process.

Steps to Conducting a Correlation in SPSS

1. Go to "Analyze" and choose "Correlate," and then choose "Bivariate."
2. You will see the following buttons: "Options," "Bootstrap," "Pearson," "Kendall's tau-b," "Spearman," "Two-tailed," "One-tailed," "Flag significant correlations," "OK," "Paste," "Reset," "Cancel," and "Help." For now, you do not need to worry about many of these options.[1]
3. To run the correlation, highlight each variable you want and move them over to the "Variables" list (you can double click on them if you want); in this case we want: articulated and latent.
4. Click on "options" and choose "means and standard deviations" and then click "OK."
5. Click "OK" on the main "Correlation" screen and you will get your outputs (15.14–15.15):

Descriptive Statistics

	Mean	Std. Deviation	N
INFOSEEKING	2.2062	.77723	337
assertiveness	2.5163	.70534	337

Output 15.14

Correlations

		INFOSEEKING	assertiveness
INFOSEEKING	Pearson Correlation	1	.597**
	Sig. (1–tailed)		<.001
	N	337	337
assertiveness	Pearson Correlation	.597**	1
	Sig. (1–tailed)	<.001	
	N	337	337

**. Correlation is significant at the 0.01 level (1–tailed).

Output 15.15

Output 15.14 shows the means, standard deviations, and number of individuals who completed each of your variables. You can see the means and standard deviations for info seeking (M = 2.21; SD = .78) and for assertiveness (M = 2.52; SD = .71). Output 15.15 is the correlation output. This figure shows how info seeking and assertiveness are positively correlated (r = .60, rounded up from .597). Next to the correlation you will notice **. If you look at the bottom of the output, you will see a note a saying "** Correlation is significant at the 0.01 level (2–tailed)." We can interpret this correlation as: there was a significant positive correlation between information seeking and assertiveness (r =.60, p < .001).

Bakker and de Vresse (2011), in an analysis of 16- to 24-year-olds, found that a variety of Internet uses are positively related to numerous kinds of political participation. For example, online social networks and online forum use are positively related to political participation. During the 2020 presidential election, both sides of this debate used social networks and social media to reach out to potential voters.

Regression

The second relational statistic takes correlation a step further and tests how a variable or variables predict(s) another variable. **Regression** is predicting a dependent variable from one or multiple independent variables. Regression analysis is all around us. If any of you has tried to buy a car and gone into negotiations, you have probably heard about a credit score. This term puts fear into the hearts of many but is basically a regressions score. The score tells creditors how likely you are to pay back debt. The score is based on various indicators including your previous debt, payment history, number of bills/debts, and demographics. Creditors, like a car dealer or mortgage company, will look at your score and make a risk analysis about you and the item you want to buy.

If you are doing a regression, you are basically plotting out a line of best fit or to fit a model that best predicts the dependent variable with your independent variable(s). The equation for this line of best fit (the regression equation) is: $Y = a + bX + \varepsilon$. Y is the dependent variable (what you are trying to predict). Alpha or a is the value of Y when the value of X equals 0. Beta or b is the slope of the regression line, which is how much Y changes for each unit change in X. X is the value of the independent variable (what is predicting Y). ε is the amount of error; for simplicity, we assume ε is 0 in regression analyses.

Let's take an example of how to predict argumentativeness related to levels of religiousness. Y equals the level of argumentativeness. The alpha (a) equals an individual's average level of argumentativeness, lets' say 25. The beta (*b*) is the impact on *Y* for each increase in an individual's level of religiousness; let's say +5 on Infante and Rancer's (1982) argumentativeness scale. *X* is an individual's level of religiousness. For every three levels of religiousness (*X* = 3), *Y* = 25 + (5)(3) = 25 + 15 = an argumentativeness level of 40. Other variables may also predict argumentativeness (ε), but this regression only predicts the effect of religiousness on argumentativeness.

As with a correlation, visually representing the data is helpful. You can do this with a scatterplot. Here are examples of scatterplots showing one variable (*X*) predicting *Y*. In (a) you can see a positive correlation, which can represent *X* having a strong positive effect on *Y*. In (b), you can see a slightly negative correlation, meaning *X* has a slight negative effect on *Y*. In (c), we see a perfect negative correlation, so *X* predicts *Y*. In (d) there is no real relationship between *X* and *Y*, which means *X* does not predict *Y*.

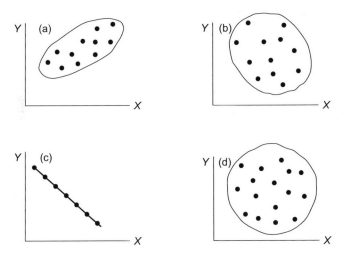

Figure 15.4

Principles of Simple Linear Regression

1. The dependent variable (what you are predicting) needs to be an interval or ratio variable.
2. The independent variables will normally be interval or ratio variables. In more advanced kinds of regression, you can have independent variables that are nominal or ordinal. We will not spend time on this right now, as using these kinds of variables can get rather complicated.
3. The sample you collect to conduct a regression should be as representative as possible of the population.
4. The variables should be normally distributed; there should not be high levels of skew or kurtosis.
5. Strive for as large a sample as possible to best represent the population.

Running a regression analysis, like many statistical tests, is not a complex procedure if you know your dependent and independent variable. Returning to COVID-19, let's look at some data from Italy. Research has explored for many years the link between a person's willingness to speak publicly on an issue and the extent to which they believe others share their opinions. When we think others share our opinions, we are more likely to speak our minds publicly. When we think we are in the minority, we are less likely to speak out; we fear being ostracized. Stephen and his team explored this relationship on the topic of COVID-19 and government responses.

Steps to Conducting a Simple Linear Regression in SPSS

1. Go to "Analyze," then choose "Regression," then choose "Linear."
2. Once in the "Linear" regression box, you will see the following commands: "Statistics," "Plots," "Save," "Options," "Bootstrap," "Previous," "Next," "Enter," "Reset," "Paste," "Cancel," and "OK."
3. Choose your "Dependent variable" and "Independent variable(s)." The analysis for this example is data looking at how much belief that you share your opinion with others predicts willingness to speak in Italy. The dependent variable is "willingness to speak." The independent variable is "share opinion with others." With this data file, highlight the dependent variable and move it over to "Dependent:". Click on the independent variable you want and move it over to "Independent(s):".
4. For a basic linear regression, you do not need to click on anything else. If you want to do more advanced regressions you can use other buttons, but that is something called Multiple Regression. So, at this point press "OK." You will get the following four outputs (15.16–15.19):

Variables Entered/Removed[a]

Model	Variables Entered	Variables Removed	Method
1	ShareOpinion[b]	.	Enter

a. Dependent Variable: WillingnesstoSpeak

b. All requested variables entered.

Output 15.16

Model Summary

Model	R	R Square	Adjusted R Square	Std. Error of the Estimate
1	.505[a]	.255	.252	.96132

a. Predictors: (Constant), ShareOpinion

Output 15.17

ANOVA[a]

Model		Sum of Squares	df	Mean Square	F	Sig.
1	Regression	97.534	1	97.534	105.541	<.001[b]
	Residual	285.558	309	.924		
	Total	383.093	310			

a. Dependent Variable: WillingnesstoSpeak

b. Predictors: (Constant), ShareOpinion

Output 15.18

Coefficients[a]

Model		Unstandardized Coefficients		Standardized Coefficients	t	Sig.
		B	Std. Error	Beta		
1	(Constant)	1.290	.214		6.019	<.001
	ShareOpinion	.565	.055	.505	10.273	<.001

a. Dependent Variable: WillingnesstoSpeak

Output 15.19

Output 15.16 shows the variables entered into the regression. "Variables Entered" shows the independent variable, and beneath that the dependent variable is listed. Output 15.17 shows the relationships, predictive nature of the two variables, and the standard error. You will first see the correlation between the two variables (.505, rounded up to .51). If you square the correlation, you get the coefficient of determination, the R^2. The R^2 explains how much one variable predicts the other variable. In this case, the R^2 is .26 (rounded up from .255). This means 26% of an individual's willingness to speak about COVID-19-related government policies in Italy are predicted by the extent to which they believe their opinions are shared by others. The Output also contains the R^2_{adj}. This is the R^2 adjusted/modified taking into consideration the number of independent variables and the sample size. The smaller your sample size and the more independent variables you have, the more likely your R^2_{adj} will drop significantly from the original R^2. The R^2_{adj} is a more conservative–and, in many ways, a more realistic–value of the total prediction in the regression.

Output 15.18 is an ANOVA table; it should look similar to the one from a few pages earlier. You can see the F-value, the alpha (p) and the df. The F and p tell you the regression is significant, $F = 105.54, p < .0001$.

Output 15.19 shows the beta (b or slope) value and how significant the beta is. Most researchers will report the standardized coefficient, in this case .51 (rounded up from .505),[2] $p < .0001$. This can be interpreted as perception of sharing opinions increases an individual's willingness to speak in China ($b = .51$). You should consider the importance of the statistical significance and the practical significance of your regression. In this case, our independent variable predicts that 26% of the dependent variable and is statistically significant. This is both practically and statistically significant. However, in some cases you might have a regression that is statistically significant but might only predict 1–10%, for example. In such cases, you should temper the interpretation by saying that, while the practical results are limited, the result is statistically significant.

This is how you can write up regression results:

Belief that others' share an opinion regarding COVID-19 was a statistically significant predictor of an individual's willingness to voice an opinion about such policies in Italy $F(1, 310) = 105.54, R^2 = .26, R^2_{adj} = .25$. Belief that others share an opinion regarding COVID-19 significantly increased willingness to voice an opinion on the topic ($b = .51$).

Regression is one of the most-used statistical methods in communication and social scientific research. Yanovitzky et al. (2006), for example, found that alcohol use by peers was a strong predictor of students' personal alcohol use. Hollander (2010) found that Americans who perceived President Obama as a Muslim in September 2008 were more likely to see him as a Muslim in November 2008 during the election. The point of these two random articles is to show the diversity of regression in research.

During the lead-up to the 2020 election, pollsters were canvassing the U.S. to report on who they predicted would win the vote. Through a combination of various independent variables, pollsters reported how, on different days, one side would be ahead of the other. In the end, these polls, as have polls in many other political events, demonstrate how error (human behavior, for example) influences our decisions and behaviors and thus final results.

Summary

This chapter was a how-to guide for inferential statistics. Generally, statistics are used by social scientific researchers but can sometimes be used by interpretive and critical/cultural researchers depending on the focus of the study. Hopefully, after reading this chapter and the accompanying student paper, you feel comfortable enough to try to conduct inferential statistics.

Key Steps and Questions to Consider

1. Inferential statistics make inferences or help us make conclusions about data.
2. There are two main kinds of inferential statistics: tests of difference and tests of relationship/prediction.
3. There are two kinds of *t*-tests, the dependent and the independent *t*-test. Both help us better understand mean differences between two groups. The result of a *t*-test is a *t*-value.
4. A one-way analysis of variance (ANOVA) is a way to explore mean differences between more than two groups. With ANOVA you conduct an *F*-test.
5. To understand differences between groups when conducting ANOVA you need to perform post-hoc analyses, such as Scheffé or Tukey's.
6. The Chi-square test is a test where you compare the observed frequencies of a variable against the expected frequencies to see if there is a statistical difference between the two. This is a nonparametric test.
7. A correlation is a statistical measure of the degree to which two or more variables (interval or ratio) in a sample are related to one another. Correlations range from -1.0 to +1.0.
8. A regression is predicting a dependent variable from one or multiple independent variables.

Activities

1. Spend one week collecting examples of inferential statistical you see in your everyday life. Keep an eye on the shows you watch, the papers and books you read, the statements people make. Remember, sayings like "9 out of 10 dentists recommend . . ." are statistical statements! Notice how often inferential statistics permeate our lives.

2. Try tracking down the study, which provided one or more of the inferential statistics you collected from Activity 1. Review the statistical tests used in the study. Were the appropriate statistical tests used in the study?
3. Make a chart of the different statistical tests, which identifies when each is appropriate to use. Consider the data type (e.g., interval, ratio level), type of variable, form of distribution, etc.
4. Special Challenge: See if you can find a research study that supports the "9 out of 10 dentists recommend/prefer/agree" statement!
5. Work through the following Chi² example. You are interested in the soda preference of students on your campus. You ask 90 students to take a taste test. 50 people prefer Diet Coke, 17 prefer Coke Zero, and 23 prefer Coca-Cola. What should be the expected frequencies? What are the observed frequencies? Is there a statistical difference? In the online companion, we go through how to enter this data and the answer.

Discussion Questions

1. Review the provided student paper by Jessica Sturtevant. Sturtevant identified a number of reasons her study did not provide statistically significant results. Discuss how your class could replicate the study with modifications to generate different results and insights.

Key Terms

Analysis of Variance (ANOVA)	Independent Samples *t*-test	Regression
	Inferential Statistics	Scheffé Test
Chi-Square	Nonparametric	S.S. Between Groups
Correlation	Numerator *df*	S.S. Within Groups
Denominator *df*	Parametric	*T*-test
Dependent Samples *t*-test	Post-hoc Comparisons	Tukey's

References

Bakker, T. P., & de Vresse, C. H. (2011). Good news for the future? Young people, internet use, and political participation. *Communication Research, 38*, 451-470. https://doi.org/10.1177%2F0093650210381738

Brashers, D. E., Haas, S. M., & Neidig, J. L. (1999). The patient self-advocacy scale: Measuring patient involvement in health care decision-making interactions. *Health Communication, 11*, 97-121. https://doi.org/10.1207/s15327027hc1102_1

Croucher, S. M., Kelly, S., Condon, S. M., Campbell, E., Galy-Badenas, F., Rahmani, D., Nshom, E., & Zeng, C. (2018). A longitudinal analysis of the relationship between adaptation and argumentativeness. *International Journal of Conflict Management, 29*, 91-108. doi: 10.1108/IJCMA-0502017-0045

Croucher, S. M., Kelly, S., Zeng, C., Burkey, M., & Galy-Badenas, F. (2020). A longitudinal examination of validity and temporal stability of organizational dissent measurement in France.

Journal of Intercultural Communication Research, 49, 107-118. doi:10.1080/17475759.2020.1716827

Hollander, B. A. (2010). Persistence in the perception of Barack Obama as a Muslim in the 2008 Presidential Campaign. *Journal of Media & Religion, 9*, 55-66. https://doi.org/10.1080/15348421003738769

Infante, D. A., & Rancer, A. S. (1982). A conceptualization and measure of argumentativeness. *Journal of Personality Assessment, 46*(1), 72-80. https://doi.org/10.1207/s15327752jpa4601_13

Ivanov, B., Parker, K. A., & Pfau, M. (2012). The interaction effect of attitude base and multiple attacks on the effectiveness of inoculation. *Communication Research Reports, 29*, 1-11.

Kassing, J. W. (1998). Development and validation of the organizational dissent scale. *Management Communication Quarterly, 12*, 183-229. https://doi.org/10.1177%2F0893318998122002

Steimel, S. (2012). Connecting with volunteers: Memorable messages and volunteer identification. *Communication Research Reports, 30*, 12-21. https://doi.org/10.1080/08824096.2012.746220

Yanovitzky, I., Stewart, L. P., & Lederman, L. C. (2006). Social distance, perceived drinking by peers and alcohol use by college students. *Health Communication, 19*, 1-10. https://psycnet.apa.org/doi/10.1207/s15327027hc1901_1

Yun, K. A., Constantini, C., & Billingsley, S. (2012). The effect of taking a public speaking class on one's writing abilities. *Communication Research Reports, 29*, 285-291. https://doi.org/10.1080/08824096.2012.723270

Undergraduate Student Paper

Students' Use of Online Media and Attitude toward Intellectual Property

Jessica Sturtevant

Abstract

As the use of online media has become more popular, issues such as online copyright and illegal downloading have become more prevalent. College students, as avid users of online media, are a key population in these developments. This study surveyed college students about their use of online media and their attitudes towards intellectual property issues and looked for patterns among the results. Although no statistically significant connections emerged, by examining both the actual media use and the abstract opinions of students, this study shows the importance of this issue and of future research in the area.

> The study shows an important reason for conducting research. Even when the results do not prove a hypothesis or research question, the study is still worthwhile. Such studies show us what is *not* connected or relevant.

Introduction

The use of online media, including listening to music and watching videos online, has become common, especially among young adults. As the use of and the market for media online has spread, so have issues concerning copyright. The increasing availability of music and video online has affected how consumers acquire media and how they view it. This study focused on college students, a group at the forefront of media use and innovation. Participants were questioned about their use of online media and their attitudes towards issues of online copyright. The results were analyzed for patterns and correlations.

The first factor the researcher looked at was gender and its effects on media use. Gender has been linked to use of the Internet in previous studies, for example Su-Yen Chen and Yang-Chih Fu's (2008) study of Internet use and academic achievement among Taiwanese adolescents. Chen and Fu found males used the Internet more frequently than females, and males and females used the Internet for different purposes: males were more likely to play online games, and females were more likely to search for information or socialize online (Chen & Fu, 2008). This study and others like it prompted the first research question:

RQ1: Does the gender of a student affect the amount of online media use?

The goal of this study was to see if there are connections between the use of online media and attitudes toward issues of online copyright. These issues include the idea of intellectual property—what rights does an artist have to a work, and how should those rights be protected online? Studies such as Friedman (1996), Jones (2000), and Oberholzer-Gee and Strumpf (2007, 2009) discussed these issues in a general sense and try to offer solutions, but little research has been done that looks specifically at the relationship between media use and attitudes of copyright and intellectual property. To study this relationship the study asked:

RQ2: Are students who use more online media more likely to support having media generally available online?

RQ3: Are students who use more online media more likely to support lenient punishments compared to those who use less online media?

> The student has a nice lead into the research questions. The reader is guided to the RQs.

Method

Students' use of online media and opinions about online copyright issues were measured using a two-part questionnaire. The first section used a Likert scale ranging from "never" to "often (almost every day)" to measure frequency of online media use in seven categories, including listening to music online, downloading and buying music online, watching TV shows and movies online, and watching clips on YouTube. Students were also asked about use of Netflix, iTunes or other subscription services. The scores were averaged together to get a comprehensive score of each participant's media use.

> Review the data standards for using an independent samples *t*-test and a Spearman correlation analysis. Remember, you have an unbalanced data comparison with 17 males and 30 females. Does the data fit with the selected tests?
>
> The sample size is fairly small for statistical analysis. Be sure to check with your teacher/advisor about her/his expectations for sample size. The sample size for this study was appropriate for the parameters set by her professor.
>
> Refer to the chapter on Data and ask yourself the following questions: do 18–20-year-olds represent all college students? Is a door-to-door sampling from one section of a dorm representative of college students? The student could address the questions by tightening up the research questions (e.g., "Are 18–20 year old college students . . . . ") or addressing them as limitations at the end of the paper.

The second section of the questionnaire addressed students' opinions about online copyright. Participants were asked if they believed media should be generally available online, what compensation artists should receive, how they felt about punishments for illegal downloading, and how informed they felt themselves and the public to be about these issues.

> The first section used a Likert scale, but we're in the dark about the second section. Description of the method section should be thorough so the reader can gather a comprehensive overview of data collection. The questions in the second section look solid, but what format was used to gather the data—as you have and will continue to discover in your understanding of methods—can be a critical in research design.

The questionnaire was administered to 47 second-year students at Marist College. Participants were between the ages of 18 and 20; 17 were male and 30 were female. The researcher went door to door in one section of the dorms to get a sample of Marist students. All surveys were completed anonymously to encourage honesty and detailed responses.

The data for this study were analyzed using three separate tests, one for each research question. For research question one, an independent samples t-test was conducted comparing participant gender and media use. For research questions two and three, a Spearman correlation analysis was used to compare participant media use and opinion of whether media should be generally available or not, and participant media use opinion about punishments (Wrench et al., 2008).

Results and Discussion

The gender of the participant did not have a significant effect on the amount of online media use, $t (22.863) = -.20, p = ns$. Both men ($M = 3.4534, SD = .68292$) and women ($M = 3.4877, SD = .35718$) had very similar rates of media use. This is contrary to what Chen & Fu, 2008) discussed; however, this may be due to the smaller sample and different age group (college students compared to adolescents) and to the fact Chen and Fu looked at all different uses of the Internet and the current study focused only on media use. The use of a comprehensive score for media use may have made the results slightly less accurate than comparing the use of each type of media between participants.

> Normally, all the statistical results are provided in their own section of the paper. Then limitations, interpretations, and alternate interpretations are provided in a separate section of the paper. Shifting to limitations and explanations in the middle of providing results may lead to confusion.

The prediction that students who use more online media would be more likely to support having media available online was not verified by the results, $r (45) = -.01, p = ns$. Most of the students supported having media accessible, regardless of how often they personally used online media (39 students responded media should be available; four said it should not be available; and four said it should be available with conditions). However, all of the students reported using online media on a regular basis, so this study only compared whether the frequency of online media use was a factor, not whether people who use online media differ in their opinions from those who do not use it at all.

Finally, participant media use was not significantly related to opinion about punishments for illegal downloading or file sharing, $r (45) = -.05, p = ns$. However, it seems logical that those who use more online media (and may use it illegally) would be more likely to support fewer or more lenient punishments than those who use less media, and this result, though not statistically significant, was closer to being significant than either of the others, so it is possible that with a larger sample there may be a correlation.

Conclusion

Though this study did not make any significant connections between students' use of online media and attitudes towards issues of copyright and intellectual property, it did begin to examine an important and multifaceted issue. All the students in the study reported using online media, with most students using some form almost every day and many using all seven types described. All the students surveyed expressed some opinion about copyright issues, with most in favor of media being generally available online but many proposing solutions to meet the needs of the artists as well as the needs of the consumers. There are connections and patterns among these results, though they may not be statistically significant.

Further research is needed to look at the relationship between media use and attitudes toward intellectual property in more depth, examining larger samples and audiences other than college students to see if these results hold true, or if the trends change in a larger sample.

Notes

1. There are three options we want to explain. Spearman and Kendall's tau-b are kinds of correlations you can run when you have nonparametric data. When your data is not-normally distributed or you are working with ordinal data, these tests can be run instead of Pearson, which is the one used for parametric data. Two-tailed versus one-tailed is the other issue we want to clarify at this point. When you have a directional hypothesis, choose a one-tailed test; when your hypothesis is non-directional, choose a two-tailed. The difference is that a two-tailed is used when you cannot predict the nature of correlation.
2. Do you remember this number from Output 15.17? It's the R, or the correlation between your independent and dependent variable.

References

Chen, S.-Y., & Fu, Y.-C. (2008). Internet use and academic achievement: Gender differences in early adolescence. *Adolescence, 44*, 797–812.

Friedman, A. J. (1996). Summary: Five solutions to intellectual property issues in a digital age. *Leonardo, 29*(4), 321–322.

Jones, S. (2000). Music and the internet. *Popular Music, 19*(2), 217–230.

Oberholzer-Gee, F., & Strumpf, K. (2007). The effect of file sharing on record sales: An empirical analysis. *Journal of Political Economy, 115*(1), 1–42.

Oberholzer-Gee, F., & Strumpf, K. (2009). File sharing and copyright. In J. Lerner & S. Stern (Eds.), *Innovation policy and the economy 2009* (Vol. 10). MIT Press.

Wrench, J. S., Thomas-Maddox, C., Richmond, V. P., & McCroskey, J. C. (2008). *Quantitative research methods for communication*. Oxford University Press.

16 Experimental Design

What Will I Learn About Experiments and Experimental Design?

When we think about experiments, we typically imagine people in labs wearing white coats and tinkering with flammable liquids and chemicals. We all have images of such experiments. We have seen them in movies and television and maybe even conducted a few experiments in a physics or chemistry class. The purpose of such experiments is to test the effects of one or more variables on another variable (when you mix chemical X with chemical Y, what happens?). While such experiments typify the "average" science experiment, they are not the only kinds of experiment on the block.

Conducting an experiment is a process. To perform an experiment, you should consider various questions. 1) What variables are under investigation? 2) What data is being collected and analyzed? 3) Where is the source of your data? 4) How is the experiment being conducted? 5) How will the experimental data be analyzed? We explore these questions and others in Chapter 16 on experimental research.

What Is Experimental Design in Communication Research?

Experiment

The focus of this chapter is experimental design. An **experiment** is a methodological design process to test how one or more variables that have been manipulated by a researcher influence another variable. A researcher should attempt to control any other variables that might affect

DOI: 10.4324/9781003109129-19

the relationship between the variables. The purpose of an experiment is to identify any causal relationships between the variables. We know there is a lot to digest in this definition. Don't worry, we are going to break down all the elements in this chapter.

Causality

An experiment is a process where a researcher investigates a possible cause-and-effect relationship between variables. A **causal argument** is not an easy thing to make. In order to make a causal argument, you must meet the following three criteria. First, there must be a manipulation of an independent variable before a change happens in the dependent variable. Second, changes in the dependent and the independent variables must be correlated (happen together). When the independent variable changes, the dependent variable should change soon afterward. Third, any change in the dependent variable should be explainable only by the independent variable and not by any other **intervening variable** or alternate factor/explanation.

> Let's consider the following example: when an anesthesiologist gives a patient anesthesia for a surgery (independent variable), the intended effect is for the patient to go to sleep for the surgery (dependent variable). The amount of anesthesia given depends on a lot of factors: the patient, the type of surgery, etc. Before and during the procedure, the anesthesiologist is careful to monitor the level of anesthesia to make sure the patient has the right amount for the desired duration of unconsciousness. We trust anesthesia will knock us out and that the effect is not caused by some other intervening variable. Through numerous trials and experiments, researchers have proven the reliability and "safeness" of anesthesia.

When conducting experiments to make causal claims, researchers follow a careful step-by-step process. We will outline this process in Figure 16.1 and then describe more in-depth each aspect of the process.

Figure 16.1 Basic Steps of Experimental Research

1. Preparation
   A. State the research problem and the hypotheses/research questions
   B. Decide if experimental methods are appropriate
2. Variable and Method Selection/Definition
   A. Define the independent and dependent variables
   B. Identify any potential intervening variables
   C. Choose the appropriate measures, surveys, etc. to use in the experiment
3. Experiment Design
   A. Experimental Control
   B. Comparison groups, random assignment, pretest and posttests
   C. Types of Designs
4. Evaluate the Experiment
   A. Internal Validity
   B. External Validity
5. Analyze the Data

Experiment Preparation

Before conducting an experiment, you must consider two main questions. First, what is the broad research problem (issue)? Second, what hypotheses/research questions are you interested in studying? In Chapters 3-7 we discussed various issues related to how you formulate and generate hypotheses/research questions. Before you begin an experiment, you need to know what you want to study.

Second, ask if an experiment is necessary. After you have done some preliminary research and determined the general topic(s) of interest, you must ask a very important question: is an experiment necessary? Remember, an experiment helps us determine causality. Causality means one or more variables cause or lead to a change in another variable. In many research studies you want to show causality, while in other studies you are not interested in showing causality.

Flip back a few pages to Chapter 15 on Inferential Statistics. In that chapter, we reference various studies. One study that did not use an experimental design was by Yanovitzky et al. (2006). The authors were interested in sampling college students for their perceptions about alcohol use based on distant versus proximate peers in predicting college students' drinking behavior. The study used a cross-sectional design. In Yun et al.'s (2012) study on the effects of taking a public-speaking class on writing abilities, the researchers used a longitudinal experimental design. The researchers were interested in the effects of taking a university public-speaking course on a student's writing abilities. Thus, testing the students' writing abilities was essential at the start of the course (a pretest) and then at the end of the course (a posttest).

Think about any medicine you have taken in your life . . . aspirin, ibuprofen, nurofen, a prescription from a physician. All of these medications have gone through what we call a clinical trial. To test the safety, governments require drug developers to test medications strictly. The first step is for the developers of the medications to state what the medications will do (their intended purpose). The second step is a clinical trial (and experiment) and is required. We will outline the next steps later in this chapter.

Variable and Method Selection/Definition

You need to define your independent and dependent variables in many studies. With experiments in particular, you may also need to identify intervening variables. You must also choose appropriate measures to explore those variables.

You need to define your variables of interest. With experiments, you are exploring the effects of one or more independent variables on a dependent variable. You may need to consider any potential intervening variables that may affect the causal relationship between the independent and the dependent variables. In Yun et al.'s (2012) study of the effects on writing abilities of taking a public-speaking class, the following five hypotheses were posed (p. 287):

H1: Individuals exposed to a public-speaking class will have greater gains in their writing skills of <u>writing context</u> than those not exposed to a public-speaking class.

H2: Individuals exposed to a public-speaking class will have greater gains in their writing skills of <u>content development</u> than those not exposed to a public-speaking class.

H3: Individuals exposed to a public-speaking class will have greater gains in their writing skills of <u>writing structure</u> than those not exposed to a public-speaking class.

H4: Individuals exposed to a public-speaking class will have greater gains in their writing skills in <u>use of sources and evidence</u> than those not exposed to a public-speaking class.

H5: Individuals exposed to a public speaking class will have greater gains in their writing skills in <u>control of syntax</u> than those not exposed to a public speaking class.

In each hypothesis, exposure or not to a public speaking class is the independent variable. The dependent variable in each hypothesis has been underlined; the dependent variable for each hypothesis focuses on an aspect of writing ability. You will find that, in well-written experimental studies, the researchers take care clearly to identify and explain their variables in the "Method" section of the article.

Yun et al. (2012) did not identify any potential intervening variables in the method section or in the review of literature. However, as only two of their hypotheses were supported (we will talk more shortly about data analysis), the researchers offered a potential intervening variable in the discussion section. The researchers noted that the outcomes of public-speaking and writing classes are different, and thus future studies should take into consideration the different outcomes. Therefore, if they conducted another experiment on the same topic, the researchers may alter their materials to consider the pedagogical differences between public-speaking and writing courses.

Think back to Chapter 13–Surveys and Chapter 5–Data. One of the issues discussed in both chapters was the different methods available for collecting data using a survey. You have many tools at your disposal if you want to conduct an experiment: self-report or other-report surveys, observations, and other codeable forms of data. Many researchers collect self-reports or other-reports from participants at various points in time (longitudinal data). Some prefer to observe human behavior. Yun et al. (2012) had students write a 3–5 page paper at the start and the end of the semester (about 12 weeks apart). The papers were on a variety of topics. The papers were then graded based on a standardized writing rubric by trained coders. You have many experimental measures available in a study. The key is to choose the most appropriate ones for your study. The choice will be based on your literature review of what other researchers have done and on your knowledge of the subject.

When conducting a clinical trial to determine the effectiveness and safety of a new medication, researchers have to ask themselves a few questions related to variables. What independent, dependent, and intervening variables could affect our understanding of how the medication affects the human body? Let's say researchers are testing a new headache pill. The researchers assert: Patients exposed to "Headache Pill X" will have less headache pain than patients exposed to other headache pills. The independent variable is "Headache Pill X" exposure, and the dependent variable is the level of headache pain. When doing the trials, the researchers must determine if any intervening variables could affect their causal argument that "Headache Pill X" reduces headache pain. We will talk more about how researchers do this shortly. Finally, the researchers have lots of ways to measure the pain relief of the pill. They could use self-reports from volunteers who take the pills, they could observe the volunteers, or they could take measurements of their blood pressure or other vitals of the patients to measure pain. Medical researchers think about all these things.

Types of Experiments (Design)

Experimental Control

So, you've decided to conduct an experiment. You've defined your variables and chosen the appropriate measures for the experiment. The next step is to choose the design of your experiment. You can conduct an experiment in myriad ways. The purpose of an experiment is to establish a causal relationship between variables. To do this, the independent variable must be manipulated in some way. Experimental design is the key because causality cannot be established without **experimental control**. Experimental control is evaluating the manipulation of the independent variable for effectiveness and to ensure you have controlled for (removed the effects of) alternative variables. You can take multiple steps to check for effective manipulation of the independent variable(s). The options are called **manipulation checks**. These steps, often statistical procedures, check (test) if the participants perceived the independent variable(s) the way a researcher intended. In Ivanov et al.'s (2012) examination of inoculation, the researchers conducted *t*-tests as manipulation checks of their inoculation messages (the independent variables).

To achieve experimental control, three things are essential: comparison groups, random assignment of participants to independent variable conditions, and pretest-posttest testing.

Comparison and Control Groups

When conducting an experiment, some of the participants need to be exposed to (given) the independent variable, and some should not be exposed. The group exposed to the manipulated levels of the independent variable(s) are called the **comparison group**. In the Yu et al. (2012) study on the relationship between writing and taking a public-speaking class, the comparison group was participants in the public-speaking class. The participants completed the writing assignment at the start of the semester and then at the end of the semester, so the researchers could see if the public-speaking class had any effect on their writing abilities. The researchers then compared the scores of the comparison group to a separate group called the control group. A **control group** is not exposed to the independent variable(s). In the case of Yu et al., the control group was students enrolled in a history class. The researchers excluded history students who had already taken a public-speaking class. The control group completed the same writing assignments as the comparison group. Comparing the control and the comparison groups allowed Yu et al. to argue the effects of the public-speaking class on writing abilities.

In both of the Yu et al. (2012) groups, the participants knew they were being measured for some kind of experiment. In some experiments, the participants do not know if they have been exposed to the independent variable(s). A **placebo** is when an individual thinks they have received a treatment, but they have not. Often in medical studies, researchers will give volunteers sugar pills. The pills, which have no effects on the body, are given to help differentiate the true effects of medications. People often believe a medication is working when in fact they are getting the placebo (and thus the phrase "placebo effect"). Placebo groups are sometimes used in social scientific and communication research.

Random Assignment

Remember, one of the goals in an experiment is to compare the results of the control and the comparison groups on some measures (generally pre- and posttests, which we will discuss in a bit). To facilitate the most reliable and valid comparison and to ensure your groups are equivalent, you should randomly assign participants. This is called **random assignment**. If your groups are not equivalent, you could have selection bias or other characteristics present in one group that are not present in another group. Think back to the discussion of random sampling from Chapters 5-7. While random assignment is slightly different, many of the same principles apply. You want to be confident your groups represent your population as closely as possible. The best way to do this is by randomly assigning.

Pre- and Posttests

Researchers often use pretests and posttests. A **pretest** is a measure (test) of the dependent variable before the manipulated independent variable. A **posttest** is the same exact measure (test) of the dependent variable given after the delivery of the manipulated independent variable. The purpose of giving a pre- and posttest is to determine if a change has occurred in the participant from the time of the pretest to the time of the posttest. If the participants in the comparison group have been exposed to the manipulated independent variable, the researchers can attribute the change in participant behavior to the independent variable, causality (as long as a few other conditions are met, of course, which we talked about earlier). In the Yu et al. (2012) study, the researchers had all the students in the comparison and the control groups write a three to five page paper at the start of the class (pretest) and at the end of the class (posttest). The researchers then analyzed the papers based on a writing rubric. They then compared the results for students in the history class (control group) and the public-speaking class (comparison group) to see if there were improvements in student writing skills.

To show causality, researchers need to control the manipulation of the independent variable(s). Utilizing comparison and control groups, random assignment, and pre- and posttests, along with manipulation of the independent variable(s), help researchers make causal claims. When studies are conducted with all of these elements, the studies are true experimental designs. If one or more of these elements is absent from the design, the study is considered a pre-experimental or quasi-experimental design. We discuss these types of designs next.

Pre-Experimental Designs

Pre-experimental designs lack one of the three elements we listed earlier: comparison and control groups, random assignment of participants to groups, and/or pretests and posttests. We will outline two examples of pre-experimental design: the one-shot case study and the one group pretest posttest design.

One-Shot Case Study

The **one-shot case study** is a design where some manipulation of the independent variable occurs, and after the manipulation the measurement of the dependent variable is taken. For example, imagine you want to measure the effectiveness of a political campaign on voting behavior. After the election, you give a survey to a group of voters and you ask them about their perceptions of the candidate. Your research tries to argue, based on the results of the survey, that the campaign had an effect on the voters' political opinions. However, without a measure of the voters' opinions before the campaign, a researcher cannot show causality.

One-Group Pretest Posttest

The **one-group pretest posttest design** adds the element of a pretest to the one-shot case study. In this type of design, the researcher administers a pretest of the dependent variable, the independent variable is manipulated, and then the dependent variable is measured again (posttest). Take the study on the effectiveness of a political campaign on voting behavior. With a one-group pretest posttest design, you would measure individuals' opinions about the political candidate before the start of the campaign (pretest), the campaign happens (the independent variable), and then you measure the opinions about the political candidate after the campaign (posttest). Finally, you compare the results of the pretest and the posttest for changes in political opinion and attribute these changes to the manipulated independent variable. This type of design is a more sophisticated design than the one-shot case study design because it has the pretest component, which provides for a point of comparison. This is what happened in the Yu et al. (2012) study on the effects of taking a public-speaking class on writing skills. See Figure 16.2 for a visual depiction of the pre-experimental designs.

Figure 16.2 Pre-Experimental Designs

One-Shot Case Study   X   O
One-Shot Pretest Posttest   O   X   O
O = Measurement of Dependent Variable
X = Independent Variable Manipulation
Source: Campbell and Stanley (1963)

While a pre-experimental design provides for statistical reliability and validity, it is difficult to absolutely state that the independent variable caused a change in the dependent variable. Quasi-experimental designs take pre-experimental designs a step further in sophistication. We will outline two designs: the time-series design and the nonequivalent control group design.

Quasi-Experimental Designs

Time-Series Design

The **time-series design** measures the dependent variable at various points of time before and after the manipulation of the independent variable. The purpose of measuring the dependent variable at various points in time is to assess degrees of change in the dependent variable over time. This kind of design is needed or useful when you are interested in measuring the development or change in the dependent variable. Let's return to the impact of a political campaign on voters' opinions about a candidate. It would be advantageous to measure the voters' opinions at various stages before a major debate (let's say once a week before the debate), and then the debate takes place. After the debate, measure the opinions again (this time every three weeks). This type of measurement design may reveal changes in opinions toward the candidate before and after the debate. While this kind of design is more sophisticated than the pre-experimental designs, it is still subject to problems. The design lacks random assignment and a control group, and thus the researcher should not claim causality.

Nonequivalent Control Group Design

A **nonequivalent control group design** has two groups—a control and a comparison group. Both groups are given a pretest and a posttest. However, only the comparison group is exposed to the independent variable. In the Yu et al. (2012) study on the effects of taking a public-speaking class on writing skills, the researchers used this kind of design. Both groups were given a pretest and posttest (the writing assignment graded by independent coders). The comparison group was exposed to the independent variable (the public speaking class). The control group (the history class) was not exposed to the independent variable. This design, like the time-series design, is more sophisticated than pre-experimental designs. However, the approach lacks random assignment, which limits its ability to prove causality. See Figure 16.3 for a visual depiction of the quasi-experimental designs.

Figure 16.3　Quasi-Experimental Designs

Time-Series Designs	O_1	O_2	O_3	X	O_4	O_5　O_6
Nonequivalent Control Group	$\underline{O_1}$	X	$\underline{O_2}$	O_3	O_4	

Source: Campbell and Stanley (1963)

The quasi-experimental designs provide more evidence for causality than the pre-experimental designs. However, neither the pre- nor the quasi-experimental designs incorporate random assignments. The lack of random assignment threatens the reliability of the experiments and limits the causal argument. True experiments, on the other hand, incorporate all the necessary elements for the best cause-and-effect argument. We will outline three designs: the pretest-posttest control group design, the posttest-only control group design, and the Solomon Four-Group Design.

True-Experimental Designs

Pretest-Posttest Control Group Design

The **pretest-posttest control group design** uses pretests and posttests, comparison and control groups, and random assignment to assess the effects of an independent variable(s) on a dependent variable. The design is identical to the nonequivalent control group, except that it includes random assignment of study participants into either comparison or control groups. Pieterse et al. (2006) used this design to assess communication messages during cancer genetic counseling. The study involved offering counselors feedback on counseling. However, not all the counselors (participants) received feedback during the study. Those who did not receive feedback were the control group. The purpose of giving some counselor feedback/training was to assess the effectiveness of the communication messages. A weakness of this experimental design is that, even though participants are randomly assigned to groups, the researchers may not know enough information about the participants to determine if differences in the group affected the outcomes. The assignment of participants to groups, even random assignment, may lead to limited statistical power.

Posttest-Only Control Group Design

The **posttest-only control group design** includes random assignment, posttests, comparison and control groups, and random assignment. Beckie (1989) used this design in an analysis of the impact of an educative telephone program on levels of knowledge and anxiety of patients undergoing coronary artery bypass surgery after hospital discharge. With a posttest-only control group design, patients were randomly assigned to either an experimental or a control group. A significant difference between the state anxiety level of the experimental and the control group was evident. While this type of design does use random assignment, without a pretest it is impossible to measure a change in behavior due to the manipulation of the independent variable.

Solomon Four-Group Design

The **Solomon Four-Group design** contains two extra control groups, comparison groups, random assignments, two pretests, and four posttests. The Solomon is the most sophisticated design possible in experimental designs. The Solomon eliminates many of the validity threats we will discuss in the next section of this chapter. The combination of comparison and control groups permits researchers to ensure rival variables have not affected the final results. Kvalem et al. (1996) studied adolescent condom use and employed this kind of design. They evaluated the effectiveness of a school sex education program in Norway. The results showed that an interaction between the pretest and the intervention (independent variable) affected condom use (dependent variable). The Solomon's main limitation is the amount of time and effort required compared to other designs. See Figure 16.4 for a visual depiction of the true-experimental designs.

Figure 16.4 True-Experimental Designs

Pretest-Posttest Control	R	O_1	X	O_2
Group Design	R	O_3	O_4	
Posttest-Only Control	R	X	O_1	
Group Design	R	O_2		
Solomon Four-Group	R	X	O_2	
Design	R	O_1	O_4	
R	O_3	X	O_5	
R	O_6			

Source: Campbell and Stanley (1963)

When conducting medical experiments, you will find a variety of different experimental designs used. One of the keys for showing that a drug "works" is to have control and comparison groups. It is essential for pharmaceutical companies to be able to say that the drug functioned this way in one group and this way in another group. If the company and the doctors doing the trials can show medically that the comparison groups had benefits from the drug that were not present in the control groups . . . they can show some causality.

Evaluating Experiments

Since experiments are concerned with showing causality, researchers are particularly concerned with being sure experiments have high validity and reliability. Reliability and validity are critical to accurately state that an independent variable(s) causes any change in a dependent variable. Look back to Chapter 6 and the discussion of reliability and validity. Reliability is the notion that instruments should perform the same way over time. Validity is the extent to which a test measures what it's supposed to measure. The same threats to reliability present in other kinds of social scientific inquiry are present in experiments: 1) errors in data entry, 2) instrument confusion, and 3) random human differences.

Numerous threats to validity are unique to experiments. In order for a measure to have validity in an experimental design, you must be sure the measures are not biased because you are trying to show causality. To show causality, you must rule out rival or intervening variables that interfere with demonstrating the causal relationship. You should be aware of two kinds of bias that can affect an experiment's ability to show causality (Cook & Campbell, 1979): time progression effects and reactivity effects.

Time Progression Effects

Experiments, unlike one-shot studies, take place over a period of time. The period of time can be short or long. As the study is taking place, time itself is a variable that must be considered. **Time progression effects** are the factors that act like separate independent variables as causes or effects because an experiment does take place during a period of time. We will identify six time progression effects: history, instrumentation, maturation, mortality, statistical regression, and testing.

History refers to an event(s) happens during the experiment that is outside of the study but may affect the outcome of the study. One way to try to counter for the history effect is to have a control-and-comparison group exposed to all the same elements/events. If an outside event happens and if differences exist between the groups, you can assess those differences as caused by the independent variable(s) and not the outside events. Take the Yu et al. (2012) study on the relationship between taking a public-speaking class and writing ability. Two of their five hypotheses were confirmed. It is possible outside events in the students' lives may have influenced the experiment: taking another course may have affected writing ability, or some students in the control group may have joined a writing club or something.

Instrumentation is when the instrument (measure) is changed during the course of the experiment. Let's say you give the pretest and then notice some things in the instrument you want to change. So, you change some of the questions and then give the posttest with the revised instrument. Can you adequately compare the results of the pretest and the posttest since you changed the instrument? The change brings into question issues of validity and reliability. If you notice something you MUST change, we recommend you change it and then test the group two more times. Let the first test serve as a pilot "dry run" and not your pretest.

Maturation is a naturally occurring process in experiments. Participants develop mentally, physically, emotionally, etc. The developmental process itself thus serves as an independent variable when trying to argue that some trait, behavior, or process causes a change in another trait, behavior, or process. For example, let's say you want to argue that an individual's religiosity (religious devotion) causes them to use certain kinds of media. You may find that religiosity is an evolving part of our lives. Thus, it would be very, very hard to show that it causes media usage.

If you wanted to show that exposure to violent media causes children to be violent, you would need to consider how children's minds and emotions develop rapidly. Therefore, some children will learn to understand the differences between fact and fiction faster than others. You will need to consider the developmental process in your study.

Mortality is the simple fact that some participants will start an experiment but not finish. For a variety of reasons people drop out of experiments. Stephen started an experiment on cultural adaptation in 2006 in France. He had 529 Muslim immigrants complete a survey. In 2012, 398 of those 529 original participants completed the follow-up survey. He was unable to find some of the original participants: they moved, did not respond to phone calls or e-mails, did not want to participate, and a couple had died in those six years. Participants have the right to drop out of an experiment. In 2018, when Stephen returns to collect more data, he knows he will lose some participants but hopes not too many.

Statistical regression is when your sample includes participants who represent the extremes of the dependent variable. Let's say you have a measure ranging from 0 to 100. If a person scores a 0 on the pretest, where can they go on the posttest except for up? One could argue that, in the Yun et al. (2012) study, individuals who were extremely poor in writing at the start of the semester would only get better, no matter what class they were taking in college (public speaking, history, or English). Thus, statistical regression acts like another independent variable to consider.

The **testing** effect is more likely to happen when participants complete a pretest and a posttest. What happens is participants become sensitized to the answers or procedure. As the participants have already taken the pretest, they know—or think they know—the "right answers." Therefore, the participants can often get a higher or more appropriate score the second or subsequent time around because they already had practice taking the measure. Think about any time you have had the chance to retake an exam, particularly the *same* exam. Since you took the exam once before, you should have done better on it the second time around because you had a "trial run."

Reactivity Effects

When people participate in an experiment, they respond to many elements of the experiment's conditions. People are asked to do all sorts of things they would not do in their normal everyday lives. **Reactivity effects** are a set of threats to an experiment's validity that center on participants' responses to the design of an experiment. We will discuss six reactivity effects: compensation behavior, demand knowledge, experiment apprehension, researcher attributes, selection, and treatment diffusion.

Compensation behavior becomes a threat to validity when the control group finds that the comparison group is being treated differently than they are. If the control group finds out the comparison group is getting paid more for the study, the control group may become angry and underperform, or the group may perform better to try to get the same kind of payment. Either way, this knowledge alters their natural experimental behavior. You can control this by taking steps to make sure members of each group do not communicate with one another and/or share information about the study with each other.

Demand knowledge is a threat to a study because you may not want participants to know the goals of the study. If participants think they know the goals of a study, they may provide answers they think the researchers want, or they may provide opposite answers to play with the research team. When trying to show causality, we do not want this kind of bias in a study. What we want is for the participants to answer questions as honestly as possible. However, when participants are aware of the goals of a study or think they are, the answers are not going to be as honest. Research has demonstrated that when individuals know they are being watched in the workplace, their productivity goes up. This is known as the Hawthorne Effect.

Some people are also apprehensive about being in experiments. **Experiment apprehension** is when participants are nervous or excited about participating in an experiment. Along with being nervous or excited, some questions in experiments can be very personal. Many people will alter their answers to appear more favorable to the experimenters. This process of altering answers to look more favorable is called the social desirability bias; we talked about it in Chapter 13 on Surveys. Building trust with participants is key to help them feel comfortable in giving honest answers.

Sometimes the researchers have personal characteristics that can affect the data collection process; this is the threat of **researcher attributes**. For example, if, when conducting research among female rape victims, you have female members on the research team, it would be advantageous. Survivors of sexual assault are generally more comfortable sharing personal/intimate details about such violence with individuals of the same sex.

The **selection** threat happens when a researcher is unable to randomly assign participants to comparison or control groups. Yu et al. (2013) were not able to randomly place students into a public-speaking or a history class. The researchers were "stuck" with the students they had that semester in the different classes. Thus, as the authors pointed out, any potential differences between the students could be attributed to a selection bias.

Treatment diffusion, also known as contamination, happens when participants in the treatment group tell people in the control group about the treatment. The discussion of the treatment contaminates the control group. For example, Kvalem et al.'s (1996) study on condom use in Norway had four groups: two control and two comparison. Two groups received the treatment (the training) and were then measured on their condom use. Discussions between the comparison group and the control group may have biased the study since the control group represented people not receiving condom-use education.

Looking at this laundry list of validity threats to experiments, we can understand why it can take so long for new drugs to be tested. The Food and Drug Administration (FDA) is rigorous when it comes to verifying the safety of vaccines. Whenever a vaccine is put on the market, 99.9% of the time we can about be certain it will work for us. We say 99.9% because there is always an element of error we talked about in earlier chapters. Error is present in experiments because of all of the threats to validity. We have all heard of the many COVID-19 vaccines out there. There will always be a risk when getting a vaccine. Clinical trials reveal some of these threats. The threats to experiments help us recognize the need for rigorous experimental design. In medical research and science, a failure to set up a valid and reliable design could lead to death. In communication and the social sciences, such a failure could lead to poor results, misreporting, and even unethical reporting.

Summary

This chapter was a how-to guide to experiments. The focus of experiments is on showing causality. Experiments are a very social scientific way of doing research. Hopefully after reading the chapter you have a better understanding of experiments. While experiments are a tall order, maybe you feel comfortable enough to try one out after reading this chapter and the ones before it. The next chapter, Chapter 17 is a how-to guide for mixed-methods research.

Key Steps and Questions to Consider

1. An experiment is a methodological process to test the effects of one or more variables that have been manipulated by a researcher on another variable.

2. You must meet three criteria to make a causal argument: manipulation of the independent variable before a change happens in the dependent variable, the changes in the dependent and the independent variables must happen together, and any change in the dependent variable should only be explainable by the independent variable, not by an intervening variable.

3. Before conducting an experiment, formulate the broad research problem and the hypotheses/research questions. Then ask yourself if an experiment is necessary.

4. Many tools are available if you want to conduct an experiment: self-report or other-report surveys, observations, and other codeable forms of data.

5. Experimental control is evaluating the manipulation of the independent variable for effectiveness and to ensure you have controlled for alternative variables.

6. Three things are needed for experimental control: comparison groups, random assignment of participants to independent variable conditions, and pretest-posttest.

7. The group of participants who are exposed to the manipulated levels of the independent variable(s) is called the comparison group.

8. A control group is not exposed to the independent variable(s).

9. A placebo is when an individual thinks they have received a treatment but have not.

10. A pretest is a measure (test) of the dependent variable before the manipulated independent variable. A posttest is the same exact measure (test) of the dependent variable given after the delivery of the manipulated independent variable.

11. A one-shot case study is a design where manipulation of the independent variable occurs, after the manipulation the measurement of the dependent variable is taken.

12. A one-group pretest posttest design is when the researcher administers a pretest of the dependent variable, the independent variable is manipulated, and then the dependent variable is measured again (posttest).

13. A time-series design measures the dependent variable at various points of time before and after the manipulation of the independent variable.

14. A nonequivalent control group design has a control and a comparison group. Both groups are given a pretest and a posttest. Only the comparison group is exposed to the independent variable.

15. A pretest-posttest control group design uses pretests and posttests, comparison and control groups, and random assignment to assess the effects of an independent variable(s) on a dependent variable.

16. A posttest-only control group design includes random assignment, posttests, comparison and control groups, and random assignment.

17. A Solomon Four-Group design contains two extra control groups, comparison groups, random assignments, two pretests, and four posttests. In experimental design, the Solomon is the most sophisticated design available.

18. Time progression effects are factors that act like separate independent variables as causes or effects because an experiment does take place over a period of time. The six time progression effects are: history, instrumentation, maturation, mortality, statistical regression, and testing.
19. Reactivity effects are a set of threats to an experiment's validity that center on participant's responses to the design of an experiment. The six reactivity effects are: compensation behavior, demand knowledge, experiment apprehension, researcher attributes, selection, and treatment diffusion.

Activity

Major Challenge! Develop a chart for easy reference of all the different experimental design options available to a communication researcher.

Discussion Questions

Pick one of the articles mentioned in the chapter. Look up the article in your library (your instructor or a reference librarian can help you find it). Your instructor may decide to divide up the class into groups with each group assigned a different article.

1. Consider how your article could be adapted to meet at least three different experimental designs.
2. Identify the specific strengths and weaknesses for your study in each of your three chosen experimental designs.
3. Which experimental is the best option and why?

Key Terms

Casual Argument
Comparison Group
Compensation Behaviors
Control Group
Experiment
Experimental Control
History
Instrumentation
Intervening Variable
Manipulation Check
Maturation

Mortality
Nonequivalent Control Group
One-Shot Case Study
One-Group Pretest Posttest
Placebo
Posttest-Only Control Group
Pre-Experimental Design
Pretest
Pretest-Posttest Control
Random Assignment Group

Posttest
Reactivity Effects
Researcher Attributes
Selection
Solomon Four-Group design
Statistical Regression
Testing
Time Progression Effects
Time-Series Design
Treatment Diffusion

References

Beckie, T. (1989). A supportive-educative telephone program: Impact on knowledge and anxiety after coronary artery bypass graft surgery. *Heart Lung, 18*(1), 46–55.

Cook, T. D., & Campbell, D. T. (1979). *Quasi-experimentation: Design and analysis issues for field settings.* Rand McNally.

Ivanov, B., Parker, K. A., & Pfau, M. (2012). The interaction effect of attitude base and multiple attacks on the effectiveness of inoculation. *Communication Research Reports, 29,* 1–11. https://doi.org/10.10180/08824096.2011.616789

Kvalem, I. L., Sundet, J. M., Rivo, K. I., Eilertsen, D. E., & Bakketeig, L. S. (1996). The effects of sex education on adolescents' use of condoms: Applying the Solomon Four-Group Design. *Health Education & Behavior, 23,* 34–47.

Pieterse, A. H., van Dulmen, A. M., Beemer, F. A., Ausems, M. G. E. M., & Bensing, J. M. (2006). Tailoring communication in cancer genetic counseling through individual video-supported feedback: A controlled pretest-posttest design. *Patient Education and Counseling, 60,* 326–335. https://doi.org/10/1016/j.pec.2005.06.009

Yanovitzky, I., Stewart, L. P., & Lederman, L. C. (2006). Social distance, perceived drinking by peers and alcohol use by college students. *Health Communication, 19,* 1–10. https://doi.org/10.1207/s15327027hc1901_1

Yun, K. A., Constantini, C., & Billingsley, S. (2012). The effect of taking a public speaking class on one's writing abilities. *Communication Research Reports, 29,* 285–291. https://doi.org/10.1080/08824096.2012.723270

17 Mixed Methods

Malynnda Johnson

For as long as I can remember, I have always asked complicated questions. I was rarely the "but why?" kid. I asked questions like "I wonder how many people do that?" "What makes some do it and not others?" When I started my career as a communication researcher, I again found myself asking complex questions requiring more than a survey or interview. While using one method provides valuable insight, I always needed more than one method to answer the questions I asked. I focus my research in health communication, and much of the work done in my field is considered applied research and naturally lends itself to complex questions. For example, how many people are engaged in a risky behavior, and what makes them do so? Are medical practitioners abiding by guidelines, and what are their motivations? To gain the fullest understanding of complex problems, a mixed-methods study needs to be conducted.

Why Complex Ideas Require Complex Methods

To understand any aspect of life, do you rely on mathematical equations? Does your opinion of a political figure come from what the media says? Are the stories your mother told you about the dangers in life the only way you have learned what not to do? Most will answer no to the questions. For instance, your mother shares her firsthand account of the dangers of riding a bike without a helmet and showing you scars from when she crashed into a tree. However, if no one else has crashed a bike into a tree, you may not feel a need to wear a helmet. Similarly, if the only reason you wear a helmet is the number of people with head injuries, but you never heard a personal story or saw the impact of not wearing a helmet, your behavior is unlikely to change. In other words, we often seek more than just numbers or just a personal story. Before we know anything to be true, we seek out many facts and perspectives. Once the pieces are assembled and can be examined as a whole, then fuller understanding is achieved.

As discussed in other chapters, we can understand the world around us by considering multiple paradigms. From a social science perspective, theories are applied, data is collected, and numbers are tested. Seeking to understand through the stories and experiences of others, interpretive scholars interview and observe people and surroundings as a way to paint a picture of a culture or society. Critical scholars, on the other hand, interpret a variety of texts including speeches, magazines, and even film to build arguments about the ways people persuade, influence, and use their power and privilege. Each paradigm offers a lens through which we can understand the world. But each is limited to only explaining one piece of the communication puzzle.

Take, for example, the use of masks to prevent against contracting COVID-19. A social scientist can examine the use of masks and face coverings before and after a state mandate. Or a researcher might consider multiple versions of an intervention to determine if one was more successful. However, by only considering the number of people who responded to the intervention by changing behaviors, the researcher doesn't know what actually motivated the individuals. What about the intervention worked? Why did others choose not to wear a mask? These "why" questions cannot be answered by numbers alone and must be addressed by conducting qualitative research. The rich stories collected through qualitative methods provide a deeper understanding of the motivations behind the choice to wear masks. However, conducting interviews takes time and the willingness of participants to talk about their behaviors. While each of the studies provides vital knowledge about COVID prevention, the risk is readers not seeing both studies. However, if the two methods are brought together, then a reader gains understanding from both the numbers of new mask wearers and the motivations behind engaging in the behavior. By mixing the methods, we gain a better understanding of the complex issues communication researchers often tackle.

Mixed Methods Defined

The mixed approach to research is comparatively new beginning in the 1950s, most notably starting with Campbell and Fiske's (1959) work extending the conceptual framework on triangulation and gaining traction in the 1980s (Creswell & Plano Clark, 2011; Teddlie & Tashakkori, 2003). However, researchers were conducting mixed-methods studies much earlier (Small, 2011). For example, mixing qualitative and quantitative methods as a means of solving social problems has been traced back to the early 19th century (Alastalo, 2008). Maxwell (2016) argued that Galileo's measurement and observations of the sun and planets are mixed methods. Seeking to address a vast array of issues, social scientists across the field of communication are combining methods. In many areas including health, policy, and organizational communication the application of mixed methods is a practical necessity (Fielding, 2010).

At the most fundamental level, a **mixed-methods** study is one "in which the investigator collects and analyzes data, integrates the findings, and draws inferences using both qualitative and quantitative approaches or methods in a single study or program of inquiry" (Fetters & Molina-Azorin, 2018). For example, imagine you are measuring college students' perceptions of binge drinking. After surveying your peers, you have a feeling the scores are not telling you the whole story. If only you could talk to some of the participants to see why they chose their answers. Then you could hear the story behind the score and have a fuller understanding of their perceptions. In this example, the mixture of methods is two steps: data collected from the survey and then adding an interview or focus group for the stories. Thus, mixed methods are occurring during the design and data-collection phases of the research process and in the data analysis and interpretation phases (Creswell & Plano Clark, 2011). By combining the survey with an interview, you can triangulate the data. **Triangulation** is a central piece of mixed-methods research for identifying corroboration between two sets of findings or to describe a process of studying a problem using different methods to gain a more complete understanding (Flick, 2018). Here we see how triangulation contributes to the **verification** of data—the process of checking data for accuracy and inconsistencies—by describing what is learned (Mathison, 1988). In other words, the use of quantitative and qualitative approaches in combination provides a better understanding than only using quantitative or qualitative approaches alone (Creswell & Plano Clark, 2011; Morse & Niehaus, 2009). In a mixed-methods design, each set of methods provides valuable information that would be absent without the use of both methods (Pluye & Hong, 2014; Teddlie & Tashakkori, 2003).

What to Consider When Planning a Mixed-Methods Study

A key to any successful mixed-methods study is careful consideration of intentions of the study and logistical planning. As any research advisor will tell you, selecting a method begins with the question you are asking. Whether convergent (complex problems focusing on societal needs), explanatory (explaining the aspects of your study in a detailed manner), exploratory (investigating a problem that has not been studied), or transformative (examining ideas, discoveries, or tools that alter our understanding of the world around us) research designs, mixed-methods research can answer your research questions (Creswell & Plano Clark, 2011). The key is ensuring your questions warrant multiple methods. After determining the multiple methods are appropriate, carefully consider how the study will be done. Mixed-methods studies can take many forms, and no one combination may meet a researcher's goals. Therefore, you must plan ahead and remain flexible when planning your strategy. To help you plan a mixed-methods study, the remaining chapter will guide you through the planning process.

Scope of the Study

Combining methods occurs when research questions are outside the scope of one method. Second, you could choose mixed methods when your topic prompts multiple viewpoints. Let's say you are interested if the number of "likes" a picture has on social media impacts the perception of a person in the photo. Mixed methods are not suitable if the question is focused on observing a specific change. Any number of single measures can test if the number of "likes" correlates to the overall perception of a photo. If the research asks, "Are people influenced by the number of 'likes' a picture has on social media?" then a mixed methods study could be useful. By shifting and widening the focus from testing *if* change was occurring, the question gains complexity and increases the opportunity for multiple methods. A researcher can then investigate if the number of "likes" impacts perceptions, followed by interviewing participants about their perceptions of the images. The initial data provides answers for the *if* portion of the question, while the interviews provide a deeper understanding of *how* and *why*. By combining the elements of multiple approaches, we gain a fuller understanding of how the "likes" impact social-media users.

Exploring the Scope

Previous research argues that acceptance by peers is an important part of children's positive school experience (Masten & Coatsworth, 1998). Additionally, social acceptance is believed to be positively linked to many measures of children's well-being, including academic success and self-confidence (Estell et al., 2002; Ladd et al., 1997). Given the tendency for individuals to gravitate toward and befriend like-minded, similar peers (Martin et al., 2013; Shrum et al., 1988), Braun and Davidson (2016) sought to understand the importance of social acceptance by peers in middle childhood from a social constructionist perspective.

Focusing on gender (non)conformity in middle childhood, the goal was to examine the associations among gender, gender-typed behavior, and peer preference in children (9-10 years old). The researchers explored the extent to which girls and boys differed in terms of masculine- and feminine-typed behavior. Second, they examined whether engagement in gender-typed behavior is associated with children's gender and preference for a hypothetical new classmate.

Questions:

1.   Do the goals of the study warrant a mixed methods design?
2.   Given the goal, what methods would you use and in what order?

Study Outcomes

Along with understanding the scope of a study, a researcher must consider the **outcomes**. Outcomes are the goals for the study. Think back to the chapters on paradigms. Each paradigm has specific goals to achieve. For instance, a social scientist tests a theory to better predict a behavior. Thus, a **primary outcome measure** includes specific key measurement(s) or observation(s) to measure the effect of experimental variables. For example, say the goal of a study is to describe patterns of a disease associated with specific risk factors. Many outcomes lend themselves to mixed methods, including understanding participants' perspectives or providing effective contextualization of instruments, measures, or interventions. Given that this chapter's goal is to provide a broad overview, let's explore four additional mixed-methods outcomes more closely.

The first outcome is providing an in-depth explanation of quantitative results. Statistical analysis provides direction and insight yet cannot provide cultural context and relevance. Additional data can provide a deeper explanation. The second outcome is merging databases to show how data converge or diverge. In these cases, we are seeking to compare different perspectives from multiple angles. The previous example of "likes" for a photo could fall into this outcome. When seeking to promote change, studies may work toward the third outcome of identifying where a population stands on a topic and what it may take to get the group to act. In such instances, a transformative approach provides the needs and challenges of a group. Finally, when an outcome involves proving both formative and summative evaluation, mixed methods can be essential. Combining pretest and posttest data to observations provides a full picture of what is being assessed and offers multiple levels to evaluate the impact of an intervention.

Integration of Data

Mixed methods research is more than types of data collected but rather how the data is analyzed and interpreted. As Maxwell (2016) argued, regardless of the research strategies, as long as the data is mutually informative rather than kept separate, the study is mixed methods. Careful consideration regarding how the data will be integrated is vital to labeling research as mixed methods. **Integration** occurs when the datasets are either merged, connected, or embedded. Integrated data is a conversation between the qualitative and quantitative components of the study. Statistical results provide a precise objective voice, while qualitative results provide a deeper understanding to the numbers. How one chooses to integrate the data will depend on the choices made when planning the study. The first choice is to merge the data. **Merging** the data can be achieved by comparing sets, transforming one set by the other, or simply joint display. The second option is **connecting** data, which requires the analysis of one dataset to guide the collection of the other. For example, results from an initial survey can identify specific groups of people when selecting interview or focus group participants. Johnson (2016) surveyed 487 young adults about their HIV knowledge and readiness to be HIV tested. Using contemplation ladders (a scale where a participant selects a level describing their behavior), she identified three categories of people: 1) those who had never thought about HIV testing, 2) those who had yet to seek testing, and 3) those who had been tested. She was able quickly to contact and interview participants with the three groups within each category, adding their stories to the numbers collected. Finally, the third means of integrating data is by **embedding**. Embedded data occurs when multiple smaller sets of data are combined within a larger framework, essentially collecting extra information in addition to the question responses. Take, for example, survey questions about a presidential election. Smaller sets of information about voting habits, political viewpoints, or amount of time researching a candidate help you gain a deeper understanding of the larger questions. By embedding the data, you are able to look at multiple pieces under one umbrella.

All three integration options can produce a successful mixed-methods study, although each change how the data will be collected and analyzed. Thus, timing is a third question to consider when planning a mixed-methods study.

Timing of Data Collection

Carefully consider the timing of mixed-methods research. **Timing** in a mixed-method study is related to when each type of data will be collected and analyzed. One approach is to collect all the data **concurrently**, meaning all phases of data collection occur at the same time. The concurrent approach offers efficiency in time; however, it may not be appropriate for all studies. However, if initial surveys provide information for creating focus groups, then a **sequential** study is appropriate. In a sequential study, the researcher implements the study in distinct phases, with one method viewed as dominant or primary and the other viewed as secondary (Morse & Niehaus, 2009). In the first phase, a researcher collects data to be analyzed and used in the next phase of study. Finally, you can combine both timelines into a **multiphase** study. Employing both concurrent and sequential commonly consists of multiple rounds of data collection.

As you can see, several considerations are involved when conducting mixed-methods research. But the question remains: how does one conduct the research? In the following section, let's walk through the process step by step.

Conducting Mixed-Methods Research

Step One: Study Design

Step One starts with selecting from one of three study designs: Convergent Parallel, Explanatory Sequential, or Exploratory Sequential. A **Convergent Parallel** design keeps the quantitative and qualitative data collection and analysis separate and then merges and compares after the completion of the study. The goal is to interpret the convergence/divergence of the two sets of data using one type of data to validate or confirm conclusions of the other type of data (also known as triangulation) (Palinkas & Cooper, 2018). Such a design is efficient in terms of time required for data collection, and each type is collected and analyzed separately and independently. However, efficiency presents some challenges. First, careful planning and expertise are needed to ensure that equal weight is given to each data type. Second, consider the consequences of different samples and different sample sizes when merging the data. The third challenge is the process of merging two sets of different data. Finally, be prepared to handle quantitative and qualitative results that do not agree. Contradictions may provide new insights, but the differences can be difficult to overcome and may require collecting additional data.

The next design option is **Explanatory Sequential.** The goal is to explain the quantitative connections but then gather additional information from qualitative data. Thus, an Explanatory Sequential study begins with the collection and analysis of quantitative data. The results are used to structure the questions for the qualitative phase. Finally, you interpret ways the qualitative results explain the quantitative results. The structure provides a logical orientation and flow to the study. The design allows for the data to direct the second phase of study. Themes and patterns emerging out of the quantitative data guide fieldwork or the questions asked during qualitative phases. However, an Explanatory Sequential design does have challenges. Obviously, with the phases of collection and analysis occurring back to back, the amount of time is doubled. This design may raise questions from an IRB, since you cannot specify how participants will be selected for the second phase until findings from the first phase. However, you can overcome the challenge by identifying key questions for selecting phase-two participants.

Finally, the third design option is **Exploratory Sequential**. Exploratory sequential uses sequential timing. In contrast to an explanatory design, the exploratory design begins with the collection and analysis of qualitative data emphasizing depth and richness. Building from the qualitative results, you seek to test or generalize the initial findings by conducting a second quantitative study. An exploratory sequential design provides a straightforward way to describe, implement, and report each phase of study.

Advanced designs might be required depending on the complexity of the topic. The three most common are embedded, transformative, and multiphase. Let's briefly explore each (for detailed explanation see Creswell, 2014). The embedded design occurs when the quantitative and qualitative data are collected and analyzed at the same time. The design includes qualitative data to answer a secondary research question within the quantitative study. This design can be helpful when a researcher does not have sufficient time or resources for extensive quantitative and qualitative data collection. The design provides supplemental data that the researcher can use to improve the larger design. The transformative framework runs data collection and

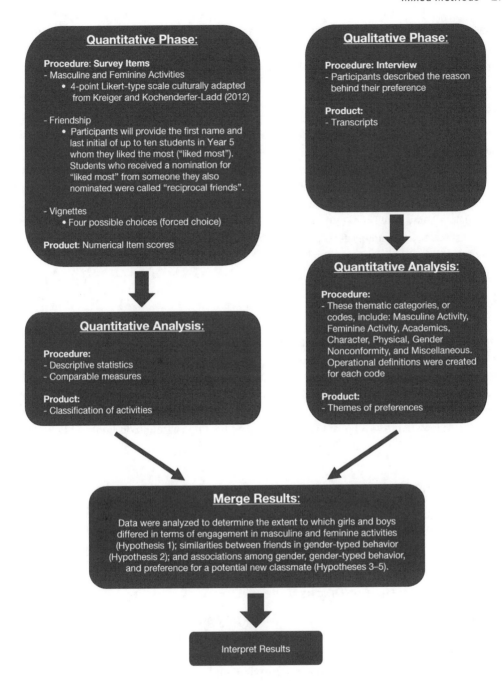

Quantitative Phase:

Procedure: Survey Items
- Masculine and Feminine Activities
  • 4-point Likert-type scale culturally adapted
    from Kreiger and Kochenderfer-Ladd (2012)

- Friendship
  • Participants will provide the first name and
    last initial of up to ten students in Year 5
    whom they liked the most ("liked most").
    Students who received a nomination for
    "liked most" from someone they also
    nominated were called "reciprocal friends".

- Vignettes
  • Four possible choices (forced choice)

Product: Numerical Item scores

Qualitative Phase:

Procedure: Interview
- Participants described the reason
  behind their preference

Product:
- Transcripts

Quantitative Analysis:

Procedure:
- Descriptive statistics
- Comparable measures

Product:
- Classification of activities

Quantitative Analysis:

Procedure:
- These thematic categories, or
  codes, include: Masculine Activity,
  Feminine Activity, Academics,
  Character, Physical, Gender
  Nonconformity, and Miscellaneous.
  Operational definitions were created
  for each code

Product:
- Themes of preferences

Merge Results:

Data were analyzed to determine the extent to which girls and boys
differed in terms of engagement in masculine and feminine activities
(Hypothesis 1); similarities between friends in gender-typed behavior
(Hypothesis 2); and associations among gender, gender-typed behavior,
and preference for a potential new classmate (Hypotheses 3–5).

Interpret Results

Figure 17.1 Braun and Davidson Convergent Parallel design

analysis concurrently *or* sequentially. Typically, a transformative design is used when specific theoretical frameworks (for instance feminist theory) require particular structures.

Finally, consider your audience when designing the study. Will your readers have a predisposition to one method? Second, consider your ability and understanding of the different methods. Your own tendencies and experiences will likely influence the design you choose. Your timeline plays a significant role in designing the study. Finally, carefully consider the complexity of the design. Again, based on your skillset for each method and the number of variables, research questions, and other aspects of the study, you want to ensure you think through how you will analyze the various datasets you will collect.

Step Two: Study Diagram

Developing a study diagram is helpful for mapping out each stage of the study. Your diagram should include the methods, collection procedures, and the datasets. For example, Braun and Davidson (2017) investigated the associations among gender, gender-typed behavior, and peer preference. Using a Convergent Parallel design, the following map plots how data was collected at each step and then compared to determine findings.

Mapping a study may seem optional yet provides an important visual for your study. Seeing the pieces in place can aid in keeping track of data and steps and forces you to think through all the steps in your study.

Step Three: Data Collection

Your data-collection process will follow the path of the selected design. The key is to create a plan for keeping the data organized and manageable. Some of the specific challenges when conducting concurrent designs (merging quantitative and qualitative research) include adequate sample sizes, using comparable samples, and employing a consistent unit of analysis across the databases. When considering sequential designs (one phase of qualitative research builds on the quantitative phase or vice versa), the issues determine what results from the first phase to use in the follow-up phase, choosing samples and estimating reasonable sample sizes for both phases, and interpreting results from both phases.

Step Four: Integrating the Data

How you choose to integrate the data you have collected is again dependent on the design and outcomes of the study. When choosing to merge data, researchers commonly report each dataset followed by a discussion of how the sets confirm or refute each other.

Step Five: Write-Up and Discussion

Just as all with research studies, the results section is followed by a detailed discussion. By drawing connections across the literature, theory, and results, the discussion provides clarity of how the datasets were combined and how they build an argument for the research. By integrating multiple methods, you can discuss the various viewpoints of a topic or provide a narrative for numerical data. By collecting and integrating across methods, the discussion of findings has the opportunity to offer insights, verify objective realities, and enrich the understanding of multiple realities.

Summary

This chapter provided an overview of the reasons why one might consider conducting a mixed-methods study. Broadly speaking, a mixed-methods study is chosen when the topic is complex in nature, calling for more than one type of data to fully answer your research questions.

A researcher might select this type of study to obtain multiple perspectives on the same topic, thus offering both depth and richness in the data and in generalizability. Important questions to consider when planning a mixed-methods study are discussed, as well as an overview of key study designs.

Key Steps and Questions to Consider

1. Choose and research your topic.
2. Ask yourself if the topic is reaching a complex level requiring multiple methods.
3. Identify the types of data needed to answer your research question(s) or hypothesis.
4. Decide on how you will collect the data (e.g., interviews, surveys, or existing datasets).
5. Which phases of the study involve human subjects? Will you be required to obtain approval from your Human Subject Review Board or Institutional Review Board?
6. What is the order of data collection? Will the data be collected simultaneously or in phases?
7. Depending on the types of data being collected, you will want to return to those chapters and review the steps and questions for those specific methods.
8. How and when will you analyze the data? Will you examine the data at the end of each phase or after all data is collected?
9. Reflect on each phase of the research (if conducted in phases). Self-reflection provides direction on the areas of focus for the additional steps in the process.
10. How will you triangulate the data? Remember that the whole point of mixing methods is to allow you to compare and build from different datasets. You must combine or look across your data.
11. Throughout the whole process, you have hopefully already identified and developed connections to the previous research. Be sure you make note of the connections; the connections are the start of your discussion section of your paper.

Activities

1. Select a topic commonly discussed in the media (television, newspaper, music, or social media), for example violence, politics, gender representation, or sexual health. Over a weekend or in a gap between classes, have groups engage with the selected media. Be sure to collect both quantitative (number of times your topic is seen) and qualitative data (ways the topic is covered, the way it made you feel, etc.). Then share findings of the initial datasets. Discuss how, by watching for a topic, you gain both sets of data yet are limited by your own viewpoint. Have each group identify ways each topic could be explained to become a mixed-methods study.
   A. Based on what is found, develop a research question requiring a mixed-methods approach.
   B. Consider the question and identify which design best works for your study.
   C. Map out the steps of conducting the study including the procedures and products of each step.

2. Have students conduct a mixed-methods scavenger hunt. In groups, have students select an area of communication likely to generate complex questions. Within the area, brainstorm topics complex enough for mixed methods. Using your school's library and/ or online databases, have students seek out examples of mixed-methods studies in those areas.

Videos

What is Mixed Methods Research According to Creswell
www.youtube.com/watch?v=1OaNiTlpyX8

Discussion Questions

1. How does the combination of methods provide a better understanding of an issue?
2. Why does the timing of data collection play a crucial role in the analysis of the data?
3. What is the essential difference between mixed-methods research and simply using multiple methods in a study?

Key Terms

Concurrent	Explanatory Sequential	Primary Outcome
Connecting Data	Integration	Measure Outcome
Convergent Parallel	Merging Data	Sequential Timing
Embedded Data	Mixed Methods	Triangulation
Exploratory Sequential	Multiphase	Verification

References

Alastalo, M. (2008). The history of social research methods. In P. Alasuutari, L. Bickman, & J. Brannen (Eds.), *The Sage handbook of social research methods* (pp. 26–41). Sage.

Braun, S. S., & Davidson, A. J. (2017). Gender (non) conformity in middle childhood: A mixed methods approach to understanding gender-typed behavior, friendship, and peer preference. *Sex Roles, 77*(1-2), 16–29. https://doi.org/10.1007/s11199-016-0693-z

Campbell, D. T., & Fiske, D. W. (1959). Convergent and discriminant validation by the multitrait-multimethod matrix. *Psychological Bulletin, 56*(2), 81–105. https://doi.org/10.1037/h0046016

Creswell, J. W. (2014). *A concise introduction to mixed methods research.* Sage.

Creswell, J. W., & Plano Clark, V. L. (2011). *Designing and conducting mixed methods research.* Sage.

Fetters, M. D., & Molina-Azorin, J. F. (Eds.). (2018). Description. *Journal of Mixed Methods Research.* https://au.sagepub.com/en-gb/oce/journal-of-mixed-methods-research/journal201775#description

Fielding, N. (2010). Mixed methods research in the real world. *International Journal of Social Research Methodology, 13*(2), 127–138. https://doi.org/10.1080/13645570902996186

Flick, U. (2018). Triangulation in data collection. *The SAGE handbook of qualitative data collection* (pp. 527-544). Sage. https://dx.doi.org/10.4135/9781526416070.n34

Johnson, M. A. (2016). Asking numbers to speak: Vrbal markers and stages of change. *Qualitative Health Research, 26*(13), 1761-1773. https://doi.org/ 10.1177/1049732316665349

Mathison, S. (1988). Why triangulate? *Educational Researcher, 17*(2), 13-17. https://doi.org/ 10.3102/0013189X017002013

Maxwell, J. A. (2016). Expanding the history and range of mixed methods research. *Journal of Mixed Methods Research, 10*(1), 12-27. https://doi.org/ 10.1177/1558689815571132

Morse, J. M., & Niehaus, L. (2009). *Mixed method design: Principles and procedures.* Left Coast Press.

Palinkas, L. A., & Cooper, B. R. (2018). Mixed methods evaluation in dissemination and implementation science. In R. C. Brownson, G. A. Colditz, & E. K. Proctor (Eds.), *Dissemination and implementation research in health: Translating science to practice* (pp. 335-353). Oxford University Press.

Pluye, P., & Hong, Q. N. (2014). Combining the power of stories and the power of numbers: Mixed methods research and mixed studies reviews. *Annual Review Public Health, 35,* 29-45. https://doi.org/10.1146/annurev-publhealth-032013-182440

Small, M. L. (2011). How to conduct a mixed methods study: Recent trends in a rapidly growing literature. *Annual Review of Sociology, 37,* 57-86. https://doi.org/10.1146/annurev. soc.012809.102657

Teddlie, C., & Tashakkori, A. (2003). Major issues and controversies in the use of mixed methods in the social and behavioral sciences. In A. Tashakkori & C. Teddlie (Eds.), *Handbook of mixed methods in social & behavioral research* (pp. 3-50). Sage.

Sample Paper: Television and Terror

By Jenna Bludorn

Review of Literature

Terrorism has power over us. In the post-9/11 world that we live in, fear reigns. Even our political candidates inspire fear into the populous in order to give themselves an edge in the election. Some experts assert that the threat of terrorism is very real and present in our everyday lives, while others argue that, although real, the threat of terrorism is overstated and perpetuated by the media. Media reaches into each and every part of one's life. From Facebook, Twitter, and other social media to print news, television news, and radio news, it seems that there is no place safe from the media's influence. Concerning the aspect of terrorism, the media may or may not have an influence on peoples' perceptions.

> Jenna has identified a complex and important problem that will easily lend itself to a mixed-methods study.

The media basically decides the overall significance of an event. This phenomenon is called media framing. A media frame is an "interpretive package that prioritizes a certain explanation or significance of an event. Any occurrence may be presented in several different ways, and the media make a purposeful choice to emphasize certain elements of the reality and suppress others" (Yarchi et al., 2013). The media uses these frames to put terrorists front and center because their stories are sensational, or they draw a lot of attention. These frames make the public terrified of Muslims in general, and according to Chaudhry (2016), it is a direct fuel for Islamophobia. This helps terrorists in the end because it draws a lot of attention to their cause.

Groupthink sets the stage of media influence. According to Janis (2005), this theory unites all the members of a group to one way of thinking. Therefore, in relation to terrorism, if "the media says that Muslims are violent ad all my friends think they are violent; they must be violent", again giving direct power to the media as an influencer. This idea that the media has all of the power is supported by the media equation, which says that what is portrayed in the media is equal to what is true in real life. To even further the media's power, agenda setting theory comes into play. According to McCombs and Shaw (2015), "the media tell us (1) what to think about, and (2) how to think about it. The first process (agenda setting) transfers the salience of items on their news agenda to our agenda. The second process (framing) transfers the salience of selected attributes to prominence among the pictures in our heads." With all of these theories working together, it is simple to see how the media influences perceptions of terrorism.

Building upon research that has already been completed, this study seeks to identify (1) the relationship between the type of media consumption and perceptions of terrorism, (2) the amount of media consumption and perceptions of terrorism, and (3) the relationship between age and perceptions of terrorism in the media. Although research has been completed on these topics, there are holes in what has been found and it is not up to date in the advanced technological and media-focused world that is today's society.

> Given these goals, the mixed-methods approach may not be clearly argued. The wording leans heavily on the quantitative side and does not fully create a framework for the qualitative piece.

Method Choice

When contemplating which type of study to choose, it was necessary to understand that a deeper look into the data must be obtained. Therefore, mixed methods was chosen. At first, it was assumed that the emphasis would be on the qualitative data, with the quantitative data there for support. After the study began, however, the emphasis shifted to the quantitative data with the qualitative there for support. The quantitative part of the study encompassed more people, points of view, and valuable information. The qualitative data is still extremely valuable, but it will ultimately be used for support and for the advertising campaign part of the final project. Both quantitative and qualitative methods used will be thoroughly explained in the "procedure" part of this paper.

> Given the ongoing challenges about mixed-methods approaches, it is vital a detailed rational for this approach is offered. A sentence or two more would allow the reader to understand which structure of mixed methods will be used as well as why this structure was required.

Participants

Of 118 participants, 95 (80.5%) were female, 20 were male (16.9%), and three (2.5%) preferred not to say. 50% of participants (59 participants) were of ages 18–28.21 participants (17.8%) were 29–39, 15 (12.7%) were ages 40–50, 15 (12.7%) were ages 51–61, 7 participants (5.9%) were 62–72, and finally 1 participant was 72+. 50 participants (43.1%) identified as Democrat, 38 participants (32.8%) identified as Republican, 4 participants (3.4%) identified as Libertarian, and 24 participants (20.7%) identified as "other".

For religion, Christian, Buddhist, Atheist, Hindu, Islam, and "other" were listed as options. 21 participants (26.3%) identified as "other". The majority of respondents (76, 64.4%) identified as Christian. Ten respondents (8.5%) identified as Atheist, and one respondent identified as Buddhist.

Options for race included: white, African-American/black, Middle Eastern, Asian, Hispanic/Latino, mixed, and "other". The majority of respondents (112, 94.9%) were white. Two respondents (1.7%) were Asian, two were mixed, one (.8%) was Hispanic/Latino, and one identified as other.

Procedure

For the qualitative part of the study, interviews were conducted. Overall, seven people participated in the interviews. Though limited in number a snow-ball sample approach was implemented, therefore participants were not chosen at random. Five of the participants were male, and two were female. All participants were white. One was a freshman, five participants were juniors, and one participant was a senior. All were students of a small private Midwestern university.

Interviews were conducted with word associations to test the question of media frames and how they affect the general American public. Media buzzwords and known media biases were tested to draw conclusions about media influence. The media sways and changes peoples' opinions using media frames, and groupthink makes all of this possible. It was important to be able to speak with participants after the word associations and ask them a series of pre-defined questions to determine how the media has affected their personal views of terrorism, and to do this quantitatively would not have had as much depth or accuracy. Participants were read known media buzzwords and asked to reply with their immediate reaction. The buzzwords and follow-up questions can be found in the appendix. Participants generally replied with 2–5 words or phrases for each word they were given. After the word associations were complete, participants were asked a set of pre-determined questions concerning the media, terrorism, and media bias. These questions were to be answered in full sentences. Overall, each interview lasted about 5–8 minutes.

Additional information is missing as well as how this phase of data collection was used in the following phase. Is the data being merged later? Or is the information from one phase shaping the focus of the next?

For the quantitative part of this study contributing to the public relations plan, a survey was given to reach people of all age groups above the age of 18. It aimed to reach people of varying ethnicities and genders as well. The link to the survey was spread through all forms of social media, specifically Facebook and Twitter. This was chosen because it was an appropriate way to reach more people about more sub-topics in a reasonable amount of time. The demographic questions asked at the end were asked in hopes to more clearly define the survey responder to accurately interpret the data. Demographics included: gender, all ages, all ethnicities political orientation, and religious affiliation.

Survey respondents were asked to define how much news they watch, where they get their news, and through what channels in order to form correlations between these factors and the perceptions of terrorism. This survey in included a total of 21 questions, including demographic questions. All questions were multiple choice or had a scale to respond to. In any question with "other" as a response option, the responder was asked to specify and define this "other". The survey was open for over a month. After the survey, analysis was conducted.

Data Analysis

ANOVAs and independent t tests were run. To determine the relationship between the type of media consumed and perceptions of terrorism as a real threat, a three-way ANOVA between "what is the primary source for your news, what is your perception on terrorism, and how accurate is the threat of terrorism happening in your country?" was run. A t-test comparing the variables of age and primary source of news was the second test completed. Various other t-tests and ANOVAs were completed, which held no significance. Finally, a t-test comparing the source of news and the accuracy of the threat of terrorism in the respondent's country was run to support the results from the significant ANOVA. The dependent variable in this research was the perception of terrorism in the general public. The independent variables were (1) amount of media consumed, (2) type of media consumed, and (3) age. The goal of this survey was to test if these independent variables effect the dependent variable.

> With the heavy interest in the quantitative aspects, the mixed-methods approach seems to get lost. We need a discussion of how the data is coming together. Where is the triangulation?

Results

The three-way ANOVA between "what is the primary source for your news, what is your perception on terrorism, and how accurate is the threat of terrorism happening in your country?" showed a .925 significance level in the two tailed-test, which is very significant on the significance scale. This suggests that there is a relationship between these variables, and this information is crucial to FAIR's public relations program. The t-test comparing the variables of age and primary source of news showed no significant results. Based on this, the target public for the program will have to be broader. Finally, the t-test comparing the source of news and the accuracy of the threat of terrorism in the respondent's country was run to support the results from the significant ANOVA, and the results were very significant with a .980 significance level. All of these tests support the hypothesis that there is a relationship between the type of news consumed and the viewer's opinion of the threat of terrorism. By this nature, if a person only views one outlet, he or she will be biased in a certain way. The public relations plan will work to inform people of this media bias predicament and give them tools to broaden their media horizons.

Data, however, is not significant without communication theory to support it. Groupthink sets the stage of media influence. According to Janis (2005), this theory unites all the members of a group to one way of thinking. Therefore, in relation to terrorism, if "the media says that Muslims are violent ad all my friends think they are violent; they must be violent", again giving direct power to the media as an influencer, as it can be used to silence groups into believing the media's message without verifying and comparing the information. This way of thinking can also work positively for FAIR's public relations campaign. For example, if "all my friends are checking their sources and scrutinizing their information, then I should too". FAIR's ideas will spread across demographics more quickly with this theory fueling them. This idea that the media has all of the power is supported by the media equation, which says that what is portrayed in the media is equal to what is true in real life. To even further the media's power, agenda setting theory comes into play. According to McCombs and Shaw (2015), "the media tell us (1) what to think about, and (2) how to think about it. The first process (agenda setting) transfers the salience of items on their news agenda to our agenda. The second process (framing) transfers the salience of selected attributes to prominence among the pictures in our heads." Media framing applies to FAIR's research findings perfectly. People that viewed certain media outlets reported a correlation to their thinking about terrorism. With all of these theories working together, it is simple to see how the media influences perceptions of terrorism and why there is a need for people to be aware of how they are influenced. Therefore, FAIR conducted research to create a plan to raise awareness and help fight media bias.

References

Chaudhry, A. A. (2016). How do the media fuel Islamophobia? *Media Development*, 6–10. https://doi.org/0143-5558

Janis, I. (2005). Groupthink. In *A first look at communication theory* (pp. 235–238). McGraw-Hill.

McCombs, M., & Shaw, D. (2015). *Agenda setting theory*. Retrieved October 13, 2016, from www.afirstlook.com/edition_7/theory_resources/by_theory/Agenda_Setting_Theory

Reporters, T. (2014, November 4). *How terrorists are using social media*. Retrieved October 13, 2016, from www.telegraph.co.uk/news/worldnews/islamic-state/11207681/How-terrorists-are-using-social-media.html

Survey summary: What are the effects of media reporting on the public. (2000, January). Retrieved November 18, 2016, from www.my3q.com/research/emmaculata/2259.phtml

Terrorism and Australia. (n.d.). Retrieved November 20, 2016, from www.questionpro.com/a/show SurveyLibrary.do?surveyID=37892

Yarchi, M., Wolfsfeld, G., Sheafer, T., & Shenhav, S. R. (2013). Promoting stories about terrorism to the international news media: A study of public diplomacy. *Media, War & Conflict, 6*(3), 263–278. https://doi.org/10.1177/1750635213491179

18 Rhetorical Criticism

What Will I Learn About Rhetorical Criticism?

Arguments about gay marriage now seem like old news since the U.S. Supreme Court settled the matter in a landmark five to four ruling in *Obergefell v. Hodges* (2015). Since the court handed down its ruling, opposition to same-sex marriage remains (Wolf, 2020). States and lower courts have continued to try to chip away at the right to marry. Before the court ruled, the issue was hot across many states. The previous photos show yard signs supporting opposite sides of a proposed state constitutional amendment to legally restrict marriage in Minnesota.

The issue of gay marriage swept across the United States, with different states taking a wide range of positions. Some states supported gay marriage, others offered a compromise called civil unions (or civil partnerships), and a few had laws barring gay marriage. The state of Minnesota passed a law in 1997 prohibiting marriage between persons of the same sex and voiding any

DOI: 10.4324/9781003109129-21

contractual rights if married in a different state (Minnesota Statutes, 2007). However, members of the legislature believed the law could be overturned by state courts and wanted to imbed the prohibition into the state constitution.

Organizations sprang up supporting and opposing the proposed amendment to the Constitution of the State of Minnesota. The competing organizations hosted fundraisers, had spokespersons, created (and updated) websites, produced and distributed paraphernalia (yard signs, buttons, stickers), and engaged across the range of social media (e.g., YouTube, twitter, and Facebook). Individuals sustained their cause in house parties, letters to editors, rallies, and, of course, on social media. The yard signs that started the chapter were just the "tip of the iceberg." The process of persuading voters continued on many fronts for many months and costing many dollars.

> In an interesting twist, the address www.minnesotaformarriage.com seen on one of the yard signs is now a marriage advice website. The switch is a cautionary tale about citing websites.

Consider the recent U.S. presidential campaigns between Joe Biden and Donald Trump. We saw political ads, political rallies, news stories on TV and in newspapers, brochures, fliers, and yard signs. We saw President Trump flex his preference for name-calling (e.g., Sleepy Joe, Crazy Bernie, Nasty Kamala, and the racist slur "Pocahontas" against Elizabeth Warren). President Trump did not stop with the Democrats, calling Kim Jong Un "Rocket Man" and "Sloppy Steve" Bannon. The speeches, ads, stories, rallies, documents, debates, yard signs, and name-calling are examples of rhetoric and opportunities for communication scholars to engage in rhetorical criticism. In this chapter, you will learn how to conduct a rhetorical criticism as a form of communication scholarship.

Introduction to Rhetoric and Rhetorical Criticism

Rhetoric and rhetorical criticism are the oldest forms of scholarship in the communication discipline, dating back to the ancient Greeks who were focused on determining what constituted an effective speech. The study and practice of rhetoric was so important for the ancient Romans, it was listed as part of a core Classical education. A Roman citizen studied rhetoric, grammar, and logic (by the Medieval period, the three disciplines together were called the **trivium**) (Salisbury, 1180/2009). The study of rhetoric has continued, in one form or another, for thousands of years since.

Rhetorical criticism is different from most other forms of communication scholarship in two ways. First, rhetoric and rhetorical criticism are major areas of study in the discipline. Unlike other forms of research methods, rhetoric and rhetorical criticism stand alone within communication studies. Some communication scholars focus their entire careers on the study of rhetoric and rhetorical criticism, and entire organizations are dedicated solely to the study of rhetoric (e.g., Rhetoric Society of America, International Society for the History of Rhetoric, and the Canadian Society for the Study of Rhetoric). In fact, one organization, the **Kenneth Burke Society**, focuses solely on the writings of just one scholar. Second, rhetorical criticism is more subjective than other communication research methods. A criticism is, at its core, an argument about how a symbol can be understood using a theory as a filter. The criticism/

argument provides a new way to understand the world and identify better ways to engage with others.

The study of rhetoric and rhetorical criticism is a daunting task. Rhetoric and rhetorical criticism have a close relationship with many of our sister disciplines including philosophy, English (particularly composition, poetics, and literary theory and criticism), sociology, religion, anthropology, and psychology. The inter-disciplinary connections make rhetoric and rhetorical criticism a robust field of study. However, the breadth and depth also make rhetoric and rhetorical criticism a complicated and complex area of study. For example, the *Encyclopedia of Rhetoric and Composition* is devoted to listing, defining, and explaining the specialized language and concepts of rhetoric (Enos, 2011). Dan and Stephen remember when they first started studying rhetorical theory. The terminology and the range of theoretical concepts was intimidating and can quickly overwhelm a young scholar. We highly recommend you start your own glossary of rhetorical terms for continual development and reflection as you expand your repertoire in rhetoric and rhetorical criticism. We are not, obviously, going to cover every aspect of rhetoric and rhetorical criticism in this chapter. We do provide a good starting framework. Take your time as you begin to explore rhetoric and rhetorical criticism. Learn which theories "speak" to you, and then take the time to explore those theories in more detail. You may decide if rhetoric and rhetorical criticism is your place in the discipline.

Defining Rhetoric

Before we look closer at rhetorical criticism as a research method, we need to spend some time with the word "rhetoric." As we talked about earlier, rhetoric is an ancient concept dating back to the ancient Greeks in the 5th century BCE.

The modern word "rhetoric" has several negative associations. From the politician who is "all rhetoric and no action," to a speech "full of rhetoric" but lacking substance, to rhetoric as deceptive practice. However, to a communication scholar, rhetoric and rhetorical criticism are powerful parts of our discipline. Scholars have long viewed rhetoric as the art of persuasion. For example, in the 4th century BCE, Aristotle defined rhetoric as "the faculty of observing in any given case the available means of persuasion" (Aristotle, 4th Century BCE/1991). Modern scholars have defined rhetoric in a similar fashion. Cathcart (1991) argues that

> rhetoric . . . refers to a communicator's intentional use of language and other symbols to influence or persuade selected receivers to act, believe, or feel the way the communicator desires" (p. 2). Kuypers (2005) defines rhetoric as "the strategic use of communication, oral or written, to achieve specifiable goals.

> (p. 5)

Foss (2004) takes the process one step further, noting that rhetoric has the power to shape how we perceive reality. Foss says, "reality is not fixed but changes according to the symbols we use to talk about it. What we count as real or as knowledge . . . depends on how we chose to label and talk about things" (p. 6). Rhetoric is an important part of our discipline, with the power to change our beliefs, attitudes, and actions and even alter how we understand people, politics, cultures, and, well . . . reality. The criticism of rhetoric plays an important role in understanding how people may be influenced by symbols. A rhetorical critic, therefore, seeks to recognize how people understand and respond to symbols and how the use of symbols shapes our perceptions of reality.

Defining Rhetorical Criticism

Rhetorical criticism as part of modern education started in the early 1900s and focused on speakers and their speeches. The most common rhetorical research is the "Great Man" criticism (e.g., an important person giving an important speech on an important occasion). We admit that sexism was involved in "Great Man" criticism, but, at this point in history, men gave most of what were considered significant speeches. However, as we all know, times change, and powerful women giving momentous speeches are now part of our society.

The scope of what contemporary rhetorical scholars critique has expanded considerably since the 1900s. We've moved well beyond just looking at speeches (though criticism of a speech is still part of rhetorical criticism). The critiqued communication is called an **artifact**. An artifact is an identifiable moment of communication from a specific time, place, and person(s). As Foss (2004) notes, an artifact is any tangible evidence that a communication act occurred.

Possible artifacts include

1. A compelling speech
2. A fascinating sermon
3. An effective essay
4. A thought-provoking interview
5. An interesting narrative or story
6. An engaging television show (or a group of similar television shows)
7. A stimulating public demonstration
8. An inspiring song lyric (or set of lyrics)
9. A curious political campaign
10. An eye-grabbing billboard
11. Any other artifact from a communication moment, which surround us every day!

Consider our opening situation with the gay marriage yard signs. We have a broad variety of artifacts for a rhetorical criticism. We could stick with just the yard signs, but the limited text may not provide enough communication for a beginning rhetorical scholar. So, let's consider what other related artifacts we can choose. We could critique the websites or the Facebook presence of either/both campaigns; we could critique a collection of editorials or letters to editors about gay marriage from major newspapers. We could critique a speech (or multiple speeches) from one (or more) politicians. We could critique statements from popular figures in society (e.g., athletes, actors, and musicians).

As we move closer to the actual process for conducting a rhetorical criticism, we must distinguish between a **popular critic** versus a **rhetorical critic**. Pierce (2003) argues that popular critics evaluate based on personal preference or taste. A popular critic seeks to influence the general public's perception. For example, movie reviews, ESPN commentaries, and ratemyprofessors.com are sources of popular criticism. A rhetorical critic, however, evaluates based on rhetorical theories and principles. According to Pierce, a rhetorical critic must be prepared to defend their analysis and criticism, defend the standards/methods used to conduct their criticism, and defend their effectiveness of the criticism.

Part of your task as a rhetorical critic is selecting an artifact for analysis. Hart and Daughton (2005) and Foss (2004) provide a good process for a beginning scholar for selecting an artifact. Foss recommends starting the process by listing what you like or dislike. Yes, you can critique something you find annoying. In fact, some scholars prefer to select an artifact they dislike. Prepping and writing a rhetorical criticism is a time-consuming task. If you start off with something you like, you may be tired of the subject by the time you are finished with the criticism. Picking something you dislike, on the other hand, has no similar downside. Foss also suggests that you may decide to select something you find confusing and want to better understand or something that grabs your interest. However, Hart and Daughton (2005) caution that you must have a solid argument for why you selected a specific artifact. Not all artifacts are created equal, and we must avoid "criticism-by-whim" (Hart & Daughton, 2005, p. 32). Your argument for selecting an artifact may focus on the historical importance, the societal influence, or the political prominence of the artifact.

Our Minnesota gay marriage artifacts have the advantage of drawing on historical (there is potential to amend a state constitution), societal (gay marriage has broad social implications), and political (politicians have taken sides on the issue).

Selecting an Approach for a Rhetorical Criticism

Once you have selected your artifact, you need to select a rhetorical theory to frame your criticism. A rhetorical theory is used to filter the symbols in the artifact so that we can see new insights. The theory is really a set of standards used for evaluating the artifact. Selecting a theory is important since the theory guides the direction of the criticism. Don't worry about selecting the best theory. No particular theory is "best" for analyzing an artifact. A lot depends on what about the artifact you find interesting. What questions do you have about the artifact? Your interest and questions should help determine the approach appropriate for your analysis.

We do not have the space in one chapter to provide details of all the possible approaches available for a rhetorical criticism. Dozens of books and entire undergraduate and graduate classes are devoted to exploring rhetorical theories. You may decide that rhetoric and rhetorical criticism is your "thing" and end up reading the books and taking many of the courses. Instead, we provide a framework for three of the most common methods used in rhetorical criticism. When you pick your specific rhetorical theory, you may need to do some additional readings on the method to expand your understanding to perform the criticism.

Neo-Aristotelian Criticism

The first rhetorical approach we "unpack" comes from our classical Greek roots. An understanding of neo-Aristotelian criticism (also known as classical or traditional criticism) is based on the classics of ancient Greece and Rome, primarily the writings of Aristotle and Cicero. You may decide to use a neo-Aristotelian approach if your artifact is a speech. A neo-Aristotelian approach has limited use for other types of artifacts.

Neo-Aristotelian criticism focuses on the **five canons of rhetoric** and is primarily used for critiquing speeches. The Greeks developed the concepts imbedded in the five canons, and the

Romans codified the five canons as part of rhetorical education. Cicero is recognized as the first person formally to list the canons in his work *De Inventione*. The five canons are *inventio* (invention), *dispositio* (organization), *elocutio* (style), *pronuntiatio* (delivery), and *memoria* (memory), though memory gets little attention in contemporary neo-Aristotelian criticism and is ironically referred to as the "forgotten" canon.

Most neo-Aristotelian criticism focuses on the canon of invention. Invention in rhetoric is different than our popular understanding of creating something new (e.g., building a better mousetrap). **Invention** in rhetoric is the discovery of ideas and arguments for use in a persuasive appeal. Invention critiques how a speaker uses logos, ethos, and pathos to persuade an audience toward a speaker's goal. Aristotle's *Rhetoric* is the foundation for logos, ethos, and pathos as **artistic proofs** used in persuasion. **Inartistic proofs** are factual, such as laws, statistics, oaths, and contracts. Inartistic proofs can be used to build an argument, but artistic proofs are more adaptable to the persuasive goal of the speaker.

Logos critiques the speaker's reasoning, arguments, and use of evidence. **Ethos** evaluates the speaker's credibility and character, especially as related to the topic, occasion, and audience for the speech. Ethos is rather unique, since the standards for critiquing pathos are more in the hands of the audience than speaker. **Pathos** explores the speaker's attempts to emotionally connect with the audience. Weak pathos may induce sympathy with the speech; strong pathos will arouse empathy. For example, the speaker may tell a moving story and hope the audience will bond with characters or situation in the story.

Reinard (2010) provides an effective neo-Aristotelian checklist based on the work of Lewis and Tabor (1966).

Neo-Aristotelian Checklist

1. Ethos:
    Is the speaker intelligent?
    Does the speaker reveal good character?
    Is the speaker a person of good will?
    Is the speaker telling the whole truth?
    Is the speaker credible?
    Does the speaker's reputation enhance the speech?

2. Pathos:
    Does the speaker establish identification with the audience?
    What types of appeal are used?
    Are appeals specific and concrete?
    Does the speaker stimulate attention and interest?

3. Logos:
    Does the speaker proceed from assumption and hypotheses that are fair and reasonable?
    Is the speaker's analysis of the subject complete and clear?
    What types of argument are used?
    Does the speaker's reasoning meet appropriate tests of validity?
    Are the supporting materials sufficient?
    Are data sufficiently documented?
    Does the speaker substitute emotional appeals for evidence and argument?

The marriage amendment issue had plenty of supporters on both sides of the issue. A neo-Aristotelian criticism focusing on one or more political candidates who had taken a stance on the issue is a good approach. We could easily collect statements from newspapers, statements made during political debates, and statements from candidates' standard stump speech (and every politician has a standard stump speech). The Internet is a blessing to rhetorical critics, who can collect all sorts of artifacts with a series of web searches. Once we have the information, we can decide if we want to focus on just one speech or a composite drawn from the variety of artifacts at our disposal. Remember, we need to have a good argument for why we decided to limit or expand the scope of what we include as our artifact. Then we can use the Reinard's (2010) checklist to work our way through the neo-Aristotelian criteria and see what criticism emerges.

Metaphor Criticism

The second rhetorical approach we explore is metaphor criticism. A metaphor is used when the qualities of one concept are used to characterize the nature of a person, thing, or idea. A critic needs to be careful of confusing a simile with a metaphor. A simile is easily identified by "like" and "as". An example may be helpful.

Metaphor = My friend is a tiger on the dance floor stalking its prey.
Simile = My friend moved across the dance floor *like* a tiger stalking its prey.

While we do not encourage the use of *Wikipedia* for scholarly work, the site does provide an effective list of common metaphors (http://en.wikipedia.org/wiki/List_of_English_language_metaphors). A few minutes reviewing the list may prove helpful for identifying metaphors in an artifact.

A critic using the metaphor approach analyzes artifact(s) by using metaphor(s). The critic evaluates the metaphor(s) to better explain how the communication may persuade our beliefs, values, and actions. The key in metaphor criticism is to determine what qualities are highlighted or repressed by the metaphor and what those qualities say about the artifact. Consider our earlier example about the tiger-friend. The animal metaphor has many qualities about a tiger—a tiger is a large, powerful, and strong carnivore and predator who attacks and feeds on other animals. A quick critique of our tiger-friend on the dance floor does not paint a pretty picture. Consider how the critique may change if the artifact is "my friend is a tiger on the football field stalking its prey." What may have been an unflattering image of a dancer turns to a compelling picture of an athlete.

Let's consider an approach for how we might conduct a metaphor criticism. The marriage amendment produced a bounty of posts on social media sites—from Facebook, to Twitter, to Tumblr, and other sites—we could gather the posts from one or multiple sites and analyze what metaphors are in play. Metaphor criticism is a good opportunity for visual analysis. A web images search of "vote no Minnesota" and "vote yes Minnesota" produces thousands (actually, hundreds of thousands!) of hits. Identifying, analyzing, and drawing out the implications for the dominant metaphors in each position might be a fascinating study.

Fantasy Theme Analysis

The third popular rhetorical approach we explore is fantasy theme analysis (also known as **symbolic convergence theory**). Fantasy theme analysis is part of a larger group of theories defined by Brock et al. (1990) as dramaturgy. If you choose to continue your studies in rhetorical criticism, you will explore narrative analysis and Burkeian dramatism, the other areas of dramaturgy.

The fantasy theme approach to rhetorical criticism was developed by Dr. Ernest Bormann at the University of Minnesota. Fantasy theme analysis is an effective method if your interest is how communication (evident in your selected artifact) can shape perceptions of reality. Fantasy theme analysis works from the concept that a group can develop a shared viewpoint called a "rhetorical vision" (Bormann, 1972, p. 398).

A rhetorical vision occurs when a series of fantasy themes merges to form a cohesive viewpoint. The rhetorical vision provides the participants with shared expectations, which are revealed in their shared vocabulary. A critic can work to build a shared vocabulary by identifying the heroes, villains, victims, storylines, scenes, repeated stories, insider humor, and other commonalities within the group's communication. While a fantasy theme analysis can develop from a single artifact, the approach works well when you have a set of artifacts all from the same group. The rhetorical vision emerges when similar patterns emerge across the various artifacts.

Finally, what artifacts might we consider if we were interested in a fantasy theme analysis of the marriage amendment question? Let's return to social media. Facebook has become a dominant method for gathering together people who share opinions on social issues. Both Minnesota campaigns have Facebook pages to support their cause. The pages have posts from supporters and detractors. Sometimes the posts are simple statements of support (e.g., "I'm voting no!" or "I support the 'Vote Yes' campaign."). However, a number of the posts are personal stories about how a yes/no vote will impact their personal lives, families, and communities. The stories are a perfect opportunity for a fantasy theme analysis. We can use the stories for identifying the heroes, villains, victims, and other components that form a fantasy theme.

Other Approaches in Rhetorical Criticism

A variety of other approaches are available to rhetorical critics. Just a few are social movement criticism, genre criticism, cluster criticism, feminist criticism, Marxist criticism, cultural criticism, ideological criticism, and postmodern criticism. Now we can see how a scholar can spend an entire career studying rhetoric and rhetorical criticism!

One final note on rhetorical criticism. Boundaries between the various rhetorical approaches are subjective, and concepts may cross over between the approaches. While one criticism may use a Marxist theory and another uses a feminist theory, this does not mean that the criticisms are in conflict. The various approaches each provide their own insights into the artifact(s). Indeed, a rhetorical critic may employ more than one approach in a variety of combinations.

Organizing a Rhetorical Criticism

Writing up a rhetorical criticism can take many forms. However, a basic criticism does follow some general guidelines. Following the structure we outline in the following box will help a beginning critic ensure all the bases are covered. (See how we slipped a sports metaphor into the explanation?)

Rhetorical Criticism Outline

1. Your description of the communication/artifact/symbols. Your description may include a justification for the artifact you've selected. What makes the artifact worthy of your (and your readers') time and attention?
2. Your description of the situation where the communication occurred—what social, historical, economic, political, and other circumstances are relevant to the artifact?
3. Your explanation of the rhetorical approach, which will guide your criticism. You may need to include a justification for the rhetorical approach you selected. Be thorough and detailed in explaining the rhetorical approach. Your explanation sets the standards for implementing your criticism.
4. You may choose to include a section discussing other studies, which have used the same rhetorical approach.
5. Your critique of the artifact using the selected rhetorical approach. Include specific examples from the artifact to illustrate how the criticism applies.
6. Your discussion of the implications of the criticism—so what can we learn from your criticism? The implications are critical. Zachry (2009) argues that rhetorical criticism must be more than just identifying and labeling the parts in an artifact. The criticism needs to provide an interpretation of what the identified/labeled parts mean.

Do not worry if you have the "correct" interpretation in your criticism. Artifacts can have many meanings, and different critics may see different meanings. Your obligation is to present strong arguments, which support your critical insights. The strength of an argument is critical in rhetorical criticism. Since we do not have objective standards of analysis in rhetorical criticism, you arguments and how well you support your arguments are the key.

Summary

This chapter was a how-to guide to rhetorical criticism. Rhetorical criticism is a more critical/cultural method, but it can also lean interpretive or social scientific depending on the researcher's approach. It is a multifaceted method. Hopefully, after reading the chapter and the accompanying student paper, you feel comfortable enough to try your own rhetorical criticism. The next chapter, Chapter 20, is a how-to guide to critical/cultural methods.

Key Steps and Questions to Consider

1. There are numerous definitions of rhetoric.
2. Rhetorical criticism is conducting an analysis of a rhetorical "act."
3. What is the difference between being a popular critic and a rhetorical critic?
4. The communication that critics "critique" is called an artifact.
5. No particular theory is "best" for analyzing an artifact.
6. Neo-Aristotelian criticism focuses on the five canons of rhetoric and is primarily used for critiquing speeches.

7. Logos critiques the speaker's reasoning, arguments, and use of evidence.
8. Ethos evaluates the speaker's credibility and character, especially as related to the topic, occasion, and audience for the speech.
9. Pathos explores the speaker's attempts to emotionally connect with the audience.
10. A critic using the metaphor approach analyzes artifact(s) by identify metaphor(s) used by the artifact.
11. Fantasy theme analysis is an effective method if your interest is how communication (evident in your selected artifact) can shape perceptions of reality.

Activities

1. Selecting Artifacts. Review the list of possible artifacts provided in the chapter and think about all the forms of communication you are inundated by each day. Take just one day and make your own list of possible artifacts for rhetorical criticism. Pay attention to the music you listen to, the TV shows you watch, the news you read, and the billboards, signs, posters, and fliers you see around you. Bring your list of artifacts to class and see who can make the strongest argument for why an artifact is worthy of criticism.
2. Selecting a Rhetorical Approach. Using one of your artifacts from Activity 1 (or the gay marriage artifacts), discuss how each of the three approaches we reviewed in the chapter may provide diverse critical insights.
3. A Rhetoric Dictionary. Starting with the list of terms in Key Questions, develop (individually or as a class) your own dictionary of terms in rhetoric. Continue to build on the dictionary as your study of rhetoric and rhetorical criticism progresses.

Discussion Questions

1. What other artifacts could we collect and critique as part of the Minnesota marriage amendment?
2. How does activity 1 illustrate how each approach illuminates different persuasive strategies? Remember, no one rhetorical approach is best, nor is any critique the "correct answer." Each approach provides different viewpoints of the artifact(s).

Key Terms

Aristotle	Invention	Rhetoric
Artifact	Kenneth Burke Society	Rhetorical Criticism
Artistic	Logos	Symbols
Criticism-by-Whim	Metaphor	Trivium
Ethos	Neo-Aristotelian	Symbolic Convergence
Fantasy Theme Analysis	Pathos	Theory
Five Canons of Rhetoric	Popular Critic	
Inartistic Proofs	Proofs	

References

Bormann, E. G. (1972). Fantasy and rhetorical vision: The rhetorical criticism of social reality. *Quarterly Journal of Speech, 58*, 396–407. https://doi.org/10.1080/00335637209383138

Brock, B. L., Scott, R. L., & Chesebro, J. W. (1990). *Methods of rhetorical criticism: A twentieth-century perspective* (3rd ed.). Wayne State University Press.

Cathcart, R. S. (1991). *Post-communication: Rhetorical analysis and evaluation*. Bobbs-Merrill.

Enos, T. (2011). *Encyclopedia of rhetoric and composition: Communication from ancient times to the information age*. Taylor & Francis.

Foss, S. K. (2004). *Rhetorical criticism: Exploration and practice* (3rd ed.). Waveland Press.

Hart, R. P., & Daughton, S. (2005). *Modern rhetorical criticism* (3rd ed.). Pearson.

Kuypers, J. A. (2005). *The art of rhetorical criticism*. Pearson.

Lewis, W. E., & Tabor, R. R. (1966). *Guidelines: Rhetorical criticism*. Cerritos College.

Minnesota Statutes. (2007). Chapter 517: Domestic relations. *Minnesota legislature–office of the revisor of statutes*. www.revisor.leg.state.mn.us/bin/getpub.php?pubtype=STAT_CHAP&year=2007&section=517#stat.517.03.0

Obergefell v. Hodges. (2015, June 6). *Oyez*. www.oyez.org/cases/2014/14-556

Pierce, D. L. (2003). *Rhetorical criticism and theory in practice*. McGraw Hill.

Reinard, J. C. (2010, June 15). *Traditional criticism checklist of starting questions*. http://commfaculty.fullerton.edu/jreinard/bookweb/traditio.htm

Salisbury, J. (2009). *The Metalogicon: A twelfth-century defense of the verbal and logical arts of the trivium* (D. McGarry, Trans.). Paul Dry Books. (Original work published 1180).

Wolf, R. (2020, June 25). Supreme Court's same-sex marriage ruling turns 5: Acceptance, advancement, but opposition remains. *USA Today*. www.usatoday.com/story/news/politics/2020/06/25/lgbtq-rights-five-years-after-gay-marriage-ruling-battles-continue/3242992001/

Zachry, M. (2009). Rhetorical analysis. In F. Bargiela-Chiappini (Ed.), *The handbook of business discourse* (pp. 68–79). Edinburgh University Press.

Undergraduate Student Paper

Secondhand Smoke and the Five Canons of Rhetoric

Steven Arning

Smoking cigarettes has been determined through scientific research to be harmful to a person's health. Smoking has since been determined as being the number one cause of preventable death in the United States. Organizations now provide information about smoking and help in people's efforts to quit smoking. One television advertisement put on the air by the American Cancer Society concerns the risks associated with secondhand smoke will be discussed. Rhetorical criticism will be provided on the advertisement using the "Five Canons" rhetorical criticism method. The advertisement's invention, organization, style, delivery, and memory will be analyzed. The use of pathos in this advertisement is the most relevant aspect and its effectiveness will also be explored.

The student has a nice introduction. He leads us into the paper with a crisp attention getter and significance about the issue and sets up the rhetorical approach—the Five Canons with a specific focus on pathos.

A brief summary of the advertisement is a crucial part in understanding the criticism on the ad. The TV spot opens with a white screen and the words, "smoking sections in restaurants . . ." in the center of the screen. There is a sound of people talking in the background; the sound is much like that of a restaurant. The screen then shows a man's face, probably in his early 30s, and he says with sarcasm, "A smoking section in a restaurant?" He then says, "that's like a peeing section in a pool." The ad then flashes to images of cigarettes burning on the edge of a dinner plate, and a man exhaling cigarette smoke. A fact is then displayed on the screen, "a half hour exposure to 2nd hand smoke dramatically increases a person's short term risk of a heart attack." The American Cancer Society's logo is displayed on the screen. The man then says "Hey it's your air."

The student's description of the artifact is solid. His description provides both the text and effective visual descriptions, so a reader can "see" what occurs in the TV ad. He can strengthen the section by explaining how the ad is significant and worthy of criticism. He might argue significance by listing the amount of money spent airing the ad or responses from supporters, critics, and the general audience to the ad.

The first aspect of the advertisement to be discussed is the invention of the commercial, or the speaker's lines of arguments or ideas. The speaker makes a metaphor to describe a similar situation to a smoking section in a restaurant. The situation described in the metaphor is simple and one everyone, no matter what audience, is familiar. His message is simple, display the facts, "a half hour exposure to 2nd hand smoke dramatically increases a person's short term risk of a heart attack." And let people think about it for themselves. The message uses pathos extremely effectively and will be discussed in further detail later in this criticism. His use of inartistic proofs, such as facts lies mainly in the one line about exposure to secondhand smoke, and the credibility lies in the company that is backing the advertisement, The American Cancer Society. It is a company that is largely recognizable and credible.

> The student reintroduced us to his chosen rhetorical approach. Notice how he plans to weave metaphor in with his use of the neo-Aristotelian criticism. Steven could use more description and explanation of both the neo-Aristotelian approach and metaphor to enhance his criticism. The section gets a little confusing, since it starts with a focus on invention but then shifts more to metaphor. He may have considered moving the sentences about the organization's credibility to the previous section when he describes the artifact. The credibility can help support significance for critiquing the ad.

The organization of the advertisement was very effective. A metaphor was used to catch the attention of the audience, which for this particular commercial is just about anyone who goes to restaurants occasionally. They caught the audience's attention and then provided facts to back up the metaphor, a very effective order. The images of the burning cigarettes and the person exhaling smoke give the viewer time to take in the metaphor and begin to understand it before they are told the facts to support the claim. The commercial would not be as effective had it been in the opposite order. The audience may not have "tuned in" as early on had they not had that "attention grabbing" metaphor at the start of the commercial.

> The student's critique of the ad's organization relies extensively on metaphor. As he was developing his criticism, he may have decided that metaphor may have been a stronger approach than using the Five Canons of Rhetoric.

The style of the advertisement is definitely an aspect that adds to the feeling of the ad—fear of the facts. The whole ad is in black and white and there is no music, and the crackling sound of the burning cigarettes is amplified. It appears to be very serious from the start and it's clearly not going to provide "happy" news. There is simply a feeling of fear; the information you are hearing is going to scare you. The ad is blunt, and simply puts out the facts. There are little distractions throughout the 30 seconds of video. The words are clearly displayed on blank backgrounds which forces people to read the facts with nothing else to look at.

> The student's section on style is effective. The description and analysis combine to provide a strong critique. However, since the two previous sections worked in metaphor, the reader may wonder why the metaphor approach was not integrated here as well.

The delivery of the information is very effective in its "down to earth" style. The speaker in the advertisement speaks in a simple, everyday way that could never been seen as hard to understand. He uses no sophisticated words and speaks of metaphors anyone could relate to. He speaks in a sarcastic tone, as though the things he is saying are common sense. It gives off the feeling that he is casually telling you something he has realized, as most people find out new facts, hearing them by word of mouth from another friend or affiliation. The speaker also has a smirk of sorts on his face when he discusses the metaphor, again implying that having a smoking section in a restaurant is a ridiculous idea that should never have been implemented, and has been the wrong way of doing things for years. The fact that the typed words on the screen have ". . ." at the end of each line is also an effective way to keep the viewer anxious to hear what's coming next. They are again, "tuned in" to hear the next line.

The memory for the advertisement is probably the most difficult part to understand. The speaker appears to have a basic knowledge of what secondhand smoke can do to a person. He knows a slightly more than the average person because he is trying to explain a fact to people that not many people know. There was obviously research performed by the American Cancer Society in order to provide true and accurate facts. The ad will stand out in viewers mind in the future because of the new information they have learned, that even sitting in a restaurant can be harmful to a person's health and secondly the overall feel of the commercial will hopefully stand out in the audiences' minds. The overall feel of the advertisement ushers in the final topic, the use of pathos in the ad.

> The student has discovered why the canon of memory is often neglected in neo-Aristotelian criticism. Critiquing the effectiveness of a speaker's memory, especially when the artifact is more than a speech, can be complicated. The student, however, is effective in critiquing memory from the dual perspectives of both the speakers in the ad and the viewers/audience who watch the ad.

The use of pathos in this advertisement is the most dominant aspect of the advertisement. Pathos can be defined as "the quality or power, especially in literature or speech, of arousing feelings of pity, sorrow, etc." In this particular advertisement the feeling that is portrayed is one of fear, and anxiousness. Viewers are realizing that they have possibly been in danger the last time they were in a restaurant and they will potentially be placed back in that same danger the next time they go out to a restaurant or event. The fear is that are helpless in a restaurant where they are slowly inhaling smoke with every breath. The way the ad is designed adds to the fear. The black and white look to the ad and the manner by which the speaker presents the information create a feeling this is a serious deal, and not a joke. The image of the person exhaling the smoke is frightening because it portrays the idea a person sitting in the non-smoking section of the restaurant is inhaling and is possibly unaware.

> The student identifies a central purpose for the American Cancer Society advertisement. The ad is more than informative. The ad is designed to influence viewers' attitudes about secondhand smoke and maybe compel viewers to action. The student may find a tighter application for the critique by focusing on pathos and metaphor instead of all five canons. Finally, the student should have provided a source citation for the quotation defining pathos.

This is a very effective and educational advertisement for the American Cancer Society. The arguments are clearly displayed with the use of a metaphor as well as clearly stated facts to support the overall argument. The imagery is simple, yet effective in providing fear-invoking scenes. Most Americans have a simple understanding of what smoking does to a person's body; if you smoke, you are slowly killing yourself. This commercial adds onto that general knowledge by describing a situation the average viewer has most likely been subjected to and describes the dangers associated with that situation.

Reference

American Cancer Society. (2011, May 10). *YouTube—broadcast yourself.* www.youtube.com/watch?v= zJ0PUB2bhCU>.

19 The Process of Critique

James P. Dimock

<table>
<tr><td>

Chapter Outline

- What Is a Critique?
- Postmodernism vs. Historical Materialism: A Matter of Perspective
- Summary
- Key Steps and Questions to Consider
- Activities
- Discussion Questions
- Key Terms
- Undergraduate Student Paper

</td><td>

</td></tr>
</table>

What Will I Learn About Critical Theory in This Chapter?

In 1843, Marx (1978) observed that, in his German homeland, "everything is being forcibly repressed" (p. 12) and so it was necessary to engage in "a ruthless criticism of everything existing, ruthless in two senses: The criticism must not be afraid of its own conclusions, nor of conflict with the powers that be" (p. 13). The concept of "ruthless criticism" defines critical theory, and critical research is called **critique** (sometimes spelled "kritik" to acknowledge the German origins and to separate critical theory research from other forms of criticism such as literary criticism or rhetorical criticism). In this chapter you will learn how to engage in critique from both a Marxist and a postmodern perspective.

What Is a Critique?

Criticism must begin with something to criticize. This focus of our criticism, often called an **artifact** or a **text**, is something we are interested in evaluating. The "text" is the communication act or event we wish to study. Because we are communication scholars, we are interested in **symbolic** objects (the use symbols to influence the way people understand and interact with the world). A text may be narrowly defined (a single speech or communication situation) or broadly defined (the discourse of a given period or epoch). Typically, for a text to be an object of critique, it must have some boundaries—something that separates the text from the **context** (the objects that surround the text and are not part of it).

DOI: 10.4324/9781003109129-22

The process of identifying a text begins with a **description** of the text. If the text is well-known, the description may not be detailed. An unfamiliar text, however, requires that the critic depict the text in enough detail that readers can understand and appreciate it. The description is then typically followed by a **justification** for the criticism. The critic must explain why this particular text is suitable or appropriate for criticism. The importance and relevance of some texts is immediately obvious, but other lesser-known or seemingly insignificant texts will require the critic to explain why this criticism should be undertaken.

Jim, Dan, and Kirstin published a critique of the movie *Brokeback Mountain* in 2013. The movie was fairly well known, received critical acclaim, and was nominated for eight and won three Academy Awards (won for Best Director, Best Original Score, and Best Adapted Screenplay). They did not have to spend a lot of time describing the movie. However, just winning a stack of awards does not mean a movie (the text) is suitable for criticism. Jim, Dan, and Kirstin argued that the film had the capacity to influence perceptions of same-sex partners and same-sex marriage (an issue that has seen monumental shifting of opinions in recent years). Once the text has been described and the decision to critique it has been justified, we are ready to begin the actual critique.

In our everyday language we often think of criticism as being some kind of negative judgment about us or our work, but not all criticism is negative. Say, for example, I think Ridley Scott's film *Alien* is better than the sequel, *Aliens* directed by James Cameron. I am engaging in a basic form of criticism by comparing and contrasting two similar texts. My criticism of the films is **impressionistic**, since it reflects my impressions or feelings about the two films—I like *Alien* better than *Aliens*. While I like both movies, the original appealed to me in ways the sequel did not. You may disagree because the first film lacked the fast-paced action sequences of Cameron's follow up. Because we are both reporting our impressions about the films, your feelings are just as valid as my feelings. When we engage in impressionistic criticism, we are really saying much more about ourselves than we are about the object of our criticism. I may like the more cerebral horror sci fi while you like action-packed shoot 'em ups. But in order to engage in critique at a scholarly level, we need to move beyond talking about our own personal feelings. Our criticism must become **reflexive** and be based on some criteria or standard of criticism.

What the critic does next depends on how he or she identifies. A historical materialist or Marxist critic is more than likely engaging in **extrinsic** criticism. For such critics, the warrant for "good criticism" is its utility. Does the criticism assist the activist or organizer in the task of making social change? For most academics and scholars—including you!—critiques are typically **intrinsic**. Extrinsic criticism considers texts and artifacts in relation to some **normative** standard. The normative standards are transhistorical and transcultural principles by which a communication practice can be judged, such as emancipation (see Chapter 6). So a Marxist critique, which holds that contemporary industrial practice is wrong because it steals the workers' *labor*, thereby *alienating* the working class, is applying standards that should exist in all times, in all places, and for all persons regardless of the historical or cultural context. All workers own their labor, and to alienate them from their labor is, by definition, oppression.

Postmodern critics, skeptical of metanarratives upon which these norms are based, are much more likely to engage in intrinsic criticism. Every text, every system of discourse, has a logic and organization of its own. Intrinsic criticism confines the focus on the text itself. Recall that Hegel and Marx both maintained that within an object lies its negation, the internal contradiction that threatens the integrity of the text. By identifying these contradictions, dilemmas, and paradoxes, the postmodern critic destabilizes meanings and invites new interpretations of the text.

Postmodernism vs. Historical Materialism: A Matter of Perspective

Marxism and postmodernism share a commitment to ethical and political ends. Their differing perspectives lead them to approach research in different ways and to undertake research for different reasons. Marx did not believe genuine reform could come from academics and intellectuals. Only the proletariat, the workers themselves, could truly change the conditions of their lives and throw off oppression. In the *Communist Manifesto*, Marx and Engels (1964) wrote:

> The socialistic bourgeois want all the advantages of modern social conditions without the struggles and dangers necessarily resulting therefrom. They desire the existing state of society minus its revolutionary and disintegrating elements. They wish for a bourgeoisie without a proletariat. The bourgeoisie naturally conceives the world in which it is supreme to be the best.
>
> (p. 107)

Intellectuals and academics are members of the petite bourgeoisie and thus their interests, according to Marxists, will always be those of the bourgeoisie. Their aim is not to restructure the society so that there is no longer class and thus no longer class conflict but to provide the working class with the material benefits of the modern, industrial world while maintaining themselves as a privileged elite.

A historical materialist approach to communication research, then, would emphasize the practical application of theory to the material conditions around us. Because Marxism is a materialistic, historical, and scientific theory, Marxist researchers can avail themselves of any of the social scientific methodologies you have read about in this book. It is not the methods of research that matter as much as the motivation for the research and the ends to which research is used. If research works to strengthen working-class and proletarian unity, it is Marxist.

Other theorists see a more active role for academic and communication scholars. Chomsky (1987), one of the most outspoken critics of the capitalist system, argued that intellectuals do not have special privileges but responsibilities:

> Intellectuals are in a position to expose the lies of governments, to analyze actions according to their causes and motives and often hidden intentions. In the Western world at least they have the power that comes from political liberty, from access to information and freedom of expression. For a privileged minority, Western democracy provide leisure, the facilities, and the training to seek the truth lying hidden behind the veil of distortion and misrepresentation, ideology, and class interest through which the events of current history are presented to us.
>
> (p. 60)

Cloud (1994) argued along the same lines that the task of a cultural critique is "to unmask the shared illusions of a society as ideas promulgated by and serving the interests of the ruling class, or those who control the production and distribution of material goods" (p. 145). Ideology is a false consciousness, a screen that separates us from the reality of the human condition. The better we can see and understand the relations of production and understand the workings of power, the more able we are to resist them. Thus, the role of the critic is not to lead the fight for change but to participate in it using his or her understanding of communication to support the struggle for change.

Like Marxist critics, postmodernists are concerned with power and praxis. Their concern differs from Marxists. The postmodernist critic has no specific vision of what society without oppression may look like or if one is even possible. Marxism attempts to construct a basis upon which a socialist society can be built. Postmodernism, on the other hand, is **deconstructionist** and seeks to deconstruct the systems and forms of oppression (Foucault, 2006).

In his work on "critical rhetoric," McKerrow (1989) offers one of the best explanations of what a critical theorist does. The critic has two tasks. The first is the critique of domination or the "demystifying the conditions of domination" and the critique of freedom or "a self-reflexive critique that turns back on itself even as it promotes a realignment in the forces of power that construct social relations" (McKerrow, 1989, p. 91). Critical communication scholars look at the practices of domination from a variety of perspectives while at the same time turning criticism back on itself, continually inviting more criticism rather than declaring that the final judgment has been passed on a subject.

Summary

This chapter introduced you to how to conduct a critical/cultural critique. As you can see from the chapter, you can approach a critical/cultural critique in numerous ways. The key is to pick one which is a good fit for your research point of view or theoretical stance. We hope after reading the chapter you feel a little more prepared to carry out this type of study. On a final note, think back to the introduction and the story of Sir Edmund Hillary and that remember "even the fearful can achieve." We wish you all the best in your future research and scholarly endeavors. Stephen and Dan look forward to seeing your work presented at conferences and published in the journals.

Key Steps and Questions to Consider

1. Identify the artifact or text to be criticized.
2. Describe the text or artifact so the readers can get a full understanding of it.
3. Justify why the text is worthy of criticism.
4. Explain the purpose and what you hope to accomplish through the critique.
5. Determine if you are engaging in extrinsic criticism or intrinsic criticism.

Activities

1. Let's return to our activity from Chapter 4 on the Critical Paradigm. Pull out the activity notes from your backpack/notebook/computer/tablet from the Chapter 4 activity. The notes may help streamline this activity.
2. Divide everyone into groups. Each group is given a different issue. The issues are slavery, prohibition, women's suffrage, same-sex marriage, and child sex abuse by priests.
3. Each group will prepare a brief presentation using the process of critique described in this chapter.

Discussion Questions

1. What similarities and differences do you see between rhetorical criticism and the critical process?
2. How will your research claims about truth and reality be different between an experimental study and a critical/cultural study?
3. Think about what is happening in current politics, sports, or the arts. What events may be relevant for critique?

Key Terms

Artifact	Extrinsic	Reflexive
Context	Impressionistic	Symbolic
Critique	Intrinsic	Text
Deconstruction	Justification	
Description	Normative	

References

Chomsky, N. (1987). The responsibility of intellectuals. In J. Peck (Ed.), *The Chomsky reader* (pp. 59–82). Pantheon Press.

Cloud, D. (1994). The materiality of discourse as oxymoron: A challenge to critical rhetoric. *Western Journal of Communication, 58*, 141–163.

Foucault, M. (2006). Truth and power. In *The Chomsky-Foucault debate on human nature* (pp. 140–171). The New Press.

Marx, K. (1978). Capital, volume one. In R. C. Tucker (Ed.), *The Marx-Engels reader* (2nd ed., pp. 294–438). Norton.

Marx, K., & Engels, F. (1964). *The communist manifesto*. Washington Square Books.

McKerrow, R. (1989). Critical rhetoric: Theory and praxis. *Communication Monographs, 56*, 91–111.

Undergraduate Student Paper

The Ethics of Pimpthisbum.com

Suzanne (Lumberg) White

"When Sean Dolan saw signs being carried by homeless people," he didn't see a economic crisis. According Sabo (2009) "[H]e saw an opportunity" (para. 1). Sean and his father, Kevin, had approached a homeless man named Tim Edwards with a proposition. Exchange his usual "will work for food" sign with one reading "Pimpthisbum.com." For his efforts, the Dolan's would then pay him $100 a day.

So a website dedicated to helping the homeless was born. Visitors to the website can buy him anything from a cheeseburger to laser hair removal to a college education. Edwards joked to CBS (2009) that he is "the world's first online bum" (para. 10). But, as Cullers (2009) has pointed out, "some homeless advocates are upset over the word 'pimp' and are alleging that Tim is being exploited" (para. 1). The Dolan's website has gotten the attention they wanted. Attention for their advertising firm. They have made the front pages of newspapers all over the world and appeared on nearly every single major news network. The Dolan's have achieved their ultimate goal of proving that they can sell anything. So if Pimpthisbum. com is able to raise money to help the homeless, isn't a little bit of exploitation OK? While some have argued that pimpthisbum raises our awareness of the homeless and puts a needed face on the issue, I argue, based on the critical ethical theory of German philosopher Jurgen Habermas, that the Dolan's have engaged in unethical communication.

> In the first two paragraphs, Suzanne does two things. First, she gives her readers a description of the text she has selected for criticism. Her description provides readers with enough information about the text to be able to understand what is going on without getting bogged down in with unnecessary details. Second, Suzanne justifies the text as an object of criticism. On one hand, the website is trying to do something about the problem of homelessness, but Suzanne questions the ethics of this sort of appeal.

Habermas's philosophy of ethical communication is, to quote Burleson and Kline (1979) "formidable," "obscure," "dense and technical" but Habermas is also one of the most important social philosophers of the 20th century and one of the most important of the critical theorists. Because his work concerns both communication and ethics, his framework is appropriate to use in critiquing pimpthisbum.com.

For Habermas, communication is unethical when it undermines what he called the lifeworld and, according to Foss et al. (2001) the lifeworld entails communicative action. Habermas asserted that when communicative action is blocked, unethical impersonal systems take over. Marmura (2008) points out that while all complex societies require some level of systems, "social inequality and ultimately . . . social pathology originate" when those systems become "unmoored from the interests and values of the communities" (p. 4). In order to prevent the colonization of the lifeworld by systems, we need to engage in communicative rationality which requires the use of constetives, regulatives, and avowels.

First, ethical communicative action requires the use of regulatives. Regulative utterances negotiate the relationship between the people. So when I ask you if you're ready for me to speak, it says something about what I think of the relationship between us. These regulatives result is mutual understanding. Unethical communication systematizes the relationship, defining it through noncommunicative means like power differences and structures.

Second, ethical communication must involve avowels. Avowels are speech acts relative to our feelings, affections, and intentions. Foss et al. (2001) explain that avowals don't refer to the world around us or to our relationships with others but reflect our internal states and the validity of an avowal is determined by "the sincerity of the stated intentions" (p. 259). Unethical communication, then, involves the use of dishonest or insincere avowals.

Finally Burleson and Kline (1979) claimed that in order to present an ethical message, the author must present constatives. Habermas says in *Communication and the Evolution of Society* that constatives "imply an unmistakeable validity claim, a truth claim" (as cited in Foss et al., 2001, p. 257). For instance, this round has five people. These statements that can be validated protect the world from manipulative systems. Unethical communication occurs when regulative are inappropriate, when avowals are insincere, and constatives are not valid.

Now that we understand Habermas's criteria for ethical action we can now apply those criteria to pimpthisbum.com.

Suzanne does a good job of explaining a complicated critical theorist like Habermas, although some might argue she has oversimplified his work. Others will see her explanation as appropriate for undergraduate research. She does make an effort to justify using Habermas' theory of ethical communication as a normative standard by which to evaluate the ethics of a communicative act. Habermas is an important figure in critical theory. Suzanne could spend more time developing a review of Habermas' work and could strengthen her paper if she used more primary sources instead of relying on secondary sources.

First, unethical messages, involve inappropriate regulatives, or a distorted understanding of relationships. It is important to bear in mind the purposes of the relationship between Edwards and the Dolans. It is about raising the profile of the Dolan's marketing firm. By making Tim popular, they say, "we can make anything popular." And pimpthisbum is riddled with links to major media outlets that have covered the story. But what this does is to commodify Edwards, to turn him into an object to be marketed and sold for the Dolan's profit. Thus the relationship between them is inappropriate and pimpthisbum is unethical according this criteria.

Second, a rhetor must use sincere avowals. In public statements, Sean and Kevin Dolan and Ascendgence Tactical Online Marketing, repeatedly depict pimpthisbum as a way to help the homeless. For example, Edwards has said, "The whole idea of this project is to get people off the street" (as cited in CBS, 2009, p. 10). But we already know that isn't true. The whole idea is to raise the public profile of the Dolan's and their advertising firm, Ascendgence. More importantly, it undermines our ability to treat Edwards's avowals as valid. Edwards is being paid by the Dolans. We simply cannot assume that he is any more sincere than a $100 a day buys. If we can't accept Tim's avowals at face value, then we have to conclude that pimpthisbum is unethical according to yet another of Habermas's criteria.

Finally, in order to present an ethical message, the author must first present constatives- or asserted truth. In Habermas's theory of ethics, constatives are the ultimate check on systemic colonization of the lifeworld because they can be verified. We can hold statements up to reality and see if they line up. Mamura points out that when unchecked, "bureaucratic standards of rationality or the profit orientation of commercial enterprise" the "ability to question, or even recognize the rules which govern [our] actions [are] greatly diminished." By putting an altruistic mask on an entirely business motive, the Dolan's violate the third and final of Habermas's criteria.

Now that we have examined how pimpthisbum.com fails to fulfill Habermas's model, we must return to our research question: So if Pimpthisbum.com is able to bring attention to the problem and raise money to help the homeless, isn't a little bit of exploitation OK? And to answer this question we will look to two implications. First because Edwards's voice is constrained by commercial interests and second because Edwards actually obscures the face of homeless.

First, Edwards's ability to function as voice for the homeless is distorted by commercial interests. Habermas's Edwards is repeated described as funny, upbeat, educated, and does not blame others for being homeless. This explanation of homelessness is great . . . if you are ultimately not interested in dealing with the problem of homelessness. A report available at the website for the National Coalition for the Homeless (2009) demonstrates a clear link between rising homelessness and the foreclosure crisis. Certainly, some people are homeless because they made bad choices . . . many are victims of mental illness, domestic violence, lack of affordable housing and other factors beyond their control. If the faces of tragic circumstances don't sell products, this helpful exploitation will not even presented.

Finally, positioning Edwards as 'the face' of homelessness obscures important dimensions of the problem. The Dolan's have made a "homeless man the symbol of all homelessness" (Daily Write). But Edwards isn't a poster-child for homelessness the way Rosa Parks came to symbolized segregation or Matthew Shepherd became a face for victims of hate crimes. The difference is rather clear: 'the symbol of homelessness' in America should look like the homelessness in America. According Pimp this bum's (n.d.) website, they "but we humanized homelessness by focusing on a particular individual" (para. 4). This particular homeless individual, however, looks and sounds a lot more like the demographic the Dolan's are interested in than the typical homeless person. According to the National Coalition for the Homeless (2007), 51% of the homeless population are, like Tim Edwards, male. But the homeless are far less likely to be white, like Edwards. The fastest growing segment of the homeless population is families with children. Edwards, an educated and articulate white man, is not the face of homelessness and doesn't give the homeless a voice. Instead his image obscures the voices of millions of people. It isn't just that the Dolan's are capitalists. It is that they let their interest in system of profit obscure important issues and questions about an important problem that is getting worse.

Suzanne applies the extrinsic standards in her evaluation putting, her scholarship at the Marxist end of the critical spectrum. Second, she uses actual statistics about homelessness in the United States to point out the conflict between the image of homelessness created by the Dolans and the reality of homelessness. The Dolans discourse contributes to a false consciousness, which Suzanne's critique attempts to correct.

Although, the Dolans seemed to make a difference, their help has proven to be unethical, and potentially harmful to our future. The goal of my paper is to not just engage in a criticism of communication but to be a critical communicatior just as Habermas engages in communicative action. Buying someone a virtual cheeseburger does not ethically confront the issue of the homeless. To put it simply, it is not about pimping but rather caring and communicating . . . and that is something we can all do.

> In the conclusion, we get a clear indication of praxis—that Suzanne's motives are not just to critique pimpthisbum.com but to confront the problem of homelessness.

References

Burleson, B. R., & Kline, S. L. (1979). Habermas' theory of communication: A critical explication. *The Quarterly Journal of Speech, 65*, 412–428.

CBS. (2009, March 9). *Is it right to pimp this bum?* cbsnews.com

Cullers, R. (2009, March 27). Pimp this bum: Salvation or exploitation. *Adweek.* www.adweek.com/adfreak/pimp-bum-salvation-or-exploitation-14427

Foss, S. K., Foss, K. A., & Trapp, R. (2001). *Readings in contemporary rhetoric.* Waveland Press.

Marmura, S. (2008). Surveillance, mass vulture and the subject: A systems/lifeworld approach. *Democratic Communiqué, 22*(2), 1–18.

National Coalition for the Homeless. (2007). *Who is homeless?* www.nationalhomeless.org/publications/facts/Whois.pdf

National Coalition for the Homeless. (2009). *Foreclosure to homelessness 2009: The forgotten victims of the subprime crisis.* www.nationalhomeless.org/advocacy/ForeclosuretoHomelessness0609.pdf

Pimp This Bum. (n.d.). *About the PTB project.* pimpthisbum.com

Sabo, T. (2009, March 26). *PimpThisBum.com employs irony on homeless man's behalf.* CNN.com

20 Methods of Performance

Desirée D. Rowe and Michael Tristano, Jr.

Chapter Outline

- Context of Performance in Communication Studies
- The Body as Method and Theory
- Performative Writing
- Mixed Method Performance
- Performance Pedagogy
- Performance as Method of Resistance
- Links to Great Performance
- Key Steps and Things to Consider
- Activities
- Discussion Questions
- Key Terms

The Empty Space, a black-box performance area for students, faculty, and collaborators in the Hugh Downs School of Human Communication at Arizona State University.

What Will I Learn About Performance?

Performance is where our words and bodies come together as a site for understanding. This chapter might be a bit different from other chapters because performance is both a method and theory. Don't worry, we won't make you read too much about theory! In this chapter, you will learn different ways to approach performance as a way of gathering and presenting qualitative data.

Remember, performance is both a method *and* a theory. As a method:

- Performance is a way of collecting data in the field.
- Performance is a way to represent data.
- Performance is a way to resist the status quo.
- Performance is a way to communicate data and/or analysis to an audience.
- Performances are a type of artifact to analyze.

Performance is also a theory. Performance as a theory helps us understand, complicate, resist, and interrogate how individuals, groups, or cultures are represented and constituted. We discuss

DOI: 10.4324/9781003109129-23

in the following chapter a long history and lots of scholarship about how communication studies scholars theorize performance. Here are just a few of the examples of the "performance turn" in theory you might have come across:

- Goffman's anticipatory socialization.
- Performances of culture and rituals (e.g., funerals, celebrations, milestones).
- Performances of speech acts (e.g., "hey you!").
- Performativity.
- Performances of identity.
- Protests and other performances of resistance.

Context of Performance in Communication Studies and Beyond

Performance Studies is an interdisciplinary field, meaning that performance studies scholars come from a wide range of different academic backgrounds. Performance researchers can be found in theatre, ethnic studies, art, English, and, of course, communication studies. Performance work is most often found within the **critical paradigm** of communication studies. The critical paradigm asks us to question the status quo and advocate for social change, and the work of performance studies scholars regularly questions how assumptions about performances of identity (for example) are constituted and reconstituted through culture. If we were to stop there—with the answer to the question and then the investigation of the performance, performance would be within the interpretivist paradigm. However, performance studies scholars regularly (but not always) keep going to advocate for social change. In the next section, we talk about the context of performance within the communication studies discipline and how performance is also a uniquely interdisciplinary method.

Today, performance studies as a field intersects with theories and methods found under the banners of queer theory, postcolonial studies, women and gender studies, and critical race studies, to name a few. For these reasons, one might consider the origins of performance studies a messy womb, one that cannot be pinned down to one academic field of study. So locating the beginnings of performance as theory and method is difficult. However, many argue that performance methods have a strong tradition in oral interpretation.

Oral interpretation, sometimes referred to as dramatic reading or interpretive reading, is the process of speaking aloud—or performing—a piece of text, traditionally while holding a manuscript. For instance, if you have ever seen a poet perform a reading one of their poems, they are engaging in oral interpretation. This was an important intervention for performance scholars, who argued that performing a text out loud changed the performers' and audiences' relationship to the text, and therefore literary theories were no longer sufficient to explain how and what happens when texts became *performed*. Oral interpretation became a cornerstone for performance studies, displaying the importance of performance as both theory and method.

If oral interpretation was the beginning, the next invention was **performing identity**. Performance scholars quickly realized that performance is paramount in understanding one's identity in several different ways. First, Goffman (1956) thought to describe face-to-face interactions as theatrical performances, as scenes. In a scene, the actors are everyday people engaging in everyday actions or conversations. Note, however, that people have the desire and the ability to present themselves in particular ways. For example, as a student in a classroom, you may want to communicate that you are prepared and studious, and therefore you make choices about your behavior. In other words, you perform "good" student. The insight led performance scholars to coin the phenomena called performativity. **Performativity** refers to repeated speech acts or nonverbal communication that becomes a cultural script for different types of identities. For example, Butler (1990) argues that gender is socially constructed and that the norms we have for how a man, for instance, should behave, look, or speak are performative. With this in mind, some performance scholars argue we are all always performing—even if we never take the stage!

Performing identity can also refer to *creating* an identity through the act of performing. Performance scholars argue that by writing, staging, and crafting autobiographical narratives, people have the ability to perform and communicate their stories and identities. The method is called **performed autoethnography**. The purpose of the method is to use personal experiences and narratives to comment on broader cultural discourses and systems of power. For example, Benge (2019) writes and performs an autoethnography that relates to her personal experience of being born to an abusive mother, navigating the foster care system, having a child of her own, and ultimately confronting civil and criminal proceedings leading to losing custody of her daughter. Benge's work integrates systems of classism, ableism, heterosexism, and racism embedded within the custody-legal-foster system constellation. Valuable autoethnography must consider what broader cultural discourses you are speaking about, critiquing, or interrogating. As you prepare a performed autoethnography, think about how to stage and present your autoethnography for an audience. Scholars argue that your relationship to your personal experiences and your writing will change when you decide to perform these experiences for others (Spry, 2016). Therefore, performed autoethnography values the writing and staging equally as part of the method.

Next, identity and performance can intersect as we understand ourselves in relationship to different types of performances. For instance, Dimitriadis (2009) explains how youth are fashioning self and community through hip hop. Dimitriadis argues performances that by hip hop artists like Eightball & MJG and Three 6 Mafia become a touchstone for how youth socialize, make sense of the world, and foster community-centered values. Performances by artists and musicians are more than a way to pass the time or relax; they are deeply connected to who we are as people and how we understand our own identities.

Finally, performance studies scholars research by studying **cultural performances**. Cultural performances refer to performance events—concerts, dances, sporting events, rituals, speeches—representing a moment in culture. For example, Ammaturo (2015) conducted an analysis of gay pride parades in the United Kingdom and Italy. She explored how members of the lesbian, gay, bisexual, transgender, and queer (LGBTQ) community create identities within the context of pride parades. Ultimately, she argued that pride parades can challenge a dominant political status quo, yet LGBTQ community members may fall prey to commodification and homonationalism, which may undercut the subversive potential of the parades.

In short, the word "performance" can mean a plethora of different ideas. "Performance" is complex, slippery, and employed differently by different people. The complexity is, however, what makes methods of performance so rich; the variety of ways to do performance research methods produces a wide range of projects, theories, and knowledge production.

The Body as Method and Theory

Performance studies explores how our bodies move, interact, persuade, influence, desire, communicate, transform, and, well, just *are* in the world. As a site of research, we can look at:

1. How our own performances of identity circulate in the world through autoethnography and performative writing.

2.   How performances outside of our own bodies make meaning through performance ethnography, oral interpretation, and performance critique.

We focus so much on the feelings and resonances of the body because for performance studies scholars the performance is **epistemic**. This means we don't separate how we *think* (the mind) from how we *feel* (the body). Epistemic emerges from the Greek word *episteme*, which means knowledge. Epistemic questions ask how we know what we know and how we build this "knowing" from experiences around us. Performance methods are an expressive epistemic. In other words, performance methods investigate how both the mind *and* the body make sense of the world. As Bell (2008) explains, "Performance as an epistemology, then, is a different, and often maligned, way of knowing the world" (p. 22). Think about how your body feels at a protest, or a funeral, or even graduation. Performance methods ask us to critically understand the movement and entanglements of bodies and the performances of identity within these rich scenes. As an expressive epistemic, performance methods investigate how our bodies and minds, together, shape and create meanings.

For example, when a femme person walks down the street late at night, she might experience people harassing her with "hey baby" or "looking good." She may be angry, or scared, or just ignore the yelling. Two experiences are intertwined in the moment—the experience of sexual harassment and the how the experience impacts her performance of self. Does she walk faster? Does she yell back? Does she change the way she dresses? Does she pass down lessons to her own daughters about how to safely perform femme-ness on a dark street late at night?

Performance as epistemic emphasizes how we combine theory and methods about the body because they are really difficult to separate in academic contexts but, most importantly, how we live our lives as people. People whose bodies communicate race, sexuality, ability, nation, and gender all just by moving between spaces. We cannot separate the two.

Performance as epistemic is important for you as the researcher. All scholars (regardless of methodological orientation) should be **reflexive.** Reflexivity is part of the epistemological foundation of performance studies and part of the research process. Reflexivity ensures that the researcher understands the influence of their own position within the research. A reflexive researcher acknowledges how your identity and your performance of self influences the research. Let's return to the earlier example. How might the research be influenced if you (the researcher) had also experienced harassment? Or if you had been a witness to the event? Finally, reflexivity is an ethical standpoint. Reflexivity asks us to be honest about biases, about privilege, and to communicate our own social position clearly to our participants within our research design and analysis.

Performative Writing

Like all research methods, the writing process is critically important to performance methods. Different from other types of methods, however, performance methods rely on the concept of performative writing. **Performative writing**, at its core, asks readers to *feel* the text (Calafell, 2007). What exactly does it mean to feel a text, though? To understand, we turn to **aesthetic**, another key concept within performance-studies research. Aesthetic performance or aesthetic communication, in the most general sense, refers to the artistic beauty of a performance. Aesthetic performance, although difficult to define, can be thought of as the combination of creativity and technique that inspires a reader or audience member to react.

Let's use an example to help illustrate the idea: imagine you are at a small music venue to see your favorite recording artist. After the opening act, the lights change dramatically, a low hum of a cord begins, smoke billows out from the sides of the set, and the artist rises up from beneath the stage. The artist begins to sing their newest hit single in all its glory with the rest of the band accompanying them, and you find yourself awestruck in the moment. The feeling in the pit of your stomach as you respond is aesthetic performance. Aesthetic performances beg us to feel and become engaged with the power of art. Methods of performance rely heavily on the creativity of aesthetic communication to impact their readers and audiences. Scholarship produced using methods of performance can very much look, feel, and sound like art. And while the performance, staging, and execution are a part of creating an aesthetic, it is vital we begin with performative writing as a method to create one.

Let's go back for a minute to performative writing, which asks the reader or audience to feel the text. Much like watching your favorite artist, the goal of performative writing invites the reader or audience to have a response. The example of the musical artist is useful. You know all the lyrics and the notes, and, when they reach your ears, you have an emotional response. Maybe the lyrics speak to your own experiences or respond to your mood. Similarly, performative writing attempts to evoke personal and cultural memory. Often, performance-studies scholars use their own experiences as the catalyst for performative writing. In this way, performative writing compels the author to write from/through the body. Essentially, performative writing is one way to theorize from your own body. The idea relies heavily on the work of woman-of-color feminists who argue, "a theory of the flesh means one where the physical realities of our lives—our skin color, the land or concrete we grew up on, our sexual longings—all fuse to create a politic born of necessity" (Moraga & Anzaldúa, 2015, p. 19). It becomes one important way performance scholars, particularly marginalized scholars, translate the personal creatively on the page. Performative writing may take the form of prose, poetry, lyrics, drama, or something totally different. The writer decides how best to communicate their ideas.

Here is an example of performative writing from Tristano's (2020) dissertation (one of the chapter authors). His research investigated how queer and trans bodies of color responded to the 2016 Pulse Night Club shooting.

> Sitting in a small seminar hall at a major research university in central Illinois, I prepare to perform on panel entitled *Politics of Resistance 'Post-Pulse': Resuscitating the Heartbeats of Neglected Queer Bodies and Beings* as part of a large, international academic conference. The panel is noted as a "Spotlight" panel in the conference program, and I am eager to take in how other academics are thinking and writing about Pulse in 2019. Three years feels like a long time, I think to myself. The spotlight designation makes it feel like there might be some groundbreaking work or at the very least sparkly potentialities for the future of research about Pulse. It makes it feel important. Before the panel begins, I read over the panel rationale once more:
>
> More than two years have passed since the tragedy at Pulse Nightclub, the gay cultural space in Orlando, FL where 49 innocents were murdered by a lone gunman. This massacre took a real and material toll on culture and cultural beings. Yet the attention given to Pulse has dwindled to nearly nothing. Questions remain concerning issues of violence, discourse, silence, marginalization, political engagement, just for starters, leading us to ask: what is the sound of Pulse's heart beat today? In this panel five participants draw on a number of conceptual and methodological approaches to examine one

or more of these issues. We represent a diverse range of backgrounds, from doctoral students to senior scholars, and share a commitment to inquiry that generates inclusive understandings of this massacre, and cultural inquiry more generally. This panel will leave plenty of time for discussion with/for those in attendance.

There is potential, I think cheerfully. And yet I feel a flutter in my chest as I recall the context of how the invitation to join this panel was extended to me.

The particular performance I am going over in my mind before the start of the panel, *Embodying the Performative Afterlife of Pulse*, is a co-authored piece with the person who invited me on to the panel. I recall receiving a text from them months earlier in which they shared they have been invited to be on a panel about Pulse and to their knowledge there were no other queer and/or trans people of color currently scheduled to appear. They wanted to mark a particular and necessary politic of ensuring that queer and/or trans voices of color were a part of this scholarly conversation (Calafell, 2017; Johnson, 2017).

Indeed, as I look around the room my co-author and I are the only self-identified queer and/or trans people of color who are on this panel. The flutter in my chest dies down a bit and feels more like a weight in the pit of my stomach. The absence of a multitude of queer and/or trans voices of color in this room echoes in the place of my body that remembers their voices absent after June 12, 2016. I wonder what most people would say about that absence. Most likely they would say they do not know where to find those voices. They are just not looking in the right places, I think to myself.

After completing our performance that detailed preliminary findings and ideas about this dissertation project, my co-author and I sit and engage with a performance that is presented as an (auto)ethnographic endeavor to explore how one relates (or does not relate) to the physical and spiritual presence of Pulse in Orlando today. In other words, how, when one goes to visit the place where Pulse stood, does one identify (or not) with it and the people that surround it. I sit there and listen to a scholar talk about his social position as it relates to Pulse; he is a white gay man who is located in Florida. As I mull over his use of Muñoz in this project, my mind drifts, if only for a moment, to be with my own thoughts, until I am immediately pulled back in when the white gay scholar utters, "as a gay man who primarily dates Latin men, I could have been there."

I stop breathing. I want to stand up, bang my hands on the table, shout, run out of the room, snatch his script out of his hand.

"How dare you? How dare you decide to perform a double gesture that simultaneously homogenizes and fetishizes a group of queer folks of color and (re)centers your own whiteness. You should be ashamed," I want to spit back at him.

Instead, I ease myself back into breathing and I try to catch a glance of anyone else who might have heard his last sentence. In this moment, I feel the power of whiteness in this academic space. I felt it from the scholar's body and utterance and now I feel it in my own choice not to say anything. I choose to perform 'good academic' rather than face the consequences of deviating from the norm (Carrillo Rowe & Malholtra, 2007).

I stop listening to the performances and I look back at the program with the list of participants for this panel. Three gay white men, two straight brown women, one straight (non-American) white man, and my co-author and I: two mixed raced queer/trans people of color. I feel and quite literally see the structures of whiteness and heteronormativity

> that underpin this academic space and conversation. I think back to the subtitle of the panel: *Resuscitating the Heartbeats of Neglected Queer Bodies and Beings*. I make a quick edit in my mind: *Neglected Queer Bodies and Beings*.

Performative writing is a compelling way to critique cultural discourses and systems of power. Performative writing, like any other method, takes practice, time, and precision. While performative writing relies heavily on creativity and aesthetic communication, it is very much a skill that must be worked and polished. You are attempting to get an audience or reader to feel, to think, to respond with their own bodies; it requires thinking, drafting, and redrafting. Activity 2, located at the end of the chapter, is an exercise to help you start practicing performative writing.

Performative writing, which often turns into performed autoethnography, is often staged as **solo performance**. Solo performance is a way for a researcher to stage a show featuring themselves and their writing. However, the value of performative writing means that the show is also performed on the page. A reader can feel the aesthetic of the communication and respond to the writing itself. In sum, performative writing is an effective method used in a variety of ways and utilized widely by scholars of performance.

Mixed-Method Performance

Performance works well when paired with other methods. A mixed-method performance is one way to bring an embodied approach to your research. The mixed-method chapter earlier in your textbook provides details and the steps for completing a mixed-methods project. Performance can pair with a lot of the other methods you have read about. You could pair with interviews, focus groups, or ethnography. For example, Madison (2010) used performance and ethnographic field work to stage her analysis. Madison's performance *Water Rites* argues that access to water is a human right. She utilizes ethnographic field work and conversation in Ghana as the basis of her performance. Watch her performance at www.youtube.com/watch?app=desktop&v=Pett8CBAjhg.

A **performed ethnography** means that your ethnographic data is scripted into an accessible staged performance. The performance is a way to report your findings back to participants, to engage in activist work, and to make academic research more accessible. Connecting to practical and embodied ways of knowing and connecting with participants (and people generally) is an important step for performance studies scholars. As Conquergood (1991) explained, "performance-centered research takes as both its subject matter and method the experiencing body situated in time, place, and history. The performance paradigm insists on face-to-face encounters instead of abstractions and reductions" (p. 187).

Adding performance to your research fulfills Conquergood's call to center how our bodies make sense of the world. Your performance could be a solo show, could incorporate lots of digital media and technology, or could be an ensemble production. A performed ethnography has no rules except that you need to represent the work accurately and fairly. Don't make up results just because they make for an interesting performance!

Desirée (one of your chapter authors) translated research for the stage using qualitative data collected by Dr. Linda Lederman on undergraduate students' use of alcohol on college campuses. Rowe (2009) scripted an interactive, audience-centered performance for undergraduates at Arizona State University to "walk through" various scenarios and choose what they would do when encountering conflicts. The scenarios, the characters within the scenarios, and the conflicts were based on Linda Lederman's qualitative data. Instead of just reading about the negative impacts of binge drinking, for example, undergraduates walked through those impacts and hopefully made better decisions in the future.

Performance Pedagogy

The connection between performance and pedagogy—or the method of practice and teaching—is one scholars believe is paramount. Often, we think of pedagogy as something that happens within the confines of the classroom. However, performance pedagogy is more complex. As Alexander (2006) noted,

> Performance pedagogy as a theoretical construct focuses both on pedagogy of teaching performance in performance studies, and on engaging performance as strategic pedagogy: performance as a way of knowing, performance as a strategic analytic; performance as a way of seeing and understanding the nuanced nomenclature of human social dynamics.
>
> (p. 253)

Put another way, **performance pedagogy** is not simply about classroom instruction, it is about how performance can be utilized as a tool of teaching and learning within larger societal contexts.

Performance pedagogy is closely related to **performance of possibilities**, a concept proposed by Madison (1999). The performance of possibilities is a method for imagining what our world can be. I am sure many of us are concerned with issues of social justice; performance, then, becomes a method in which we might imagine a more just world. In this way, performance is pedagogical, because as audience members and performers we are teaching and learning about what we want for our society. Take for example, Mojisola Adebayo's play *The Integration of Sandra Bland*, in which Adebayo (2019) sat down and transcribed verbatim the dash cam recording of the arrest of Sandra Bland, a 28-year-old Black woman, on July 10, 2015. Bland was pulled over by police officer Brian Encinia for failure to signal. As events escalated, Bland was forcefully arrested and taken into custody. The next day, Bland was found hanged in her cell in Waller County, Texas. Abebayo requests that Encinia is played by one white man and that Bland is played by 100 Black women. The casting enables audience members to reimagine the interaction between Bland and Encinia; begs them to grapple with issues of race, policing, and power; and forces them to imagine what is possible with the strength of 100 Black women. Performance methods are pedagogical because they aid us in fighting for futures that are net yet here.

Performance as Method of Resistance

The Integration of Sandra Bland is a stark reminder that performance is also a method of resistance. With its roots in activist theatre, performance-studies scholars use performance as a way to imagine the future alongside the audience. Dr. Augusto Boal was a Brazilian activist and organizer whose Theatre of the Oppressed (1974) is a key development in imagining those future possibilities. Theatre of the Oppressed is a technique grounded in engagement with the audience. Theatre of the Oppressed has six "branches"; in each branch the audience has different levels of involvement. Boal (1979) called the audience "spect-actors," because (depending on the type of performance) the audience worked with the actors to change the outcomes of the performances and practice imagining—and embodying—a potential future. Activity 1, discussed later, is derived from one of the branches of Boal's Theatre of the Oppressed and is a great beginning exercise for reimagining the role of the audience in resisting the status quo.

If you want to keep exploring different techniques of resistance for the stage, Dr. Linda Park-Fuller's (2003) Playback Theatre is another technique. Playback Theatre "involves a blurring of roles where performers become audience members and audience members become performers; it provides a metaphorical language where performances 'answer' performances; and it invites a performative method of research and reporting that features interrogating over evaluating" (p. 288). Within Playback Theatre, the audience is involved in the re-creation of performances of events or experiences provided by the audience. The performers and actors work together to tell the story, stop the story, and, sometimes, rewrite the story. Together, in conversation with the "conductor," stories are told and retold magnifying moments of resistance or foregrounding another perspective.

While both the Theatre of Oppressed and Playback Theatre are methods of performance with an audience, performance studies scholars can take a wide range of approaches to performing resistance. (Of course they can!) Performance-studies scholars consider all texts as **polysemic.** This means a text can speak in multiple voices. Performances and texts tell us, as researchers, multiple stories about how they are circulated in the world. It is our job, as researchers, to help understand and contextualize those stories.

Performance studies scholars don't only look at the performance stage as a text, as we discussed earlier; we also look at the performances of everyday life. And, in this way, performances that resist the status quo are within those every day acts. For example, Erincin's (2016) special issue of *Liminalities: A Journal of Performance Studies* explored how stillness and silence can be seen as a performance of resistance within nonwestern and transnational contexts. The essays in the special issue examine stillness and silence within texts using performance as a theoretical frame to conduct a rhetorical or content analysis, examine stillness and silence through a documentary film, and explore the author's own life as a site of resistance through performative writing.

Because performance-studies scholars are attending to the stage, the page, and the body within a framework of resistance, we must also be attuned to how our bodies and the bodies of those around us are expected to perform within the status quo. **Queer of Color critique** is a central tool for this understanding. Performance studies scholars have also taken up Ferguson's (2003) charge to "interrogate of social formations at the intersections of race, gender, sexuality, and class, with particular attention in how those formations correspond with and diverge from nationalist ideals and practices" (p. 149). Queer of Color critique doesn't have a step-by-step guide. Queer of Color critique is a politic of foregrounding the imbalances of power within performances of identity, and "for critical communication researchers, it would be advantageous to consider the many ways that bodies are enacting multiple identities at once and having to negotiate various levels of power in order to simply live life" (Valles-Morales & LeMaster, 2015, p. 79). Queer of Color critique demands that we, as researchers, step up and examine the surface-level performances and that we dig deeper to see the impacts of the cultural formations of race, nation, sexuality, gender, economics, and ability on our understanding of what types of bodies should be enacting what types of performances.

Links to Great Performances

1. *Fred Astaire's Dancing Lessons* by Goltz (2020) at http://liminalities.net/16-3/fredastaire.html.

2. *The Storyteller Project: Digital Storytelling for Women of Color* edited by Boylorn et al. (2019) at http://liminalities.net/15-4/.
3. *Ekkreinen: A Stop Motion Capsule Performance* by Rowe (2018) at http://liminalities. net/14-4/ekkreinen.html.

Summary

Performance is a method that asks the researcher to be reflexive of their subject position, their relationship to participants, and how knowledge is co-constructed by all of our collective performances. Performance is a method for representing autoethnographic data or field work from interviews or focus groups or to study cultural performances. Through our discussion of possible performance paths, we've shined the light on performance as a creative and embodied way of making sense of the world.

Key Steps and Things to Consider

1. Performance has many definitions.
2. Performance studies researchers must be reflexive about their positionality.
3. Performance is political.
4. Performance studies is an interdisciplinary field.
5. Performance can be understood as both theory and method.
6. Performance has an intrinsic relationship with art and creativity.

Activity #1: Sculptures of the Self

This activity is adapted from Rowe et al. (2019). In this activity, each student brings 10 objects of personal significance to class in a brown paper bag. The students place their bags on the perimeter of the room and select someone else's bag. Students examine the objects from their chosen bag and build/create a sculpture they think represents the identity of the person who provided the objects. Rowe, Rudnick, and White explain:

> They can build the sculpture however they wish, but they should try to demonstrate why these objects might matter to the person who provided them. For example, often a student will place a religious text at the center of the sculpture to emphasize an assumed high importance of spirituality, or wrap a blanket around the outer boundary of the other objects to communicate the blanket is a comfort object. Once all students are finished building their sculptures, the class "tours the museum." Each artist will describe the sculpture they created and why they believe the work accurately represents the person's identity. Other class members are then invited to share their own interpretation of the sculpture. The owner of the items should not indicate their identity. After all sculptures have been viewed, students are asked to go stand by their objects and take

a photo of the initial sculpture. Students will then re-sculpt the objects into a sculpture they feel accurately describes their own identity and take a second photo of the sculpture. For example, one student moved a centered religious text to the periphery of the sculpture to illustrate a loss of faith, and another crumpled the blanket into a disheveled ball to capture emotions regarding a parents divorce. When all are finished with the second sculpture, students should silently tour the museum again on their own. Ask them to take notes about differences they observed in the new sculptures.

(p. 3)

Activity #2: Writing the Self as Object

This activity is designed to provide students the opportunity to practice writing from the body and, in turn, performative writing. Sit, close your eyes, and pay attention to how you are feeling today. What object do you feel like? It can be any type of object. Draw the object. The drawing is an important step because you need to clearly visualize the object. Take 5-10 minutes to write down adjectives associated with the object. For example, Michael visualized a kettle and wrote down "hot," "black," and "heavy." Remember, the words are not about how you are feeling, they are words you associate with the object. Next, write a story that personifies the object and makes the object the protagonist. Use the adjectives to help direct how the story progresses. For example, I might wrote a story identifying reasons a kettle might be feeling heavy; what's weighing it down? The final step is to reflect on your story. Answer the question: how does the story resonate with your own personal experiences and why? The reflection is an exercise in writing from the body and can be turned into pieces of performative writing. Feel free to repeat the activity several times with different objects that they feel like on any particular day.

Discussion Questions

1. Think about a time when you were in a large group. How did you make sense of your identity among others? Did you share performances of identity? Did you learn anything about your own performance of identity? How could this be an expressive epistemic?
2. Can you think of a reading or discussion from one of your classes that might make for an impactful performance? How can a research text be "translated" for the stage?
3. Performance can be many things at the same time. What are some of the benefits of its multiple meanings? Drawbacks? How does it make you feel about doing performance research?
4. What social issues might you want to integrate into a performance-methods project? How might you create a performance of possibilities that touches on the issues you care about?
5. Performances of resistance are also everyday acts. Have you ever engaged in a performance of resistance? How can you be reflexive about that experience?

Key Terms

Aesthetic

Critical Paradigm

Cultural Performances

Epistemic

Oral Interpretation

Performance of Possibilities

Performance Pedagogy

Performance Studies

Performative Writing

Performativity

Performed
Autoethnography

Performed Ethnography

Performing Identity

Polysemic

Queer of Color Critique

Reflexive

Solo Performance

References

Adebayo, M. (2019). *Mojisola Adebayo: Plays two: I stand corrected; Asara and the sea-monsters; oranges and stones; the interrogation of Sandra Bland; STARS*. Oberon Books.

Alexander, K. B. (2006). Performance and pedagogy. In D. S. Madison & J. Hamera (Eds.), *The Sage handbook of performance studies* (pp. 253–260). Sage.

Ammaturo, F. R. (2016). Spaces of pride: A visual ethnography of gay pride parades in Italy and the United Kingdom. *Social Movement Studies, 15*(1), 19–40. https://doi.org/10.1080/147428 37.2015.1060156

Bell, E. (2008). *Theories of performance*. Sage.

Benge, L. (2019). For the love of: A motherhood of state violence and affective residues. In C. Beyer & A. L. Robertson (Eds.), *Mothers without their children* (pp. 43–52). Demeter Press.

Boal, A. (1979). *Theatre of the oppressed* (A. Charles & M.-O. L. McBride, Trans.). Theatre Communications Group.

Boylorn, R. M., Williams, V., & Raimist, R. (Eds.). (2019). The storyteller project: Digital storytelling for women of color. *Liminalities: A Journal of Performance Studies, 15*(4). http://liminalities. net/15-4/

Butler, J. (1990). *Gender trouble*. Routledge.

Calafell, B. M. (2007). *Latina/o communication studies: Theorizing performance*. Peter Lang.

Calafell, B. M. (2017). Brown queer bodies. *Qualitative Inquiry, 23*(7), 511–512. https://doi.org/10.1 177%2F1077800417718290

Carrillo Rowe, A., & Malhotra, S. (2007). (Un)hinging whiteness. In L. M. Cooks & J. S. Simpson (Eds.), *Whiteness, pedagogy, performance: Dis/placing race* (pp. 271–298). Lexington Books.

Conquergood, D. (1991). Rethinking ethnography: Towards a critical cultural politics. *Communication Monographs, 58*, 179–194. https://doi.org/10.1080/03637759109376222

Dimitriadis, G. (2009). *Performing identity/performing culture: Hip hop as text, pedagogy, and lived practice*. Peter Lang.

Erincin, S. (2016). Introduction: On minorities, silence, stillness, and resistance. *Liminalities: A Journal of Performance Studies, 12*(3), 1–7.

Ferguson, R. A. (2003). *Aberrations in black: Toward a queer of color critique*. University of Minnesota Press.

Goffman, E. (1956). *The presentation of self in everyday life*. Doubleday.

Goltz, D. B. (2020). Fred Astaire's dancing lessons. *Liminalities: A Journal of Performance Studies, 16*(3). http://liminalities.net/16-3/fredastaire.html

Johnson, A. (2017). Pulse: From death to resurrection and back again. *Qualitative Inquiry, 23*(7), 483–487. https://doi.org/10.1177%2F1077800417718292

Madison, D. S. (1999). Performance, personal narrative, and the politics of possibilities: Visions and revisions. In S. J. Dailey (Ed.), *The future of performance studies: Visions and revisions*. National Communication Association.

Madison, D. S. (2010). *Acts of activism: Human rights as radical performance*. Cambridge University Press.

Moraga, C., & Anzaldúa, G. (2015). *This bridge called my back: Writings by radical women of color* (4th ed.). SUNY Press.

Park-Fuller, L. (2003). Audiencing the audience: Playback theatre, performative writing, and social activism, *Text and Performance Quarterly*, *23*(3), 288–310. https://doi.org/10.1080/1 0462930310001635321

Rowe, D. D. (2009, March). Writer and director. *Drink, Drank, Drugged*. A live performance based on college drinking research conducted by Linda Lederman. Empty Space Theater, Arizona State University.

Rowe, D. D. (2018). Ekkreinen: A stop motion capsule performance. *Liminalities: A Journal of Performance Studies*, *14*(4). http://liminalities.net/14-4/ekkreinen.html

Rowe, D. D., Rudnick, J. J., & White, L. (2019). Images of identity: Performing power and intersectionality. *Communication Teacher*, *34*, 312–319. https://doi.org/10.1080/17404622.2019.1 690156

Spry, T. (2016). *Body, paper, stage: Writing and performing autoethnography*. Routledge Press.

Tristano, M. (2020). *After the 49: Pulse's performative afterlife* (Publication No. 28030316) [Doctoral dissertation, Arizona State University]. ProQuest Dissertation Publishing.

Valles-Morales, J. I., & LeMaster, B. (2015). On queer of color criticism, communication studies, and corporeality. *Kaleidoscope: A Graduate Journal of Qualitative Communication Research*, *14*(8), 77–81.

Index

Numbers in *italics* denotes a figure on the corresponding page.